Realistic Revolution

Between 1989 and 1993, with the end of the Cold War, Tiananmen, and Deng Xiaoping's renewed reform, Chinese intellectuals said goodbye to radicalism. In newly-founded journals, interacting with those who had left mainland China around 1949 to revive Chinese culture from the margins, they now challenged the underlying creed of Chinese socialism and the May Fourth Movement that there was 'no making without breaking'. *Realistic Revolution* covers the major debates of this period on radicalism in history, culture, and politics from a transnational perspective, tracing intellectual exchanges as China repositioned itself in Asia and the world. In this realistic revolution, Chinese intellectuals paradoxically espoused conservatism in the service of future modernization. They also upheld rationalism and gradualism after Maoist utopia but concurrently rewrote history to re-establish morality. Finally, their self-identification as scholars was a response to rapid social change that nevertheless left their concern with China's fate unaltered.

ELS VAN DONGEN is Assistant Professor of History at Nanyang Technological University, Singapore.

Realistic Revolution changes our understanding of Chinese conservatism in the post-Mao period. Based on a comprehensive and critical reading of Chinese thinkers and writers, van Dongen brings to life the Chinese critique of radicalism during the critical years after Tiananmen. Lucidly written, acutely analytical, this is a wonderfully rewarding read.
Professor Timothy Cheek, University of British Columbia

Shocked by the violence of Tiananmen and the collapse of the Soviet Union, China's intellectuals began exploring the roots of radicalism and the meaning – or usefulness – of conservatism. In this carefully researched and wonderfully written book, van Dongen excavates the international conversation that unfolded over the next decade. This book should be in every class on contemporary China.
Professor Joseph Fewsmith, Boston University

Realistic Revolution
Contesting Chinese History, Culture, and Politics after 1989

Els van Dongen
Nanyang Technological University, Singapore

CAMBRIDGE
UNIVERSITY PRESS

University Printing House, Cambridge CB2 8BS, United Kingdom

One Liberty Plaza, 20th Floor, New York, NY 10006, USA

477 Williamstown Road, Port Melbourne, VIC 3207, Australia

314-321, 3rd Floor, Plot 3, Splendor Forum, Jasola District Centre, New Delhi - 110025, India

79 Anson Road, #06-04/06, Singapore 079906

Cambridge University Press is part of the University of Cambridge.

It furthers the University's mission by disseminating knowledge in the pursuit of education, learning and research at the highest international levels of excellence.

www.cambridge.org
Information on this title: www.cambridge.org/9781108421300
DOI: 10.1017/9781108367783

© Els van Dongen 2019

This publication is in copyright. Subject to statutory exception and to the provisions of relevant collective licensing agreements, no reproduction of any part may take place without the written permission of Cambridge University Press.

First published 2019

A catalogue record for this publication is available from the British Library

Library of Congress Cataloging in Publication data
Names: van Dongen, Els, author.
Title: Realistic revolution : contesting Chinese history, culture, and politics after 1989 / Els van Dongen, Nanyang Technological University, Singapore.
Other titles: Contesting Chinese history, culture, and politics after 1989
Description: First edition. | Cambridge, United Kingdom : New York, NY, USA : University Printing House, 2018. | Includes bibliographical references.
Identifiers: LCCN 2018049324| ISBN 9781108421300 (hardback) | ISBN 9781108431729 (pbk.)
Subjects: LCSH: Revolutions–China–History–20th century. | Radicalism–China–History–20th century. | China–Intellectual life–1976–
Classification: LCC DS774.5 .D66 2018 | DDC 951.04–dc23
LC record available at https://lccn.loc.gov/2018049324

ISBN 978-1-108-42130-0 Hardback
ISBN 978-1-108-43172-9 Paperback

Cambridge University Press has no responsibility for the persistence or accuracy of URLs for external or third-party internet websites referred to in this publication, and does not guarantee that any content on such websites is, or will remain, accurate or appropriate.

To my friends and family, without whom
nothing to my name
一无所有

Table of Contents

Acknowledgments	*page*	viii
Notes on Transliteration		xi
Abbreviations		xii
1 Goodbye Radicalism: The Early 1990s		1
2 Neoconservatism and Doing Things with *-Isms*		34
3 Xiao Gongqin and the Yan Fu Paradox		67
4 A Tale of Two Revolutions		94
5 Chen Lai and the Max Weber Dilemma		131
6 Of Post-*Isms* and May Fourth		164
7 The Double Nature of Realistic Revolution		196
Biographies of Prominent Intellectuals		218
Glossary		225
References		232
Index		270

Acknowledgments

This account of how thought travels has been shaped by my own voyages across continents and the people, institutes, and organizations that made them possible. Axel Schneider first opened my eyes to the world of Chinese intellectuals and provided me with the opportunity to write a doctoral dissertation under his supervision, from which this book project developed. During these years at Leiden University, I benefited considerably from stimulating group discussions with Chiara Brivio, Curtis Anderson Gayle, Chris Goto-Jones, Tze-ki Hon, Joel Joos, Rikki Kersten, Ya-pei Kuo, Ethan Mark, Lewis Mayo, Viren Murthy, Kiri Paramore, Christian Uhl, and Torsten Weber. I am above all grateful to Tze-ki, Viren, and Torsten for their multiple suggestions for improvements. From the "Arsenaal" and "CNWS," for contributing to this project in manifold ways, I further thank Karin Aalderink, Tryfon Bampilis, Ilona Beumer, Vincent Breugem, Amnon Bruck, Woei-Lien Chong, Francesca Dal Lago, Valentina Georgieva, Jeroen Groenewegen, Hui Guo, Ingmar Heise, Michael Laver, Marc Matten, Dirk Meyer, Oliver Moore, Chris Nierstrasz, Paramita Paul, Annika Pissin, Lena Scheen, Florian Schneider, Chunyan Shu, Bas Snelders, Maghiel van Crevel, and Jeroen Wiedenhof.

The Netherlands Organisation for Scientific Research (Nederlandse Organisatie voor Wetenschappelijk Onderzoek or NWO) generously funded my dissertation project at Leiden University. I also thank the Fulbright Foundation in Amsterdam for financial support that enabled me to spend six months in Boston for research. At Boston University, Joseph Fewsmith spared both time and effort to provide me with invaluable feedback and reading suggestions. During my visits to Beijing and Shanghai, a great number of Chinese intellectuals thoughtfully answered my questions and received me with hospitality. Sincere thanks go out to Chen Lai, Jia Xiaoye, Jiang Yihua, Luo Zhitian, Ma Yong, Tao Dongfeng, Wang Hui, Wang Yuechuan, Xiao Gongqin, Xu Jilin, Yue Daiyun, Zhang Yiwu, and Zheng Min. At Peking University, which provided financial research assistance during my stay, Zhang Qi and Zhang Zikai helped out on various fronts and immersed me in campus life.

Nanyang Technological University in Singapore provided important financial support to complete this project in the form of a Postdoctoral Fellowship

Acknowledgments

and later Startup Grant. My utmost gratitude goes to Hong Liu, then chair of the School of Humanities and Social Sciences, for his guidance during and after this period. I further thank Kang K. K. Luke and Alan K. L. Chan, in their capacities as head of the School of Humanities and dean of the college, respectively, for funding opportunities for follow-up research trips. I would have never completed this book without the thoughtful direction of Evelyn Hu-Dehart, who provided detailed comments on the manuscript and made time for discussions. Gregor Benton, who never ceased to encourage me, offered precious instruction about writing. I further express thanks to my colleagues in History—Scott Anthony, Song-chuan Chen, Zach Fredman, Geok Yian Goh, Jessica Hinchy, Sinae Hyun, Keng We Koh, Joey Long, Sandra Manickam, Wen-Qing Ngoei, Farish Noor, Lisa Onaga, Hyung Wook Park, Miles Powell, Michael Stanley-Baker, Hallam Stevens, Venus Viana, Ivy Yeh, and Taomo Zhou—for the stimulating exchange of ideas and wonderful advice.

Acknowledgments are also due to those colleagues with whom I discussed this project at various stages and whose input made a difference. They include Shigeru Akita, Salvatore Babones, Daniel Bell, Beatrice Botero, Hok Yin Chan, Yuan Chang, Shuxia Chen, Meng-hsuan Chou, Evan Dawley, Carine Defoort, Xiaoping Fang, Fredy Gonzalez, Sabrina Hao, Baogang He, Christopher Holman, Said Islam, Olivier Krischner, Chenyang Li, Mary Mazzilli, Weichong Ong, Kerstin Pannhorst, Erik Schicketanz, Kamal and Ranjana Sheel, William Sima, Nicolas Standaert, and Kristin Stapleton. In addition, I thank Miaw-fen Lu and Marlon Zhu of the Modern History Institute at the Academia Sinica who made it possible for me to complete the writing of this book in Taiwan through a Visiting Fellowship. For inspiring me intellectually since my graduate days, I am furthermore indebted to Geremie Barmé, Timothy Cheek, and Gloria Davies.

The staff members at the Leiden University Library, the Harvard-Yenching Library, the National Library in Beijing, Peking University Library, the Humanities and Social Sciences and Chinese libraries at Nanyang Technological University, and the various libraries of the Academia Sinica were indispensable in collecting the materials for this research. Special credit is due to Hanno Lecher at Leiden University and Kiak Peng Ng at Nanyang Technological University for patiently dealing with my countless requests.

Finally, I thank the two anonymous reviewers for their constructive comments. At Cambridge University, editor Lucy Rhymer skillfully guided me throughout the process and Lisa Carter and Amy Mower oversaw production. Nancy Hearst of Harvard's Fairbank Center and Joseph Dahm edited and proofread the manuscript with immense care and saved me from many embarrassments. Reuben Ang Yuheng and Huiying Dong assisted with the biographies that appear at the end of the text. For the cover design, Ryan Nussbacher kindly shared his expertise.

This book would have never seen the light without the support of my friends and family, to whom I dedicate this project. To my friends, thank you for being my final destination, always. To my parents, Jos and Denise, and my sisters Inge and An, thank you for being there, and for forever motivating me to travel along roads not taken. I save the final word of thanks for my grandfather Gaston, whose incredible sense of humor and love of the simple pleasures of life have been the finest travel companions throughout. They will be missed.

A different version of Chapter 5 was previously published under the title "Confucianism, Community, Capitalism: Chen Lai and the Spirit of Max Weber," in Tze-ki Hon and Kristin Stapleton, eds., *Confucianism for the Contemporary World: Global Order, Political Plurality, and Social Action* (Albany: State University of New York Press, 2017), 19–43.

Notes on Transliteration

For Chinese persons who are commonly known in the English-speaking world by names other than the pinyin transliteration, I have adopted the generally used spelling, for example, Chiang Kai-shek or Sun Yat-sen. For Chinese scholars publishing in English who are known by a name other than that in pinyin transliteration, the common spelling (often Wade-Giles) is used, for example, Tu Wei-ming or Yü Ying-shih.

For Chinese-language publications, mainland Chinese scholars are listed using the pinyin transliterations, citing the surname first, as in Chen Lai. For those scholars who publish both in Chinese and in English, but who are primarily known under a name that follows the Chinese convention (surname first), I have kept the Chinese convention for all publications. I have also kept the Chinese convention for English translations of works by Chinese scholars. For other English-language publications, I follow the Western convention, citing first the given name, followed by the surname. All short citations to Chinese and Western names include only the surname.

Abbreviations

CAS	Chinese Academy of Sciences
CASS	Chinese Academy of Social Sciences
CCP	Chinese Communist Party
CESRRI	Chinese Economic System Reform Research Institute
CLG	*Chinese Law and Government*
CPSU	Communist Party of the Soviet Union
CYX	Chen Lai, *Chuantong yu xiandai: Renwen zhuyi de shijie* (Tradition and Modernity: The Scope of Humanism) (Beijing: Beijing daxue chubanshe, 2006)
EAI	East Asian Institute (formerly Institute of East Asian Philosophies)
GATT	General Agreement on Tariffs and Trade
LOC	Charlotte Furth, ed., *The Limits of Change: Essays on Conservative Alternatives in Republican China* (Cambridge, MA: Harvard University Press, 1976)
KMT	Kuomintang
NPC	National People's Congress
PLA	People's Liberation Army
POCS	Samuel Huntington, *Political Order in Changing Societies* (New Haven, CT: Yale University Press, 1968)
XGQJ	Xiao Gongqin, *Xiao Gongqin ji* (Collected Works of Xiao Gongqin) (Ha'erbin: Heilongjiang jiaoyu chubanshe, 1995)
YZLG	Xiao Gongqin, *Yu zhengzhi langman zhuyi gaobie* (Parting with Political Romanticism) (Wuhan: Hubei jiaoyu chubanshe, 2000)
ZFL	Li Shitao, ed., *Zhishi fenzi lichang: Jijin yu baoshou zhijian de dongdang* (Intellectual Positions: The Turbulence between Radicalism and Conservatism) (Changchun: Shidai wenyi chubanshe, 1999)

1 Goodbye Radicalism
The Early 1990s

> What is the foundation stone of contemporary Europe which lies so brilliantly before us? It is the gift of revolutions.
>   Chen Duxiu, "Wenxue geminglun" (On the Literary Revolution)

> In the twenty-first century, we must no longer wage revolution. We must not once again yearn for, eulogize, and worship revolution as if it were sacred.
>   Li Zehou and Liu Zaifu, *Gaobie geming* (Farewell to Revolution)

Revolution, according to Mao Zedong, cannot be compared to "writing an essay, or painting a picture, or doing embroidery" because it cannot be "so refined, so leisurely and gentle, so temperate, kind, courteous, restrained and magnanimous." Revolution is an "act of violence."[1] During the decade after the death of the Great Helmsman, Chinese intellectuals began to question not only the necessity of violent revolution but also the notion of radical change. The belief that there was "no making without breaking" (*bupo buli*) had permeated not only Chinese socialist modernity, they argued, but also China's famous twentieth-century political-cum-cultural movement, the May Fourth Movement (1917–21).[2] In the historical, cultural, and political discourse of the early 1990s, intellectuals said goodbye to the radicalism of twentieth-century China.

Between 1989 and 1993, in a series of debates in leading academic journals, Chinese intellectuals engaged in the unmaking of twentieth-century radicalism, the specter of which loomed large. Why did Chinese intellectuals feel a need to unwrite the recent past at this historical juncture? This book seeks to answer

---

[1] Mao Tse-tung, "Report on an Investigation of the Peasant Movement in Hunan," in *Selected Works of Mao Tse-tung* (Peking: Foreign Languages Press, 1967), 1.44–46.

[2] I follow the periodization of Tse-tsung Chow because this is when the main events of the movement took place. In 1917, new thought and literature gained thrust, whereas after 1921, the movement was more oriented toward political action. See Chow, *The May Fourth Movement: Intellectual Revolution in Modern China* (Cambridge, MA: Harvard University Press, 1960), 6. On the complex transition from cultural action to political mobilization during May Fourth, see Shakhar Rahav, *The Rise of Political Intellectuals in Modern China: May Fourth Societies and the Roots of Mass-Party Politics* (Oxford: Oxford University Press, 2015).

that question. A series of political and socioeconomic developments render the early 1990s a pivotal period in the history of post-Mao China. The end of the Cold War and the implosion of the Soviet Union between 1989 and 1991 raised profound questions about the legacy of socialism and the legitimacy of the Chinese Revolution. The repression of the student democracy movement in the spring of 1989 ended the already severed alliance between Chinese intellectuals and the state in the service of modernization. The launch of the second reform period, with Deng Xiaoping's Southern Tour in early 1992 and followed by the Fourteenth Party Congress in October of the same year, created formidable economic, political, social, and cultural changes that existed in tension with the narratives of revolution and socialism.

In her influential work *Translingual Practice*, Lydia Liu asks, "Does theory travel? If so, how? ... Indeed, who does the traveling?[3] Japan had been a crucial node in the trajectory of Western theory traveling to China during the late nineteenth and early twentieth centuries, as were Europe and the United States thereafter, or the Soviet Union in the mid-twentieth century.[4] Throughout, however, Chinese intellectuals abroad served as interpreters of the foreign theories. During the early 1990s, different generations of Chinese émigrés in the United States attracted the attention of mainland Chinese intellectuals. In addition to those who left China before or after 1949 and who were educated in Hong Kong, Taiwan, or the United States, they also included a new generation of Chinese intellectuals who had participated in the reform era. In the case of the former, they had left China decades earlier and were eager to bring Chinese culture back from the "periphery" to the "centre" in the new economic and political climate.[5] Critical of the Maoist attitude toward Chinese tradition, these Chinese intellectuals traced the radical rejection of Chinese tradition back to the decades following the First Opium War (1839–42) and connected this period of radicalism with that of May Fourth and the Cultural Revolution (1966–76).[6]

---

[3] Lydia H. Liu, *Translingual Practice: Literature, National Culture, and Translated Modernity—China 1900–1937* (Stanford, CA: Stanford University Press, 1995), 21.

[4] This is not to say that Europe, the United States, and Japan were the only places from where or through which theory traveled. See, for example, Rebecca Karl's work on the role of colonized nations in China's identity formation and conceptions of nationalism at the turn of the century. Rebecca E. Karl, *Staging the World: Chinese Nationalism at the Turn of the Twentieth Century* (Durham, NC: Duke University Press, 2002). Also, as Liu notes, the traveling of theory was not merely one-directional or merely involving actors outside of China. Examples include China-Japan-China trajectories and trajectories involving Jesuits and Protestants based in China. See Liu, *Translingual Practice*, 32–39.

[5] Tu Wei-ming "'Cultural China': The Periphery as the Center," *Daedalus* 120.2 (1991), 1–32.

[6] This is the official Chinese periodization. Others use 1966–69, corresponding to the Red Guard movement. Guobin Yang, *The Red Guard Generation and Political Activism in China* (New York: Columbia University Press, 2016), 6. On the Cultural Revolution, see Roderick MacFarquhar and Michael Schoenhals, *Mao's Last Revolution* (Cambridge, MA: Belknap, 2006); Frank

After 1989, with China's self-identity and the identity of Chinese intellectuals both in disarray, mainland Chinese intellectuals explored novel narratives of modern Chinese history and reworked some of the ideas of Chinese intellectuals in the United States for a mainland environment. They were hence also intermediaries or "mediators" in their own right.[7] Newly launched journals, lecture tours, international conferences, and visiting professorships beginning in the 1980s, in both China and abroad, allowed for interactions among scholars in mainland China, Hong Kong, Taiwan, and Singapore, Chinese émigrés in the United States, and scholars in Europe and the United States. In addition to the decline in travel restrictions on mainland China, the reforms in Taiwan allowed visits from mainland travelers after 1987. Publications in Taiwan of works that had first appeared on the mainland led one scholar to refer to 1987 as Taiwan's year of "mainland fever." In addition, the New York–based journal *Zhishi fenzi* (The Intellectual), which was established in 1984 and published in Chinese, functioned as a bridge among scholars based on the mainland, in Taiwan, in Hong Kong, and overseas.[8]

In 1988 Yü Ying-shih, a prominent intellectual historian of China based in the United States, delivered a lecture on radicalism and conservatism in modern Chinese history at the Chinese University of Hong Kong. But it was only after 1989 that reflections on radicalism began to extend to mainland China. Also noteworthy was a 1991 conference held in New York on Chinese intellectuals during China's transitional period that brought together scholars from mainland China and elsewhere. This was followed by the publication of polemical articles by Yü Ying-shih and the mainland Marxist historian Jiang Yihua in *Ershiyi shiji* (Twenty-First Century) in 1992.[9] The latter, a Hong Kong–based scholarly journal, was founded in 1990 and served as a bridge among the various groups of scholars. Thus, a discourse that spread across Chinese-language media and that included a "China" not limited to the geopolitical boundaries of the People's Republic of China but also including Chinese communities globally began to unfold. The participants were part of the "Sinophone world" of intellectuals who made use of "China-originated languages and dialects" in attempts to make sense of the changes that were

---

Dikötter, *The Cultural Revolution: A People's History, 1962–1976* (London: Bloomsbury, 2016); Joseph W. Esherick, Paul G. Pickowicz, and Andrew G. Walder, eds., *The Chinese Cultural Revolution as History* (Stanford, CA: Stanford University Press, 2006).

[7] Peter Burke notes that, next to those who emigrate and bring back new knowledge, "stay-at-home scholars" at universities in major cities are also "mediators" in the sense that they gather and process knowledge. See Peter Burke, *Exiles and Expatriates in the History of Knowledge, 1500–2000* (Waltham, MA: Brandeis University Press, 2017), 21.

[8] John Makeham, *Lost Soul: "Confucianism" in Contemporary Chinese Academic Discourse* (Cambridge, MA: Asia Center, Harvard University, 2008), 51.

[9] Chen Xiaoming, "Antiradicalism and the Historical Situation of Contemporary Chinese Intellectuals," *Contemporary Chinese Thought* 29.2 (Winter 1997–98), 31.

taking place in China.[10] Furthermore, Chinese intellectuals in the United States simultaneously published for Anglophone audiences, and Chinese translations of these works also helped shape the Sinophone discourse of the early 1990s.

During this period, radicalism not only was rejected in its cultural and historical manifestations but, following the crisis in the Soviet Union, infiltrated political discourse about the economic reforms in China. In all cases, discussions were structured around a binary of radicalism (*jijin zhuyi* 激进主义) and conservatism (*baoshou zhuyi* 保守主义). In this milieu of such rapid change, however, what did it mean to speak about conservatism? Such discussions highlighted the question of conservatism in China, which had been repressed, together with liberalism, after the victory of the Chinese Communist Party (CCP) in 1949. The significance of the debates in the early 1990s is that they raised the issue of alternative paths to Chinese modernity in the face of the "end of history." In debates on radicalism, Chinese intellectuals dealt with questions such as Enlightenment, modernity, morality, legitimacy, and reform, themes that were investigated in relation to modern Chinese history during the 1990s.[11] Such discussions were a continuation of the reflections on socialism that had commenced after the end of the Cultural Revolution but took on a new form after 1989 and 1992.

The Meaning of 1989 and 1992

The early 1990s functioned as a hinge between the New Enlightenment Movement of the mid- to late 1980s and the period after the mid-1990s that witnessed a transformation of the intellectual landscape into two major factions of liberals and the "New Left," even if this distinction omits many of the involved complexities. It stood between the overall optimistic belief in modernization that marked the 1980s, as reflected in the 1983 Chinese translation of Alvin Toffler's *The Third Wave*, and the more dystopian climate of the 1990s, often known as the "second reform decade."[12]

---

[10] Geremie R. Barmé, "Worrying China and New Sinology," *China Heritage Quarterly* 14 (June 2008), www.chinaheritagequarterly.org/articles.php?searchterm=014_worryingChina.inc &issue=014. The term "Sinophone" has been used in various ways across different disciplines. I am using it here in the broader sense, namely to refer to Chinese-speaking communities inclusive of those in mainland China, Hong Kong, and Taiwan. See the reference to a "Sinophone Sphere" in Timothy Cheek, "The Worlds of China's Intellectuals," in Timothy B. Weston and Lionel M. Jensen, eds., *China In and Beyond the Headlines* (Lanham, MD: Rowman & Littlefield, 2012), 155, 158–60.

[11] Geremie Barmé, "The Revolution of Resistance," in Elizabeth J. Perry and Mark Selden, eds., *Chinese Society: Change, Conflict and Resistance* (London: RoutledgeCurzon, 2003), 56.

[12] Chaohua Wang, "Introduction: Minds of the Nineties," in Wang, *One China, Many Paths* (London: Verso, 2003), 11; Jing Wang, *High Culture Fever: Politics, Aesthetics, and Ideology in Deng's China* (Berkeley: University of California Press, 1996), 41.

An important marker between the two periods is the June 4, 1989, crackdown on the Tiananmen demonstrations. However, some of the trends that became dominant after 1989 had already been present during the 1980s. Furthermore, the New Enlightenment Movement of the mid- to late 1980s was an outgrowth of the Movement to Liberate Thinking of the late 1970s.[13] At the Third Plenary Session of the Eleventh Party Congress in December 1978, Deng Xiaoping reiterated the need to "emancipate thinking" and to move away from the ideological rigidity of the Mao era by "seeking truth from facts."[14] The party also declared that "socialist modernization" was part of the official agenda. During the early 1980s, these changes paved the way for a more fundamental criticism of the utopian socialism of the Mao era and a move from class as a category of analysis to an emphasis on the subject. In 1983, at the commemoration of the centenary of Karl Marx's death, Zhou Yang, the literary critic and deputy head of the CCP Propaganda Department, delivered a speech on "socialist humanism," in which he criticized the dogmatism and class determinism of the Cultural Revolution.[15] The controversial claim that alienation could also exist under socialism led to the Campaign Against Spiritual Pollution in late 1983 and early 1984. After the campaign, criticism of utopian socialism continued, but this time it was in the form of a call for "Enlightenment" that included characteristics of Western modernity.

The Democracy Wall Movement and other political campaigns of the late 1970s and early 1980s that were initiated by Chinese youth preceded the cultural movement of the 1980s. Before the Campaign Against Spiritual Pollution of 1983–84, the "antiliberal" campaign of 1981 had already targeted authors of the late 1970s "scar literature" that had repudiated the Cultural Revolution but had also laid bare the tragedies of socialism. During the 1980s, editorial committees such as Towards the Future (Zouxiang weilai) and Culture: China and the World (Wenhua: Zhongguo yu shijie), independent from

---

[13] Xu Jilin, "The Fate of an Enlightenment: Twenty Years in the Chinese Intellectual Sphere (1978–1998)," tr. Geremie Barmé and Gloria Davies, in Edward Gu and Merle Goldman, eds., *Chinese Intellectuals between State and Market* (London: RoutledgeCurzon, 2004), 183.

[14] Richard Baum, *Burying Mao: Chinese Politics in the Age of Deng Xiaoping* (Princeton, NJ: Princeton University Press, 1994), 63. Deng referred to emancipating thinking in his December 13, 1978, speech, titled "Emancipate the Mind, Seek Truth from Facts, and Unite as One in Looking to the Future," in *Selected Works of Deng Xiaoping (1975–1982)* (Beijing: Foreign Languages Press, 1984), 151–63, which marked the beginning of the reform period.

[15] Wang Ruoshui, deputy editor of *Renmin ribao* (People's Daily), and Wang Yuanhua drafted the speech. A revised version was published in *Renmin ribao*, March 16, 1983. See Xu, "Fate of an Enlightenment," 186 and 200n4. For an overview of the debate on "humanist Marxism," see Wang, *High Culture Fever*, 9–36; David A. Kelly, "The Emergence of Humanism: Wang Ruoshui and the Critique of Socialist Alienation," in Merle Goldman, Timothy Cheek, and Carol Lee Hamrin, eds., *China's Intellectuals and the State: In Search of a New Relationship* (Cambridge, MA: Council on East Asian Studies, Harvard University, 1987), 159–82.

publishing houses but affiliated with research units or working with official patrons, were central in this New Enlightenment Movement.[16] The mid-1980s witnessed the zenith of media interest in the spread of a "culture fever" (*wenhua re*), or an obsession with comparative research on the pros and cons of Chinese and Western cultures, in the form of debates, lectures, and editorials.[17] This culture fever culminated in the 1988 documentary *Heshang* (River Elegy). Although the makers of the documentary series upheld liberation from tradition through modernization and Westernization, the documentary also reflected the "apocalyptic anxiety" of a society caught in rapid transformation.[18]

A review of the intellectual landscape of the 1990s reveals a very different picture. Before 1989, different generations had passed down the "talismans" of May Fourth; they had accentuated various elements of the May Fourth legacy, but by the 1990s the legacy itself was being questioned.[19] Because of this retreat from the May Fourth agenda after 1989, both the leading New Leftist Wang Hui (b. 1959) at Tsinghua University and the liberal Xu Jilin (b. 1957) at East China Normal University have compared the 1990s to the period between the late 1920s and the outbreak of the Sino-Japanese War in 1937, when a departure from idealism and a fragmentation of the intellectual landscape substituted for the "explosive energies" of the May Fourth era.[20] The liberal Zhu Xueqin (b. 1952) at Shanghai University has further stated that the 1990s were characterized by a shift toward "neo-authoritarianism," the use of foreign discourses, and the discarding of a "critical spirit" or a "sense of intellectual responsibility," accompanied by a growing impact of market forces.[21]

---

[16] On the organizational structure of the editorial committees, see Wang Xiaoming, "The Politics of Translation: Modes of Organization in the Chinese Translation Movement of the 1980s," tr. Kenneth Dean, in Naoki Sakai and Yukiko Hanawa, eds., *Specters of the West and the Politics of Translation* (Ithaca, NY: Traces Editorial Office, Cornell University, 2001), 269–300; see also Chen Fong-ching, "The Popular Cultural Movement of the 1980s," in Gloria Davies, ed., *Voicing Concerns: Contemporary Chinese Critical Inquiry* (Lanham, MD: Rowman & Littlefield, 2001), 71–86.

[17] Especially crucial was the lecture series organized by the Academy of Chinese Culture in Beijing. For a detailed overview of the main events, see Wang, *High Culture Fever*, 48–56.

[18] Wang, *High Culture Fever*, 119.

[19] Rana Mitter, *A Bitter Revolution: China's Struggle with the Modern World* (Oxford: Oxford University Press, 2004), 273–74.

[20] Wang, "Introduction: Minds of the Nineties," 11. On Tiananmen as a watershed event, see Joseph Fewsmith, *China since Tiananmen: The Politics of Transition* (Cambridge: Cambridge University Press, 2001); Jean-Philippe Béja, "Introduction: 4 June 1989: A Watershed in Chinese Contemporary History," in Béja, ed., *The Impact of China's 1989 Tiananmen Massacre* (London: Routledge, 2011), 1–12.

[21] Zhu Xueqin, "For a Chinese Liberalism," tr. Wu Shengqing, in Wang, ed., *One China, Many Paths*, 98–99.

The politics of the intellectual discourses during the 1990s were "overdetermined by how they simultaneously came to terms with 1989 and 1992."[22] The intellectuals were responding to the relevant social, political, and economic shifts, but this is not to say that the context determined all the content.[23] The Tiananmen demonstrations in the spring of 1989 emerged from the social effects of the economic reforms, such as inflation, income inequalities, and corruption among the political elite. The government sought to redress some of the imbalances caused by the transition from plan to market through the urban reforms and the 1988 price reforms, but without success.[24] After the violent suppression of the Tiananmen demonstrations during the following year, intellectuals began struggling with the issues of their place in the reforms and their alliance with the state. Reflections on the 1980s naturally led to reflections on socialism, and such reflections were further strengthened by the decline of socialism internationally, the end of the Cold War, and the advance of global capital. The "prolonged postmortem assessment" of what had caused the implosion in the Soviet Union so as to avoid the same fate in China became an important topic of research.[25] Henceforth, the official emphasis was on stability and gradual reforms, as reflected in the formula of "crossing the river by feeling for the stones" (*mozhe shitou guohe*).[26]

Internally, Deng Xiaoping's Southern Tour in January and February 1992 also triggered reflections on revolution and on the socialist identity of a country that had turned to reform. It was during his Southern Tour that Deng called for a more forceful reform and opening up. The tour thus ended the period of uncertainty after the June 1989 Tiananmen crackdown, the string of upheavals in Eastern Europe, and the implosion of the Soviet Union in December 1991. The October 1992 Fourteenth Party Congress political report, which Joseph Fewsmith calls "the most liberal economic document in CCP history," approved the foundation of a "socialist market economy."[27] Following this landmark transformation, foreign direct investment (FDI) from

---

[22] Zhang Xudong, "The Making of the Post-Tiananmen Intellectual Field: A Critical Overview," in Zhang, ed., *Whither China? Intellectual Politics in Contemporary China* (Durham, NC: Duke University Press, 2001), 9.

[23] Benjamin A. Elman, "The Failures of Contemporary Chinese Intellectual History," *Eighteenth-Century Studies* 43.3 (2010), 378.

[24] Timothy Cheek, *Living with Reform: China since 1989* (London: Zed Books, 2003), 68, 82. On the broader causes and the impact of Tiananmen, see David S. G. Goodman and Gerald Segal, eds., *China in the Nineties: Crisis Management and Beyond* (Oxford: Clarendon, 1991).

[25] David Shambaugh, *China Goes Global: The Partial Power* (Oxford: Oxford University Press, 2013), 51.

[26] See Kalpana Misra, *From Post-Maoism to Post-Marxism: The Erosion of Official Ideology in Deng's China* (London: Routledge, 1998).

[27] Joseph Fewsmith, "Reaction, Resurgence, and Succession: Chinese Politics since Tiananmen," in Roderick MacFarquhar, ed., *The Politics of China: Sixty Years of the People's Republic* (Cambridge: Cambridge University Press, 2011), 505–6.

Hong Kong, Taiwan, and Chinese in Southeast Asia began to transform China's economy and society. These changes triggered a "consumer revolution" that even led to the commercialization of Chairman Mao's legacy in the form of a "Mao fever."[28]

In spite of this paradigm shift, however, there was no clear-cut break between the two decades. During the 1980s, a number of intellectuals had already been critical of the May Fourth Movement and the Enlightenment project. The philosopher Li Zehou (b. 1930), for example, famously argued that the "salvation" (*jiuwang*) "nationalist" element of May Fourth had repressed its "Enlightenment" (*qimeng*).[29] The "utopian" mood of the 1980s had already suffered vital setbacks prior to the 1990s. At the beginning of 1987, General Secretary Hu Yaobang was forced to resign because, due to his permissive cultural and political policies, he had allowed "bourgeois liberalization" to flourish.[30] Also in 1987, the new party general secretary, Zhao Ziyang, drawing on the ideas of theorist Su Shaozhi and faced with the challenges of inflation and corruption, stated that the country was only at the "primary stage of socialism."[31] In addition, the 1988 documentary *Heshang*, in which the filmmakers press China to embrace Western civilization, became subject to fierce criticism and brought about disputes on the reforms.[32] Amid the reform setbacks, prior to 1989 a sense of crisis had already engulfed the intellectual world. In fact, this sense of crisis had been lurking under the surface ever since the start of the reform era.[33]

Unmaking Radicalism: Realistic Revolution

Even though China's rapid transformation led to many stimulating academic and cultural debates, intellectual discourse during the reform period remains

---

[28] Ralph Litzinger, "Theorizing Postsocialism: Reflections on the Politics of Marginality in Contemporary China," *South Atlantic Quarterly* 101.1 (Winter 2002), 38. On Mao fever, see Ross Terrill (whose own study of Mao played a role in the fever), *The Life of Mao*, www.overdrive.com/search?q=E32A112B-2D31-482A-A8AA-16A00E298663; Geremie R. Barmé, *Shades of Mao: The Posthumous Cult of the Great Leader* (Armonk, NY: M.E. Sharpe, 1996).

[29] See Li Zehou, "Qimeng yu jiuwang de shuangchong bianzou" (The Double Variation of Enlightenment and Salvation), in Li, *Zhongguo xiandai sixiangshi lun* (On Modern Chinese Intellectual History) (Beijing: Dongfang chubanshe, 1987), 7–49.

[30] Geremie Barmé, "History for the Masses," in Jonathan Unger, ed., *Using the Past to Serve the Present: Historiography and Politics in Contemporary China* (Armonk, NY: M.E. Sharpe, 1993), 265.

[31] Wang, *High Culture Fever*, 37. In fact, the term "primary stage of socialism" had been used even earlier by Mao Zedong, but now it was being employed to justify the reform policies. See Henry Yuhuai He, *Dictionary of the Political Thought of the People's Republic of China* (Armonk, NY: M.E. Sharpe, 2001), 385–87.

[32] On *Heshang*, see Chapter 4 of this volume.

[33] Bill Brugger and David Kelly, *Chinese Marxism in the Post-Mao Era* (Stanford, CA: Stanford University Press, 1990), 3.

relatively understudied. Scholars such as Geremie Barmé and Gloria Davies have made pioneering efforts to bring Chinese voices to international audiences.[34] A number of studies address the broader intellectual and cultural discourse of the 1980s, 1990s, and 2000s, but few pay attention to interactions among scholars in mainland China, Hong Kong, Singapore, Taiwan, and elsewhere.[35]

Scholarship on the "conservative turn" of the early 1990s, referring to the rise of political neoconservatism and nationalism and a renewed interest in Chinese culture and tradition, can generally be divided into political and cultural discussions. For the political debates, scholars have studied neoconservatism as part of the elite struggles over reform and in relation to questions of political legitimacy and the crisis of Marxist ideology.[36] "Cultural conservatism" refers to arguments about the preservation and continuity of Chinese culture, including debates on New Confucianism, revisionist historiography, and postmodernism and language reform. Some authors have also interpreted these cultural debates as manifestations of cultural nationalism, which refers to an understanding of the nation in cultural rather than political-territorial or civic terms.[37] This distinction between political and cultural developments overlooks the fact that in actuality the two coexisted as products of the changing domestic and international environments. In contrast with the 1980s, when intellectual views were a "weathervane" about the reform policies, during the 1990s a "curious set of parallels" existed between the political and cultural discourses, such as those on radicalism, civil society, and the public sphere.[38]

---

[34] See, for example, Davies, ed., *Voicing Concerns*; Wang, ed. *One China, Many Paths*. For dissenting voices of the 1980s, see Geremie Barmé and John Minford, eds., *Seeds of Fire: Chinese Voices of Conscience* (New York: Noonday Press, 1989) and Geremie Barmé and Linda Jaivin, eds., *New Ghosts, Old Dreams: Chinese Rebel Voices* (New York: Times Books, 1992). For English translations of more recent writings by Chinese intellectuals, see the Reading the China Dream website and the accompanying project run by David Ownby, Timothy Cheek, and Joshua Fogel. www.readingthechinadream.com.

[35] Representative studies on reform-era intellectual discourse include Xiaomei Chen, *Occidentalism: A Theory of Counter-discourse in Post-Mao China* (Oxford: Oxford University Press, 1995); Gloria Davies, *Worrying about China: The Language of Chinese Critical Inquiry* (Cambridge, MA: Harvard University Press, 2007); Min Lin, with Maria Galikowski, *The Search for Modernity: Chinese Intellectuals and Cultural Discourse in the Post-Mao Era* (New York: St. Martin's, 1999); and Wang, *High Culture Fever*. For an example of a study that pays much attention to this interaction, see Makeham, *Lost Soul*.

[36] Fewsmith, *China since Tiananmen*; Gunter Schubert, "Was Ist Neokonservativismus? Notizen zum Politischen Denken in der VR China in den 90er Jahren" (What is Neoconservatism? Notes on Political Thought in the PRC during the 1990s), *Asien* (Asia) 65 (October 1997), 57–74; Brugger and Kelly, *Chinese Marxism in the Post-Mao Era*; Misra, *From Post-Maoism to Post-Marxism*.

[37] Yingjie Guo, *Cultural Nationalism in Contemporary China: The Search for National Identity under Reform* (London: Routledge, 2004), 18.

[38] Wang, "Introduction: Minds of the Nineties," 15, 16–19, 36.

Although some authors have conducted research jointly on cultural and political developments, they have nevertheless suggested that the former merely serve the latter, as in the case of the Confucian revival.[39] Studies that think of the cultural, political, and economic developments of the reform era together do not specifically discuss the early 1990s. Arif Dirlik, for example, has analyzed the rise of New Confucianism and "national studies" (*guoxue*) in relation to global changes, but this critical intervention is mainly about the meaning of 1992—capitalism—for the Chinese intellectual world.[40] Other studies that include both cultural and political developments remain oriented toward the political aspects. Peter Moody's study of conservatism includes "traditionalism," nationalism, populism, and "neo-conservatism," but does not move beyond political thought.[41] Fewsmith's *China since Tiananmen*, a wide-ranging and impressive analysis of political and intellectual changes since 1989, nevertheless mostly centers around the political-reform issue.[42]

This book analyzes the historical, cultural, and political debates of the early 1990s through the lens of the paradigm shift of "anti-radicalism" that connected these debates. In intellectual debates, the term "radicalism" refers not only to China's socialist modernity but also to its liberal past in the form of the May Fourth Movement, often considered modern China's most influential intellectual and political movement. This critique of radicalism was not only a critique of revolution per se but also a critique of a progressivist mode of thought, according to which destruction was a prerequisite for development. The rise of anti-radicalism was directly related to the broader sociopolitical and socioeconomic changes heralded by the implosion of the Soviet Union, by June Fourth, and by the acceleration of the economic reforms. Engagement with the Chinese revolutionary past not only was related to economic reconfigurations in East Asia but also was part of the global challenges to the universalism of Enlightenment in the framework of what Dirlik calls "Global Modernity."[43]

After 1989, reflections on radicalism were more than manifestations of self-censorship. There were certainly limits on the objects of inquiry, the methodology, and expression of discussions during the reform era.[44] The blacklisting,

---

[39] Werner Meissner, "New Intellectual Currents in the People's Republic of China," in David C. B. Teather and Herbert S. Yee, eds., *China in Transition: Issues and Policies* (New York: St. Martin's, 1999), 18–19.

[40] Arif Dirlik, *Culture and History in Postrevolutionary China: The Perspective of Global Modernity* (Hong Kong: Chinese University Press, 2011).

[41] Peter Moody, *Conservative Thought in Contemporary China* (Lanham, MD: Rowman & Littlefield, 2007), 14.

[42] Fewsmith, *China since Tiananmen*.

[43] Dirlik, *Culture and History in Postrevolutionary China*, x–xi.

[44] Michael Schoenhals, *Doing Things with Words in Chinese Politics: Five Studies* (Berkeley: Center for Chinese Studies, Institute of East Asian Studies, University of California, 1992), 106–9.

sudden "transfers," dismissals, or demotions of academics had continued under the reforms, with the difference that those affected could now continue to write as freelance writers and under pseudonyms or could publish in Hong Kong and, beginning in the late 1990s, on the Internet.[45] At the same time, some journals, such as the literary periodical *Tianya* (Frontiers), published in the southern province of Hainan, were less restricted than those in Beijing. Journals could also receive private funding. The ideological climate of the time allowed for discussions that were more abstract and theoretical, but more than political quietism, the debates on radicalism were an engagement with socialism. The methodology behind the debates, which involved a highlighting of the function of ideas in twentieth-century history, also brought up Marxist responses, in which the debates were criticized for manifesting "idealist" tendencies.

However, many of the relevant texts in the debates were not published on mainland China. Those who criticized revolution explicitly, such as the philosopher Li Zehou and the literary critic Liu Zaifu in their famous 1995 account *Gaobie geming* (Farewell to Revolution), were published in Hong Kong.[46] Second, the debates appeared primarily in the Hong Kong journal *Ershiyi shiji* or in other more independent journals, such as *Dongfang* (Orient), which were less constrained by mainland censorship. In addition, academic publications were generally less sensitive than more public outlets such as newspapers because the number of readers was more limited.[47] Even though *Ershiyi shiji* was a highly influential journal and a vital medium for the debates, it was a scholarly journal with a circulation of only about 3,500, as compared to, at its peak, a circulation of up to 120,000 for *Dushu* (Reading).[48] Nevertheless, some of the intellectuals who took part in the debates of the early 1990s still faced censorship or had to publish outside of mainland China.

Debates about radicalism involved questions of legitimacy, relations between the state and the individual, the role of intellectuals, and the very nature of Chinese modernity. In several respects, they constituted what I refer to as a "realistic revolution." First, "realistic" refers to the fact that Chinese intellectuals, following the official turn to pragmatism, advocated commonsense approaches to change. This was a move away from the utopianism of the Mao era. Second, intellectual reflections on radicalism were also revolutionary

---

[45] Émilie Frenkiel, *Conditional Democracy: The Contemporary Debate on Political Reform in Chinese Universities* (Colchester: ECPR Press, 2015), 19–23; Merle Goldman, "Repression of China's Public Intellectuals in the Post-Mao Era," *Social Research* 76.2 (July 2009), 682.

[46] Li Zehou and Liu Zaifu, *Gaobie geming: Huiwang ershi shiji Zhongguo* (Farewell to Revolution: Looking back at Twentieth-Century China) (Hong Kong: Tiandi tushu youxian gongsi, 1995).

[47] Frenkiel, *Conditional Democracy*, 18.

[48] Wang, "Introduction: Minds of the Nineties," 28, 56. This was before the journal became available online, as it is today.

in that they did not shy away from challenging the need for revolution in the past. This was different from the official solution, which firmly preserved the status of the revolution in the past (as will be further explained below). Third, the term "realistic revolution" also refers to the practice of juxtaposing revolutions and identifying the most realistic revolution to rewrite China's past and future course. This juxtaposition of revolutions need not surprise us, for revolutionaries are often familiar with previous revolutions. They can serve as "models or counter-examples," or, in the words of Keith Michael Baker and Dan Edelstein, as "scripts" to be transformed: "Marx rewrote the script of the French Revolution; Lenin revised Marx; Mao revised Lenin; and so on and so forth."[49] Rather than comparing revolutions, as in the sociological tradition, Chinese intellectuals looked upon revolutions as scripts that had to be rewritten in order to improve an unsatisfactory reality.

Whereas the French Revolution and its ideals of liberty, equality, and fraternity were invoked positively in China of the 1980s, both the French and Russian revolutions were criticized after 1989 when several Chinese intellectuals identified the Glorious Revolution (1688–89) as the only realistic revolution. During the Glorious Revolution, King James II of England was overthrown by the Dutch stadtholder William III and British parliamentarians. It resulted in the establishment of a constitutional monarchy and an English bill of rights. The traditional view in historiography is that the revolution was "glorious" and "bloodless" because allegedly it was a peaceful, gradual, and evolutionary transition, unlike the violent revolutions on Continental Europe. In Whig history accounts, the victory of the revolutionaries represented a victory over the old England, divided by, among others, class and religion, and the new England of liberty.[50] Recent scholarship has challenged the notion of a "sensible" revolution and instead has placed the Glorious Revolution in a broader European perspective and in a longer time frame. Seen from this perspective, the Glorious Revolution was no less violent or modern than its French counterpart.[51]

Relying on the conventional view, a reference to the Glorious Revolution as a model in China in the 1990s was the expression of a will to progress in a more rational and stable manner. It was perceived as having avoided the violence of the French Revolution, now used as a counter-model that represented the irrational course of the Chinese Revolution, and as a belief in the transformational power of the human will. Chinese intellectuals henceforth utilized the

---

[49] Keith Michael Baker and Dan Edelstein, "Introduction," in Baker and Edelstein, eds., *Scripting Revolution: A Historical Approach to the Comparative Study of Revolutions* (Stanford, CA: Stanford University Press, 2015), 2.

[50] Stuart E. Prall, *The Bloodless Revolution: England, 1688* (Madison: University of Wisconsin Press, 1985), x.

[51] Steven C. A. Pincus, *1688: The First Modern Revolution* (New Haven, CT: Yale University Press, 2011).

modern meaning of the Chinese term *geming* (revolution). Before the modern period, *geming* had referred to dynastic change, the overthrow of the Mandate of Heaven (*tianming*), and the existence of cosmically determined cycles. Therefore, it was tied to political and moral legitimacy.[52] In its modern meaning, however, after having gained momentum following the failure of the 1898 Reform Movement, through the Japanese use of *geming* (*kakumei*) to denote "revolution," the origin of the character *ge* (革) was relevant. The character "philologically originated from the act of peeling off skin from a beast, designating a break or a drastic detachment."[53] During the 1990s, even though intellectuals challenged the modern meaning of revolution as drastic and radical change, the original meaning of *geming* was also present in that the debates were about morality, legitimacy, and the loss of "ultimate concerns."[54]

Fourth, realistic revolution refers to the tensions between the intellectuals' advocacy of a more rational, objective, and moderate course, and idealism, moralism, and future-oriented visions. I argue that, in spite of the ubiquitous references to conservatism, intellectuals continued to project change into the future and integrated conservatism into a vision of modernization that was no less linear. Also, arguing for a "detached" scholarship instead of political activism, the debates reveal a continuation of the idea that the Chinese intellectual was a moral guardian responsible for the fate of the nation. As for the form of the discussions in which this belief was expressed, the discourses of the early 1990s were highly evaluative and prescriptive, with, in spite of calls for an "objective" scholarship, a continuation of what Davies and Cheek have referred to as the "moral extremism" and "black-and-white judgements" of the Mao era.[55] In brief, we cannot make sense of reform China without relating it to both its "traditional" and its more recent radical past.[56]

Projecting Change into the Future

Amid the rapid modernization and the transition to globalization, conservatism was a framework in which to discuss the long-standing conundrum of how to modernize yet remain Chinese. For over a century, this question had been at

---

[52] Jin Guantao and Liu Qingfeng, *Guannianshi yanjiu: Zhongguo xiandai zhongyao zhengzhi shuyu de xingcheng* (Studies in Conceptual History: The Formation of Key Modern Chinese Political Terms) (Hong Kong: Dangdai Zhongguo wenhua yanjiu zhongxin, Chinese University Press, 2008), 18–19, 585–86.
[53] Chen Jianhua, "World Revolution Knocking at the Heavenly Gate: Kang Youwei and his Use of Geming in 1898," *Journal of Modern Chinese History* 5.1 (June 2011), 91, 94.
[54] Jin and Liu, *Guannianshi yanjiu*, 19, 357–61.
[55] Davies, *Worrying about China*, 3, 118; Cheek, *Living with Reform*, 50–51.
[56] Catherine Lynch, Robert B. Marks, and Paul G. Pickowicz, "Introduction: Chinese Radicalism in Historical Context," in Lynch, Marks, and Pickowicz, eds., *Radicalism, Revolution and Reform in Modern China: Essays in Honor of Maurice Meisner* (Lanham, MD: Lexington, 2011), 8–9.

the heart of the endeavors of Chinese intellectuals, and it had found expression in formulas such as *tiyong*—borrowing foreign technology for "application" but relying on Chinese learning for the "essence." During the May Fourth era, intellectuals had vigorously debated the place of Chinese culture in modernization, followed by a continuation of these discussions in the form of the topic of "cultural construction" during the 1920s and 1930s.[57] The issue became most pressing when the twentieth-century narratives about China's progress, namely Marxism and the Chinese "Enlightenment" of May Fourth, lost their appeal after 1989 and 1992. It was at this historical juncture that a re-evaluation of the past gained urgency. During the late nineteenth and early twentieth centuries, debates on Chinese modernity emerged amid feelings of national humiliation and the transition from empire to nation-state. During the 1990s, the debates were prompted by China's changing self-identity within the broader ideological landscape of the "end of history," China's economic rise following the "East Asian miracle," and the nation's integration into the global economy.

Modernity, in the words of Arif Dirlik, is "the fluid product of a changing topography of economic, political, social, and cultural relationships" and its very fluid nature means that it is difficult to define. Dirlik distinguishes between three "phases" of modernity, namely "Eurasian modernities," "Euromodernity," and "contemporary Global Modernity." Euromodernity, characterized by Europeans relying on slavery and colonization to spread the values of science and capital, had been the prominent global form since the eighteenth century. Euromodernity is relevant here because it was also the modernity that Chinese intellectuals encountered during the late nineteenth century and led them to rewrite the past based on modern ideas of time.[58] This modern interpretation of the relation between past, present, and future also became the object of discussions on twentieth-century radicalism, which marked the period of China's transition from modernization to "Global Modernity." However, in spite of this transition, discussions remained trapped in the modernization framework, and conservatism was interpreted within this linear perspective. Even when, in the mid-1990s, the discussions moved from the issue of modernization to the issue of modernity, intellectuals continued to search for a better path to Chinese modernity.

According to the German conceptual historian Reinhart Koselleck, under modernity the past is perpetually re-created in terms of new explanations of the present, whereas the present is interpreted in light of future possibilities. Modernity opens up new "horizons of expectations" (*Erwartungshorizont*) that

---

[57] On *tiyong* and the debates on "cultural construction," see Q. Edward Wang, *Inventing China through History: The May Fourth Approach to Historiography* (Albany: State University of New York Press, 2011).

[58] Dirlik, *Culture and History in Postrevolutionary China*, 20–22.

exist in tension with experience; it is marked by new "temporalizations" of history.[59] In the 1990s, Chinese intellectuals questioned the fascination with progress and linear development that had been dominant under the May Fourth and revolutionary paradigms, but this challenge was limited because it occurred under conditions of China's integration into the global capitalist system. Here it is useful to refer to Koselleck's concept of "past future" (*Vergangene Zukunft*), more commonly translated as "futures past." In China, futures imagined by past generations, and the May Fourth generation in particular, were reclaimed, but the relation between past, present, and future under modernity remained unchanged. In this sense, history, as Keith Tribe puts it, is not about "simple facticity" but rather about "possibilities."[60]

The binary of radicalism and conservatism that was prominent in the debates of the early 1990s, as an *-ism* (*zhuyi*), also reflected a fixation on the future that had underpinned the *-isms* in China ever since they were introduced through Japan in the early twentieth century. As with *-isms* elsewhere, they were the product of an age of revolution and nationalism.[61] The *-isms* in early twentieth-century China, as Ivo Spira explains, were, referring to Koselleck, "concepts of movement" (*Bewegungsbegriffe*): "History came to be seen as something that progressed purposefully and that could and should be shaped by the human will."[62] This reflected a new historical consciousness of change projected into the future, as opposed to the cyclical cosmology of the Chinese dynastic periods. The latter contained references to a "Golden Past" but not to a "Golden Future."[63] In Maoist China, a "Marxist-inspired utopianism" had given the future further purpose and meaning and had justified sacrifice and hardship by an "accentuation of the future."[64] During the debates of the early 1990s, in spite of rejections of drastic historical ruptures, the reconception of the relation between past and present still served to make the past more useful in the present.

---

[59] Keith Tribe, "Introduction," in Reinhart Koselleck, *Futures Past: On the Semantics of Historical Time*, tr. Keith Tribe (New York: Colombia University Press, 2004), xviii; Koselleck, *Futures Past*, 10, 258.

[60] Tribe, "Introduction," xi.

[61] Ivo Spira, *A Conceptual History of Chinese -Isms: The Modernization of Ideological Discourse* (Leiden: Brill, 2015), 2; Koselleck, *Futures Past*, 222–54.

[62] Spira, *Conceptual History of Chinese -Isms*, 6.

[63] Ibid., 47–48. This is not to say that the cyclical view of history was the only view of history that existed in dynastic China, as has been noted by, among others, Michael Puett and Prasenjit Duara. See Michael Puett, "Classical Chinese Historical Thought," and Prasenjit Duara, "Empires and Imperialism," in *A Companion to Global Historical Thought*, ed. Prasenjit Duara, Viren Murthy, and Andrew Sartori (Hoboken, NJ: Wiley-Blackwell, 2014), 34–46 and 384–98.

[64] Jiwei Ci, *Dialectic of the Chinese Revolution: From Utopianism to Hedonism* (Stanford, CA: Stanford University Press, 1994), 3–4. On utopianism and Mao's "voluntarism," see also Maurice Meisner, *Marxism, Maoism, and Utopianism: Eight Essays* (Madison, WI: University of Wisconsin Press, 1982). On the emphasis on voluntarist or Marxist elements in Maoism, see Nick Knight, *Rethinking Mao: Explorations in Mao Zedong's Thought* (Lanham, MD: Lexington, 2007).

The only book-length study in English on modern Chinese conservatism is the 1976 volume *The Limits of Change*, edited by Charlotte Furth.[65] This volume, the outcome of a 1972 conference at Harvard University on "Intellectuals and the Problem of Conservatism in Republican China," was widely referred to in the discussions of the early 1990s.[66] This was the case because it dismissed the argument put forward by historian Joseph Levenson that after China's encounter with the West, its resort to tradition could have arisen only from emotional and psychological needs.[67] For Levenson, the arrival of the West had distorted the balance between Chinese "history" and universal "values," and the embrace of Chinese tradition served to restore this balance. Levenson's "traditionalism" is reminiscent of how the term was used by sociologists Karl Mannheim and Max Weber, namely as an unreflective and psychological clinging to tradition.[68] *The Limits of Change* argues that the resort to tradition in modern China was instead a modern phenomenon based on conscious choice and reflection. In addition, whereas Chinese conservatives had previously been evaluated as being obstacles to modernization under the impact of the revolutionary paradigm, the 1976 volume argues that conservatives in China had not opposed change.

Two centuries after it was published, *Reflections on the Revolution in France* (1790) by Edmund Burke (1729–97) figured prominently in debates on modern Chinese history and culture.[69] Whereas Burke cared about historical particularity and the natural and gradual growth of institutions, during the 1990s intellectuals both within and outside of mainland China invoked Burke's works to advocate reform. This brings us to the wider question of conservatism in China, a topic that remains understudied given China's dominant narrative of revolution and the spread of modernization theory and Marxism internationally during the Cold War period. In this environment, conservatism meant opposing change. Mary Wright, in her 1957 book on the

---

[65] Charlotte Furth, ed., *The Limits of Change: Essays on Conservative Alternatives in Republican China* (Cambridge, MA: Harvard University Press, 1976) (hereafter cited as *LOC*).

[66] Most of the essays in *The Limits of Change* are translated in Zhou Yangshan and Yang Suxian, eds., *Jindai Zhongguo sixiang renwu lun: Baoshou zhuyi* (Modern Chinese Thought and People: Conservatism) (Taipei: Shibao wenhua chuban shiye youxian gongsi, 1980).

[67] Joseph R. Levenson, "'History' and 'Value': The Tensions of Intellectual Choice in Modern China," in Arthur F. Wright, ed., *Studies in Chinese Thought* (Chicago: University of Chicago Press, 1953), 146–94.

[68] Karl Mannheim, "Conservative Thought," in Kurt H. Wolff, ed., *From Karl Mannheim* (New York: Oxford University Press, 1971), 152–56; Max Weber uses the term in both *The Protestant Ethic and the Spirit of Capitalism*, tr. Stephen Kalberg (New York: Columbia University Press, 2011) and his studies on religious sociology.

[69] Edmund Burke, *Reflections on the Revolution in France and on the Proceedings in Certain Societies in London Relative to that Event: In a Letter Intended to Have Been Sent to a Gentleman in Paris* (London, 1790), reprinted in Frank M. Turner, ed., *Reflections on the Revolution in France* (New Haven, CT: Yale University Press, 2003).

Tongzhi Restoration (1862–74), titled *The Last Stand of Chinese Conservatism*, argues that conservatism had unique traits, such as the belief in a rational natural order and the innate goodness of man, the importance of group interests and customs, and the concept of the universal state. In other words, Wright's conservatism was the preservation of a Confucian order.[70] In his 1969 book *Chinese Intellectuals and the Revolution of 1911: The Birth of Modern Chinese Radicalism*, Michael Gasster associates the term "radicalism" with the birth of a new intelligentsia and the quest for rapid and profound modernization. Gasster contrasts this "modern radicalism," marked by the creation of utopian goals in the future and reformist and revolutionary optimism, with the "traditional conservatism" that was not so keen about innovation.[71]

In their introduction to the volume, Charlotte Furth and Benjamin Schwartz argue that a Western interpretation of conservatism, based on the accounts of the German sociologist Karl Mannheim and the "founding father" of conservatism Edmund Burke, can also be applied to modern China. Mannheim had asserted that conservatism in Germany could be portrayed as a "style of thought" that opposed the rationality and abstract thought of the Enlightenment and replaced it with an embrace of particularity and the historically grown. Whereas the progressive movement was marked by a belief in the "consciousness of the possible," conservatism clung to the concrete and the qualitative.[72]

Basing her argument on Mannheim, Furth proposes that modern Chinese conservatism was characterized by a "style of thought," or a historical consciousness, according to which change through individual action could have only limited bearing on the environment.[73] Furthermore, Furth and Schwartz both argue that modern Chinese conservatism was primarily a "cultural conservatism"; it was not a Burkean conservatism aimed at preserving the entire sociopolitical status quo.[74] The decline of the "mystique of the imperial monarchy" since the 1890s had separated the political order from the moral and cultural orders.[75] Apart from this distinction between culture and politics, Furth also divides conservatives into "nativists," for whom Chinese culture was particular, and "universalists," for whom Chinese values were primarily

---

[70] Mary Clabaugh Wright, *The Last Stand of Chinese Conservatism: The T'ung-Chih Restoration, 1862–1874* (Stanford, CA: Stanford University Press, 1957).
[71] Michael Gasster, *Chinese Intellectuals and the Revolution of 1911: The Birth of Modern Chinese Radicalism* (Seattle: University of Washington Press, 1969), viii, xvii.
[72] Mannheim, "Conservative Thought," 132, 155.
[73] Charlotte Furth, "Culture and Politics in Modern Chinese Conservatism," in *LOC*, 51.
[74] Benjamin Schwartz, "Notes on Conservatism in General and in China in Particular," in *LOC*, 16.
[75] Furth, "Culture and Politics," 25.

universal. Using this framework, the book includes articles on scholars who embarked on a search for a "national essence" (*guocui*), such as Liu Shipei (1884–1919), on political modernizers such as Yuan Shikai (1859–1916) and the Kuomintang (KMT), on "New Confucians," who based their reading of Confucianism on the Neo-Confucianism of the Song (907–1279) and Ming (1368–1644) dynasties, and on "modern historicism." The latter refers both to the social evolutionism of historian Tao Xisheng (1899–1988) and to the cyclical view of history of writer Zhou Zuoren (1885–1967) and his retreat from the public sphere.

Furth argues that these different manifestations of conservatism, including that of modernizers such as Yuan Shikai, were united by what she terms "presumptions of continuity."[76] Schwartz poses the question, "Can people who are wholeheartedly committed to modernization ever be considered conservative?"[77] For Schwartz, the answer is positive, since modernization is a process independent of human will, a process that requires stability and an awareness of the unique nature of Chinese historical culture.[78] For Furth, both a subscription to continuity for practical reasons and a defense of continuity based on the belief that things are historically grown are manifestations of conservatism. As Arif Dirlik's article on Tao Xisheng demonstrates, it was perfectly possible to combine an advocacy of historical continuity with the promotion of progress and voluntarism.[79] But in this sense was conservatism really a belief in the "limits of change"?

In addition, interpretations of conservatism differ widely in the various chapters of this volume. Guy Alitto, for example, in his chapter on Liang Shuming (1893–1988), one of the scholars critical of Western civilization after World War One, treats Chinese conservatism as part of a global reaction against modernization as rationalization.[80] In late-modernizing countries such as China, Alitto argues, modernization was perceived of as a Western product; the result was a cultural conservatism that joined hands with nationalism.[81] In the same volume, Tu Wei-ming and Chang Hao posit that New Confucianism was either an intellectual construct or a reaction to an intellectual crisis that in actuality was a crisis of meaning.[82] Finally, Lloyd Eastman's article on the KMT defines conservatism as a backing of the status quo, and relying on

---

[76] Ibid., 50.   [77] Schwartz, "Notes on Conservatism," 12.   [78] Ibid., 14, 18–19.
[79] Arif Dirlik, "T'ao Hsi-sheng: The Social Limits of Change," in *LOC*, 305–31.
[80] Guy Alitto, "The Conservative as Sage: Liang Shu-ming," in *LOC*, 213–41.
[81] Alitto also formulates this argument in *The Last Confucian: Liang Shu-ming and the Chinese Dilemma of Modernity* (Berkeley: University of California Press, 1987 [1979]). See also Guy S. Alitto [Ai Kai], *Shijie fanwei nei de fan xiandaihua sichao: Lun wenhua shoucheng zhuyi* (Anti-modernization Thought in the Global Spectrum: On Cultural Conservatism) (Guiyang: Guizhou renmin chubanshe, 1991).
[82] Tu Wei-ming, "Hsiung Shih-li's Quest for Authentic Existence," in *LOC*, 242–75; Chang Hao, "New Confucianism and the Intellectual Crisis of Contemporary China," in *LOC*, 276–302.

Clinton Rossiter's argument that there is no conservatism in rapidly modernizing societies, Eastman argues that the KMT created a new and modern order and hence it was not conservative.[83]

In spite of these limitations, *The Limits of Change*, which also includes writings by China-born intellectuals in the United States, became a reference work for Chinese scholars who conducted research on the topic in later decades. In reform China, which reached its peak in the 1990s, there was a renewed interest in scholars of the Republican period who had engaged in various forms of *guoxue*, or national studies, as part of cultural and historical construction.[84] This "new *guoxue*" included research on those scholars who congregated around *Guocui xuebao* (Journal of National Essence, 1905–12), such as Deng Shi (1877–1945?), Liu Shipei, Huang Jie (1873–1935), and Zhang Taiyan (1869–1936).[85] It also involved those who had expressed criticism of May Fourth in the debates on Eastern and Western cultures and in the 1923 Debate on Science and Metaphysics. In the latter, critics such as Zhang Junmai (Carsun Chang, 1887–1969) opposed the all-powerfulness of science in favor of a perspective of human life (*renshengguan*) or *Weltanschauung*.[86] Among the critics of May Fourth who engaged in the debates on Eastern and Western cultures, especially after 1921, were the late Liang Qichao (1873–1929), Zhang Shizhao (1881–1973), Du Yaquan (1873–1933), and Liang Shuming, who took issue with the materialism, utilitarianism, progressivism, and scientism of Western modernity. These thinkers instead looked to the philosophers Bergson, Eucken, and Russell.[87] After traveling to Paris for the Paris Peace Conference and visiting several other European countries, Liang Qichao recorded, in his *Ouyou xinying lu* (Impressions on a Trip to Europe, 1919), his findings about the ruins of

---

[83] Lloyd Eastman, "The Kuomintang in the 1930s," in *LOC*, 191-212; Clinton Rossiter, *Conservatism in America* (Melbourne: Heinemann, 1955), 219.

[84] See Axel Schneider, "Bridging the Gap: Attempts at Constructing a 'New' Historical-Cultural Identity in the PRC," *East Asian History*, no. 22 (December 2001), 129–44.

[85] *LOC*, 57–89, includes a chapter on "national essence" by Laurence A. Schneider, titled "National Essence and the New Intelligentsia." On national essence, see Tze-ki Hon, *Revolution as Restoration: Guocui Xuebao and China's Path to Modernity, 1905–1911* (Leiden: Brill, 2013); on Zhang Taiyan, see Viren Murthy, *The Political Philosophy of Zhang Taiyan: The Resistance of Consciousness* (Leiden: Brill, 2011).

[86] The 1923 Debate on Science and Metaphysics, also referred to as the Debate on Science and the Philosophy of Life (*Kexue yu renshengguan*), took place between February and December 1923. The main participants were Zhang Junmai, Ding Wenjiang, Liang Qichao, Hu Shi, and Wu Zhihui. For an overview of this debate, see D. W. Y. Kwok, *Scientism in Chinese Thought, 1900–1950* (New Haven, CT: Yale University Press, 1965), 135–68.

[87] Chow, *May Fourth Movement*, 327. Liang Qichao is most famous for his involvement in the 1898 Reform Movement, but he was also a journalist and scholar. Zhang Shizhao is primarily known for establishing *Jiayin zazhi* (Tiger Magazine) in 1914 and *Jiayin zhoukan* (Tiger Weekly) in 1925. Du Yaquan was the founder and editor of the journal *Dongfang zazhi* (Eastern Miscellany).

postwar Europe. Research by scholars of the Republican period also includes work on the New Confucians of the 1920s and 1930s, such as Liang Shuming, who, in his *Zhong Xi wenhua ji qi zhexue* (Chinese and Western Cultures and Their Philosophies, 1921), famously criticizes Western civilization.[88]

One group that received much attention in the "new *guoxue*" of the 1990s was the group of scholars congregating around the journal *Xueheng* (Critical Review, 1922–33). Even though these scholars, the most prominent to criticize May Fourth, were subject to various interpretations in China during the 1990s, what is relevant for our purposes is that the discussions concentrated on the position of *Xueheng* in modern Chinese conservatism. In addition, some *Xueheng* scholars became associated with the ideal of independent scholarship of the early 1990s.[89] Part of the discussion on May Fourth radicalism included a reassessment of the *Xueheng* scholars as modern scholars whose ideas, it was argued, had emerged from intellectual exchanges. They had not rejected Western culture in toto, it was now claimed, but rather had tried to selectively integrate it with Chinese culture.

Even though the interpretation of conservatives as moderns was not a new argument, its meaning was significant in the early 1990s. It represented a re-evaluation of "conservative" Republican figures, such as the *Xueheng* scholars, who had been dismissed by their contemporaries, such as Hu Shi and Lu Xun, and later repressed during the Mao period. By the 1990s more nuanced perspectives portrayed these scholars as supportive of the May Fourth project and as advocates of the integration of Chinese and Western learning.[90] The re-evaluation of May Fourth conservatives formed part of the broader re-examination of the Republican period that took place after China's 1978 reform and opening up, and especially after the 1989 Tiananmen events, with a

---

[88] I include in the "new *guoxue*" those scholars in Schneider, "Bridging the Gap," 133.

[89] Drawing on Shen Songqiao and his own research on *Xueheng*, Axel Schneider divides the scholars involved in the *Xueheng* journal into three groups. They are (1) the "New Humanists" who studied with Irving Babbitt in the United States, namely Mei Guangdi, Wu Mi, Hu Xiansu, and others; (2) the school of historical geographers, including Liu Yizheng, Miao Fenglin, Zheng Hesheng, Zhang Qiyun, and others; and (3) those historians loosely associated with *Xueheng*, including Wang Guowei, Chen Yinke, Tang Yongtong, and Zhang Yinlin. One interpretation of *Xueheng* involves the first group and analyzes the position of *Xueheng* within Chinese conservatism and survival of the national spirit. Culture in this instance was static and the scholar was seen as a spiritual leader who was not separate from the political realm. Another interpretation regards the historians and the scholarship loosely associated with *Xueheng* as an example of Sino-foreign exchanges and the dynamism of Chinese culture. This interpretation, with its emphasis on historiographical methodology, regards the scholar as the guardian of Chinese culture. See Schneider, "Bridging the Gap," 135–38. On Chen Yinke, see Axel Schneider, "Between *Dao* and History: Two Chinese Historians in Search of a Modern Identity for China," *History and Theory* 35.4 (December 1996), 54–73.

[90] Yü Ying-shih, with Josephine Chiu-Duke and Michael S. Duke, eds., *Chinese History and Culture, Volume Two: Seventeenth Century through Twentieth Century* (New York: Columbia University Press, 2016), 210–11.

resort to nationalism and increased attention to reunification with Taiwan.[91] What concerns us regarding the 1990s' reassessment of Republican conservative figures is the argument that these Republican figures had global and cosmopolitan outlooks. In discussions of the May Fourth conservatives, mainland Chinese scholars argued that their ideas were no less formed by international currents and scholarship outside of China than had been the ideas of the May Fourth progressives.

Beginning in the 1990s, scholars outside of mainland China also deconstructed the simplistic distinction between Chinese conservatives, liberals, and radicals and emphasized the former's worldly outlook. In a 1994 article on "national history" in the early twentieth century, intellectual historian Yü Ying-shih depicts the *guocui* (national essence) scholars as pioneering modernizers who were receptive to new ideas. Lydia Liu analyzes the *Guocui* and *Xueheng* scholars from the perspective of how they related themselves to the West discursively rather than as conservatives. In a more recent volume on the *Guocui* scholars, Tze-ki Hon continues to argue for an interpretation of these scholars beyond the confines of the "teleology of revolution." In a study on cultural and political thought in Republican-era China, Edmund Fung draws on Schwartz's chapter in *The Limits of Change* to argue that the advocates of conservatism, liberalism, and socialism all operated within the same framework: all were responding to the "crisis of modernization" and all were preoccupied with saving the nation.[92] Singling out the global dimensions of the ideas of the May Fourth intellectuals went hand in hand with the new explorations in scholarship on the meaning of May Fourth in places such as Hong Kong and Singapore and other studies on the transnational dimensions of the May Fourth Movement.[93]

The volume *The Limits of Change* therefore is relevant in two respects. First, it paved the way for a reinterpretation of Republican conservatism as modern and global, which would continue both inside and outside of

---

[91] Qiang Zhang and Robert Weatherley, "The Rise of 'Republican Fever' in the PRC and the Implications for CCP Legitimacy," *China Information* 27.3 (2013), 277–300. I thank William Sima for bringing this article to my attention.

[92] See Yü Ying-shih, "Changing Conceptions of National History in Twentieth-Century China," in Erik Lönnroth, Karl Molin, and Ragnar Björk, eds., *Conceptions of National History: Proceedings of Nobel Symposium 78* (Berlin: Walter de Gruyter, 1994), 155–74; Liu, *Translingual Practice*; Hon, *Revolution as Restoration*; Edmund S. K. Fung, *The Intellectual Foundations of Chinese Modernity: Cultural and Political Thought in the Republican Era* (Cambridge: Cambridge University Press, 2010).

[93] Chen Xueran, *Wusi zai Xianggang: Zhimin qingjing, minzu zhuyi ji bentu yishi* (May Fourth in Hong Kong: Colonial Context, Nationalism and Local Consciousness) (Xianggang: Zhonghua shuju, 2014); David L. Kenley, *New Culture in a New World: The May Fourth Movement and the Chinese Diaspora in Singapore, 1919–1932* (London: Routledge, 2003); Erez Manela, *The Wilsonian Moment: Self-Determination and the International Origins of Anticolonial Nationalism* (Oxford: Oxford University Press, 2007).

mainland China in later decades. Second, it exposed some of the topics involved in the use of conservatism amid rapid change. The question was one of how a critique of modernity and an embrace of historical continuity could be relevant for the early 1990s. Paradoxically, the rejection of progressivism could be part of an effort to advocate a Chinese modernization theory. In addition, it argued that conservatism in Republican China was not about defending the sociopolitical order as a whole; some Chinese intellectuals would reiterate this argument during the 1990s as part of their efforts to protect Chinese culture from political and commercial intrusions.

The Crisis of the Intellectual

The unmaking of radicalism was also a realistic revolution because of the tensions between advocacy of a "pure" scholarship and the continuation of the tradition of public and politically engaged intellectuals responsible for the fate of the nation. Unmaking radicalism was a strategy to criticize the political engagement of intellectuals during the 1980s. Here we see an overlap with the *Xueheng* debates that centered on intellectuals as scholars detached from politics. The highlighting of scholarship served to reinstate the cultural and moral authority of intellectuals in response to their political and social "marginalization."[94] In the Maoist period, numerous intellectuals had been persecuted during the Anti-Rightist Campaign (1957–58), or during the mass campaigns of the Cultural Revolution when intellectuals were designated as the "Stinking Ninth" category. It was not until after 1976 that intellectuals were finally treated as valuable partners in the reform project. However, after Tiananmen and with the rise of experts, specialization, and professionalization in the 1990s, intellectuals were once again marginalized.

What do we mean by "intellectuals" in the setting of the early 1990s? The Western term "intelligentsia," which emerged in Russia in the 1860s, refers to public engagement and service to the nation.[95] The modern Chinese term for "intellectual," or "knowledgeable elements" (*zhishi fenzi*), was allegedly derived from the Russian reference. Earlier classical Chinese only had terms such as "literati," "scholar," and "gentry."[96] Before the abolition of the examination system in 1905, scholars were directly linked to the power-holders

---

[94] Gloria Davies, "The Self-Made Maps of Chinese Intellectuality," in Davies, ed., *Voicing Concerns*, 18.
[95] Zhidong Hao, *Intellectuals at a Crossroads: The Changing Politics of China's Knowledge Workers* (Albany: State University of New York Press, 2003), 377–85.
[96] Shiping Hua, *Scientism and Humanism: Two Cultures in Post-Mao China, 1978–1989* (Albany: State University of New York Press, 1995), 28.

because they were trained to serve the bureaucracy.[97] During the May Fourth period, such scholars would become independent intellectuals. Under Mao, when they served as intellectual cadres or "establishment intellectuals," they were both institutionally and discursively controlled by assignments to administrative work units, or *danwei*, and the need to engage in permanent "ideological work."[98] It was during this period that the term *zhishi fenzi* was widely used in official discourse to refer to mental workers. However, the term was expansive and included a range of various social groups, and it also contained ambiguities.[99] During the 1980s, intellectuals were partially rehabilitated and considered as valuable as workers, peasants, and soldiers, as reflected in the dictum "Respect knowledge, respect talent" (*zunzhong zhishi, zunzhong rencai*).[100]

With the repression of the 1980s' "New Enlightenment" after June 4, 1989, relations between intellectuals and the state once again underwent a dramatic change. The period between 1989 and 1991 was marked by oppression and ideological controls, with many intellectuals seeking refuge in the United States or elsewhere. Those who remained in mainland China refrained from direct confrontation with the state and engaged in self-reflection. As Timothy Cheek argues, the "ideological moment" of the period was one of "correcting revolutionary errors" and discussing systemic reform that could avoid the disasters of the Cultural Revolution and the state socialism of the Soviet Union.[101] After Tiananmen and the end of the Cold War, this issue gained new urgency.

During the early reform period, intellectuals were party-state public officials. As the reforms unfolded, the "disaggregation" of intellectuals signified the emergence of a broader variety of roles for intellectuals and the loss of their public impact; they could not be defined simply as critics or supporters of the

---

[97] This claim requires some nuance because the majority of degree holders did not obtain positions within the bureaucracy; instead, they played active roles in local communities. In addition, serving the state did not mean that the traditions of professionalism or of critical intellectuals were absent. See Merle Goldman and Timothy Cheek, "Introduction: Uncertain Change," in Goldman, Cheek, and Hamrin, eds., *China's Intellectuals and the State*, 1–20.
[98] Timothy Cheek, *The Intellectual in Modern Chinese History* (Cambridge: Cambridge University Press, 2015), 89, 129–30; Litzinger, "Theorizing Postsocialism," 36–37. Litzinger draws on Sheldon Hsiao-peng Lu, "Postmodernity, Popular Culture, and the Intellectual: A Report on Post-Tiananmen China," *Boundary 2* 23.2 (1996), 139–69. On "establishment intellectuals," see Carol Lee Hamrin and Timothy Cheek, eds., *China's Establishment Intellectuals* (Armonk, NY: M.E. Sharpe, 1986).
[99] Eddy U, "The Making of Chinese Intellectuals: Representations and Organization in the Thought Reform Campaign," *China Quarterly*, no. 192 (2007), 971–89. The category "student" was no less ambiguous. On the formation of this category during May Fourth, see Fabio Lanza, *Behind the Gate: Inventing Students in Beijing* (New York: Columbia University Press, 2010).
[100] Wang, *High Culture Fever*, 113.
[101] Cheek, *Intellectual in Modern Chinese History*, 217, 221.

Chinese state.[102] It was during this period that some established their own organizations, think tanks, and business and consulting firms that were independent of the state, and others forged alliances with social groups outside of the political establishment. What did not change, however, was a meandering between political commitment and a quest for intellectual autonomy.[103] Even those intellectuals who were not "establishment intellectuals" did not necessarily criticize the government; rather, they sought "to discover and transmit the truth" about the objects of their research.[104]

Mannheim and others divide intellectuals into several generations with a common consciousness. However, as Mannheim notes, this common consciousness came into being only following exposure to drastic change, and it was by no means uniform. Instead, we see the emergence of "generation units."[105] Wang Gungwu famously devised the notion of six generations of intellectuals, which was then introduced into China by the liberal intellectual Xu Jilin.[106] In this study, most mainland Chinese intellectuals belong either to the Cultural Revolution generation, born in the 1950s, whose education was interrupted when they became sent-down youths to the rural areas (*zhiqing*), or to the following generation, those born in the 1960s. The Cultural Revolution was, so to speak, "a birthmark for those of the Tiananmen generation."[107]

Even though the Cultural Revolution was the defining formative event for the generations born in the 1950s and 1960s, there are considerable differences in how Chinese intellectuals responded to these experiences due to factors such as class and/or geographic location.[108] The idea of a Cultural Revolution generation is hence insufficient to explain the diversity of intellectual thought in the early 1990s. In addition, the main voices of the anti-radicalism with which this generation engaged belonged to an older generation that was born in the 1930s and that had left China around 1949. The main representatives of this generation relevant for our discussion on radicalism are Yü Ying-shih (b. 1930), Lin Yü-sheng (b. 1934), and, slightly younger, Tu Wei-ming (b. 1940). Having received their educations in Hong Kong, Taiwan, or the

---

[102] Cheek, *Living with Reform*, 95–96; Timothy Cheek, "Xu Jilin and the Thought Work of China's Public Intellectuals," *China Quarterly*, no. 186 (June 2006), 406.

[103] Goldman and Cheek, "Introduction," 3.

[104] Edward Gu and Merle Goldman, "Introduction: The Transformation of the Relationship between Chinese Intellectuals and the State," in Gu and Goldman, eds., *Chinese Intellectuals between State and Market*, 12.

[105] Karl Mannheim, "The Problem of Generations," in Paul Kecskemeti, ed., *Essays on the Sociology of Knowledge* (London: Routledge and Paul, 1952 [1927–28]), 306.

[106] See Wang Gungwu, *The Chinese Intellectual: Past and Present* (Singapore: Faculty of Arts and Sciences, National University of Singapore, 1983); Xu Jilin, *Xu Jilin zixuanji* (Self-Selected Works of Xu Jilin) (Guilin: Guangxi shifan daxue chubanshe, 1999).

[107] Rowena Xiaoqing He, *Tiananmen Exiles: Voices of the Struggle for Democracy in China* (New York: Palgrave Macmillan, 2014), 118.

[108] Frenkiel, *Conditional Democracy*, 50.

United States, these intellectuals had been exposed to both liberalism and the movement to preserve Chinese culture and Confucianism outside of mainland China following the destruction of Chinese culture under the Communist regime after 1949. Paying attention solely to the Cultural Revolution denies the relevance of the interactions that took place between this older generation and the Cultural Revolution generation in the discourses of the 1990s.

Zhidong Hao makes a further distinction between "humanistic" and "technocratic" intellectuals based on their professional orientations.[109] Humanistic intellectuals, in Schumpeter's words, "talk or write about subjects outside their professional competence."[110] Whereas during the 1990s both professionalization and commercialization impacted the role of intellectuals in society, their self-perception as moral agents in the tradition of the Confucian literati (*shi*) remained unchanged. These "humanistic" intellectuals raised their voices from within universities and government think tanks, such as the Chinese Academy of Social Sciences (CASS), in contrast to the publishing houses and editorial committees that had played a significant part in the 1980s cultural discourse.[111] In this study, we primarily examine humanistic intellectuals, but the discussion on neoconservatism also includes some technocratic intellectuals as well as those who continued to serve as intellectual cadres during the reforms.

Most of the humanistic intellectuals were male, despite the fact that at that time there was an increase in the number of women pursuing education and entering academia. By the 1990s, even though over 30 percent of students in higher education were women, at the doctoral level the figure was as low as about 10 percent. Without graduate degrees, women remained among the lower ranks of the academic system, accounting for only about 9 percent of the some seventeen thousand full-time professors.[112] Nevertheless, some of these women were highly influential and were major actors in debates on radicalism. For example, Chapter 6 discusses the role of poetess Zheng Min (b. 1920) in the debate on the literary revolution.

During the 1990s, those in scholarly circles identified themselves as scholars (*xuezhe*) instead of as intellectuals (*zhishi fenzi*), the latter of which had the more "radical" connotation of political engagement. Philosopher Li Zehou has famously stated that the 1990s was an era in which "thinkers fade out,

---

[109] Hao, *Intellectuals at a Crossroads*, 1–72.
[110] Joseph A. Schumpeter, *Capitalism, Socialism, and Democracy*, 5th ed. (London: Allen & Unwin, 1976 [1942]), 146.
[111] Wang, "Introduction: Minds of the Nineties," 14. On the Chinese Academy of Social Sciences during the reform era, see Margaret Sleeboom-Faulkner, *The Chinese Academy of Social Sciences (CASS): Shaping the Reforms, Academia and China (1977–2003)* (Leiden: Brill, 2007).
[112] Ruth Hayhoe, *China's Universities 1895–1995: A Century of Cultural Conflict* (Hong Kong: Comparative Education Research Centre, University of Hong Kong, 1999), 130–31.

scholars protrude" (*sixiangjia danchu, xueshujia tuxian*).[113] The heroes of the 1990s included the historians Chen Yinke (1890–1969) and Wang Guowei (1877–1927), who came to be celebrated as advocates of intellectual independence and guardians of Chinese culture, unlike the more politically engaged May Fourth thinkers such as Hu Shi, Lu Xun, and Chen Duxiu. This change is also reflected in the popularity of the 1995 volume *Chen Yinke de zuihou ershi nian* (Chen Yinke's Last Twenty Years), which discusses Chen Yinke's struggle for intellectual freedom under the CCP between 1949 and 1969.[114] Nonetheless, advocacy of autonomy was by no means apolitical: a goal of scholarly excellence now turned to political reform. For this reason, the present study refers to the self-proclaimed scholars of the 1990s as intellectuals who were publicly engaged and passionate about the nation.

With the resort to scholarly endeavors, the attention to the quality of knowledge production, and the establishment of "academic norms" (*xueshu guifan*), new academic journals, such as the independent *Xueren* (The Scholar)[115] and *Yuandao* (True Way), ran articles on topics related to Chinese culture.[116] *Xueren*, for example, aimed to "retrieve the history of modern Chinese scholarship (*xueshushi*)."[117] In response to the scholarship of the 1980s, in journals such as *Xueren* and *Zhongguo shehui kexue jikan* (China Social Sciences Quarterly), scholars discussed the matter of "academic standardization."[118] Discussions on radicalism were directly related to efforts to create a new knowledge through a critique of existing epistemologies. Radicalism, it was argued, had wrongly been based on romanticism and abstract rationalism; what was needed instead was knowledge based on empiricism and experience.

Apart from the question of what constitutes an intellectual in these circumstances, there is also a related question: what is a *Chinese* intellectual? In the words of Timothy Cheek, "When is a Chinese intellectual Chinese and when

---

[113] Li Zehou, "Li Zehou dawen" (Li Zehou Answers Questions), *Yuandao* (True Way) 1 (1994), 1.
[114] Lu Jiandong, *Chen Yinke de zuihou ershi nian* (Chen Yinke's Last Twenty Years) (Beijing: Sanlian shudian, 1995). Historian Chen Yinke had been trained in Berlin, Paris, and the United States, and he was loosely associated with *Xueheng*. His research is concerned with the development of the Chinese "national spirit" between the third and tenth centuries. Also see Schneider, "Between *Dao* and History," 54–73.
[115] Sometimes also translated as "Scholars."
[116] Davies, "Self-Made Maps," 19. *Yuandao* came out in book form; the first volume (Beijing: Zhongguo shehui kexue chubanshe, October 1994) was edited by Chen Ming. Other academic journals that were established during the early 1990s include *Xueshu jilin* (Scholarship Collection) and *Yuanxue* (Original Studies).
[117] Wang, "Introduction: Minds of the Nineties," 17. *Xueren* is a book series published under the editorship of Chen Pingyuan, Wang Hui, and Wang Shouchang (Jiangsu: Jiangsu wenyi chubanshe, 1991–2000).
[118] Tang Yijie, "Some Reflections on New Confucianism in Mainland Chinese Culture of the 1990s," tr. Gloria Davies, in Davies, ed., *Voicing Concerns,* 125.

does one become foreign?"[119] In the early 1990s, this question was highly relevant given that Chinese intellectuals who had left China during various periods—before or after 1949, during the reform period, or before or after 1989—left their mark on discourses in China. In addition, Chinese scholars in China and those based at universities abroad argued about who had the right to represent China. Therefore, discussions on radicalism also reflected the impact of transnational forces in the transformation of Chinese intellectual identity. This occurred due to increasing global connectivity, due to the influence of the Chinese communities outside of mainland China, and due to the growing mobility of Chinese academics, many of whom were receiving their education abroad, working at foreign universities, or spending time at foreign institutions.

Especially Taiwan and Hong Kong, as part of the economic, political, and cultural geographies of what has been referred to as "Greater China," occupied a unique space in the intellectual exchanges of the 1980s and 1990s.[120] During the Cold War, Taiwan and Hong Kong served as places of refuge for those fleeing the Communist regime. However, seeking to revive Chinese culture in Taiwan and Hong Kong was challenging because they both had been under colonial rule and resident Chinese scholars had been cut off from the mainland. In addition, under the Cold War binary of capitalism versus Communism, their writings had an anti-Communist agenda.[121] During the reform period, however, these places became central capitalist nodes in a network of economic and cultural exchanges, which brought to the surface questions about Chinese identity. In addition, terms such as "Cultural China," which imagined a China beyond geopolitical boundaries and inclusive of Chinese communities globally, reflected the new realities of capitalist development and the redefinition of Chineseness from the margins.

Concepts and "Counter-Concepts"

This study centers around Chinese understandings of the terms "radicalism" and "conservatism" in the early 1990s. Despite its importance in Chinese

---

[119] Cheek, *Living with Reform*, 97.

[120] There is no consensus on the meaning of the term "Greater China," but because of the connotations of expansionism, scholars such as Wang Gungwu have expressed skepticism toward the term. For different interpretations of the term, including a "weaker" definition of "Greater China" as various processes of interaction between mainland China, Hong Kong, Macao, Taiwan, and, for some, also Chinese overseas, see *China Quarterly*, no. 136, Special Issue: Greater China (December 1993).

[121] Tze-ki Hon, "Introduction: Confucianism for the Contemporary World," in Tze-ki Hon and Kristin Stapleton, eds., *Confucianism for the Contemporary World: Global Order, Political Plurality, and Social Action* (Albany: State University of New York Press, 2017), xiii.

political and academic discourse, few studies have placed language at the center of analysis. Nevertheless, in the *Analects* we already find a connection between "rectifying names" (*zhengming*) and putting the affairs of state in order.[122] Paying attention to the relevance of language in political, cultural, and historical Chinese discourse, this study adopts a conceptual history approach. The merit of the approach of Reinhart Koselleck and others in their monumental work *Geschichtliche Grundbegriffe* (Basic Historical Concepts) is that it connects the history of concepts with social and political history and treats concepts as contested constructions.[123] Koselleck is especially interested in notions of time under modernity and how past, present, and future relate to one another. His term of "future expectations" is particularly relevant to the 1990s and explains the paradox of historical re-evaluations that were utterly unhistorical. In other words, Koselleck's "historico-conceptual comprehension" is suited to an analysis of the changing engagements with the past during a period of rapid transition.[124]

These conceptual changes reflect the broader sociostructural changes in the making of a postsocialist China amid global capitalism. It was precisely during periods of rupture that old words gained new meanings and that neologisms appeared.[125] The meaning of the term "conservatism," as Wang Hui notes, changed rapidly in the environment of reform. During the late 1970s, to be "conservative" meant to support Mao Zedong, as opposed to the "reformers" who were supporters of Deng Xiaoping. Those who were dubbed "reformers" during this period, however—such as Deng Liqun and Hu Qiaomu—became "conservatives" during the 1980s. After Tiananmen, the distinction between conservatives and reformers was difficult to uphold.[126] A principal change, however, was that intellectuals consciously identified with the terms "conservatism" and "neoconservatism." Conservatism could refer to a positive and healthy attitude toward gradual reform.

---

[122] See, for example, Schoenhals, *Doing Things with Words in Chinese Politics*, 2, where he refers to the *Analects*. Another study that pays attention to discourse in Chinese politics is David E. Apter and Tony Saich, *Revolutionary Discourse in Mao's Republic* (Cambridge, MA: Harvard University Press, 1994).

[123] Otto von Brunner, Werner Conze, and Reinhart Koselleck, eds., *Geschichtliche Grundbegriffe: Historisches Lexikon zur politisch-sozialen Sprache in Deutschland* (Basic Historical Concepts: A Dictionary on Historical Principles of Political and Social Language in Germany) (Stuttgart: Klett-Cotta, 1972–97). For an introduction to Koselleck and his works, see Niklas Olsen, *History in the Plural: An Introduction to the Work of Reinhart Koselleck* (New York: Berghahn Books, 2012).

[124] Tribe, "Introduction," xiv.

[125] Koselleck, *Futures Past*, 79. On the formation of neologisms in China, see Liu, *Translingual Practice*; Spira, *Conceptual History of Chinese -Isms*.

[126] Wang Hui, "The New Criticism," in Wang, ed., *One China, Many Paths*, 57–58.

Another reason why Koselleck's conceptual history is particularly useful for a study of China in the early 1990s is because of his idea of "counter-concepts" (*Gegenbegriffe*).[127] As Koselleck explains, counter-concepts are utilized for self-definition; those who apply counter-concepts are attempting to create unity through a reliance on simplistic dualisms. In some instances, such dualisms are unequally antithetical or asymmetric, and those who establish the dualism present their own stance in such a way that readers cannot but identify with their stance and negate the counter-concept. Moreover, those who are associated with a certain counter-concept generally do not identify with this position.

During the early 1990s radicalism functioned as a counter-concept against which the concepts of conservatism and neoconservatism (*xin baoshou zhuyi*) were projected. This is reflected in the title of the volume in which the main texts in the debate are collected, namely *Zhishi fenzi lichang: Jijin yu baoshou zhijian de dongdang* (Intellectual Positions: The Turbulence between Radicalism and Conservatism).[128] Instead of the triangle of liberalism, the New Left, and New Confucianism that was not yet present during the early 1990s, there was an engagement with "totalistic iconoclasm," a moderate preoccupation with socialism's negative effects, and a nativist turn.[129] Radicalism was one of the themes on which establishment intellectuals and humanistic intellectuals "initiated discussions separately, yet converged pragmatically."[130]

Sources and Overview of the Chapters

This study relies on journal articles, official newspapers, monographs, and edited volumes published in mainland China, Taiwan, Hong Kong, Singapore, and the United States. The sources were obtained from the Harvard-Yenching Library, the Sinological Institute of Leiden University, the National Library in Beijing, the library of Peking University, the Humanities and Social Sciences and Chinese libraries of NTU in Singapore, and Academia Sinica in Taipei. The study also draws on a series of interviews, conducted in Beijing and Shanghai, with the main scholars involved in the debates.

---

[127] For an explanation and some examples of "counter-concepts," see Reinhart Koselleck, "The Historical-Political Semantics of Asymmetric Counterconcepts," in *Futures Past*, 155–91.
[128] Li Shitao, ed., *Zhishi fenzi lichang: Jijin yu baoshou zhijian de dongdang* (Intellectual Positions: The Turbulence between Radicalism and Conservatism) (Changchun: Shidai wenyi chubanshe, 1999) (hereafter cited as *ZFL*).
[129] See Davies, "Self-Made Maps"; Gan Yang, *Tong santong* (Unifying the Three Traditions) (Beijing: Shenghuo, dushu, xinzhi sanlian shudian, 2007); Geremie Barmé, *In the Red: On Contemporary Chinese Culture* (New York: Columbia University Press, 1999).
[130] Wang, "Introduction: Minds of the Nineties,"16–17.

Journal articles include those published in newly founded academic journals, such as the leading Hong Kong academic journal *Ershiyi shiji* and the newly founded mainland journals, such as Hainan-based *Tianya*, *Dongfang*, and *Zhanlüe yu guanli* (Strategy and Management). It also includes articles in older journals, such as *Dushu*, which was established in 1979. Some discussions were conducted in more specialist journals, such as *Zhexue yanjiu* (Philosophy Research) or *Wenxue pinglun* (Literary Review). Edited volumes in which relevant articles from the debates are collected constitute another type of primary source. Apart from the main edited volume *Zhishi fenzi lichang* referred to above, these include volumes on May Fourth published in Taiwan and Hong Kong, and collections of Chinese debates on modern Chinese history or on specialized topics, such as neo-authoritarianism or postmodernism. Finally, collections of writings by Chinese intellectuals served as relevant primary sources.

Debates on radicalism reached a peak between 1989 and 1993, so these are our central years of concern. But both the formation and outgrowth of these debates transcend this narrow time frame. Based on the major political transitions, Wang Chaohua divides the 1990s into three distinct periods, namely, the period from June 4, 1989, to the international decline of socialism (1989–91), the period beginning with Deng's Southern Tour and ending with his waning power (1992–95), and, finally, the period when Jiang Zemin was unchallenged leader (1995–2003).[131] This book analyzes the debates during the former two periods. Chapters 2 and 3 cover the period from 1989 to 1991 and revolve around the dominant theme of politics. The defining contexts in which these discussions took place were the repression of the Tiananmen demonstrations and the implosion of the Soviet Union. Chapters 4, 5, and 6 center on the 1992–95 debates that followed the deepening of the economic reforms in 1992. The chapters demonstrate the changes in thinking about the economic, political, cultural, and historical aspects of Chinese modernity throughout the main periods of 1989–91 and 1992–95.

Chapter 2 discusses the political theory of neoconservatism in relation to its perceived counterpart of radicalism during the 1989–91 transitional period. The chapter compares use of the theory as a "label" with two main "banners," or advocacies, of the theory. The first advocacy is that of neoconservatism by the political theorist and historian Xiao Gongqin. The second advocacy is a 1991 policy document titled "Realistic Responses and Strategic Options for China after the Soviet Upheaval," which has been connected to the ideas of a group of "princelings," or the offspring of highly placed officials with vast networks in the CCP, government, or business, in response to the failed Soviet

---

[131] Wang, "Introduction: Minds of the Nineties," 14–15.

coup of August 1991. The chapter argues that these advocacies were linked in their rejection of radicalism and in their resort to non-Marxist theories of legitimation. However, Xiao Gongqin's theory of neoconservatism was coined in relation to problems of modernization and the Tiananmen demonstrations, whereas "Realistic Responses" was drafted in response to the Soviet coup of 1991 and the crisis of socialism. Furthermore, only Xiao's theory of neoconservatism can be considered the continuation of the theory of neo-authoritarianism and, more specifically, of the version of the so-called Southern School.

Chapter 3 looks at Xiao Gongqin's theory of neoconservatism from the perspective of its rejection of radicalism in modern Chinese history. Xiao Gongqin is a central figure in this chapter because it was he who first coined the term *xin baoshou zhuyi* in the post-Tiananmen situation to refer to a theory of modernization. This historical take on neoconservatism elaborates on the argument in this chapter, namely that we need to understand it more broadly as part of the discourse on modernization in China. The chapter questions Xiao's indebtedness to Edmund Burke in his advocacy of historical continuity because it was mediated through the figure of Yan Fu (1854–1921), who is known for his flirtations with Social Darwinism. The chapter argues that in spite of Xiao's reference to the social organism and his defense of a strong state, his reading of Burke manifested elements of both Friedrich Hayek and Karl Popper. In addition, his conservatism was about preserving the past for the future. The chapter, and Xiao Gongqin in particular, forms the bridge between the political theory of neoconservatism from 1989 to 1991 and the historical and cultural debates between 1992 and 1995 that are represented in the following chapters.

Chapter 4 discusses one of the main debates on history in the early 1990s, that is, the debate on radicalism and conservatism in modern Chinese history. The main vehicle for this debate, which peaked in 1992, was the influential Hong Kong journal *Ershiyi shiji*, which is indicative of the growing interactions between intellectuals in mainland China and Chinese intellectuals in Hong Kong, Taiwan, Singapore, and the United States. The chapter outlines the transformation of the latter's liberal and moral critique of mainland China, where the discussion revolved around economic reform by reference to two revolutionary models—the "realistic" Glorious Revolution versus the "utopian" French Revolution (1789–99). In the discussion, participants evaluated the merits of the Cultural Revolution and a century of change in China through the lens of Edmund Burke's criticism of the French Revolution. The chapter also discusses the broader implications of the debate by linking it to the issue of a "Cultural China" impacted by the economic rise of East Asia. After renewed economic reform, conservatism as the advocacy of a strong state gradually became replaced with a conservative liberalism or the advocacy of partial and gradual economic reform and the idea that the market was a stabilizer.

Chapter 5 shows how the debates on radicalism were transformed after renewed economic reform in 1992 and the perceived cultural radicalism of the May Fourth Movement. The chapter looks into the formation of debates on May Fourth during the period of its seventieth anniversary and during the 1989 protest movement. It shows the entanglement of the debates on May Fourth radicalism with the reassessment of Confucianism on mainland China amid the increasing commercialization and growing moral vacuum in society. The key figure in the chapter is the philosopher Chen Lai because of his prominence in these discussions. Furthermore, he indicates that he was intellectually influenced by Tu Wei-ming, which, as shown in Chapter 3, illustrates the trajectory of Chinese thought during the reform period, making its way to mainland China through China-born scholars based in the United States. The chapter argues that advocacies of New Confucianism were no less a manifestation of the realistic revolution of the time in their attempt to demonstrate the place of Confucianism in modernization and to redefine the role of the intellectual. In this chapter, these questions are discussed through the lens of Max Weber.

Continuing the reassessment of the May Fourth Movement in Chapter 4 and the impact of commercialization on intellectual life between 1992 and 1995, Chapter 6 looks at the engagement with radicalism and neoconservatism in discussions on the literary revolution, which was part of the May Fourth Movement. The assessment of the May Fourth legacy took the form of engagement with Chinese language and modernity to raise questions about cultural identity. Amid globalization, rapid commercialization, and the Marxist crisis of faith, postmodernist theories entered the debate as part of a broader effort to rethink Chinese modernity and the Chinese knowledge model. Specifically, the chapter discusses the role of the poetess Zheng Min in the discussion, as well as her exchanges with intellectuals in China and abroad. Behind these exchanges we discover anxiety about the place and identity of Chinese intellectuals during reform. The chapter argues that post-theories became part of a conservative argument about historical continuity because both postmodernism and reflections on radicalism engaged with socialist and liberal manifestations of modernity in China. Paradoxically, post-theories also became incorporated into a modernization narrative.

Chapter 7 concludes by revisiting the theme of realistic revolution from the perspective of the three main tensions in the debates: that between radicalism as a criticism of change that was made in the service of modernization; that between the quest for a more "objective" scholarship and the continued inherent moralism; and that between the self-proclaimed "scholars" and the remaining public engagement of intellectuals. It further evaluates the meaning and implications of the unmaking of radicalism. The debates, in spite of their limitations, questioned the merits of violent and permanent revolution, reflected a new divide among intellectuals with respect to the meaning of reform, and signified a crucial step in the transformation of Chinese academic discourse from the uncritical embrace of modernization in the 1980s to the more thorough criticism of Chinese modernity after the mid-1990s. The conclusion further engages critically with the field of Chinese intellectual history as an exercise in moral evaluation and offers some reflections on the function of history in Chinese intellectual debates. The chapter ends with a brief overview of intellectual developments after the mid-1990s and some final thoughts on the debates from the angle of developments in global intellectual history.

2 Neoconservatism and Doing Things with -*Isms*

> The major political event of the twentieth century is the death of socialism.
> Irving Kristol, *Neoconservatism: The Autobiography of an Idea*
>
> No one created a doctrine and called himself a neoconservative.
> Seymour Martin Lipset, "Neoconservatism: Myth and Reality"

"Be firm promoters of the Four Modernizations," encouraged a 1980 *Renmin ribao* (People's Daily) editorial that compared the task of modernizing agriculture, industry, national defense, and science and technology to a new Long March.[1] With the "Four Modernizations" (*sige xiandaihua*) written into the party and state constitutions in 1978 and 1979, respectively, the CCP shifted the primacy of politics and class struggle to economic development.[2] The famous Third Plenum of the Eleventh Central Committee of the CCP in December 1978 consolidated China's economic reforms as a focal point of policy, and the political elite attempted to justify ideologically both the economic shift and the leading part of the intellectual elite. This took place in the form of debates on practice, the stages of socialism, the idea of class, and class struggle.[3] Reform had to be presented as a continuation of past revolutionary practices, thus complicating the evaluation of Mao Zedong and the Cultural Revolution. As a solution, both Marxism-Leninism and Mao Zedong Thought remained part of the guiding ideology, as included in Deng Xiaoping's March 1979 "Four Basic Principles," namely socialism, the dictatorship of the proletariat, the leadership of the CCP, and Marxism-Leninism-Mao Zedong Thought, and rejecting the "extreme" Leftism that had originated in the 1950s. The "utopian" Marxism that resulted in the Cultural Revolution was

---

[1] "Be Firm Promoters of the Four Modernizations," *Renmin ribao* editorial, February 1, 1980, in James T. Myers, Jürgen Domes, and Milton Yeh, eds., *Chinese Politics: Documents and Analysis, Vol. 3: The Death of Mao (1976) to the Fall of Hua Kuo-feng (1980)* (Columbia: University of South Carolina Press, 1995), 433–38.

[2] The notion of the Four Modernizations is generally dated to Zhou Enlai's report to the Fourth National People's Congress (NPC) in 1975. However, Zhou had already proposed modernization in these four areas during the Third NPC in 1964. See Immanuel C. Y. Hsü, *China without Mao: The Search for a New Order*, 2nd ed. (Oxford: Oxford University Press, 1990), 92–93.

[3] Misra, *From Post-Maoism to Post-Marxism*, 10, 13.

now presented as an "aberration" and the current course was featured as a return to normalcy and "rationality."[4]

It was this double engagement with the CCP's revolutionary legacy that would return with a vengeance in 1989–91, the period at the center of this chapter. Faced with a domestic legitimacy crisis following the Tiananmen crackdown and with the decline of socialism internationally, neoconservatism in political discourse emerged as an alternative ideology that turned to traditional Chinese culture as a source of cohesion and that advocated stability and statism. Tiananmen, the revolutions of 1989, and the dissolution of the Soviet Union in 1991 exacerbated what had been a long-standing ideological crisis and lack of popular support for the regime. The latter was revealed in the "three belief crises"—of faith in socialism, of belief in Marxism, and of trust in the party.[5] In addition, attempts to justify change ideologically were inconsistent and were not supported by a majority of the political and intellectual elite.[6]

The period from 1989 to 1991, when the legitimacy crisis reached a peak, was an interlude between the repression of the Tiananmen demonstrators on June 4, 1989, and the deepening of the economic reforms following Deng Xiaoping's Southern Tour in early 1992. Domestically, following the repudiation of the Tiananmen demonstrations as a "counterrevolutionary disturbance" (*dongluan*) in the notorious April 26 editorial in *Renmin ribao*, underscoring stability became paramount. Internationally, the August 1991 Soviet coup in Moscow that heralded the end of the Soviet Union and the Communist Party of the Soviet Union (CPSU) further revealed the precarious nature of reform under Communist party leadership.

To understand the significance of the Soviet upheaval in particular, we need to briefly outline what it entailed. Mikhail Gorbachev, general secretary of the CPSU and later president of the Soviet Union, had initiated policies of *perestroika* (restructuring) and *glasnost* (opening), calling for radical economic reform and democratization. However, the policies failed to deliver and resulted in tensions in the Soviet Union that ultimately led to protests. As a last resort, the opponents of the reforms staged a coup. The coup began on August 19, the day before some Soviet republics were to sign a revised Union Treaty that envisioned a devolution of central power. Even though Boris Yeltsin, one of the opponents of Gorbachev's reform program who had recently been elected to the newly created post of president of the Russian Soviet Federative Socialist Republic, called for opposition to the coup, the

---

[4] Davies, *Worrying about China*, 113.
[5] Suisheng Zhao, "A State-Led Nationalism: The Patriotic Education Campaign in Post-Tiananmen China," *Communist and Post-communist Studies* 31.3 (1998), 288.
[6] Misra, *From Post-Maoism to Post-Marxism*, 4; X. L. Ding, *The Decline of Communism in China: Legitimacy Crisis, 1977–1989* (Cambridge: Cambridge University Press, 1994).

coup resulted in the end of both the CPSU and the Soviet Union. In December 1991, Gorbachev stepped down from his position as president, and the Soviet Union was formally dissolved on December 31.[7]

Chinese hard-liners feared that China's economic and political reforms would meet a fate similar to that of Gorbachev's "revolutionary" reforms.[8] The fate of Tiananmen in China and of reform in the Soviet Union had already become entangled during the historic visit of Gorbachev to Beijing on May 15, 1989. The 1989 events in China were followed by the collapse of the Communist regimes in Eastern Europe and the fall of the Berlin Wall in November 1989, but, unlike China, most of the regimes in Eastern Europe did not use military repression. However, in August 1991, as in June 1989 in China, Soviet leaders brought in the military to suppress the demonstrations and to end the coup.[9] Hence there was a fear of history coming full circle: with the collapse of Communism in Eastern Europe following on the heels of the Tiananmen demonstrations and the 1991 coup in Moscow, would Beijing be next?

Even though very few scholars paid much attention to ideology in the debates during the reform era, we cannot understand the rise of neoconservatism without relating it to the ideology and legitimacy crisis after 1989.[10] However, as argued below, we can discern crucial distinctions between the two main advocacies of neoconservatism, one of which was related to the post-Tiananmen setting and the problems of reform, and the other of which was connected to the events in the Soviet Union. Nevertheless, they shared a rejection of what they both referred to as "radicalism," that is, rapid economic reform and political democratization. In addition, amid crisis, both advocacies emphasized the importance of a strong state and both, to varying degrees, resorted to non-Marxist modes of legitimation. In this chapter, the contextualization of both advocacies, or "banners," of neoconservatism will be contrasted with the use of the "label" of neoconservatism in existing research, a distinction I borrow from Jin Yuanpu.[11] I argue that because the status quo was one of transition, the use of neoconservatism as a label led to its application to a

---

[7] Richard Sakwa, *The Rise and Fall of the Soviet Union, 1917–1991* (London: Routledge, 1999), 474–94.

[8] For the impact of these events on the CCP, see John W. Garver, "The Chinese Communist Party and the Collapse of Soviet Communism," *China Quarterly*, no. 133 (1993), 1–26.

[9] Timothy Brook, *Quelling the People: The Military Suppression of the Beijing Democracy Movement* (Stanford, CA: Stanford University Press, 1998), 14.

[10] Misra, *From Post-Maoism to Post-Marxism*, 4, 6–7. Misra lists Arif Dirlik, Maurice Meisner, Mark Selden, Joseph Fewsmith, Bill Brugger, and David Kelly as examples of scholars who paid attention to ideology during the reform-era debates.

[11] Jin Yuanpu, "He yi 'baoshou zhuyi' er you 'xin'?" (Why "Conservatism" and Why "Neo"?), in *ZFL*, 385.

range of positions that vary from Leftism or a move away from Leftism to nationalism and that extend much beyond the period 1989–91.

I further argue that a narrow interpretation of neoconservatism on a Left-Right axis based on pre-existing definitions of the theory ignores the historical dimension of neoconservatism as part of a century-old discourse on modernization. In fact, Chinese scholars involved in discussions on China's political transformation have already argued for an interpretation of neoconservatism along these lines. In his Columbia University dissertation, Wang Juntao, a well-known Tiananmen activist who was sentenced for thirteen years for his counterrevolutionary activities but was released in 1994 and exiled to the United States, links the theory of neoconservatism to discussions about reform and modernization.[12] The modernization dimension of the discussion will be elaborated in more detail in Chapter 3. Before analyzing the two main "banners" of neoconservatism in political discourse from the perspective of criticism of radicalism during the 1989–91 transitional period, we must first examine the neoconservatism label that has been applied in current studies.

Neoconservatism as the Middle Path

In existing research, one tendency has been to understand neoconservatism as a middle position between the political factions, as a modus vivendi among various groups, including the new interest groups from the reforms, such as the capitalists, the rulers, and the liberal intellectuals.[13] However, the labeling of groups in Chinese politics during the reform era is problematic because of the changes in language, the fluidity of factions, and the cycles of opening and tightening. In such a situation, Leftism would refer to conservatism and Rightism would refer to liberalism.[14] Neoconservatism is then an "intermediate" ideology, a "middle position" or a "middle path" between

---

[12] Wang Juntao, "Reverse Course: Political Neo-conservatism and Regime Stability in Post-Tiananmen China" (Ph.D. diss., Columbia University, 2006), 19. See also Li Ping, ed., *Zhongguo xia yi bu zenyang zou: Dangdai jingying da lunzheng* (What Is the Next Step for China? The Big Debate among the Contemporary Elite) (Toronto: Mingjing chubanshe, 1998). This book resulted from a project initiated by Wang Juntao and Chen Ziming, the other Tiananmen activist who was sentenced to thirteen years. Chen Ziming was also released in 1994 but was later rearrested and remained under house arrest until 2002. He died of pancreatic cancer in 2014. On the role of Wang and Chen in the Tiananmen demonstrations, see George Black and Robin Munro, *Black Hands of Beijing: Lives of Defiance in China's Democracy Movement* (New York: John Wiley, 1993).

[13] Gu Xin and David Kelly, "New Conservatism: Intermediate Ideology of a 'New Elite,'" in David S. G. Goodman and Beverley Hooper, eds., *China's Quiet Revolution: New Interactions between State and Society* (New York: St. Martin's Press, 1994), 231; Barrett L. McCormick and David Kelly, "The Limits of Anti-liberalism," *Journal of Asian Studies* 53.3 (August 1994), 805.

[14] Baum, *Burying Mao*, 14–15.

"conservatives"—which in the Chinese setting refers to the Old Left, namely figures such as Hu Qiaomu, Deng Liqun, Bo Yibo, Peng Zhen, and Chen Yun—and "radical reformers" or liberals.[15] Such a reading of neoconservatism leads to the identification of Leftist positions as political centralization and statism as well as a range of nationalist advocacies, including neoconservatism.

In addition to political centralization, advocacies of economic liberalism can also be associated with the theory of neoconservatism because economic liberalization is considered to be a "re-emergence," "remaking," or "reworking" of the late 1980s' neo-authoritarianism, which argued for both strong rule and economic reform.[16] Chinese intellectuals had already debated democracy and dictatorship in the early twentieth century, but in the late 1970s they witnessed advocacies of democracy in the form of the Democracy Wall Movement.[17] The Chinese debate on neo-authoritarianism was part of a wider debate on democracy against the background of developments in East Asia. The Four Mini Dragons of East Asia, as an example, the city-state of Singapore, had been successful in carrying out economic reforms under strong rule. Furthermore, the debate on neo-authoritarianism also emerged against the background of the dilemmas of reform, including the problems of urban reforms, social inequalities, inflation, and corruption as well as the unsuccessful introduction of price reforms in 1988.

To some Chinese neo-authoritarians, Mikhail Gorbachev was a model of a "reform-minded authority figure," and they believed that General Secretary Zhao Ziyang could play a similar role in China.[18] Zhao Ziyang reportedly introduced neo-authoritarianism to Deng Xiaoping in March 1989.[19] Scholars have regarded the debates on neo-authoritarianism as a tool in the elite struggles over reform between Deng's faction and Zhao's faction

---

[15] McCormick and Kelly, "Limits of Anti-liberalism," 821; Gu and Kelly, "New Conservatism," 220; Fewsmith, *China since Tiananmen*, 80; Michael Sullivan, "Democracy and Developmentalism: Contending Struggles Over Political Change in Dengist China, 1978–1995" (Ph.D. diss., University of Wisconsin–Madison, 1995), 342.

[16] See, for example, Schubert, "Was Ist Neokonservativismus?," 59; Youzhuo Li, "Will Neo-conservatism Dominate Post-Deng China?" *China Strategic Review* 2.2 (1997), 32; Wen-hui Tsai, "New Authoritarianism, Neo-conservatism, and Anti–Peaceful Evolution: Mainland China's Resistance to Political Modernization," *Issues & Studies* 28.12 (1992), 7; Michael J. Sullivan, "The Impact of Western Political Thought in Chinese Political Discourse on Transitions from Leninism, 1986–1992," *World Affairs* 157.2 (October 1994), 85; Joseph Fewsmith, "Neoconservatism and the End of the Dengist Era," *Asian Survey* 35.7 (1995), 637.

[17] For example, the early 1930s debates on democracy and dictatorship (*minzhu gen ducai de zhengbian*) played out between Hu Shi, Jiang Tingfu, Ding Wenjiang, and others in the journal *Duli pinglun* (Independent Critique).

[18] Li, "Will Neo-conservatism Dominate Post-Deng China?," 32–33.

[19] Sullivan, "Impact of Western Political Thought," 80–82.

and as a continuation of the advocacies of "enlightened despotism" and "political tutelage," or as an outgrowth of the earlier debates on democracy.[20] During the late 1980s, in discussions on democracy, the neo-authoritarians stressed that their ultimate goals were no different from those of the liberal democrats. After 1989, however, concerns about the establishment of a market economy were accompanied by concerns about preventing political instability.[21]

Like neoconservatism, seen on a Left-Right axis neo-authoritarianism was both a continuation of Leftist centralization and a radical economic shift to marketization. As both Shu Yun Ma and Harold Waterman assert, the elitist gradualist strategy behind neo-authoritarianism was conservative, but economically, advocating the market and private ownership, it was "perhaps the most radical doctrine that has ever been proposed in the history of Communist China."[22] Because of the role of the state and the elites and the creation of new interest groups within the state that accompanied the expansion of the market, for Leftist critic Wang Hui neoconservatism, neo-authoritarianism, and neoliberalism were all identical, even though neoliberals professed a belief in the spontaneous workings of the market.[23]

Consequently, researchers disagree about the extent to which the theory of neoconservatism moved away from Leninism. McCormick and Kelly point to the "ironies" of neoconservatism because it attempted to counter liberalism, while, at the same time, it also made "crucial concessions" to liberalism.[24] In contrast, for Wen-hui Tsai the transition from Leninism was less clear because neoconservatism resisted political democratization.[25] According to Feng Chen, neoconservatism represented a defense of a political middle ground, but with

---

[20] Sullivan, "Democracy and Developmentalism," 225. The first interpretation is present in most articles on "neo-authoritarianism." On the political entanglements of the theory, see, for example, Shu Yun Ma, "The Rise and Fall of Neo-authoritarianism in China," *China Information* 5.3 (1990), 5, 12–13 and Mark M. Petracca and Mong Xiong, "The Concept of Chinese Neo-authoritarianism: An Exploration and Democratic Critique," *Asian Survey* 30.11 (1990), 1116. For an example of the second perspective, see Arthur Waldron, "Warlordism versus Federalism: The Revival of a Debate?," *China Quarterly*, no. 121 (1990), 116–28. Merle Goldman's book *Sowing the Seeds of Democracy in China: Political Reform in the Deng Xiaoping Era* (Cambridge, MA: Harvard University Press, 1994) represents the third interpretation. See Sullivan, "Democracy and Developmentalism," 267n3–5.
[21] Kalpana Misra, "Curing the Sickness and Saving the Party: Neo-Maoism and Neo-conservatism in the 1990s," in Shiping Hua, ed., *Chinese Political Culture 1989–2000* (Armonk, NY: M.E. Sharpe, 2001), 147–48.
[22] Ma, "Rise and Fall of Neo-authoritarianism in China," 1–2, 16; Harold Waterman, "Which Way to Go? Four Strategies for Democratization in Chinese Intellectual Circles," *China Information* 5.1 (1990), 14.
[23] Wang Hui, *China's New Order: Society, Politics, and Economy in Transition*, ed. Theodore Huters (Cambridge, MA: Harvard University Press, 2003), 59–60.
[24] McCormick and Kelly, "Limits of Anti-liberalism," 821.
[25] Tsai, "New Authoritarianism, Neo-conservatism, and Anti-Peaceful Evolution," 1.

the "new" element of using a different approach and a different rhetoric.[26] For Li Youzhuo, because neoconservatism attempted to replace the ideology but to preserve the elite power structure, it was a "Communist liberalism."[27]

As already noted, in the Chinese environment conservatism, representing preservation of the status quo, refers to a Leftist position. Since the prefix "neo" can imply either an affiliation with Leftism or a move away from Leftism, neoconservatism came to embrace both, as, for example, in the 1994 book *Looking at China through a Third Eye*.[28] The alleged author is Wang Shan, who had been educated at Peking Normal University after having experienced the Cultural Revolution and then became deputy director of Peking Opera College. According to its critics, however, the book was linked to the "princelings" (*taizidang*)—a term used to refer to the offspring of government officials who often occupied key positions in government or business—in particular Pan Yue, son-in-law of General Liu Huaqing and deputy editor at *China Daily* at the time. Pan was also associated with the document "Realistic Responses" that will be discussed below.[29] *Looking at China through a Third Eye* examines the following six topics: foreign intervention in Chinese affairs, the serious peasant problem, the weakness of Chinese intellectuals, Chinese cadres, methods for social control, and China in the international community. A common theme running through all six chapters is the mounting disintegration as a result of Deng Xiaoping's reforms, which had resulted in a decline of authority, a waning of ideology and morality, and a rise of social problems. The current problems were blamed on those intellectuals who "lacked an autonomous spirit" and on the peasantry who posed a serious danger to the regime.[30]

Looking at China through a Third Eye has been labeled neoconservative because it seems to represent a "mournful elegy," marking the death of the socialist model.[31] Christopher Hughes argues that the views expressed in the book come "closest to the wholesale departure from socialism in favor of elitist

---

[26] Feng Chen, "Order and Stability in Social Transition: Neoconservative Political Thought in Post-1989 China," *China Quarterly*, no. 151 (1997), 593.
[27] Li, "Will Neo-conservatism Dominate Post-Deng China?," 39.
[28] Wang Shan, *Disan zhi yanjing kan Zhongguo* (Looking at China through a Third Eye) (Taipei: Zhouzhi wenhua, 1994).
[29] See Liu Binyan, "Ping 'Disan zhi yanjing kan Zhongguo'" (On *Looking at China through a Third Eye*), *Beijing zhi chun* (Beijing Spring), no. 17 (October 1994), 23–39; He Pin, "'Disan zhi yan' haishi 'disan zhi shou'? Liu Huaqing nüxu Pan Yue he 'Disan zhi yanjing kan Zhongguo'" (A "Third Eye" or a "Third Hand"? Liu Huaqing's Son-in-law Pan Yue and *Looking at China through a Third Eye*), *Beijing zhi chun*, no. 17 (October 1994), 21–22.
[30] Wang, *Disan zhi yanjing kan Zhongguo*, 147.
[31] Suisheng Zhao, *A Nation-State by Construction: Dynamics of Modern Chinese Nationalism* (Stanford, CA: Stanford University Press, 2004), 263.

authoritarianism," as expressed in some neoconservative advocacies.[32] Author Wang Shan criticizes both Deng Xiaoping and Jiang Zemin for not taking correct measures with regard to the weakening of the state as a consequence of the reform and opening up. Nationalism was one part of the new ideology in the "third eye" perspective; the other two were Social Darwinism and Marxism. In general, as Hughes rightly argues, the book is neoconservative because of its advocacy of elitist nationalism to guide the market reforms and its stress on the relevance of the middle class in reform. However, neoconservatives certainly dismissed the anti-intellectualism of the book.

Although Peter Moody also regards Wang Shan's book as an expression of neoconservatism, he applies the label for different reasons. For Moody, the book was part of a trend of "conservative populism," or "radical conservatism," which was identified with *Leftist* tendencies. In his definition of conservatism, Moody includes "Leftist" tendencies because they were a "conservative populist critique of market liberalism."[33] Hence, for Moody, Wang Shan's book belongs to the same type of criticism of "conservative" reform as the so-called "Ten-Thousand-Character Manifestos" that circulated among party and government leaders in 1995 and that were attributed to the Marxist ideologue Deng Liqun. These manifestos warned of the national security dangers posed by the reforms, especially since 1992, in terms of ownership structure, class, ideology, and the future of the CCP.[34] Here we can see how use of neoconservatism on a Left-Right axis can be confusing in a Chinese situation—for some, Wang Shan's book marked the decline of Leftist tendencies, whereas for others it represented Leftist criticism of the reforms.

Another theme associated with neoconservatism is that of a centralized state. Hu Angang and Wang Shaoguang have been linked to neoconservatism because of their 1993 research report on China's state capacity.[35] Wang

---

[32] Christopher R. Hughes, *Chinese Nationalism in the Global Era* (London: Routledge, 2006), 93. Hughes also mentions support for the book from Chen Yuan, son of party elder Chen Yun, and Pan Yue.

[33] Moody, *Conservative Thought*, 7.

[34] The official title of the manifesto is "Yingxiang woguo guojia anquan de ruogan yinsu" (Various Factors Influencing Our Country's National Security). For a translation, see *China Quarterly*, no. 148 (December 1996), 1426–41. Deng Liqun claimed that he did not write the document; it was followed by three similar documents that circulated between 1995 and 1997. See He, *Dictionary of the Political Thought*, 295–96.

[35] Wang Shaoguang and Hu Angang, *Jiaqiang zhongyang zhengfu zai shichang jingji zhuanxing zhong de zhudao zuoyong: Guanyu Zhongguo guojia nengli de yanjiu baogao* (Strengthening the Guiding Role of the Central Government in the Transition to a Market Economy: A Research Report on China's State Capacity) (Shenyang: Liaoning renmin chubanshe, 1993). The report was also published in Hong Kong (Oxford University Press, 1994). Translated by Joseph Fewsmith as "Wang Shaoguang Proposal (I) and (II)," in *Chinese Economy* 28.3 (May–June 1995) and 28.4 (July–August 1995). A shorter version of the report appears in *Ershiyi shiji*, no. 21 (February 1994), 5–14, under the title "Zhongguo zhengfu jiqu nengli de xiajiang ji qi houguo" (The Decrease in the Extractive Capacity of the Chinese Government and

Shaoguang, a political scientist educated at Cornell University, was working at Yale University at the time. Hu Angang, an influential economist, was first based at the Chinese Academy of Sciences (CAS), but as a postdoctoral researcher at Yale he became familiar with Wang Shaoguang. In their report, they argue that the central state's capacity to extract state revenue had been weakened due to the tax reforms of the 1980s.[36] Deng Xiaoping's reforms had led to decentralization—or, more specifically, to "devolving authority and granting benefits" (*fangquan rangli*)—and thus the authors advocated a more centralized reform.[37]

The differences between Wang and Hu's report and the views of the Old Leftists become clear if we compare the report to, for example, the several Ten-Thousand-Character Manifestos that appeared between 1995 and 1997. These manifestos regarded the decline of the public sector, the emergence of a "non-governmental bourgeois class," and the embryonic "new bureaucrat comprador bourgeoisie" as threats, whereas Wang Shaoguang and Hu Angang are not opposed to these changes.[38] As Fewsmith correctly points out, the "neo-statists" shared some positions with the "popular nationalists"—both wanted to give the people a voice and to deconstruct the special interests of the privileged.[39] It is noteworthy that Hu Angang and Wang Shaoguang collaborated with Kang Xiaoguang, who had graduated from the Department of Ecology at the CASS.[40] During the 1990s, Kang Xiaoguang researched poverty and poverty relief as well as semi-independent social organizations, topics about which he published in the journal *Zhanlüe yu guanli*. Hu Angang and Wang Shaoguang's advocacy of a strong state and their attentiveness to social justice once again reveal that the label "neoconservatism" refers to an amalgamation of

---

Its Consequences). Wang Shaoguang replies to the criticisms expressed in the debate, in "Zai lun Zhongguo zhengfu jiqu nengli—Jianda Yang Dali, Cui Zhiyuan, Rao Yuqing, Xiao Geng zhu xiansheng" (Further Discussion on the Extractive Capacity of the Chinese Government: Reply to Yang Dali, Cui Zhiyuan, Rao Yuqing, and Xiao Geng), *Ershiyi shiji*, no. 22 (April 1994), 129–36.

[36] Fewsmith, *China since Tiananmen*, 134–35.

[37] Wang and Hu, *Guanyu Zhongguo guojia nengli de yanjiu baogao*. See also Wang Shaoguang and Hu Angang, *The Political Economy of Uneven Development: The Case of China*, ed. Mark Selden (Armonk, NY: M.E. Sharpe, 1999).

[38] Fewsmith, *China since Tiananmen*, 136.   [39] Ibid., 139–40.

[40] In 2005 Kang became professor of regional economics and politics at Renmin University. He is also known for his writings on Falungong and Confucianism. I thank Joseph Fewsmith for bringing Kang to my attention and for sharing some of Kang's writings, such as Kang Xiaoguang, *Xin baoshou zhuyi zhenglunji* (Collected Political Essays on Neoconservatism) (Beijing: n.p., 2002). See Hu Angang, Wang Shaoguang, and Kang Xiaoguang, *Zhongguo diqu chaju baogao* (A Report on China's Regional Disparities) (Shenyang: Liaoning renmin chubanshe, 1995).

themes, some of which do not differ from those in the official media or from Old Leftism.

Neoconservatism and Nationalist Advocacies

A second related interpretation of neoconservatism is associated with the theory of nationalism, as for example in a 1997 issue of *Chinese Law and Government* titled "Nationalism and Neoconservatism in China in the 1990s," edited by Stanley Rosen of the University of Southern California.[41] Whereas the nationalism favored by the neoconservatives arose in the specific milieu of the period between 1989 and 1991, the nationalism of some of the authors in this issue of the journal appeared during a later period and was not related to the fear of political instability of the post-Tiananmen years. In addition, this advocacy of nationalism was also part of the official discourse and during the early 1990s could be found across the entire political spectrum.[42] This issue of *Chinese Law and Government* also includes articles by liberal intellectuals, who use the label neoconservatism to discredit the nationalists. As Rosen explains, during the 1990s intellectual independence was considered a badge of honor, and the various factions accused one another of aligning with the government.[43] Therefore, the issue includes articles by both advocates of neoconservatism and by nationalists who were also labeled neoconservatives.

The issue also features one 1996 article by Wang Xiaodong, a graduate of Peking University who wrote on politics, economics, and international relations and who later became editor of the journal *Zhanlüe yu guanli*, one of the main sources of the debates on nationalism. Allegedly representing the views of the military,[44] the journal organized several conferences on nationalism during the early 1990s. Using the pseudonym Shi Zhong, Wang Xiaodong argues that the rise of nationalism during the 1990s was a necessity and a return to normalcy after the "national nihilism" of the 1980s.[45] Wang defends Chinese nationalism from its portrayals in the Western media and from

---

[41] Stanley Rosen, ed., "Nationalism and Neoconservatism in China in the 1990s," *Chinese Law and Government* (hereafter cited as *CLG*) 30.6 (November–December 1997), 3–100.

[42] Hughes, *Chinese Nationalism in the Global Era*, 8; Geremie Barmé, "To Screw Foreigners Is Patriotic: China's Avant-Garde Nationalists," *China Journal*, no. 34 (July 1995), 215.

[43] Stanley Rosen, "Guest Editor's Introduction," in Rosen, "Nationalism and Neoconservatism in China in the 1990s," 7.

[44] Suisheng Zhao, "Chinese Intellectuals' Quest for National Greatness and Nationalistic Writing in the 1990s," *China Quarterly*, no. 152 (December 1997), 736.

[45] Shi Zhong (Wang Xiaodong), "Zhongguo de minzu zhuyi he Zhongguo de weilai" (Chinese Nationalism and the Future of China), *Mingbao Yuekan* (Mingbao Monthly), no. 9 (1996), tr. in *CLG* 30.6 (November–December 1997), 8–27 (translated from the original, which differed from the version published in *Mingbao Yuekan*).

references by Chinese liberals to its authoritarian and antidemocratic nature. Nationalists underscored order and state power because, as the events in the former Soviet Union and Eastern Europe had shown, they knew that in the event of chaos the West surely would not come to their rescue.[46]

Similarly, the article on nationalism by economist Sheng Hong referred to in the above-noted issue of *Chinese Law and Government* was not linked to the neoconservative leitmotifs of the post-Tiananmen period. Instead, the label was derived from his introduction of institutional economics to China, which was used to reject the reform "shock therapy" of the Soviet Union.[47] In his article, Sheng Hong discusses the cultural strategies of nationalism and "cosmopolitanism" (*tianxia zhuyi*) from the perspective of global economic efficiency.[48] Sheng Hong insists that China had been a cosmopolitan cultural civilization ever since unification under the Qin dynasty (221 BCE–206 CE), whereas divided Europe had known nationalism and rule only by "warring states."[49] In response to the "bullying and humiliation" by the Western powers ever since the First Opium War (1839–42), China had no choice but to embrace nationalism, but this was a defensive rather than an expansionist nationalism.[50] Like Wang Xiaodong, Sheng Hong also published his nationalist advocacies in the journal *Zhanlüe yu guanli*, thereby provoking criticism from liberal intellectuals such as Xu Youyu.[51] Sheng Hong also upheld that the expansion of Western civilization, distinct from that of Chinese civilization, was based not on the rules of free trade but rather on brute force and Social Darwinism.

This promotion of nationalism clearly was not related to the themes of political legitimacy and stability as expressed between 1989 and 1991. Wang Xiaodong and Sheng Hong were writing in the environment of growing pride as a result of China's economic successes and of a perception that after two incidents in 1993 other nations were growing hostile to China. The first incident was the *Yinhe* incident, when the Chinese cargo ship *Yinhe* was stopped by the US Navy in the international waters of the Indian Ocean because intelligence had suggested that it was carrying materials to produce chemical weapons. The second incident was the awarding of the 2000 summer Olympics to Sydney rather than Beijing. Additional factors that had also given rise to this nationalism were opposition to China's bid to enter the General

---

[46] Ibid., 19, 21–22, 24–25.   [47] See Fewsmith, *China since Tiananmen*, 80–82.
[48] Sheng Hong, "Cong minzu zhuyi dao tianxia zhuyi" (From Nationalism to Cosmopolitanism), *Zhanlüe yu guanli*, no. 1 (1996), 14–19, tr. in *CLG* 30.6 (November–December 1997), 31–42.
[49] Sheng, "From Nationalism to Cosmopolitanism," 38.   [50] Ibid., 39–41.
[51] Sheng Hong, "Shenme shi wenming" (What Is Civilization?), *Zhanlüe yu guanli*, no. 5 (1995), 88–98. For Xu Youyu's criticism, see "Shi jingjixue tiaozhan lishi, haishi luoji daiti shishi" (Is Economics Challenging History or Is Logic Replacing Empirical Facts), *Zhanlüe yu guanli*, no. 2 (February 1996), 94–97.

Agreement on Tariffs and Trade (GATT) as well as the Taiwan Straits crisis of 1995 and 1996. This popular nationalism was more in accord with anti-American and anti-Japanese sentiments rooted in their perceived containment policy, as expressed in the 1996 best seller *China Can Say No* than with neoconservative sponsorship of political stability and centralization after Tiananmen.[52] In addition, this popular nationalism also contained an antigovernment tone, whereas neoconservatism was highly elitist in nature.[53]

He Xin (b. 1949), a former researcher at the Institute of Modern History and the Institute of Literature of CASS, is also often considered to be representative of neoconservatism. The political liberal Liu Xiaobo (1955–2017) referred to He Xin as "the most visible symbol of China's so-called neo-conservatism movement" in the aftermath of June Fourth.[54] Whereas Liu Xiaobo applied the term to voice political criticism of He Xin's support for the government crackdown in 1989, others used it because of the themes of statism, nationalism, gradual economic reform, and Realpolitik in his writings.[55] Fewsmith refers to He Xin as an example of a "muscular" neoconservatism because his nationalist writings are more extreme than those of other nationalists.[56]

There are some similarities between He Xin's criticism of the radicalism of the 1980s and the Cultural Revolution, and the criticism of the radicalism by other neoconservatives, as discussed below.[57] But He Xin also embraced Marxism (he even argued that Marxism should become a religion) and his views were used to support such media campaigns.[58] For example, according to a January 1991 article in *Zhongguo qingnianbao* (China Youth Daily), He Xin favored a gradual modernization and a creative transformation of Chinese culture. He also sought to expose the "latent strategic interests" behind the Western bourgeoisie's "peaceful evolution."[59] In various other writings, He

---

[52] Song Qiang, Zhang Zangzang, Qiao Bian, et al., *Zhongguo keyi shuo bu: Lengzhan hou shidai de zhengzhi yu qinggan jueze* (China Can Say No: Political and Emotional Choices in the Post–Cold War Era) (Beijing: Zhonghua gongshang lianhe chubanshe, 1996).

[53] Fewsmith, *China since Tiananmen*, 156.

[54] Liu Xiaobo, "China's Neo-political Conservatism in the 1990s," *China Strategic Review* 1.9 (December 1996), 12.

[55] On statism, see, for example, He Xin, *Lun zhengzhi guojia zhuyi: He Xin jinqi zhenglun* (On Political Statism: Recent Political Commentaries by He Xin) (Beijing: Shishi chubanshe, 2003).

[56] Fewsmith, *China since Tiananmen*, 93.

[57] See He Xin, "Wode kunhuo yu youlü" (My Perplexities and Concerns), *Xuexi yuekan* (Study Monthly), no. 12 (1988), 36–37; He Xin, "A Word of Advice to the Politburo," tr. Geremie R. Barmé, *Australian Journal of Chinese Affairs*, no. 23 (January 1990), 49–76, 54–55.

[58] David Kelly, "Chinese Marxism since Tiananmen: Between Evaporation and Dismemberment," in Goodman and Segal, eds., *China in the Nineties*, 27. By doing so, He was responding to the merger of Marxism and science during the reform era that had allowed intellectuals to discuss certain issues more openly and to move beyond the framework of dialectical materialism and the theory of consciousness. See ibid., 27.

[59] Fang Wang, "Huaxia wenming chuantong yu zuguo xiandaihua de sikao: Lun He Xin de wenhuaxue yanjiu" (Reflections on Chinese Civilization and Culture and the Modernization of

Xin warns against the global hegemony of the United States and criticizes the "romanticism" of the Chinese reforms.[60] As David Kelly argues, He Xin's pragmatic justification of Marxism and his idealization of the 1950s were no different from the nostalgia and advocacy of Marxism among "conservative" cadres such as Hu Qiaomu.[61] It is therefore clear that references to nationalism and tradition or criticism of "radicalism" were not necessarily indicative of what researchers call the "intermediate position" of neoconservatism.

Even if we restrict the label of neoconservatism to the period from 1989 to 1991, we should note that nationalism, both in the form of patriotism and in highlighting China's unique conditions, was widely appropriated in media campaigns of the time. After the death of Hu Yaobang and the dismissal of Zhao Ziyang in 1989, "conservative" moderates, such as Jiang Zemin and Li Peng, and hard-line ideologues, such as Gao Di—then editor of *Renmin ribao*—and Deng Liqun, gained power. This power shift enabled the emergence of propaganda that emphasized patriotism, political stability, and "national conditions" (*guoqing*), thus preventing a focus on "universalist" democracy and human rights.[62] In the aftermath of Tiananmen, a consensus was formed among the various factions that the way forward would involve a slowing down of the economic reforms. Moderates also supported those propaganda campaigns that promoted stability and opposed attempts to reverse socialism. After the Soviet coup of August 1991, however, this consensus began to fall apart as disagreements about the pace of the reforms and the spread of the propaganda campaigns increased.[63]

The stress on "national conditions" was part of a patriotic education campaign that began in 1991 and peaked in 1994. At the height of this campaign, which included special courses, textbooks, magazines, journals, and even a Research Center on National Conditions at Peking University, the State Education Commission designated "One Hundred Patriotic Education Bases," which would later be increased in number.[64] The unique "national conditions" underscored in this campaign included China's overpopulation, limited natural resources, partially developed economy, and long history and cultural traditions.[65] Conservative ideologues interpreted the Soviet coup and

the Motherland: On He Xin's Research on Cultural Studies), *Zhongguo qingnianbao*, January 10, 1991, 4.

[60] See Fewsmith, *China since Tiananmen*, 93–95.
[61] Kelly, "Chinese Marxism since Tiananmen," 29.
[62] The term *guoqing*—literally meaning "the Chinese situation" (*Zhongguo qingkuang*)—had already been used in the cultural and political debates during the late nineteenth century and again during the 1930s. See Barmé, "To Screw Foreigners Is Patriotic," 212n11.
[63] Sullivan, "Democracy and Developmentalism," 324–26, 328, 332–33.
[64] See Zhao, "State-Led Nationalism," 287–302. See also Zhao, "Chinese Intellectuals' Quest," 743.
[65] Zhao, "State-Led Nationalism," 296–97.

the implosion of the Soviet Union several months later as confirmation of the Western strategy of "peaceful evolution." Against this background of calls for patriotism, stability, and "national conditions," did neoconservatism offer anything new? To answer this question, we must move away from its use as a label and analyze its two main manifestations that supported its criticism of radicalism.

Neoconservatism: Banners against Radicalism

Whereas neoconservatism emerged as a label in the American context, in the early 1990s some Chinese intellectuals actively began to identify with neoconservatism. In the United States, the term was first coined as a label to discredit political renegades—"no one created a doctrine and called himself a neoconservative," as Seymour Martin Lipset wrote.[66] In particular, the label was used to denote the intellectual trajectory of the so-called New York intellectuals between the 1930s and the 1960s. Irving Kristol, who is often considered to be the godfather of the American neoconservative movement, has described his own intellectual trajectory from "youthful socialism" to "self-critical liberalism," and then to "neoconservatism."[67] In contrast, in China some intellectuals consciously used the term to put forward alternative views of reform. This was a remarkable development; under the dominant narrative of revolution, conservatism originally signified an opposition to progress. Therefore, it is imperative to grasp why and how Chinese advocates of neoconservatism employed the term during the early 1990s. We must distinguish between neoconservatism as a "label" and neoconservatism as a "banner," as writes Jin Yuanpu, a literary scholar who obtained his doctorate from CASS.[68]

It is here that a conceptual history approach is relevant; there was a clear shift in the connotation of conservatism that was linked to the economic, political, and social ruptures. Both June Fourth and the international decline of socialism prompted a search for alternative sources of legitimacy. Conservatism (*baoshou*—consisting of *bao* 保, meaning "to protect," "to keep," and "to guarantee," together with *shou* 守, "to guard," "to defend," and "to abide by the law") initially referred to the sum of these compounds, namely, to guard, to protect, and to preserve. However, after linear visions of history

---

[66] Seymour Martin Lipset, "Neoconservatism: Myth and Reality," in Carl-Ludwig Holtfrerich, ed., *Ernst Fraenkel Vorträge zur amerikanischen Politik, Wirtschaft, Gesellschaft und Geschichte* (Ernst Fraenkel Lectures on American Politics, Economy, Society, and History) (Berlin: John F. Kennedy-Institut für Nordamerikastudien, 1988), 15.

[67] Irving Kristol, *Neoconservatism: The Autobiography of an Idea* (New York: Free Press, 1995), ix.

[68] Jin, "He yi 'baoshou zhuyi' er you 'xin'?," 385.

entered China during the late nineteenth century, conservatism came to refer to preservation of the old order and opposition to any change or reform.[69] Under Mao, conservatives became associated with "feudalism" and "backwardness." In the early 1990s, the prefix "neo" was added to conservatism, but what did this signify?

In general, the prefix "neo" is used either to provide a theory with respectability by giving it a historical dimension or to discredit a theory by linking it to an earlier theory that had negative connotations.[70] In an article included in the edited volume *Zhishi fenzi lichang: Jijin yu baoshou zhijian de dongdang*, Wang Yuechuan, professor of Chinese literature at Peking University, argues that use of the prefix "neo" in the Chinese milieu refers to the revival of conservatism after a long period of decline. It also provides a trace of acknowledgment of classical liberalism.[71] As we will see in Chapter 4, this acknowledgment of classical liberalism applied more to the later use of the term in cultural and historical discourse rather than to the political use of the term during the 1989–91 period. In contrast, in another article in the same volume, Wang Sirui argues that, as opposed to the "Burkean" and classical liberalist essence of neoconservatism in the United States, Chinese neoconservatives were antiliberal and upheld "statism" (*guojia zhuyi*), "new order-ism" (*xin zhixu zhuyi*), and nationalism.[72] Wang Sirui's claim applies more to the 1989–91 period when advocacies of conservatism included defense of a strong state and stability.

Given the negative historical connotation of the term "conservatism" in the Chinese setting, the prefix "neo" was used to indicate its difference from older forms of conservatism, as Wang Juntao argues.[73] A notable distinction between American and Chinese neoconservatism is that the former is characterized by a sense of moral and cultural crisis, whereas in China it is characterized as a legitimacy crisis. Chen Xiaoming, a researcher in the Department of Literature at CASS at the time who later became a professor at Peking University, argued that neoconservatism could engage in the construction of

---

[69] Li Guoyan et al., eds., *Dangdai Hanyu cidian* (A Contemporary Chinese Dictionary) (Shanghai: Shanghai cishu chubanshe, 2001), 32, 1024; Hanyu dacidian bianyuanhui (Chinese Dictionary Editorial Committee), ed., *Hanyu da cidian* (Chinese Dictionary), 13 vols. (Shanghai: Hanyu dacidian chubanshe, 1995), 1.1388–89.
[70] David Robertson, "Neo," in Robertson, *The Routledge Dictionary of Politics* (London: Routledge, 2004), 337–38.
[71] Wang Yuechuan, "Dangdai wenhua yanjiu zhong de jijin yu baoshou zhi wei" (The Link between Radicalism and Conservatism in Research on Contemporary Culture), in *ZFL*, 422–38, 432.
[72] Wang Sirui, "Jinri Zhongguo de xin baoshou zhuyi" (Neoconservatism in Today's China), in *ZFL*, 406–21, 412.
[73] Wang, "Reverse Course," 11.

a non-mainstream value system precisely because of the ongoing legitimacy crisis.[74] Chinese neoconservatism attempted to resolve this crisis through an instrumental reference to traditional cultural values.

A second reason why a conceptual history approach is relevant here is that in the two main advocacies of neoconservatism, the theory was based on a rejection of what advocates referred to as "radicalism." Radicalism operated as what Koselleck refers to as a "counter-concept": it was defined as such so that the reader could not but identify with the conservative position. The flexible and relatively broad meaning of the term rendered it useful in both the official media and academic discourse. In addition to the differences in meaning across these discursive spheres, the meaning of concepts also evolved as the reforms unfolded.

Here it is useful to briefly look at the meaning of radicalism as it was traced by Koselleck in the European setting and what it came to mean in China. In Europe, "radical" originally meant "deep-seated," "rooted," or "inborn," but since the eighteenth century it meant "that what goes to the root."[75] Later, it also came to refer to a priori goals or a will for renewal and progress, after which, by the mid-nineteenth century, it became an ideology linked to revolution and socialism. Radicalism followed the Enlightenment axioms and ignored reality through a faith in abstract reason.[76] In China, the term "radicalism" emerged alongside socialism and anarchism in the early twentieth century. During the May Fourth period, following the introduction of Marxism into China, radicalism became an ideology, just as it had earlier in Europe. In a discussion on "problems and *-isms*" (*wenti yu zhuyi*), Li Dazhao, who later would be a cofounder of the CCP, lamented being labeled radical (then translated as *guoji zhuyi*) because of his turn toward Bolshevism. According to Li Dazhao, the Japanese had used the term as a negative translation of Bolshevism because they adhered to militarism and capitalism. Wang Fansen, an intellectual historian at the Academia Sinica in Taiwan, has argued that the "new-*isms*" (*xin zhuyi*) from the period after May Fourth, in addition to being perceived of as total solutions to problems, were strengthened by the Bolshevik mode of organization, which became a model after the Russian

---

[74] Chen Xiaoming, "Baoshouxing yu hefahua: Pingxi dalu zheng xingcheng yizhong wenhua lichang" (Conservative Disposition and Legitimation: Review of a Cultural Position That Is Taking Shape on the Mainland), *Zhongguo luntan* (China Forum) 16 (February 1, 1992), 93–97, 96.

[75] Peter Wende, "Radikalismus" (Radicalism), in von Brunner, Conze, and Koselleck, eds., *Geschichtliche Grundbegriffe*, 5.113.

[76] On the Enlightenment, see Peter Gay, *The Enlightenment: An Interpretation* (New York: Knopf, 1966–69); Jonathan I. Israel, *Radical Enlightenment: Philosophy and the Making of Modernity, 1650–1750* (Oxford: Oxford University Press, 2001).

October Revolution.[77] The term "radicalism" hence appeared next to Bolshevism (*Bu'erzhaweike zhuyi*) in the 1923 *Xin wenhua cishu* (A Dictionary of New Culture).[78]

The Chinese compound *jijin* also reveals its progressivist connotation: the meanings of *ji* (激) include "to dash," "to arouse," "fierce," and "violent," and the meanings of *jin* (进) include "to advance," "to enter," and "to receive."[79] In its premodern use, *jin* (进 to advance, to enter) was used not in a linear sense but rather spatially, as in the sense of moving forward or entering, or in terms of a promotion.[80] As a modern compound, *jijin* (激进) came to be used in a manner similar to *jijin* (急进), to advance rapidly (*jisu qianjin* 急速前进), but both could also mean far-reaching, thorough, or radical. Lu Xun, for example, used the term *jijin* (急进) to refer to "radical" youth, whereas Mao Zedong used the term *jijin* (激进) to refer to "radical" economic and political reform that would benefit the people.[81]

Given this background, it was unusual that during the early 1990s the term came to refer to a denouncement of thorough economic and political change. Whereas earlier the connections between the various parts had been accentuated—without drastic breaks, or moving rapidly there could be no progress (*bupo buli*)—now it was believed that the first part was disconnected from the second; advancement could and should be achieved without destruction and in both a rational and gradual manner. However, considerable differences still existed between the main advocacies of neoconservatism.

Xiao Gongqin, Modernization, and Tiananmen

The first major advocate of neoconservatism was Xiao Gongqin (b. 1946), a professor of history at Shanghai Normal University and the son of a KMT general from Sichuan province. Xiao's education was interrupted during the Cultural Revolution, and it took more than a decade, spent primarily working in a factory, before he began to pursue a degree in history at Nanjing University. Noteworthy for the development of neoconservatism was the December 1990 conference on Chinese Tradition and Socialist Modernization, organized by the Ideology and Theory Department of *Zhongguo qingnianbao*.[82] Xu

---

[77] Spira, *Conceptual History of Chinese -Isms*, 160–61, 171. Spira refers to Wang Fansen [Wang Fan-shen], "'Zhuyi shidai de lailin': Zhongguo jindai sixiangshi de yige guanjian fazhan" (The Advent of the "Age of *–Isms*": A Key Development in the History of Modern Chinese Thought), *Dong Ya guannianshi jikan* (Journal of the History of Ideas in East Asia), no. 4 (2013), 3–7 and 9–88.

[78] Spira, *Conceptual History of Chinese -Isms*, 257.

[79] Li et al., *Dangdai Hanyu cidian*, 472, 545.

[80] Hanyu dacidian bianyuanhui, *Hanyu da cidian*, 10.978–79. [81] Ibid., 6.172, 7.459–60.

[82] Sullivan, "Democracy and Developmentalism," 231n.

Weicheng and Yuan Mu, two former Cultural Revolution propagandists, reportedly attended the conference.[83] According to Hong Kong media, the literary critic and political commentator He Xin and affiliates of *Zhongguo qingnianbao* also attended.[84] Nevertheless, it remains unclear to what extent there was political support for Xiao's neoconservatism. Xiao's neoconservatism also featured extensively in the Taiwan-based *Zhongguo shibao zhoukan* (China Times Weekly) in 1992 and again in 1993.[85]

Xiao's theory of neoconservatism was a post-1989 reworking of the theory of neo-authoritarianism, debates on which go back to 1986.[86] Xiao Gongqin reportedly first used the term *xin quanwei zhuyi* (neo-authoritarianism) at an August 1988 conference organized by, among others, the Shanghai-based *Shijie jingji daobao* (World Economic Herald) and *Guangming ribao* (Enlightenment Daily) on the problems facing Chinese intellectuals. *Shijie jingji daobao* was published with the support of the Shanghai Academy of Social Sciences and was a supporter of Zhao Ziyang's reform program. At the conference, Xiao Gongqin presented neo-authoritarianism as one of three policy choices, the other two being policy renewal under the traditional system and "parliamentary romanticism" (*yihui langman zhuyi*). Through the "visible hand" of authoritarian rule, Xiao argued that neo-authoritarianism could create the "invisible hand" of a market economy and conditions for democratic rule.[87] He also presented his ideas on neo-authoritarianism to Jiang Zemin—party

---

[83] Xu Weicheng was a vice mayor of Beijing. According to the Hong Kong press, he was also the person behind the editorial "Bixu qizhi xianming de fandui dongluan" (We Must Take a Firm Stand and Oppose Turmoil), *Renmin ribao*, April 26, 1989, 1.

[84] "Behind the CCP Princes Party," *Pai-hsing* (The People), no. 260 (March 16, 1992), 32–35. Translated in *Inside China Mainland* (Taipei) 14.5 (May 1992), 6–10. Xiao Gongqin allegedly received the support of vice minister of telecommunications Chen Haosu, who was the son of Marshal Chen Yi (1901–72). Chen Yi had been a commander in the Chinese army during the 1930s and 1940s, and later was appointed a marshal in the People's Liberation Army (PLA), and vice premier and minister of foreign affairs between the 1950s and the 1970s. Xiao Gongqin is also believed to have had contact with associates of Jiang Zemin and the offspring of several officials.

[85] See *Zhongguo shibao zhoukan bianji* (editors of *China Times Weekly*), "Dalu xin baoshou zhuyi de jueqi: Fangwen dalu 'di'er sichao' lilunjia Xiao Gongqin" (The Rise of Mainland Neoconservatism: An Interview with Mainland "Second Trend" Theorist Xiao Gongqin), *Zhongguo shibao zhoukan*, January 26, 1992, 66–69 and February 2, 1992, 98–100; Xiao Gongqin, "Zouxiang xin baoshou zhuyi" (Toward Neoconservatism), *Zhongguo shibao zhoukan*, February 21, 1993, 46–51 and February 28, 1993, 36–39.

[86] Zhang Bingjiu used the term "semiauthoritarian" (*banjiquan*) in 1986. During the late 1980s, Wang Huning also argued in favor of a strong government and gradual democratization. See Qi Mo, ed., *Xin quanwei zhuyi: Dui Zhongguo dalu weilai mingyun de lunzheng* (Neo-authoritarianism: Debates on the Future Fate of Mainland China) (Taipei: Tangshan chubanshe, 1991).

[87] Xiao Gongqin, "Zixu," in *Yu zhengzhi langman zhuyi gaobie* (Parting with Political Romanticism) (hereafter cited as *YZLG*) (Wuhan: Hubei jiaoyu chubanshe, 2001), 6.

secretary of Shanghai at the time—at a bimonthly gathering of intellectuals held in November 1988.[88]

On January 16, 1989, an article by Wu Jiaxiang, an economist and researcher in the General Office of the Central Committee of the CCP and an adviser to Premier Zhao Ziyang, appeared in *Shijie jingji daobao*.[89] Wu Jiaxiang proposed an intermediate stage of neo-authoritarianism in the transition from authoritarianism to democracy. This differed from the traditional form of authoritarianism because authority would be deployed for the development of individual freedom.[90] One day later, Xiao Gongqin published his views in the Shanghai paper *Wenhui bao*.[91] The ensuing debate represented an exchange between advocates of neo-authoritarianism and liberal democrats. Whereas the former, basing their arguments on the models of development in East Asia, argued that economic reform should precede political reform, the latter argued that political reform could not be postponed.[92] After the repression of the Tiananmen Square demonstrations, the debate abruptly ended, but similar discussions continued outside of mainland China, both in private meetings and in journals published in Hong Kong, Taiwan, and elsewhere.

The publication of the articles by Wu Jiaxiang and Xiao Gongqin in January 1989 marked the official launch of the Northern and Southern schools of neo-authoritarianism, whose spokespersons were located in Beijing and Shanghai, respectively. The Northern School, the main proponents of which were Wu Jiaxiang, Chen Yizi, Zhang Bingjiu, and Yang Baikui,[93] and the Southern School, including Xiao Gongqin and Wang Huning, differed over the causes of China's socioeconomic crises, the matter of state power, and the speed of the economic reforms.[94] For the Northern School, the causes of the crisis were

---

[88] Sullivan, "Impact of Western Political Thought," 84.
[89] Barry Sautman, "Sirens of the Strongman: Neo-authoritarianism in Recent Chinese Political Theory," *China Quarterly*, no. 129 (1992), 74n8. Wu Jiaxiang's article is titled "Xin quanwei zhuyi shuping" (Commenting on Neo-authoritarianism). It was reprinted in Qi, *Xin quanwei zhuyi*, 4–8.
[90] Fewsmith, *China since Tiananmen*, 75–76.
[91] Xiao Gongqin and Zhu Wei, "Tongku de liangnan xuanze: Guanyu 'xin quanwei zhuyi' lilun dawenlu" (A Painful Dilemma: A Record of Questions and Answers on "Neo-authoritarianism"), *Wenhui bao*, January 17, 1989.
[92] For English translations by scholars residing in China prior to 1989, see Stanley Rosen and Gary Zou, eds., "The Chinese Debate on the New Authoritarianism," *Chinese Sociology and Anthropology* 23.4 (Summer 1991). For criticisms by democrats residing in the United States after Tiananmen, see ibid., 24.1 (Fall 1991).
[93] Chen Yizi was the director of the Chinese Economic System Reform Research Institute (CESRRI) (Zhongguo Jingji Tizhi Gaige Yanjiusuo) under the State Commission for Restructuring the Economy. Zhang Bingjiu was a Ph.D. candidate at Peking University. Yang Baikui was a political scientist at CASS and a research assistant for the democrat Yan Jiaqi, who at the time was the director of the Institute of Political Science at CASS. Wang Huning was a professor of international politics at Fudan University.
[94] Sullivan, "Democracy and Developmentalism," 247, 249, 257.

inflation and corruption, whereas the Southern School attributed the inflation and corruption to a crisis in authority and a dearth of independent social organizations. The Northern School advocated strong rule to stabilize the market and to enable quick-paced reforms, whereas the Southern School favored gradual reform to develop an independent middle class and to preserve continuity with China's traditional culture.[95] The Northern School also highlighted the universal applicability of neo-authoritarianism, whereas the Southern School argued that the theory was applicable only to late-modernizing countries at the early stages of modernization. Finally, some members of the Northern School—notably Wu Jiaxiang and Chen Yizi—were advisers to Zhao Ziyang, whereas members of the Southern School had no clear political affiliations, but reportedly some members were in contact with Jiang Zemin.[96]

Whereas after Zhao Ziyang's downfall in 1989 members of the Northern School were either arrested or left China, Xiao Gongqin remained in China and continued to promote a new form of neoconservatism—gradual reform under strong rule. In the post-Tiananmen setting, such advocacy of gradual reform could be used to criticize Zhao Ziyang and to support order and stability. Following the events in the Soviet Union and Eastern Europe in late 1989 and thereafter, debates on neoconservatism suited the needs of some intellectuals who felt that there should be a move away from Leninism.[97]

An extended version of Xiao Gongqin's speech at the December 1990 conference appeared in *Zhongguo qingnianbao* in February 1991 under the title "Yan Fu's Reflections on China's Modernization and Its Enlightenment."[98] In this article, Xiao argues that the nineteenth-century translator Yan Fu (1854–1921) had been a proponent of "gradualist" or "incrementalist" modernization (*jianjin zhuyi de xiandaihua*). Unlike the "radical modernizers," Yan Fu did not believe that Chinese traditional culture and values were obstacles to modernization. In fact, he regarded them as indispensable levers during the process of modernization.[99] In Xiao Gongqin's February 1991 article, he summarizes the advocacy of the "gradual modernizers" as the following:

By using enlightened despotism as an authority lever to push Chinese modernization and by considering traditional cultural value symbols as intermediaries for

---

[95] Ibid., 248–49, 256–57.
[96] Wang Huning became head of the Central Policy Research Office of the Central Committee of the CCP under Jiang Zemin. He was also an adviser to Jiang Zemin, Hu Jintao, and Xi Jinping. He became a member of the Politburo in 2007 and a member of the Politburo Standing Committee in 2017.
[97] Sullivan, "Democracy and Developmentalism," 331–33.
[98] Xiao Gongqin, "Yan Fu dui Zhongguo xiandaihua de sikao ji qi qishi" (Yan Fu's Reflections on China's Modernization and Its Enlightenment), *Zhongguo qingnianbao*, February 6, 1991, 3.
[99] Ibid.

modernization, they [the gradual modernizers] propose to induce the growth and maturation of endogenous modernization factors. They do this in order to allow them to become harmonized with the corresponding new system and to form a development mechanism with the endogenous as a mainstay.[100]

In this edited version of his speech, the term "neoconservatism" does not appear; it is replaced by "neo-gradualism" or "neo-incrementalism" (*xin jianjin zhuyi*). Use of "gradualism" was more in accord with the official advocacy of slower reforms and the complementary use of tradition as part of a nationalist response to the legitimacy crisis of 1989. However, in the longer version of the speech that appears in Xiao Gongqin's *Collected Works* (1995), "neoconservatism" appears in the title of the article.[101]

Tradition not only could function as a lever in the introduction of foreign elements, but also could strengthen political cohesion. For Xiao, during the transitional period of modernization, nationalism in a broad sense—loyalty to one's nation—could function as a coagulating force, or a "'natural' political resource."[102] The problem with Chinese nationalism since modern times, Xiao argues, is precisely that it rejects "mainstream culture" (*zhuliu wenhua*), namely Confucianism. Since the "mainstream culture" was a collective experience in response to challenges, and since it represented the "national character" (*guoxing*) of the nation, it was particularly useful in terms of strengthening legitimacy.[103] During the reform era, anti-imperialism or scientific and technological achievements as sources of nationalism or patriotism were no longer sufficient.[104]

Xiao Gongqin states that his neoconservatism is rooted in his criticism of radicalism. This has generally been neglected or interpreted as "democratic radicalism," but Xiao's interpretation of the term exceeds this and should be understood in relation to the history of Chinese modernization.[105] Xiao distinguishes between three kinds of radicalism, namely "psychological radicalism" (*xintaishang de jijin zhuyi*), "system determinism" (*zhidu juedinglun*), and "political romanticism" (*zhengzhi langman zhuyi*).[106] The first type,

---

[100] Ibid., 3.
[101] Xiao Gongqin, "'Yan Fu beilun' yu jindai baoshou zhuyi biange guan" (The "Yan Fu Paradox" and the Conservative View of Change in Modern Times), in Xiao, *Xiao Gongqin ji* (Collected Works of Xiao Gongqin) (hereafter cited as *XGQJ*) (Ha'erbin: Heilongjiang jiaoyu chubanshe, 1995), 18–41.
[102] Xiao Gongqin, "Minzu zhuyi yu Zhongguo zhuanxing shiqi de yishi xingtai" (Nationalism and Ideology during China's Transitional Era), in *XGQJ*, 350–58, 351.
[103] Ibid., 352.
[104] On economic performance as a source of legitimacy, see, for example, Feng Chen, "The Dilemmas of Eudaemonic Legitimacy in Post-Mao China," *Polity* 29.3 (1997), 421–40. See also Ci, *Dialectic of the Chinese Revolution*.
[105] See, for example, Chen, "Order and Stability in Social Transition," 599.
[106] Xiao Gongqin, "Zixu" (Preface), in *XGQJ*, 9.

"psychological radicalism," stands for reform plans based on a sense of anxiety instead of on a realistic assessment of affairs, which results in rash and impetuous actions. This type of radicalism often manifests itself in times of crisis, when those who resort to sudden action use it to obtain peace of mind. As Xiao explains,

> In reality, this "psychological" radicalism implies that when people demand a bold and resolute destruction of the old order and the old system, and when they demand the import of new systems through swift and violent battle-style methods that seek to accomplish the task in one stroke, subconsciously they often consider this way of doing things to be a strategy for psychological balance and self-comfort.[107]

"System determinism" was "radical" in that it advocated the import of Western systems without taking into account that every institution or system is the product of a long process of social and historical growth. According to Xiao, if one were to transplant a system without the supporting elements of the society of which it is a product, the result in another environment would be different; it could even lead to social disorder. Xiao describes this type of radicalism as follows:

> In the West, a certain system A produces a certain effect B. For this kind of causal relation, it is necessary that a number of social, economic, and cultural elements internal to the society function as supporting conditions. When people, in order to obtain the effect described above in China, import a certain Western system in isolation, because Chinese society lacks the relevant Western social supporting conditions the outcome will not only be that it is impossible to produce the causal relation between system A and effect B, but also that the old and new systems will both be unable to carry out the integration of social order. This is because the original old system has already been artificially destroyed and because the new system lacks the supporting conditions and cannot be established or operate.[108]

Finally, "political romanticism" implies a notion of reform based on abstract principles and blueprint designs of the society, as in French revolutionary rationalism. This type of reform fails because it ignores the particular and the historically grown.

Under the effects of aspirations and projections, people with this mentality are likely to often regard certain principles that are considered "naturally reasonable" abstract principles, utopian-style "natural laws," or transcendent "first moral principles" as the basis for the reconstruction of the social order. The reason why this trend is called "idealism" is that those who hold such ideas profoundly believe that history can be reconstructed or transformed according to certain a priori and self-explanatory logical

---

[107] Xiao Gongqin, "Lishi jujue langman: Zhongguo gaige di'er sichao de jueqi" (History Rejects Romanticism: The Emergence of the Second Trend of Reform Thought in China), in *XGQJ*, 109–22, 115.

[108] Ibid., 116.

ideas—just like engineers design products—and that it is not necessary to take into account the empirical facts of history proper.[109]

Although here Xiao Gongqin does not mention Karl Popper, the perceived link between radicalism and "romanticism" and the imagery of the engineer in connection with social reform are two elements that are present in Popper's *The Open Society and Its Enemies*.[110] Xiao's radicalism not only referred to the political liberalism of the late 1980s and the failure of Tiananmen but also entailed certain goals and means of action dominated by a priori principles, utopianism, and abstract rationalism. In his view, the latter were also present in Leftist extremism. More than only a content of thought, Xiao's radicalism also referred to an idealist mode of thinking that was present on both sides of the ideological spectrum.

Xiao's neoconservatism appeared in the official media because of its advocacy of gradual reform and its use of traditional resources in this process, which, as we have seen, were also being officially promoted at the time. Apart from Xiao's article on Yan Fu in *Zhongguo qingnianbao*, several other articles by Xiao were published in *Beijing qingnianbao* (Beijing Youth Daily), both official publications of the Communist Youth League.[111] Xiao is also mentioned in the book *Gongheguo de di sandai* (The Third Generation of the Republic), which includes an introduction by propagandist Yuan Mu.[112] In a section on radicalism, author Yang Fan, a Beijing-based economist, defines radicalism as follows:

> It is characterized by subjective aspirations that transcend objective reality; it hopes to develop China through exceeding stages and with increasing speed ... During the era of reform and opening up, radicalism is revealed in two trends of thought. The first one is "the trend of thought of extreme democratization," which manifests itself politically in bourgeois liberalization; the second one is "the trend of thought of returning to the ancients and remembering the past," which manifests itself politically in opposition to modernization.[113]

Yang Fan explains that the trend of "extreme democratization" regards the Western model of multiple parties, private property, and a market economy as

---

[109] Ibid., 117.
[110] See Karl Popper, "Aestheticism, Perfectionism and Utopianism," in K. R. Popper, *The Open Society and Its Enemies*, 2 vols., 4th rev. ed. (Princeton, NJ: Princeton University Press, 1963), 1.157–68.
[111] Articles by Xiao Gongqin appeared in *Beijing qingnianbao*, September 4, 1990, 4, January 19, 1992, 6, and May 13, 1993, 3 (with expanded versions in *XGQJ*, 109–22 and 123–39), and also appeared in *Zhongguo xiandaihua yanjiu* (Research on Chinese Modernization), no. 12 (1994).
[112] Yang Fan, *Gongheguo de di sandai* (The Third Generation of the Republic) (Chengdu: Sichuan renmin chubanshe, 1991).
[113] Ibid., 187.

its ideal, whereas the trend of "returning to the ancients and remembering the past" is rooted in a "peasant-style utopia" and populism. The convergence of these two trends formed the intellectual basis for the June Fourth Incident. Both manifestations of radicalism were marked by an ignorance about China's "national conditions," by a subjective mentality divorced from reality, by ideal models, by praising virtue over history, by an "overcorrection," by the philosophy of struggle, by a stress on opposition, and by an appraisal of revolution at the expense of reform.

Yang further notes that *Gongheguo de di sandai* represents a defense of "gradualism" (*wenjin zhuyi*) against both "conservatives" (hence, the Old Left) and "liberals" within the party, and it is here that he invokes Xiao Gongqin. According to Yang Fan, Xiao distinguishes "gradualism" from conservatism; the basic difference between the two is that "conservatives" identify with traditional value symbols, whereas "gradualists" "merely consider these traditional value symbols, principles, and rules, along with the traditional authority form, as levers that are indispensable for orderly evolution and economic reform."[114] Hence, some elements of Xiao's theory were promoted after 1989, but the term "neoconservatism" was avoided so as to distinguish the use of traditional elements from the "conservative" identification with Chinese tradition and to emphasize the forward-looking nature of "gradualism."

"Realistic Responses" and the Soviet Upheaval

The "banner" of neoconservatism was also raised in the policy paper "Sulian zhengbian hou Zhongguo de xianshi yingdui yu zhanlüe xuanze" (Realistic Responses and Strategic Options for China after the Soviet Upheaval), written by the offspring of high officials, often referred to as "princelings," that appeared internally after the August 1991 coup in the Soviet Union.[115] The document was published by the Ideology and Theory Department of *Zhongguo qingnianbao*, the same organ that had organized the 1990 conference at which Xiao Gongqin had coined the theory of neoconservatism.[116]

Whereas, as we have seen, Xiao Gongqin's neoconservatism was a reworking of neo-authoritarianism after 1989, "Realistic Responses" was a reaction to

---

[114] Ibid., 251–55, 255.
[115] The document was leaked to the New York–based liberal Chinese journal *Zhongguo zhi chun* (China Spring), no. 1 (January 1992), 35–39. David Kelly brought this document to international attention in a special issue of *CLG* that includes an English translation of the document and criticisms by overseas Chinese intellectuals. See David Kelly, ed., "Realistic Responses and Strategic Options: An Alternative CCP Ideology and Its Critics," *CLG* 29.2 (March–April 1996), 1–96. The discussion in this chapter relies on the original document; the criticism, with reference to the original documents, relies on the translations by David Kelly.
[116] Fewsmith, "Neoconservatism," 642.

the August 1991 Soviet Coup. During the coup, the Communist "hard-liners," including the heads of the KGB, army, and police, plotted against the president of the Soviet Union, Mikhail Gorbachev.[117] Although order was restored, the *putsch* succeeded in exposing the cracks in Soviet ideology. Despite the official background of "Realistic Responses," it was published only internally: *Zhongguo qingnianbao* is under the general office of the CCP's Youth League. It never appeared in official party journals. Overseas Chinese critics have claimed that official publication would have been tantamount to publicly admitting the party's "ideological bankruptcy."[118] The alleged authors of the document are Yang Ping, head of the Ideology and Theory Department of *Zhongguo qingnianbao*, and Wang Xiaodong, but the document reportedly also had ties to the princelings Chen Yuan, the son of Chen Yun, and Pan Yue, the son-in-law of General Liu Huaqing, a Long March veteran who was then vice chairman of the Central Military Commission. As critic Hu Ping writes of the document, it had an "obvious official background," but no "official affiliation."[119]

The voice of Chen Yuan, who graduated in engineering and economics from Tsinghua University and CASS and who was a vice governor of the People's Bank of China, can be discerned in the document in the form of a critique of the radical reform of the Soviet Union. Since the late 1980s Chen Yuan had been gathering a group of "largely conservative economists and social scientists" in the Beijing Young Economists Association.[120] Even before the coup, Chen Yuan was stressing that planning and centralization were crucial to the economic reforms. He put forward the term "dukedom economy" to refer to the rise of local autonomy and monopolies under the economic reforms.[121] Chen criticized the reforms in both the Soviet Union and Eastern Europe because they were accompanied by social, economic, and political instability. Instead, Chen Yuan argued for gradual and stable reform; he found just such an example in the reform policies of Premier Li Peng.[122]

---

[117] On the Soviet coup, see Michael Mandelbaum, "Coup de Grace: The End of the Soviet Union," *Foreign Affairs* 71.1 (1992), 164–83; John B. Dunlop, "The August 1991 Coup and Its Impact on Soviet Politics," *Journal of Cold War Studies* 5.1 (2003), 94–127.

[118] Hu Ping, "Bitan Zhonggong jiebanren de gangling: Ruhe kandai 'Yingdui yu xuanze'" (Notes on the Program of the CCP Heirs Apparent: How to Treat "Realistic Responses"), *Zhongguo zhi chun*, no. 1 January 1992), 23–24, tr. in *CLG* 29.2 (March–April 1996), 35–37, 36.

[119] Ibid., 36.

[120] Willy Wo-Lap Lam, "Chen's Son Bids to Expand Power Base," *South China Morning Post*, May 19, 1992, 11. This group included scholars from CASS, scholars and cadres from the Research Office of the CCP Central Committee, and members of the former Chinese Economic System Reform Research Institute (CESRRI). Other princelings in the group included Deng Yingtao, Tang Ruoxi, and Du Ying, the son-in-law of Deng Liqun.

[121] Fewsmith, *China since Tiananmen*, 84–85; He, *Dictionary of the Political Thought*, 671.

[122] Daniel Kwan, "Stability Put Before Reform," *South China Morning Post*, May 8, 1992, 12.

"Realistic Responses" outlines the tasks that were required for China in order to avoid the fate of the Soviet Union. It describes the deeper cause of the Soviet and Eastern European upheavals as "utopian capitalism" (*kongxiang ziben zhuyi*) in the people's mode of thought.[123] It further criticizes the economic "shock therapies" (*xiuke liaofa*) of the Soviet Union and Eastern Europe, which were radical reform plans based on abstract blueprints and revolutionary methods that ignored the gradual nature of reform.[124] Apart from "utopian capitalism," the authors also discerned "utopian socialism" (*kongxiang shehui zhuyi*), which they describe as follows: "Its mode of thought is concretely manifested in thinking that as soon as some perfect system has been established, all other problems will be readily solved."[125] They further criticize the "utopian socialism" of the Great Leap Forward (1958–61) and the Cultural Revolution (1966–76).

The "realistic responses" and "strategic options" that the authors propose include the following. The CCP should be transformed from a "revolutionary party" (*gemingdang*) to a "ruling party" (*zhizhengdang*) in response to the state of socialist construction. The party should not underscore class struggle during the construction phase, and "populism" and mass movements should be avoided. The reason for this is that reforms, as Huntington writes, are often "the forerunner of revolution."[126]

The latter is a reference to Samuel Huntington's 1968 book *Political Order in Changing Societies*, which had been translated into Chinese in 1988 and had figured prominently in the Chinese debates on neo-authoritarianism.[127] Huntington's main thesis is that "rapid social change and the rapid mobilization of new groups into politics coupled with the slow development of political institutions" will lead to political instability.[128] A socialist party can learn from the experience of transformation in the "bourgeois political parties." Here, the authors contrast "Western rationalist philosophy" with "radicalism," "romanticism," and "irrationalism":

To counter-attack "socialist liberalization," and, concurrently, to eliminate the radicalism, romanticism, and irrationalism within the bourgeois camp, many bourgeois scholars came out in defense of the capitalist system. For example, Russell, Popper,

---

[123] *Zhongguo qingnianbao* sixiang lilunbu (*China Youth Daily* Ideology and Theory Department), "Sulian zhengbian hou Zhongguo de xianshi yingdui yu zhanlüe xuanze" (Realistic Responses and Strategic Options for China after the Soviet Upheaval), *Zhongguo zhi chun*, no. 1 (January 1992), 35–39.

[124] Ibid., 36.   [125] Ibid., 36.   [126] Ibid., 36.

[127] Samuel Huntington, *Political Order in Changing Societies* (hereafter cited as *POCS*) (New Haven, CT: Yale University Press, 1968). The most widely read translation of *POCS* is *Biange shehui zhong de zhengzhi zhixu* (Political Order in Changing Societies), ed. Li Shengping (Beijing: Huaxia chubanshe, 1988).

[128] Huntington, *POCS*, 6.

Hayek, and others epitomized Western rationalist philosophy and science. They played a significant role in eliminating "counter-charge" mechanisms and radical aspects from the bourgeois system, and they provided a new theoretical basis for the transformation of the bourgeoisie from a revolutionary to a ruling party and for the safeguarding of the capitalist system.[129]

The document also addresses changes at the ideological level, where transformation required a "creative interpretation" of "socialism with Chinese characteristics." The latter was first put forward by Deng Xiaoping in 1982 when he stressed that the development of productivity and economic construction were the key tasks of socialism.[130] The authors of "Realistic Responses" now argued that socialism, rooted in the caves of Yan'an, was the only remaining source of legitimacy for the CCP because the other source, namely the Bolshevik Revolution, had already atrophied. Socialism had to be reinterpreted based on China's "particular national conditions" (*teshu de guoqing*), namely, China was a huge and populous country that had been oppressed for a long time.[131] Third, these "national conditions" also dictated that gradual reform based on realism (*xianshi zhuyi*) and rationalism (*lixing zhuyi*) was the only way to carry out the process of reform and opening up. Such gradual reform would draw from the "neoconservatism in the history of reform in modern China" and Western rationalism.[132] The authors contrasted neoconservatism and "Western rationalist philosophy" with radicalism:

> By neoconservatism, we mean a view of reform that differs from that of the traditional diehard conservative forces. It stands for the use of rational elements in the traditional and current orders, and for the gradual introduction of the rational elements in Western systems in order to realize Chinese modernization. Western rationalist philosophy refers to a school different from romanticist and irrationalist philosophy. It stands for proof, instrumental rationality, and orderly, gradual advancement. It opposes romanticism and violence as well as the anti-order, anti-society, and anti-culture conduct of irrationalism. Neoconservatism and Western rationalist philosophy have always existed in opposition to radicalism.[133]

Here, referring to the realization of "Chinese modernization," the authors also note the importance of nationalism, patriotism, and national interest in the struggle against "peaceful evolution." This is in accordance with the agenda of the moderate reformers and the fears of a collapse after the events in Eastern Europe and the Soviet Union. In addition, Chinese interests, the socialist system, and modernization could be safeguarded only by the

---

[129] *Zhongguo qingnianbao* sixiang lilunbu, "Sulian zhengbian hou Zhongguo," 36–37 (my translation).
[130] He, *Dictionary of the Political Thought*, 75, 547.
[131] *Zhongguo qingnianbao* sixiang lilunbu, "Sulian zhengbian hou Zhongguo," 37.
[132] Ibid., 37.   [133] Ibid., 37 (my translation).

"creative transformation of traditional Chinese culture."[134] The Confucian tradition of collectivism and altruism in the field of ethics, its "this-worldly spirit" of common responsibility, and its "heroic manner of man" should be used as a "source of values" in the process of socialist modernization. In the economic sphere, the "radical reform view" (*jijin de gaigeguan*) should be rejected because a change in the relations of production might intensify the contradictions in the system and weaken control by the central government.

The authors further argue that the "romantic reform view" (*langman zhuyi gaigeguan*) that wanted to "resolve problems from the very basics" and the "mentality of deep-level reform," according to which the issue of ownership was key to solving the problems of reform, should be eliminated.[135] Changing Mao Zedong's famous dictum that "political power grows out of the barrel of a gun," the authors state, "the CCP must grasp not only the gun but also the asset-based economy."[136] Government and enterprise should be strictly separated, but party and government should be separated only to a certain extent. The authors further insist that a policy based on the Five Principles of Peaceful Coexistence and the "national interest" should replace a foreign policy guided by moral principles and ideology. A "greater Chinese cultural and economic sphere" should be established in response to the emergence of regional economic blocs.[137]

Because there were no open debates on neoconservatism, the only dissenting voices that could be heard were those of the liberal democrats in Hong Kong or the United States. Some denounced the document as a fascist program.[138] Others stressed that the agenda of party ownership was irreconcilable with the idea of a "Third Way" in between capitalism and socialism.[139] In this respect, the program offered nothing new; it partially supported Chen Yun's "bird-cage economy," or the view that the market economy should serve merely to sustain the planned economy, and it partially supported Deng Xiaoping.[140] Conversely, other critics pointed to the new aspects of neoconservatism: it was an attempt to formulate a new theory during a period of

---

[134] Ibid., 37.   [135] Ibid., 38.   [136] Ibid., 38.   [137] Ibid., 38.

[138] See, for example, Su Wei, "Yifen taizidang jiebian de baipishu" (A White Paper on the Princeling Faction's Succession), *Zhongguo zhi chun*, no. 1 (January 1992), 28–29, tr. David Kelly, in *CLG* 29.2 (March–April 1996), 48–51; Zhao Yuesheng, "Xin faxisi zhuyi de xuanyan" (A Manifesto of Neofascism), *Zhongguo zhi chun*, no. 1 (January 1992), 29–30, tr. David Kelly, in *CLG* 29.2 (March–April 1996), 52–54.

[139] Lu Wei, "Taizidang paozhi 'shizheng gangling' shimo" (How the Princelings Launched Their "Political Platform"), *Qianshao* (Front Line), no. 2 (February 1992), 92–93, tr. David Kelly, in *CLG* 29.2 (March–April 1996), 32–34.

[140] Chen Kuide, "Wangchao mori de 'xinzheng'" (A Doomed Dynasty's "New Deal"), *Zhongguo zhi chun*, no. 1 (January 1992), 24–25, tr. David Kelly, in *CLG* 29.2 (March–April 1996), 38–41.

"ideological bankruptcy of the CCP."[141] Seen from this perspective, the document urged a shift from a "revolutionary" to a "ruling" party and reflected this shift in terms of language.[142] As to the lack of a concrete time schedule for democracy, one critic stated, "If this speed is maintained at the same rate as that which can be reached by the mainland government, then new conservatism might as well set up office in Li Peng's toilet."[143] Other criticisms stated that neoconservatism did not provide a prescription for how to avoid arbitrary authority, it remained vague about how to achieve democracy, it was elitist, it wrongly reduced corruption and bureaucracy to problems of individual behavior, and it placed too much emphasis on political and economic order and stability.[144]

Neoconservatisms and the Events of 1989 and 1991

In sum, there were considerable differences between the two main advocacies of neoconservatism, which were directly related to the respective contexts in which these theories had been formulated. Xiao Gongqin was more interested in the conflicts within the Chinese political system that had emerged during the 1980s and that had helped trigger the Tiananmen demonstrations. His theory represented a continuation of the theory of neo-authoritarianism of the late 1980s. For Xiao, 1989 demonstrated that state building remained a prerequisite for a successful transition to democracy, but after 1989, he placed more weight on Chinese tradition. Conversely, "Realistic Responses" is noted for its advocacy of Realpolitik following the Soviet coup, which revealed the dangers of economic and political reform. The document foresees the tragedy of the dissolution of the Soviet Union, thus it seeks to advance an economic middle road. But this state building was combined with a strong agenda of party building—the party continued to control the gun.

Xiao Gongqin's own view of the relationship between "Realistic Responses" and his neoconservatism was that both examined the impact of radicalism in the

---

[141] Hu Ping, "Notes on the Programme of the CCP Heirs Apparent: How to Treat 'Realistic Responses,'" tr. David Kelly, in *CLG* 29.2 (March–April 1996), 35–37, 36.

[142] Ding Chu, "Cong 'yi' xiang 'li' de zhanlüe zhanbian" (Strategic Switch from "Principle" to "Profit"), *Zhongguo zhi chun*, no. 1 (January 1992), 30–31, tr. David Kelly, in *CLG* 29.2 (March–April 1996), 55–57, 55–56.

[143] Wang Zhaojun, "Xin baoshou zhuyi yu dalu zhishi fenzi" (New Conservatism and the Intellectuals in Mainland China), *Zhongguo luntan* 21 (July 1, 1992), 106–14, tr. David Kelly, in *CLG* 29.2 (March–April 1996), 83–96, 96.

[144] Yin Huimin, "Xin baoshou zhuyi yu Zhongguo qianjing" (New Conservatism and China's Outlook), *Jiushi niandai* (The Nineties), no. 4 (April 1993), 86–88, tr. David Kelly, in *CLG* 29.2 (March–April 1996), 77–81; Ruan Ming, "Cong xin quanwei zhuyi dao xin baoshou zhuyi" (From New Authoritarianism to New Conservatism), *Kaifang zazhi*, February 1992, 28–32, tr. David Kelly, in *CLG* 29.2 (March–April 1996), 58–70; Wang, "Xin baoshou zhuyi yu dalu zhishi fenzi."

People's Republic of China and both criticized the Cultural Revolution and Mao Zedong's policies from the perspective of the preservation of stability. Xiao added, however, that the authors of "Realistic Responses" began from their personal interests (*jieji liyi*)—the interests of the "offspring of the revolution," whose "empire" was threatened by radicalism—whereas his own underlying worries were related to China's "national interests" (*minzu de liyi*).[145] This, as indicated in the previous chapter, was a common accusation during the 1990s when intellectual independence was considered an asset. Nevertheless, even though Xiao endorsed state building and rejected a strengthening of the party, he did not make any effort to clearly separate the two.

With respect to radicalism, the princelings mentioned radicalism in the same breath as "romanticism" and "irrationalism." More specifically, rationalism was the opposite of "irrationalism" (*fei lixing zhuyi*) and relied on the positive powers of reason instead of emotions and "utopian ideals." They referred to Russell, Popper, and Hayek as representatives of "Western rationalism." The princelings adhered to rationalism because they wanted to shed light on the rational and practical nature of the party after the utopianism of the Mao era.[146] For Xiao Gongqin, however, radicalism stood for abstract rationalism (*weili zhuyi*) in an epistemological sense; it referred to knowledge gained through reason. Xiao discarded this in favor of the tradition of empiricism (*jingyan zhuyi*), which holds that knowledge is gained through experience.

A second critical difference between Xiao Gongqin and the princelings is reflected in their respective economic advocacies. From their terminology, we find that the princelings still adhered to a Marxist framework of "socialist" versus "bourgeois" thought and the "capitalist system." They disapproved of "radical" reform because it would change the relations of production. In contrast, Xiao Gongqin, very much in the spirit of the modernization fervor of the 1980s, supported market reforms if they could be gradually introduced. Furthermore, whereas Xiao subscribed to private ownership and the depoliticization of economics, the princelings argued that the party should not surrender its control over the economy. From an economic point of view, only Xiao Gongqin's neoconservatism represented a continuation of neo-authoritarianism.

In spite of these differences, Xiao and the princelings invoked the same foreign thinkers in their defense of neoconservatism, including Edmund Burke, Karl Popper, Paul Tillich, Alexis de Tocqueville, and Samuel Huntington. As Sullivan writes on the appropriation of foreign theories in neo-authoritarianism and neoconservatism, "Once entering a different political-historical context, theory often plays a role in the transformation of that society and the theory

---

[145] Interview with Xiao Gongqin, Shanghai, August 4, 2006.
[146] Davies, *Worrying about China*, 168.

itself is also recreated."[147] In China, Western theorists were often invoked as authorities to support claims, in this case to promote healthy and "rational" reform, but references to these thinkers were highly selective.

Even though the semiofficial document "Realistic Responses" was written in Marxist language, it still points to the existence of a legitimacy crisis after the 1991 coup. Officially, however, since party legitimacy was based on revolution, the party could not abandon revolution. As Arif Dirlik states, the official solution was a "negotiated settlement on the past that seeks to historicize the revolution while distancing it from the present."[148] For the "princelings," however, the revolutionary identity was part of the problem, and nationalism offered an alternative. Of course, the use of nationalism to foster cohesion was nothing new; decades earlier Mao Zedong had already discovered the potential of anti-imperialist nationalism to foster cohesion.[149] The official campaigns of the early 1990s, as we have seen, also relied on nationalism. But neoconservatism in its various forms went even further in its acknowledgment of the limits of revolution as a source of legitimacy under reform.

In this respect, there was certainly a rift between neoconservatism and official justifications of economic reform. Officially, reform continued to be justified on Marxist grounds, even though there were disputes among those who advocated a more orthodox Marxist view and those who, like Deng Xiaoping, reinterpreted socialism more pragmatically as economic construction. At the Third Plenum of the Eleventh Central Committee in 1978, the move from class struggle to economic development was first legitimated with the argument of "practice as the sole criterion of truth" (*shijian shi jianyan zhenli de weiyi biaozhun*), which was in line with Mao's own statements.[150] Furthermore, in the 1981 Resolution on Certain Questions in the History of Our Party since the Founding of the State, approved by the Sixth Plenary Session of the Eleventh Central Committee, the Mao of the Cultural Revolution period is distinguished from the Mao of the mid-1930s to the mid-1950s. The resolution denounces the former but praises the latter for his achievements in liberation and the transformation to socialism. In addition, the resolution separates Mao's individual thought from Mao Zedong Thought as the

---

[147] Sullivan, "Impact of Western Political Thought," 79.
[148] Arif Dirlik, "The Past as Ideology and Critical Resource: Politics and Historical Revisionism after the Fall" (unpublished conference paper, Workshop on Revisionism, Leiden, November 2005).
[149] Cheek, *Living with Reform*, 43, 45.
[150] An article with this title appeared in *Guangming ribao* (Enlightenment Daily) on May 11, 1978.

"crystallisation of the collective wisdom of the Party's revolutionary experience."[151] This distinction and the emphasis on the "organizational side" at the expense of the "charismatic parts" allowed for the latter to retain legitimacy during the reform period.[152] Whereas the 1981 resolution settled the question of Mao's legacy, the trial of the Gang of Four served to offer justice, heal the wounds inflicted by the violence of the Cultural Revolution, and explain historical events in a manner that allowed for a transition to a more rational era.[153]

The official justification of reform had taken on new forms over the years, but it remained based on a Marxist narrative. The phrase "socialism with Chinese characteristics," as already referred to above, first appeared at the Twelfth Party Congress in 1982. In 1987, Zhao Ziyang put forward the theory of the "primary stage of socialism."[154] Because China had never undergone a capitalist stage, it was argued, its forces of production had not developed. At the Fourteenth Party Congress in 1992, Jiang Zemin referred to a "socialist market economy."[155] These developments show that the official rhetoric was attempting to justify the economic reforms as congruent with the future goal of socialism, whereas the neoconservatives were recommending a market economy resorting to non-Marxist Western theories and referring to Chinese modernization.[156] Hence, seen from a Marxist perspective, neoconservatism was anti-Marxist and questioned the legitimacy of the Chinese revolution.[157]

As this chapter has shown, the main advocacies of neoconservatism were united in their resort to non-Marxist thinkers, their rejection of radicalism as drastic economic and political reform, their turn to Chinese tradition as a

---

[151] Arif Dirlik, "Mao Zedong in Contemporary Chinese Official Discourse and History," *China Perspectives*, no. 2 (2012), 19–20, 20.

[152] Cheek, *Living with Reform*, 58. The CCP composed its first Historical Resolution in 1945 to corroborate Mao's position as chairman and leader of the revolution. Ibid., 57.

[153] Alexander C. Cook, *The Cultural Revolution on Trial: Mao and the Gang of Four* (Cambridge: Cambridge University Press, 2016), 3.

[154] This theory was a reworking of Su Shaozhi's theory of "undeveloped socialism." See Misra, *From Post-Maoism to Post-Marxism*, 91–115. The first stage was a transition from capitalism to socialism, which was completed in the 1950s. The second stage, the "primary stage of socialism," would last until about 2050. The "primary stage" was also divided into three phases: (1) a doubling of the GNP of 1980 (which Zhao Ziyang considered to be already accomplished in 1987), (2) a doubling of the economy by 2000, and (3) a GNP at the level of the relatively developed countries by 2050.

[155] For details, see Alan R. Kluver, *Legitimating the Chinese Economic Reforms: A Rhetoric of Myth and Orthodoxy* (Albany: State University of New York Press, 1996), 39–119.

[156] Wang Shaoguang, "Qiubian paluan de xin baoshou sichao" (The Neoconservative Trend That Seeks Change and Fears Chaos), *Zhongguo shibao zhoukan*, March 8, 1992, 76–77.

[157] Chen, "Order and Stability in Social Transition," 612; Sullivan, "Democracy and Developmentalism," 330.

source of cohesion, their backing of a strong state, and their preoccupation with Chinese modernization. Furthermore, both advocated reform that was either "rational" (as opposed to "utopian") or based on "experience" instead of "reason." They were divided, however, in that they constituted responses to crises at different fronts and in their views on private property. Another crucial distinction was that Xiao Gongqin, as a historian, projected radicalism into the past. This, as we will see, was not without consequences.

3   Xiao Gongqin and the Yan Fu Paradox

> He will therefore have to use what knowledge he can achieve, not to shape the results as the craftsman shapes his handiwork, but rather to cultivate a growth by providing the appropriate environment, in the manner in which the gardener does this for his plants.
>
> Friedrich Hayek, "The Pretence of Knowledge"

The radicalism that neoconservatives condemned was not restricted to the events of 1989, 1991, or the Cultural Revolution. For the main theorist of neoconservatism, Xiao Gongqin, radicalism could be traced back to the late nineteenth century. In analyses of neoconservatism, scholars have referred to Xiao's historical writings, but they have primarily interpreted them in light of Xiao's alignment with the government or with the "neoconservative-type elites," the antiliberal characteristics of the theory, or political conservatism.[1] On Xiao's famous essay on the translator Yan Fu, which will be analyzed later in this chapter, Gu and Kelly state, "While it is couched as an essay in modern intellectual history, it is in fact a customary mode of expression for Xiao, as for many contemporary Chinese intellectuals, to deliver opinions through the mouths of historical personages."[2] Similarly, Peter Moody interprets Xiao's writings on the 1898 Hundred Days Reform as an allusion to both the turmoil of 1989 and Deng Xiaoping's radical reform program; Xiao's criticism amounts to a defense of Jiang Zemin's reform line.[3]

While Xiao certainly draws on history to write about reform China, and while the above readings raise critical questions about the place of history in Chinese academic debates, one cannot reduce Xiao's writings on history to mere instrumentalism. Xiao is also a historian who shares the fixations of other intellectuals in the humanities, and for him neoconservatism is more than a

---

[1] Sullivan, "Democracy and Developmentalism," 347; Meissner, "New Intellectual Currents," 19; McCormick and Kelly, "Limits of Anti-liberalism," 804–31; Tsai, "New Authoritarianism, Neo-conservatism, and Anti–Peaceful Evolution," 7–8; Xu Ben, *Disenchanted Democracy: Chinese Cultural Criticism after 1989* (Ann Arbor: University of Michigan Press, 1999), 169; Schubert, "Was Ist Neokonservativismus?," 61–62.
[2] Gu and Kelly, "New Conservatism," 223.   [3] Moody, *Conservative Thought*, 158–59.

political theory—it draws on the debates on Chinese modernization and the continuity of Chinese culture that have taken place since the late nineteenth century. Gu and Kelly also make reference to this direction. They note that Xiao is "concerned with three perennial sources of controversy among Chinese intellectuals," namely the topic of gradualism versus radicalism, the function of traditional values in the modernization process, and the question of who is privileged by "the modernizing social force."[4] Similarly, Feng Chen has noted that "neoconservative ideas, unlike the neo-authoritarian debate, go beyond the political domain . . . Their cultural ramifications, however, deserve a separate study."[5] However, this observation appears only in a footnote to Chen's article.

The place and function of history in Xiao's writings on the reform period is more complex than has hitherto been acknowledged. Xiao has referred to himself as a "historian who shows solicitude for the nation's fate," and, as a historian, he considers himself to be privileged: he can enter history through the door of reality and vice versa.[6] Xiao acknowledges that he is not a specialist on modern Chinese history, but history is key for his study of reform.[7] For Xiao, any politics should be rooted in history.[8] Nevertheless, Xiao was trained as a historian and, like other historians of his time, he rewrote modern Chinese history as a history of modernization. In the words of Chinese historian Ma Yong of CASS, historians who studied the 1898 Reform Movement were actually engaged in "the earliest attempts by the Chinese people in the all-round pursuit of modernization."[9] Hence, Xiao's writings also reflect the changing historiographical practices of the 1980s and early 1990s amid the growing interest in modernization. In addition, the responses to Xiao's writings also reflect the tensions between the quest for scholarly integrity and political service that intensified after 1989.

This chapter discusses Xiao's neoconservatism from the perspective of the role of history and its connection with earlier debates on China's modernization. For Xiao, the historical figure of Yan Fu was the earliest neoconservative modernizer. Even though Xiao argues that Yan Fu's theory was a Burkean plea for historical continuity, this chapter argues that his reliance on Yan Fu, who reinterpreted elements of Social Darwinism, reflects Xiao's vision of

---

[4] Gu and Kelly, "New Conservatism," 221.
[5] Chen, "Order and Stability in Social Transition," 594. [6] Xiao, "Zixu," in *XGQJ*, 12, 16.
[7] Xiao Gongqin, "Lishixue zai Zhongguo biange shidai de yiyi" (The Meaning of Historical Studies in the Era of Chinese Reform), in *XGQJ*, 359–64.
[8] Xiao Gongqin, "Dangdai Zhongguo xin baoshou zhuyi de sixiang yuanyuan" (The Intellectual Origins of Contemporary Chinese Neoconservatism), *Ershiyi shiji*, no. 40 (April 1997), 126–35, 133.
[9] Ma Yong, "Jindai lishi renwu yanjiu" (Research on Personages in Modern History), in Zeng Yeying, ed., *Wushi nian lai de Zhongguo jindaishi yanjiu* (Research on Modern Chinese History during the Past Fifty Years) (Shanghai: Shanghai shudian chubanshe, 2000), 659–83, 677.

neoconservatism as a modernization theory. In spite of Xiao's criticism of rapid and wholesale change through Yan Fu and Edmund Burke, his neoconservatism indicates that *-isms* in 1990s China remained "concepts of movement" intended to bring about change.[10] The Burke in Xiao's neoconservatism was a Burke reinterpreted through the lens of Yan Fu's evolutionism and a liberalism à la Hayek and Popper. Conservatism in this sense was to preserve the past for the future.

Xiao Gongqin and the Chinese Intellectual World

Xiao Gongqin was a professor of history at Shanghai Normal University when he began to advocate his theory of neoconservatism. He has divided his intellectual path into four stages. The first stage (1978–81) covers his years as a master's student. After the Cultural Revolution, Xiao was admitted to the History Department of Nanjing University, where he specialized in the history of the Yuan dynasty (1260–1368).[11] During the second stage (1982–87), Xiao began to research issues in modern Chinese history that were related to the problems of the contemporary reforms. He considers *The Predicament of Confucian Culture: Modern Chinese Literati and the Challenge of the West* to be his main work during this period.[12] In this book, Xiao argues that the main reason for the failure of China's modernization process was the "cultural conservatism" and the "Confucian dogmatism" of the literati under a "closed system."[13] Xiao underscores the continuity of this stage of his thought with his later advocacy of neoconservatism.[14]

During the third stage of his thought (1988–89), Xiao's interest shifts to the contribution of the reform faction to the ultimate failure of reform. He calls this research "the history of early modernization" (*zaoqi xiandaihua lishi yanjiu*), as distinguished from "research on modern history" (*jindaishi yanjiu*). At this point, Xiao becomes interested in the political choices of the Chinese reformers since modern times and criticizes their "radical mode of thought."[15] During the fourth stage (1989–present), Xiao applies his research on early modernization to a study of reform. Borrowing from political sociology, Xiao analyzes which political models are most suited to completion of the modernization

---

[10] Spira, *Conceptual History of Chinese -Isms*, 2.
[11] Xiao, "Zixu," in *XGQJ*, 2. Xiao's master's thesis, which is titled "Lun Yuandai de huangdi jicheng wenti" (On the Issue of Throne Succession during the Yuan Dynasty), is a cultural analysis of the political crisis during the Yuan dynasty (1260–1368). It analyzes the tensions between the political systems of the pastoral and farming communities respectively.
[12] Xiao Gongqin, *Rujia wenhua de kunjing: Zhongguo jindai shidaifu yu Xifang tiaozhan* (The Predicament of Confucian Culture: Modern Chinese Literati and the Challenge of the West) (Chengdu: Sichuan renmin chubanshe, 1986).
[13] Ibid., 3.   [14] Xiao, "Zixu," in *XGQJ*, 4.   [15] Ibid., 6–7.

process. For this, he draws inspiration from the French sociologist Émile Durkheim (1858–1917) and from Yan Fu, the Chinese translator of British works. With respect to Durkheim, the concept that Xiao finds most suited to explain the problems of Chinese modernization is that of "anomy" (*shifan*), which Durkheim coined in *The Division of Labor in Society* (1893) and which later reappeared in *Suicide* (1897).[16] With respect to Yan Fu, according to Xiao he was the first Chinese thinker who paid attention to the differing conditions in the Western and Chinese systems, thus rendering him the first neoconservative modernizer. This chapter discusses Xiao's research during the third and fourth stages of his intellectual path, both preceding and following June Fourth, which has been collected in volumes such as *History Rejects Romanticism: Neoconservatism and Chinese Modernization* (1998), *Reform amidst Crisis: Radicalism and Conservativism in the Process of Late Qing Modernization* (1999), and *Parting with Political Romanticism* (2001).[17]

Even though Xiao's writings were partially used to promote gradual reform in the official media, such as *Zhongguo qingnianbao* and *Beijing qingnianbao*, as discussed in the previous chapter, they also appeared in the main vehicles for intellectual debates. These debates took place in journals such as *Zhishi fenzi*, *Tianjin shehui kexue* (Tianjin Social Sciences), *Zhongguo xiandaihua yanjiu*, *Tansuo yu zhengming* (Exploration and Contention), *Zhanlüe yu guanli*, *Zhongguo shehui kexue jikan*, *Ershiyi shiji*, and *Kaifang shidai* (Open Times). Many of Xiao's writings that originally appeared in these journals were later collected in *Xiao Gongqin ji* (Collected Works of Xiao Gongqin), on which this chapter partly draws.[18]

Xiao not only participated in the mainland debates in these venues but also was clearly familiar with the work of the US-based Chinese scholar Lin Yü-sheng. Lin is famous for his thesis on the "totalistic antitraditionalism" of the May Fourth generation, which mainland scholars reworked in their reflections on radicalism, as will be discussed in further detail in the next chapter. In July 1988, Lin Yü-sheng, Xiao Gongqin, and Xu Jilin engaged in a dialogue on the May Fourth Movement.[19] In this dialogue, Lin Yü-sheng

---

[16] Ibid., 10.
[17] Xiao Gongqin, *Lishi jujue langman: Xin baoshou zhuyi yu Zhongguo xiandaihua* (History Rejects Romanticism: Neoconservatism and Chinese Modernization) (Taipei: Zhiliang chubanshe, 1998); Xiao Gongqin, *Weiji zhong de bianqe: Qingmo xiandaihua jincheng zhong de jijin yu baoshou* (Reform amidst Crisis: Radicalism and Conservatism in the Process of Late Qing Modernization) (Shanghai: Shanghai sanlian shudian, 1999); Xiao, *YZLG*.
[18] Xiao Gongqin, *Xiao Gongqin ji* (Collected Works of Xiao Gongqin) (Ha'erbin: Heilongjiang jiaoyu chubanshe, 1995).
[19] Lin Yü-sheng, Xu Jilin, and Xiao Gongqin, "'Wusi': Duoyuan de fansi: Lin Yü-sheng, Xu Jilin, Xiao Gongqin duihua lu" (Multiple Reflections on "May Fourth": Record of a Dialogue among Lin Yü-sheng, Xu Jilin, and Xiao Gongqin), in Lin Yü-sheng et al., *Wusi: Duoyuan de fansi* (May Fourth: Multiple Reflections) (Hong Kong: Sanlian shudian, 1989), 241–51.

expresses satisfaction with the shift away from wholesale antitraditionalism on mainland China. However, for him, political and economic guarantees for the creation of moral liberty and the dangers of man-made authority are equally weighty. Xiao Gongqin argues that a strong man-made authority is necessary on mainland China given that historically its modernization forces were weak. Hence, Xiao engages with debates on radicalism partly instigated by Chinese scholars abroad, but he interprets them within the framework of his theories on neo-authoritarianism and questions of reform on mainland China.

That Xiao was involved in the major historiographical debates of the times can be seen from his contributions to various major collections of writings. These include *Chongxin renshi bainian Zhongguo: Jindaishi redian wenti yanjiu yu zhengming* (A New Understanding of One Hundred Years of China: Research and Debates on Popular Issues in Modern Chinese History, 1998), *Zhishi fenzi lichang: Jijin yu baoshou zhijian de dongdang* (1999), and *Lishi de huida: Zhongguo jindaishi yanjiu zhong de jige yuanze lunzheng* (History's Response: Some Principal Debates in Research on Modern Chinese History, 2001).[20] The inclusion of Xiao's writings in leading academic journals and thematic edited volumes reveals that he took part in the dominant intellectual discussions. In addition, in a commentary on the rejection of radicalism during the early 1990s that looks at the debate retrospectively, Zheng Dahua and Jia Xiaoye of CASS include Xiao Gongqin in a section on anti-radicalism and a re-evaluation of events in modern Chinese history. The same section includes writings by CASS historian Ma Yong, philosopher Li Zehou, and writer and philosopher Wang Yuanhua, the ideas of whom all will be explored in the next chapters.[21]

Although he took part in the main intellectual debates, how did other Chinese academics perceive Xiao Gongqin? And how did Xiao himself understand his role? Xiao identifies himself primarily as an academic rather than as a political adviser and regrets being considered a representative of political forces.[22] The fascinations of the "academic faction," with which Xiao identifies, include the history of Chinese modernization and civil society,

---

[20] Feng Lin, ed., *Chongxin renshi bainian Zhongguo: Jindaishi redian wenti yanjiu yu zhengming* (A New Understanding of One Hundred Years of China: Research and Debates on Popular Issues in Modern Chinese History), 2 vols. (Beijing: Gaige chubanshe, 1998); *ZFL*; Gong Shuduo, Jin Chongji, and Song Xiaoqing, *Lishi de huida: Zhongguo jindaishi yanjiu zhong de jige yuanze lunzheng* (History's Response: Some Principal Debates in Research on Modern Chinese History) (Beijing: Beijing shifan daxue chubanshe, 2001).

[21] Zheng Dahua and Jia Xiaoye, "Ershi shiji jiushi niandai yilai Zhongguo jindaishi shang de jijin yu baoshou yanjiu shuping" (Commentary on Research on Radicalism and Conservatism in Modern Chinese History since the 1990s), *Jindaishi yanjiu* (Modern Chinese History Research), no. 4 (2005), 293–95.

[22] Xiao, "Zixu" (Preface), in *YZLG*, 8.

the transformation of traditional Chinese culture, and the Chinese national character. The "policy faction," on the other hand, according to Xiao, concentrates on the relations between central and local government, between population and resources, and between state power and democratic rule.[23] The concerns of the "policy faction" to which Xiao refers are identified in the previous chapter as the major themes in research on neoconservatism. In contrast, Xiao is more interested in intellectuals in the history of Chinese reform.[24]

From the perspective of historian Ma Yong, who has written extensively on the late Qing reforms and the 1911 Revolution, Xiao Gongqin merely utilizes history as a tool and as a new discursive strategy.[25] Nonspecialists such as Xiao, Ma Yong argues, should "give history back to the historians."[26] However, the distinction that Ma Yong makes between a genuine interest in history and an instrumental exploitation of it is not clear-cut because the explosion of interest in the 1898 Reform Movement was also triggered by the current reforms. Hence, we should understand Ma Yong's claim in relation to the shift from political engagement to academic scholarship that characterized the intellectual world of the early 1990s.

The historical scholarship of Xiao, as both a political theorist and a historian, evoked resistance because it contravened the preoccupation with disengaged scholarship that emerged after 1989. After all, as opposed to many others who had taken part in the neo-authoritarianism debates, Xiao did not have to flee China. Discussions on radicalism in modern Chinese history, as we will see in the following chapter, were not only a critique of a historical teleology but also an "articulation of frustration" following Tiananmen.[27] Rewriting modern Chinese history from the perspective of intellectuals also served to come to terms with the abrupt ending of the 1980s' intellectual movement. With this in mind, let us now turn to Xiao's reading of modern Chinese history.

---

[23] Xiao Gongqin, "Zhuanxingqi Zhongguo renwen zhishi fenzi de sizhong leixing" (Four Types of Intellectuals in the Humanities in Transitional China), in *XGQJ*, 182–89.

[24] See, for example, Xiao Gongqin, *Zhishi fenzi yu guannian ren* (Intellectuals and Men of Concepts) (Tianjin: Tianjin renmin chubanshe, 2002); Xiao Gongqin, *Rujia wenhua de kunjing: Jindai shidaifu yu Zhong Xi wenhua pengzhuang* (The Dilemma of Confucian Culture: Modern Literati and the Collision of Chinese and Western Cultures) (Guilin: Guangxi shifan daxue chubanshe, 2006).

[25] See, for example, Xiao Gongqin, *1911 nian Zhongguo da geming* (The Great Chinese Revolution of 1911) (Beijing: Shehui kexue wenxian chubanshe, 2011); Ma Yong, *1898 nian nachang weisui zhengbian* (The Aborted Coup of 1898) (Nanjing: Jiangsu renmin chubanshe, 2011).

[26] Interview with Ma Yong, Beijing, August 8, 2005 and June 6, 2006.

[27] Zhu, "For a Chinese Liberalism," 104.

The Lessons of History: Three Kinds of Radicalism

Like other intellectuals at the time, Xiao discerns several stages of radicalism in modern Chinese history, and in the process he frequently refers to Edmund Burke. The reason why Chinese intellectuals invoked Burke was, according to Xiao, that Burke was easy to understand—Chinese intellectuals read his criticism of the French Revolution as criticism of the Cultural Revolution. In contrast, the conservatism of American thinkers, such as Leo Strauss and Carl Schmitt, was not recognizable to Chinese intellectuals because China lacked the Greek tradition to which they often referred.[28] Xiao stated that he too invoked Burke because he did not oppose change, arguing that change was necessary for preservation.[29]

Xiao added that Burkean conservatism should be distinguished from its "Maistrian" counterpart, which was "reactionary" in nature.[30] Here Xiao refers to Joseph de Maistre (1753–1821), a critic of the French Enlightenment who upheld an authoritarian Catholicism, which Xiao contrasts with the liberal variant represented by Burke. Whereas Burkean conservatism was based on the existence of a civil society, such a condition was lacking in China—the purpose of Chinese neoconservatism was precisely to bring about the realization of a civil society. In China, neoconservatism had a contradictory attitude toward its own tradition: it criticized radical antitraditionalism, but in returning to tradition it was careful not to become a "fundamentalist conservatism."[31]

On radicalism, Xiao states, "One can say that the criticism, reflections, and research with regard to radicalism in the early Chinese modernization process are a historical resource for the formation of my reform thoughts, with gradualism as a basis."[32] A common pattern used in the reassessment of modern Chinese history at the beginning of the 1990s, as we will also see in the next chapter, is the three "stages" of radicalism. The beginning of the first stage is generally situated at the end of the nineteenth century, when reformers such as Kang Youwei (1858–1927), Tan Sitong (1865–98), and Liang Qichao (1873–1929) launched the 1898 Hundred Days Reform Movement (*wuxu bianfa*). The second stage centers around the 1911 Revolution, or, for some, the May Fourth Movement, which broadly refers to the cultural and political movements between 1917 and 1921. The third and final stage consists of Marxism and the Maoist excesses of the Cultural Revolution.

---

[28] Interview with Xiao Gongqin, Shanghai, August 4, 2006.
[29] Xiao, "Dangdai Zhongguo xin baoshou zhuyi de sixiang yuanyuan," 126.
[30] Ibid. The distinction between "Burkean" and "Maistrian" conservatism is taken from Peter Viereck's study on conservatism. See Viereck, *Conservatism from John Adams to Churchill* (Princeton, NJ: Van Nostrand, 1956).
[31] Xiao, "'Yan Fu beilun,'" 36, 39–40. [32] Xiao, "Zixu," in *XGQJ*, 10.

Like other Chinese intellectuals who condemned this century-old radicalism, Xiao, by looking into China's past, bids farewell to what he calls "utopianist political myths."[33] In particular, Xiao criticizes the impact of the modern model of revolutionary thought that unconsciously created a "dislocation" of reform thought. This is manifested in the mentality of an "overcorrection" (*fei jiaowang bu zuyi guozheng*), in the perception that reform is a revolution, in the dichotomy of good versus bad, and in the belief that goals can be achieved in a single step.[34] In a January article that appeared in *Beijing qingnianbao*, Xiao elaborates on his three types and stages of radicalism.[35] Xiao's article on "system determinism," which dates from as early as 1989, should be understood in relation to the Tiananmen demonstrations.[36] Two 1993 articles discuss "political romanticism."[37] Overall, Xiao's three types of radicalism are indicative of the overriding attention of intellectuals at that time to "gradualism" and incremental reform in response to the "radical" reform of 1989.

Xiao argues that his three types of radicalism can be perceived as "successive stages" in modern Chinese history.[38] The 1898 Hundred Days Reform was marked by "psychological radicalism," the parliamentary democracy of the Republic (1912) suffered from "system determinism," and during the period before and after the May Fourth Movement "political romanticism" flourished in the form of "radical antitraditionalism" (*jijin fan chuantong zhuyi*) and "wholesale Westernization theories" (*quanpan Xihualun*). The cycle that connects them thereafter reappeared in different historical conditions, and for Xiao the history of modern China and China of the 1980s especially had "similar historical structures."[39] The three types of radicalism were different aspects of one and the same "collective unconsciousness."[40] Let us now take a closer look at these three stages of radicalism.

---

[33] Xiao Gongqin, "The Political Attitudes of the Various Strata in China's Society and Their Prospects for the Future," *Chinese Economy* 32.3 (1999), 59.
[34] Xiao Gongqin, "Zouxiang chengshu: Zhongguo gaige de fansi yu zhanwang" (Toward Ripening: Reflections on and Prospects for the Chinese Reforms), in *XGQJ*, 123–39, 134.
[35] Xiao, "Lishi jujue langman," 109–22.
[36] Xiao Gongqin, "Lun dangdai Zhongguo de langman zhuyi gaigeguan: Dui 'zhidu juedinglun' de piping" (On the Romantic Reform View in Contemporary China: Criticism of "System Determinism"), in *XGQJ*, 87–108.
[37] Xiao, "Zouxiang chengshu," 123–39; Xiao Gongqin, "Cong zhengzhi langman zhuyi dao zhengzhi jijin zhuyi: Dui Zhongguo zaoqi yihui minzhu sichao de lishi kaocha" (From Political Romanticism to Political Radicalism: Historical Research on the Early Parliamentary Democracy Trend), in *XGQJ*, 265–80.
[38] Xiao, "Zixu," in *XGQJ*, 9; Xiao, "Lishi jujue langman," 117.
[39] Xiao, "Zixu," in *XGQJ*, 9–10; Xiao, "Zixu," in *YZLG*, 4.
[40] Xiao Gongqin, "Sixiangshi de meili" (The Charm of Intellectual History), in *Zhishi fenzi yu guannian ren,* 109; Xiao, "Zixu," in *YZLG*, 9.

The "Psychological Radicalism" of the 1898 Hundred Days Reformers

In "Re-examining the Hundred Days Reform Movement: Discussing the Cultural Roots of Early Political Radicalism,"[41] Xiao examines why the educational, political, economic, and military innovations that Kang Youwei and Emperor Guangxu (1871–1908) introduced between June 11 and September 21, 1898, ended with a coup d'état and a rejection of the most principal changes.[42] Xiao argues that it is wrong to reduce the failure of the 1898 Reform Movement to "unfavorable objective conditions" or to the mistakes of the conservative opposition.[43] Kang Youwei's "psychological radicalism" was at the heart of the failure of the movement. Responding to their feelings of cultural anxiety, the reformers undertook large-scale reforms to achieve a psychological balance.[44]

This feeling of crisis and urgency was related to China's sorry state of affairs after its defeat in the Sino-Japanese War (1894–95). As a result, there was a discrepancy between the reformers' subjective aspirations and what was realistically feasible. Xiao's definition of radicalism is reminiscent of that of Michael Gasster, who regards radicalism as a dissatisfaction with the present that leads to the creation of better conditions in one's mind.[45] Just as Plato compares social decay to an illness and a statesman to a physician, Xiao compares the reformers to "radical doctors" who believed that a major operation was the only solution to China's illness.[46] Because this type of radicalism was driven by anxiety, Xiao also refers to it as a "feeling-of-anxiety radicalism" (*jiaolügan de jijin zhuyi*).[47]

In Xiao's analysis of the failure of the Hundred Days Reform Movement, we can discern traces of earlier debates on neo-authoritarianism and references to Samuel Huntington's *Political Order in Changing Societies*. Xiao argues that the structure of the bureaucracy was not conducive to radical reform. There was a dual structure of authority, in which a complex amalgam of power relationships preserved the balance between the Empress Dowager Cixi (1835–1908) and the Emperor Guangxu (1872–1908). Radical reform caused

---

[41] Xiao Gongqin, "Wuxu bianfa de zai fanxing: Jianlun zaoqi zhengzhi jijin zhuyi de wenhua genyuan" (Re-examining the Hundred Days Reform Movement: Discussing the Cultural Roots of Early Political Radicalism), in *ZFL*, 121–41.
[42] For the course of the Reform Movement program, see Chang Hao, "Intellectual Change and the Reform Movement, 1890–1898," in John King Fairbank and Kwang-ching Liu, eds., *The Cambridge History of China, Vol. 11: Late Ch'ing, 1800–1911, Part Two* (Cambridge: Cambridge University Press, 1980), 274–338.
[43] Xiao, "Wuxu bianfa," 135.   [44] Xiao, "Zixu," in *XGQJ*, 9.
[45] Gasster, *Chinese Intellectuals and the Revolution of 1911*, 237–38.
[46] Xiao, "Political Attitudes," 77.
[47] Interview with Xiao Gongqin, Shanghai, August 4, 2006.

a polarization and created tensions with the Confucian bureaucratic values. In addition, the vast size of the Chinese bureaucracy negatively affected the reforms' chances of success. Samuel Huntington similarly argues that large-scale bureaucracies—for instance those in Russia, China, and the former Austrian Empire—were much more difficult to reform than noncentralized countries such as Japan.[48]

Elements of Huntington in Xiao Gongqin's works exceed the topic of bureaucracies. Xiao's suitable strategy is what Huntington calls a "Fabianist strategy," analogous to British society in the late nineteenth century that advocated a gradual approach to social democracy.[49] Huntington coined this term in relation to the modernization of Turkey, referring to the strategy of Mustafa Kemal Atatürk, whom Huntington contrasts with the approaches of Emperor Guangxu and Holy Roman Emperor Joseph II.[50] Following Huntington, Xiao argues that Kemal disentangled problems by starting with easy issues in order to secure the support of the majority.[51] After each successful reform, Kemal hinted at the next step, but from the very beginning he did not publicize his entire plan, which Huntington calls a "foot-in-the-door approach."[52] The Qing reformers, in contrast, Xiao argues, sought rapid reforms because of the sense of crisis that blurred their capacity to think rationally. Kang Youwei publicized his entire reform plan from the outset, something Huntington calls a "*blitzkrieg* approach."[53] Moreover, by taking the side of the reformers, Kang Youwei turned the officials into opponents. In brief, the reformers focused on the necessity of the reforms, but not on their feasibility.[54]

Xiao locates the roots of "psychological radicalism" in the traditional Chinese political culture of "you die, I live" (*nisi wohuo*) or "where you are, I am not" (*youni wuwo*), which prevented compromise and consensus.[55] To some extent, the connection that Xiao makes between the traditional Chinese political culture and radicalism is reminiscent of Lin Yü-sheng's analysis of the "totalistic antitraditionalism" of the May Fourth reformers, to be discussed in the next chapter.[56] Lin Yü-sheng also traces the roots of radicalism back to Chinese tradition: in the instance of the May Fourth reformers, their

---

[48] See Samuel Huntington, "Political Change in Traditional Polities," in *POCS*, 140–91, 366–67. Xiao notes, however, that his ideas on neo-authoritarianism were shaped before he read Huntington. Interview with Xiao Gongqin, Shanghai, August 4, 2006.
[49] Xiao, "Wuxu bianfa," 128.   [50] Huntington, *POCS*, 344–56.
[51] Xiao, "Wuxu bianfa," 128.   [52] Huntington, *POCS*, 346, 353.
[53] Xiao, "Wuxu bianfa," 128; Huntington, *POCS*, 346.   [54] Xiao, "Wuxu bianfa," 136.
[55] Ibid., 140. Xiao's perception of Chinese political culture resembles Tsou Tang's interpretation of Chinese politics as a "winner-take-all" conflict. See Joseph Fewsmith, *Elite Politics in Contemporary China* (Armonk, NY: M.E. Sharpe, 2001), xiv.
[56] Lin Yü-sheng, *The Crisis of Chinese Consciousness: Radical Antitraditionalism in the May Fourth Era* (Madison: University of Wisconsin Press, 1979).

radicalism was due to their "holistic" way of thinking, which led them to pursue only "ultimate goals."

The modernization framework features prominently in Xiao's account of modern Chinese history. For Xiao, the division between traditional and modern China is neither the Opium War nor the start of the technological reforms after the 1870s, but the 1898 Reform Movement. It was only then that a feeling of crisis among the literati took shape.[57] Xiao's return to this moment in history was not unique at the time; during the early 1990s, there was a true revival of interest in late Qing politics, the 1898 Reform Movement, and the New Policies (*xinzheng*) that followed the Reform Movement. The latter included the establishment of a modern education system in the aftermath of the abolition of the examination system in 1905 and reform of the judiciary and the police. Since the 1980s, Chinese historians had been using the modernization paradigm, writing about elites, top-down reforms, and modernization, rather than the revolutionary paradigm with its preoccupation with the masses or bottom-up revolution.[58]

According to the traditional paradigm of historiography, the main narrative of modern Chinese history—which stretched from the First Opium War (1839–42) to the May Fourth Movement of 1919—was a struggle against both feudalism and imperialism.[59] In this model, Chinese society was a "semi-colonized" and "semi-feudal" society and historical incidents were weighed on the basis of their struggle against or in alignment with colonization and feudal forces. This is referred to as the "two semis" (*liangban*) model. However, highlighting the revolution against imperialism and feudalism, historians now argued, concealed the other side of the story, namely that of semi-independence and semi-capitalism. Historian Liu Danian therefore rephrases the "two basic problems" of national independence and feudal rule as problems of modernization and industrialization.[60] In 1980, the framework of the three stages of development, namely the Self-Strengthening Movement, the

---

[57] One of Xiao's monographs is about reform in late Qing China, with several chapters discussing the Reform Movement of 1898. See his *Weiji zhong de bianqe*.

[58] Huaiyin Li, "From Revolution to Modernization: The Paradigmatic Transition in Chinese Historiography in the Reform Era," *History and Theory* 49.3 (2010), 336–60.

[59] The lines of demarcation in "modern Chinese history" (*jindaishi*) have changed over time. In 1950, when historian Fan Wenlan founded the Modern History Research Institute of CASS, *jindaishi* stretched from the Opium War (1840) to the May Fourth Movement of 1919. The period after 1919 was referred to as *xiandaishi*. Today, *jindaishi* usually stretches from the Opium War to the founding of the People's Republic of China in 1949. See Jiang Tao, "Wanqing zhengzhishi" (Late Qing Political History), in Zeng, *Wushi nian lai de Zhongguo jindaishi yanjiu*, 19–22. Some researchers claim that the *jindai* period actually ended with the death of Mao Zedong in 1976, after which a true period of modernization began. Another (older) viewpoint is that 1956 should be the demarcation line because that was the year when socialism was purified of its capitalist elements. Interview with Ma Yong, Beijing, June 6, 2006.

[60] Jiang, "Wanqing zhengzhishi," 38.

1898 Reform Movement, and the "bourgeois" 1911 Revolution, was referred to as the "three ladders" (*sange jieti*).[61] In challenging the existing "two semis" model, mainland historians drew on works of scholars in Taiwan, such as Zhang Yufa of the Institute of Modern History at the Academia Sinica, who in the 1970s had conducted research on modernization. One of the leading Chinese scholars on modernization theory on mainland China was Luo Rongqu (1927–96) of Peking University.[62]

The criticism of radicalism was part of an attempt by Xiao to improve modernization efforts by foregrounding gradualism and incremental reform. For example, to indicate China's lack of a response to the post-1895 challenges, Xiao refers to Eisenstadt's concept of "the breakdown of modernization" or the setback after a period of relative progress in modernization.[63] The modernization theorists upon whom Xiao draws, namely Huntington and Eisenstadt, are "revisionist" modernization theorists for whom modernization was not necessarily universal or necessary and for whom the relationship between modernization and revolution was complicated.[64] This is consistent with the views of the Southern School of neo-authoritarianism to which Xiao belonged: neo-authoritarianism was applicable to late-modernizing countries only during the early stages of modernization. This rejection of universalism also suited Xiao's theory of neoconservatism that emphasized the importance of context and historical growth.

"System Determinism" after the 1911 Revolution

In Xiao's second form of radicalism, we can discern the Burkean concentration on the historical growth of institutions and on historical particularity. However, the idea of the cultivation of growth discussed by Xiao also features in the works of Friedrich Hayek, who defended empiricism against rationalism, as will be discussed further below. In addition, Xiao's reference to "trial and error" can be found in Popper's idea of "piecemeal engineering," a concept that was also popular among other Chinese intellectuals of the early 1990s. We will come back to this in the next chapter. Historical growth in this sense was hence advocated not because institutions were considered the last chain of a

---

[61] Ibid., 37–38.
[62] Interview with Ma Yong, Beijing, June 6, 2006. See, for example, Luo Rongqu, ed., *Cong "Xihua" dao xiandaihua: Wusi yilai youguan Zhongguo de wenhua quxiang he fazhan daolu lunzheng wenxuan* (From "Westernization" to Modernization: Selections from the Debate on China's Cultural Trends and Development since May Fourth) (Beijing: Beijing daxue chubanshe, 1990).
[63] Xiao Gongqin, "Zhongguo zaoqi xiandaihua de cuozhe ji qi lishi houguo" (The Setbacks in China's Early Modernization and the Historical Results), in *XGQJ*, 222.
[64] Li, "From Revolution to Modernization," 338. "Classical" modernization theories are those of Cyril E. Black, Marion Levy Jr., and Alex Inkeles.

long historical process, but because this growth would enable a better modernization in the future. Xiao merges certain elements from Burke with ideas from both Hayek and Popper, centering around the gradual and empirical cultivation of the surrounding conditions for the growth of institutions.

Xiao argues that one of the pitfalls of institutional reform during the early twentieth century was the lack of consideration of the different conditions surrounding the political systems in the West and in China. This resulted in a naïve "transplantation" of an entire ready-made Western system. The failure was ascribed to the import being insufficiently thorough. Xiao refers to this excessive stress on the import of systems as "system determinism." He finds examples in the thought of Sun Yat-sen (1866–1925), the "father" of the 1911 Revolution, but it was also present in an earlier generation, namely in the thought of Kang Youwei and Chen Tianhua (1875–1905), the latter of whom was involved in the founding of the Revolutionary Alliance (*Tongmenghui*).[65]

What these reformers did not consider was that every system is the outcome of a long evolutionary process and that it was hence impossible for the system to produce the same effects that had been obtained in the original environment. Kang Youwei, for example, was convinced that imitating the Western economic, political, and educational systems would solve China's problems. To describe the Western systems, Chen Tianhua used the metaphor of delicacies spread out on a table that were ready to be prepared and enjoyed at once. Imitation was more successful than invention. Sun Yat-sen compared the Western political system to an advanced machine; instead of inventing a new machine, imitation of an existing machine would guarantee output after a short period of time.[66]

A basic problem of such "system determinism," according to Xiao, is that it always explained problems within its own framework; if reform did not succeed, it was only because there was a problem with the old system and this radicalism was fought with more radicalism. Reform, according to this logic, became a revolution.[67] The final result of the disorder and radicalism from such "system determinism" was social breakdown.[68] Here we also find some similarities with Gasster's reference to a type of radicalism according to which the failure of reform is regarded as proof that more reform is necessary. Gasster refers to precisely the same examples, such as Sun Yat-sen's locomotive analogy.[69]

Xiao also finds such "system determinism" behind the Chinese economic reforms of the 1980s. Mainstream thought at that time supported a large-scale import of a market system to foster market mechanisms. Nonetheless, this was

[65] Xiao, "Lun dangdai Zhongguo de langman zhuyi gaigeguan," 87–108, 89.   [66] Ibid.
[67] Ibid., 93–94.   [68] Xiao, "Lishi jujue langman," 116.
[69] Gasster, *Chinese Intellectuals and the Revolution of 1911*, 241.

a reverse logic: importing a system without the necessary social structures was like "wearing a raincoat and hoping it will rain."[70] In response, those who believed in "system determinism" proposed "economic shock therapies," or the direct import of Western-style pluralist democratic rule. Such criticism of the "shock therapies," as we have seen in Chapter 2, also appeared in the princelings' document on neoconservatism in the aftermath of the Soviet upheaval. With the 1980s' convergence of the vicious cycle of anomy leading to more radicalism and the vicious cycle of anomy leading to the decline of authority and efficacy, the social background for the Tiananmen events was created.[71]

In response to these problems of reform, Xiao put forward two basic strategies for system transplantation. The first strategy, which Xiao calls the "guidance model system" (*youdaoxing zhidu*), supports the import of a system in accordance with the maturity of the "modernizable factors" in the social organization. The system would stimulate the maturing of such factors, allowing for a gradual integration of the system and the internal factors. The second strategy, which Xiao calls the "greenhouse model system" (*wenshixing zhidu*), is that a different system would first be imported in one relatively isolated area. As in a closed environment of a greenhouse, the reaction of the old system to the new system could then be tested. Examples of this model are the special economic zones (SEZs) in southern China, the first four of which were Shenzhen, Zhuhai, Shantou, and Xiamen.[72] What these two strategies have in common for Xiao, and reminding us of both Popper and Hayek, is their empirical trial-and-error method rather than a rational design.[73]

The two types of radicalism, namely "psychological radicalism" and "system determinism," are indicative of Xiao's attention to particularity, historical growth, and gradual change. Instead of starting from systems, Xiao argues that we need to look at the surrounding conditions, which will then determine the nature of the system. In the third type of radicalism, Xiao rejects rational designs in favor of a more empiricist approach to change. He does this by juxtaposing the French and English models of change, represented by Jean-Jacques Rousseau (1712–78) and Edmund Burke, respectively. This juxtaposition, for which Chinese intellectuals drew on Hayek's distinction between French and English models of liberalism, was commonplace in 1990s debates on radicalism, as explored further in the next chapter. We will discuss this third type of radicalism in more detail because it is here that Xiao outlines the basis for Yan Fu's critique of radicalism, upon which his own neoconservatism is based.

---

[70] Xiao, "Zouxiang chengshu," 126.   [71] Ibid., 126–27.
[72] Xiao Gongqin, "Lun dangdai Zhongguo de langman zhuyi gaigeguan," 103–5.
[73] Interview with Xiao Gongqin, Shanghai, August 4, 2006.

The "Political Romanticism" around the May Fourth Movement

For Xiao, "romanticism" has two interrelated layers of meaning, namely the "mood" of breaking with existing norms and the projection of ideals and aspirations on outer objects. Because of the latter, according to Xiao, romanticists often start from a "rational" (*heli*) or orderly state that does not exist in reality. Jean-Jacques Rousseau, for example, derived his image of the Middle Ages from poems on the countryside.[74] A basic characteristic of romanticism is what Xiao calls its "subjectivism" (*zhuti zhuyi*), and he refers to the description of intellectual historian Roland Stromberg, who defines romanticism as "the participation of the mind in shaping reality."[75]

However, whereas in the West romanticism arose as a reaction against modernity, in China political romanticism arose against the background of the struggle for national survival. In this environment, Chinese intellectuals were prone to what British philosopher and mathematician Alfred North Whitehead calls the "fallacy of misplaced concreteness," or the false belief that something is a concrete reality when in fact it is an abstract belief.[76] Xiao borrows this reference to Whitehead from Lin Yü-sheng, who uses it to criticize the use of foreign concepts in the Chinese milieu.[77] Although Lin invoked the concept to criticize liberal Hu Shi (1891–1962) and New Confucian Tang Junyi (1909–78), Xiao also applies it to Chen Tianhua, Sun Yat-sen, and Wang Jingwei (1883–1944), whose parliamentary democracy was but a projection of desire.[78]

In "History Rejects Romanticism: The Emergence of the Second Trend of Reform Thought in China," Xiao refers to this third type of radicalism as French Revolution-style rationalist radicalism (*Faguo dagemingshi de weili zhuyi de jijin zhuyi*).[79] Xiao calls this rationalism because the reforms were based on abstract principles of natural law or on transcendent "first moral principles."[80] Xiao's equating of the French Revolution with "rationalism" and his discard of "first principles" can also be found in Edmund Burke.[81] This

---

[74] Xiao, "Cong zhengzhi langman zhuyi," 266.
[75] Ibid. Quote from Roland N. Stromberg, *European Intellectual History since 1789*, 3rd ed. (Englewood Cliffs, NJ: Prentice Hall, 1981), 50.
[76] Ibid., 275. Whitehead coined the concept of the "fallacy of misplaced concreteness" in his *Science and the Modern World* (Cambridge: University Press, 1953 [1926]).
[77] See, for example, Lin Yü-sheng, "Reflections on the 'Creative Transformation of Chinese Tradition,'" tr. Michael S. Duke and Josephine Chiu-Duke, in Karl-Heinz Pohl, ed., *Chinese Thought in a Global Context: A Dialogue between Chinese and Western Philosophical Approaches* (Leiden: Brill, 1999), 89.
[78] Wang Jingwei studied in Japan and was a member of Sun Yat-sen's Revolutionary Alliance. Initially a left-wing KMT politician, Wang collaborated with the Japanese from 1940 to 1945. He was also a strong opponent of Chiang Kai-shek.
[79] Xiao, "Lishi jujue langman," 109–22, 117. [80] Ibid. See Chapter 2.
[81] Frank Turner, "Introduction: Edmund Burke: The Political Actor Thinking," in Edmund Burke, *Reflections on the Revolution in France*, ed. Turner (New Haven, CT: Yale University Press,

rationalism was also a form of romanticism because unconscious ideals were projected onto a system that no longer had anything to do with reality, as in the "system determinism."[82] To point out the problems of this approach, Xiao refers to the German theologian Paul Tillich, according to whom romanticism forgets all about the limitations of men and creates blueprints that do not conform with reality.[83]

This romanticism was revealed after the May Fourth Movement in the form of theories about wholesale Westernization. In "Rethinking the Debate on 'Problems and -*Isms*' in Modern Intellectual History," Xiao argues that the period since May Fourth witnessed "an adoration of ideas" (*linian chongbai*).[84] Thinkers were convinced that the solution to all problems could be found in abstract concepts. In fact, as Xiao states, this trend also existed before May Fourth, for example in the belief since the time of the Russo-Japanese War (1904–5) that constitutionalism would save China.[85] The first Chinese intellectuals who doubted that -*isms* could solve problems were, according to Xiao, the translator Yan Fu and the May Fourth liberal intellectual Hu Shi.

In 1919 Hu Shi criticized rationalism in the journal *Meizhou pinglun* (Weekly Review).[86] For Hu Shi, -*isms* were solutions to concrete problems, a point that is also made in Lin Yü-sheng's research on Hu Shi.[87] Hu Shi objected to separating -*isms* from the concrete environment in which they originated and argued that one should first study both the background of the -*ism* and the essence of the problem in question. Xiao discerns an empiricist stance in Hu Shi's talk of "problems and -*isms*." Although one specific -*ism* that Hu targeted was socialism, according to Xiao, his criticism was much broader and more directed at general "-*ism* determinism" (*zhuyi juedinglun*).[88]

However, according to Xiao, Hu Shi failed to recognize that there are two kinds of -*isms*: empiricist-type -*isms* (*jingyan zhuyi leixing de zhuyi*) and rationalist-type -*isms* (*weili zhuyi leixing de zhuyi*).[89] Whereas the former are related to concrete problems, the latter are derived from abstract "first principles," or from ideas of the ultimate good. Only by making this division between two kinds of -*isms* can one explain why, during the early twentieth century, Chinese intellectuals were attracted only to French Revolution-style

---

2003), xxv, xliii n13. Burke contrasts "first principles" with history and circumstances in a September 27, 1780, letter to Joseph Hartford.

[82] Xiao Gongqin, "Lun dangdai Zhongguo de langman zhuyi gaigeguan," 90.
[83] Xiao, "Lishi jujue langman," 122.
[84] Xiao Gongqin, "Jindai sixiangshi shang de 'wenti yu zhuyi' zhenglun de zai sikao" (Rethinking the Debate on "Problems and -*Isms*" in Modern Intellectual History), in ZFL, 142–57.
[85] Ibid., 142.
[86] Chen Duxiu and Li Dazhao, who were both working for the recently established Peking University, founded this journal in December 1918.
[87] See Lin, *Crisis of Chinese Consciousness*.
[88] Xiao, "Jindai sixiangshi shang de 'wenti yu zhuyi,'" 152.   [89] Ibid., 153.

idealism (*Faguo dagemingshi de lixiang zhuyi*) and not to "Anglo-American-style empiricist liberalism" (*Ying Meishi jingyan zhuyi de ziyou zhuyi*).[90]

Yan Fu, by contrast, in his *Zhengzhi jiangyi* (Lectures on Politics, 1906), criticized natural law and "ideas determinism" (*linian juedinglun*) from Plato to Rousseau.[91] Since 1913, in several works, such as *Tianyan jinhualun* (Evolution Theory, 1913), *Shuodang* (On Parties, 1913), and *Minyue pingyi* (A Critique of the Social Contract, 1914), he specifically criticized Rousseau's "natural law theory."[92] In such works, Xiao argues, Yan Fu attacked the rationalist Continental tradition of philosophy. Yan Fu's most representative work in this respect is *Minyue pingyi*, in which he criticized Rousseau's social contract theory for its reliance on abstract principles and its ignorance of practical experience and historical reality. Yan Fu disapproved of the political "perfectionism" (*wanmei zhuyi*) in the rationalist tradition; he preferred the tradition of British-American empiricism, in which liberty grew out of the old society.[93]

In *Shuodang*, Yan Fu condemned the use of natural law to measure tradition because it could lead only to political radicalism. In *Tianyan jinhualun* Yan argued against the destruction of the old because, he realized, it would inevitably lead to the disintegration of both the old and the new.[94] In brief, in a clear nod to Hayek, long before other Chinese intellectuals, Yan Fu understood the struggle between Continental rationalism and British empiricism, the opposition between their respective methods of deduction and induction, and the link between rationalism and utopianism and between empiricism and gradual reform.

The "Yan Fu Paradox," or Why Cows Can Never Be Horses

Through Yan Fu, Xiao carries out an epistemological critique of the perceived rationalism underlying reform and seeks to root reform in British empiricism. At first, Xiao's interpretation of Yan Fu as a neoconservative modernizer seems quite remarkable, given that Yan Fu, upon his return from England in 1879, was an early spokesperson for Western ideas in China. Mao Zedong

---

[90] Ibid., 153.
[91] Ibid., 143. See Wang Shi, ed., *Yan Fu ji* (Collected Works of Yan Fu), 5 vols. (Beijing: Zhonghua shuju chubanshe, 1986), 5.1241–1316.
[92] Xiao, "Jindai sixiangshi shang de 'wenti yu zhuyi,'" 143. See Wang, *Yan Fu ji*, 2.309–19, 2.298–308, and 2.333–40.
[93] Xiao, "Jindai sixiangshi shang de 'wenti yu zhuyi,'" 145. On Yan Fu's reading of Rousseau along the lines of Huxley's Social Darwinism, see Fan Yun, "Zuowei fangfa de Lusuo: Xiandai Zhongguo bainian Lusuoxue de fansi" (Rousseau as an Approach: Reflections on a Century of Rousseau Studies in Modern China), *Zhejiang daxue xuebao* (Journal of Zhejiang University) 43.2 (March 2013), 160–68.
[94] Xiao, "Jindai sixiangshi shang de 'wenti yu zhuyi,'" 147–48. See Wang, *Yan Fu ji*, 4.1104–50.

placed Yan Fu on a par with personalities such as Hong Xiuquan, the leader of the Taiping Rebellion, Sun Yat-sen, and Kang Youwei—all of whom "turned toward the West to seek truth."[95] Similarly, CASS historian Zheng Dahua regards Yan Fu as an early proponent of Westernization.[96] For historian Ma Yong, Yan Fu is one of the most famous "Enlightenment thinkers" of modern China.[97] However, Yan Fu did not support the 1911 Revolution or the founding of the Republic; instead he was in favor of a constitutional monarchy. In addition, after 1912 Yan Fu supported Yuan Shikai, thereby rendering a conservative reading of Yan Fu less questionable.[98]

Some scholars, including Yan Fu's biographers Zhou Zhenfu and Tse-tsung Chow, have proposed that there is a "break" between Yan Fu's early liberalism and Westernization and his late conservatism and traditionalism.[99] However, Benjamin Schwartz contests this "break" in his well-known 1964 work on Yan Fu, *In Search of Wealth and Power*.[100] According to Schwartz, Yan Fu's most radical defense of democracy, namely his 1895 essay "In Refutation of Han Yu," a critique of the monarchy, already contained elements of his later conservatism.[101] In Schwartz's view, Yan Fu's ultimate aim was national wealth and power, and whether or not his belief in democracy was genuine, he nevertheless interpreted it as a means to reach his ultimate goal, a point also echoed by Wang Rongzu.[102] Second, for Yan Fu democracy could not be realized immediately because conditions were not yet ripe. Schwartz further notes that Yan's conservatism was much broader than "traditionalism" in the

---

[95] Mao Zedong, "Lun renmin minzhu zhuanzheng," June 30, 1949 (On the People's Democratic Dictatorship), in *Mao Zedong xuanji* (Selected Works of Mao Zedong) (Beijing: Renmin chubanshe, 1991), 4.1469.

[96] Zheng Dahua, "Xiandai Zhongguo wenhua baoshou zhuyi sichao de lishi kaocha" (A Historical Investigation into Trends in Modern Chinese Cultural Conservatism), in Feng, *Chongxin renshi bainian Zhongguo*, 2.446.

[97] Ma Yong, "Yan Fu wannian sixiang yanbian zhi chonggu" (A Re-evaluation of the Intellectual Development of Yan Fu in His Later Years), *Zhexue yanjiu*, no. 4 (1992), 46.

[98] Interview with Ma Yong, Beijing, August 8, 2005.

[99] For example, for Tse-tsung Chow, Yan Fu was a "leading liberal reformer" between 1895 and 1902, and a "conservative" from 1902. See Chow, *May Fourth Movement*, 62 ns and 64 nt.

[100] Benjamin Schwartz, *In Search of Wealth and Power: Yen Fu and the West* (Cambridge, MA: Belknap, 1964).

[101] Ibid., 215–16, 224–28. For the essay "In Refutation of Han Yu" (Pi Han), see Wang, *Yan Fu ji*, 1.32–36. On Yan's interpretation of the essay, see Peter Zarrow, *After Empire: The Conceptual Transformation of the Chinese State, 1885–1924* (Stanford, CA: Stanford University Press, 2012), 83–87.

[102] See Wang Rongzu, "Ziyou zhuyi yu Zhongguo" (Liberalism and China), *Ershiyi shiji*, no. 2 (December 1990), 33–37. Schwartz's argument that Yan Fu deliberately distorted John Stuart Mill's liberalism was criticized by Huang Kewu in his *Ziyou de suoyiran: Yan Fu dui Yuehan Mi'er ziyou zhuyi sixiang de renshi yu pipan* (The Raison d'Être of Freedom: Yan Fu's Understanding and Critique of John Mill's Liberalism) (Taipei: Yunchen wenhua shiye gufen youxian gongsi, 1998).

sense that it also contained elements of Spencerian evolution theory.[103] Like Schwartz, Theodore Huters also outlines the complexities in Yan Fu's thought by arguing that Yan Fu stressed the difference between China and the West in order to return to an ancient past, but he also used the argument of difference in a "rhetoric of alarm," namely to criticize China and to champion Westernization.[104]

Xiao draws on a reading of Schwartz and others who argue against a clear break in Yan Fu's thought. It is questionable whether Yan Fu was a liberal, according to Xiao, because he believed that wealth and power could be achieved through enlightened authoritarian rule rather than through liberalism.[105] Elsewhere Xiao notes that Yan Fu confirmed the value of liberalism. However, in the political realm Yan opposed Western liberalism.[106] For Xiao, the central aspect of Yan Fu's "gradual modernization thought" was his "theory of the social organism" (*shehui youjilun*), as expressed in, for example, his *Shehui tongquan* (A History of Politics, 1904).[107]

For Xiao, Yan Fu was a neoconservative because his theory of the social organism was an expression of Burke's "gradualist conservatism" (*jianjin zhuyi de baoshou zhuyi*). Although Xiao uses the adjective "gradualist" in Chinese, he translates the term in English as "evolutionary."[108] This indicates that Xiao already reads Burke into Yan Fu's evolutionism—Xiao even argues that Yan Fu had read Burke and that is why Xiao discerns traces of Burke in between the lines.[109] This leads us to the following question: Why was the first representative of Xiao's neoconservatism a thinker who has generally been associated with Spencerian evolution theories?

Here, a note on Yan Fu serves to clarify his understanding of change at the turn of the twentieth century. Yan's theory of the social organism shows similarities with Spencer's image of it as being analogous with a biological organism, an idea that Spencer developed in *The Principles of Sociology*.[110] It was Yan Fu who introduced the terms "grouping" (*qun*) and "society" (*shehui*) to China. As with many neologisms, this occurred through Japan. Both terms

---

[103] Schwartz, *In Search of Wealth and Power*, 84.
[104] Theodore Huters, "Appropriations: Another Look at Yan Fu and Western Ideas," *Xueren*, no. 9 (April 1996), 314.
[105] Xiao, "'Yan Fu beilun,'" 19–20.
[106] Xiao, "Dangdai Zhongguo xin baoshou zhuyi de sixiang yuanyuan," 126–35, 132.
[107] Xiao, "'Yan Fu beilun,'" 22; Wang, *Yan Fu ji*, 4.922–35. This is a 1904 translation by Yan Fu of Edward Jenks, *A History of Politics* (London: J.M. Dent, 1900).
[108] Xiao Gongqin, "Zhongguo xin baoshou zhuyi de sixiang yuanyuan" (The Intellectual Origins of Chinese Neoconservatism), in *YZLG*, 25–40, 25–26.
[109] Xiao, "Dangdai Zhongguo xin baoshou zhuyi de sixiang yuanyuan," 134; Interview with Xiao Gongqin, Shanghai, August 4, 2006.
[110] Herbert Spencer, *The Principles of Sociology*, 2nd ed. (London: Williams and Norgate, 1877–97).

stress the strength of individuals and the relationship among them. The latter was expressed through the metaphor of "crystals chemically bonded together," as contrasted with the former "loose potatoes in a sack."[111]

In late nineteenth-century China, as several authors have noted, Darwinism was used to promote collective strength.[112] For Spencer, the quality of the social organism depended on the quality of the individuals in it, and the aim of the release of physical, moral, and intellectual energies was individual happiness. Yet Yan Fu interpreted the release of energy as a means to achieve national wealth and power—the nation could be compared to one organism among many in the struggle for survival.[113] Another aspect of Yan Fu's interpretation of the theory of evolution is that he stressed its voluntarism and its Faustian-Promethean aspects rather than its determinism.[114] In a more general sense, many Chinese intellectuals gave a "Lamarckian twist" to the theory of evolution during the late Qing dynasty (1644–1911). This was not only due to the fact that this was inherent in Spencer but also because characteristics "acquired" in human societies were indeed transmitted.[115]

In Xiao's reading of Yan Fu's theory of the social organism, this organism reacted and adapted to circumstances, and the adaptation of one single element affected the entire structure. Yan Fu compared the import of a foreign system to taking the hoofs of a horse, placing them on a cow's nape, and expecting it to become a "winged steed" (*qianlima*).[116] The reason why this was impossible, according to Yan Fu, was that essence and function could not be separated from each other (*tiyong bukeli lun*). The early

---

[111] Wang Fanshen, "Evolving Prescriptions for Social Life in the Late Qing and Early Republic: From *Qunxue* to Society," tr. Joan Judge, in *Chinese Studies in History* 29.4 (Summer 1996), 75. Yan Fu used the term "grouping" in his translation of Huxley's *Evolution and Ethics* (Tianyan lun) as well as in *On Power* (Yuanqiang) and *On Liberty* (Qunxue yiyan). He first used the term "society" in *On Liberty*, in which he distinguishes it from "grouping" by adding that "society" is "grouping with laws" (Wang, "Evolving Prescriptions," 76–77, 83). Furth notes that Yan Fu's term *qunxue* is an allusion to Xunzi's idea of "groups." See Furth, "Intellectual Change: From the Reform Movement to the May Fourth Movement, 1895–1920," in John King Fairbank, ed., *The Cambridge History of China, Vol. 12: Republican China, 1912–1949, Part 1* (Cambridge: Cambridge University Press, 1983), 335. Although Yan Fu used the term *qunxue* ("collectivities" or "masses") as a translation for "sociology," the term *shehuixue* later became the standard term through the Japanese neologism *shehui*, as a translation for modern society. See Dirlik, *Culture and History in Postrevolutionary China*, 200.

[112] In addition to Schwartz, as mentioned above, see also Wang, "Evolving Prescriptions," 76. On the reception of Darwin in China, see James Reeve Pusey, *China and Charles Darwin* (Cambridge, MA: Council on East Asian Studies, Harvard University, 1983).

[113] Schwartz, *In Search of Wealth and Power*, 56, 59, 69–80.

[114] Ban Wang, *Illuminations from the Past: Trauma, Memory and History in Modern China* (Stanford, CA: Stanford University Press, 2004), 29.

[115] Charlotte Furth, "The Sage as Rebel: The Inner World of Chang Ping-lin," in *LOC*, 113–50, 130–31.

[116] Xiao, "'Yan Fu beilun,'" 23.; Wang, *Yan Fu ji*, 3.560.

reformers were mistaken in their advocacy of *Zhongti Xiyong* (Chinese learning as the substance, Western learning as the function) because *ti* and *yong* are inseparable. Instead, Yan Fu called it *Zhongxue tiyong* and *Xixue tiyong* (Chinese learning as substance and function; Western learning as substance and function).

As such, Xiao argues, Yan Fu was the first to realize the dilemma of Chinese modernization, namely, the dilemma between "single import" (*danxiang yinjin*) and "wholesale import" (*quanxiang yinjin*). Single import was impossible because each element was part of an organic system and required the support of the other elements in that system. Consequently, the import of one element automatically had to lead to the import of an entire system. However, wholesale import was also impossible because the elements that supported and defined the system were in fact endless. Even if one were to transplant onto a cow all the elements that made a horse a horse, the cow would never be a horse. Xiao calls this the "Yan Fu paradox" (*Yan Fu beilun*) because Yan Fu was the first to point out the problems of both single and wholesale import strategies. In other words, Yan Fu was the earliest Chinese neoconservative thinker who argued that gradual reform was necessary from the perspective of circumstance theory (*tiaojianlun*), even though this was not a systematic theory in his writings.[117]

Xiao describes Yan Fu's way of overcoming the Yan Fu paradox by the following: "It was that one should pay special attention to the degree of development and the ripening of new elements inside the social organism and that one should regard this as the basis for the import and use of external systems."[118] For Yan Fu, when considering reform one had to take into account customs and popular feelings because they had been shaped over a long period of time. Yan Fu had already advocated gradual reform in *Yuanqiang* (On Power, 1895), three years before the 1898 Reform Movement.[119] Xiao repeatedly quotes Yan Fu's phrase: "The new has not yet been obtained, but the old has already been destroyed."[120] Yan Fu paid attention to the growth and ripening of new elements in the social organism, but his weakness was that he did not truly transform tradition, possibly because he was still too close to the Classics.

Xiao appears truly convinced that Yan Fu's theories bore a Burkean stamp. Yan Fu and Burke do indeed overlap in the sense that both underscore experience, natural growth, and particular circumstances, all of which justify limited interference in the process of change. In addition, both in Burkean conservatism and in Yan Fu's thought, the cultural and the natural are conflated.

---

[117] Xiao, "'Yan Fu beilun,'" 29; Interview with Xiao Gongqin, Shanghai, August 4, 2006.
[118] Xiao, "'Yan Fu beilun,'" 31. [119] See Wang, *Yan Fu ji*, 1.5–1.15.
[120] For example, Xiao, "'Yan Fu beilun,'" 31; Xiao, "Zhongguo zaoqi xiandaihua," 221.

Conservatives have invoked the metaphor of a "second nature" for habits, customs, and culture in order to stress their inevitability.[121] Likewise, social evolutionists such as Yan Fu have compared social processes to natural processes. Moreover, one might argue that both social evolutionism and conservatism are preoccupied with continuity and order, and thus some theorists do find the two theories compatible.[122]

Nevertheless, as Robert Nisbet argues, social evolutionism and conservatism hold different views of change. For social evolutionists, change is continuous, directional, endogenous, necessary, and related to big, abstract entities, whereas for conservatives, change is accidental, exogenous, and related to concrete historical data.[123] Additionally, social evolutionism is determinist in that it reduces change to natural laws, thus leaving little room for human interference. Conservatives, in contrast, underscore that the processes of historical change are complicated, but they nevertheless believe that there is some room for human interference. Whereas Social Darwinists make natural analogies for the purpose of predictability, conservatives do so in order to show the inevitability of events. For Social Darwinists, nature can offer a model to analyze societies; for conservatives, although nature should be respected, culture and history play equally crucial roles, and it is culture that restrains man from natural inclinations.

Hence, Xiao's reading of Yan Fu as a neoconservative modernizer incorporates Social Darwinist notions of change in his Burkean defense of gradualism. This reflects the future-oriented nature of Xiao's advocacy of historical continuity, in which Chinese progress is a focal point. As Spira notes:

> Applying the concept of *jinbu* "progress" to characterize the preservation of the past is a significant example of what Reinhart Koselleck has termed the temporalization (*Verzeitlichung*) of concepts: although the goal of conservatism is to preserve (essential elements of) the past, it preserves them for the future; the realization of that goal lies in the future and stands in contrast to other goals set up by people taking other positions.[124]

It is this interpretation of preservation for the future that is crucial to Xiao's reading of Yan Fu. Through the figure of Yan Fu, Xiao reconciles elements from three different intellectual traditions: conservatism, social evolutionism, and liberalism. In accordance with Burkean conservatism, he underlines

---

[121] Jerry Z. Muller, "Introduction: What Is Conservative Social and Political Thought?" in Muller, ed., *Conservatism: An Anthology of Social and Political Thought from David Hume to the Present* (Princeton, NJ: Princeton University Press, 1997), 19–20.

[122] For example, Larry Arnhart, *Darwinian Conservatism* (Exeter, UK: Imprint Academic, 2005).

[123] See Robert Nisbet, *Social Change and History: Aspects of the Western Theory of Development* (Oxford: Oxford University Press, 1969), 240–304.

[124] Spira, *Conceptual History of Chinese -Isms*, 188.

gradual change and historical growth and the particularity of tradition. In addition, there is some room for Chinese culture to "filter" imported systems from other societies. However, because his neoconservatism is a modernization theory, what Xiao borrows from social evolutionism is a view of change that is directional and necessary. The social organism appears to function more as a way to predict changes in systems (in accordance with systems theory), rather than because of a conviction that change is contingent. As such, the conservative critique of linearity is missing from Xiao's gradualism, ultimately indicating that the Burke in Yan Fu is not the conservative Burke.

Xiao criticizes belief in the makeability of the French revolutionaries, but not belief in human reason. Edmund Burke is read as a representative of Anglo-American empiricist liberalism. The argument Xiao makes here is reminiscent of Hayek's comparison between two traditions of liberty in *The Constitution of Liberty* (1960).[125] For Hayek, only the British tradition is a tradition of liberty because it is based on empiricism, and he considers freedom to be the lack of oppression. The French tradition, of which Jean-Jacques Rousseau is one of the main representatives, is based on Cartesian rationalism to design society rationally and ex nihilo. In this tradition, freedom is about the realization of all-encompassing moral schemes. We will come back to this distinction between two "traditions" of liberty in the next chapter.

Xiao can be said to be closer to Hayek than to Burke in that he defends the historical growth of societies along the lines of Hayek's liberal argument: political democracy must be based on certain social structures that cannot immediately be imported. This interpretation is confirmed by Xiao's argument that Yan Fu's empiricism received influence of the tradition of English liberalism. Hayek referred to this tradition as "true liberalism," namely the empiricist tradition rooted in history.[126] Xiao also notes that Burke's conservatism was rooted in the tradition of civil society and "English-style liberalism."[127]

Xiao's emphasis on the application of new elements in a relatively isolated area and on the importance of trial and error is also closer to liberalism. This is reminiscent of Karl Popper's defense of "piecemeal engineering." In *The Open Society and Its Enemies*, Popper rejects the argument that social experiments must be conducted on a large scale. For Popper, social experiments under "laboratory conditions," or in an "isolated village," are developed by trial and error and are based on reason instead of passion.[128] Hence, in spite of the references to the social organism, Xiao's neoconservatism was also an

---

[125] See Friedrich A. Hayek, "Freedom, Reason, and Tradition," in *The Constitution of Liberty* (London: Routledge, 2006), 49–62.
[126] Xiao, "Dangdai Zhongguo xin baoshou zhuyi de sixiang yuanyuan," 130.   [127] Ibid., 134.
[128] Popper, *Open Society,* 1.162–63.

advocacy of empiricism against rationalism and of partial change against "social engineering" along the lines of Hayek and Popper.

Ambiguous Tradition: Experience, *Ren*, and Moral Autonomy

If the above demonstrates the limits of Xiao's Burkean conservatism, such limitations are manifest in his interpretation of Chinese tradition, which is central to his theory of neoconservatism. As noted in the previous chapter, tradition, according to Xiao, can function as a "lever" to introduce foreign elements, and "mainstream culture" acts as a coagulation force. Xiao uses an organic metaphor to describe the function of culture in the process of importing foreign systems:

> It is like a naturally grown ecological forest belt that encircles the throng of a certain area. It has the ecological function of buffering, filtering, and regulating the "wind, sand, rain, and dew" of external cultures. This function of ecological regulation is not the result of rational and conscious planning or design by people who have lived in the place in question for a long period of time; it is the result of a natural ecology of balancing and "screening" in the long-term process of historical evolution. If people practically destroy it because of pests, once the buffering and screening of this cultural protective screen is lost, even though on the surface external cultures can be vastly implanted without difficulty or resistance, in reality it can only result in all-round and rapid soil erosion.[129]

Apart from the reference to the "natural" function of processes of change, which, as discussed above, we see in both conservatism and social evolutionism, we find that Xiao understands culture as the product of local conditions. Given Xiao's emphasis on history and particularity, we would expect a definition of "culture" and "tradition" that is compatible with this emphasis. As will be demonstrated, this is only partially the case.

In Xiao's reference to Yan Fu, tradition is indeed particular and the product of people's specific experiences. Tradition is a "carrier," "intermediary," or "receptor" (*shouti*) of outer system elements because its basis is a "national particularity" (*minzu texing*), without which it would be but an empty shell. According to Xiao, the common culture, beliefs, virtues, and customs of a people form the "national character"—they are the "cultural soul" (*wenhua linghun*) of a nation, without which survival is impossible. National character is embodied in the collective experiences of a nation and in its "mainstream culture," value symbols, and ideology. Referring to Yan Fu, tradition is the "experience" (*yueli*) shaped in response to the challenges of the natural and social environment. Cultural tradition is a condensed "collective experience"

---

[129] Xiao, "'Yan Fu beilun,'" 36.

(*jiti jingyan*). However, this view is also somewhat reminiscent of Hayek's definition of tradition as stemming from "habits of responding."[130]

But what precisely is this "collective experience," and how does it serve to support the introduction of foreign elements? From Xiao's other writings, we can infer that he is referring to Confucianism. Many of Xiao's early works analyze how Confucianism obstructed modernization efforts. In a 1986 article, Xiao discusses how the "inertia" of Chinese culture hindered modernization.[131] A "cultural ossification" occurred after the institutionalization of Confucianism in the Qin and Han dynasties. Although attempts were made to redress such an ossification during the Song and Ming dynasties, in general the merging of Confucianism with the traditional sociopolitical system, in which a landowner economy, the examination system, and the bureaucracy were the main units, meant that society lost its self-transforming potential.[132]

In 1988, Xiao's engagement with Chinese culture shifted in relation to the early reflections on "radical antitraditionalism" on mainland China. In a preface to *The Dignity of the Sage* (1988), by the famous liberal intellectual Xu Jilin, Xiao argues that it is this radicalism that led to "cultural anomie."[133] Xiao was already analyzing how this culture could be beneficial to modernization and how a narrow "antitraditionalism" should be avoided. In relation to this, in a 1994 article Xiao links this antitraditionalism to modern Chinese nationalism that opposes mainstream Chinese culture and perceives it to be in opposition to modernity. After 1949, Confucian culture became associated with feudalism; it was only during the reform era that mainstream Chinese culture assumed the potential to be a resource for national cohesion.[134]

Xiao's emphasis on national particularity in relation to culture existed in tension with the "mainstream culture" of Confucianism, and, more particularly, with the moral autonomy (*daode zizhuxing*)—a central element in the Kantian tradition of moral philosophy—that Xiao discerned in the original Confucianism.[135] This emphasis on moral autonomy is relevant because it connects Xiao to intellectual discussions on Confucianism that were taking place during this period. It also reveals that, in spite of his call for empiricism, Xiao has traits of the Confucian scholar who considers himself to be

---

[130] Friedrich A. Hayek, *The Collected Works of F.A. Hayek, Vol. 1: The Fatal Conceit: The Errors of Socialism*, ed. W. W. Bartley III (Chicago: University of Chicago Press, 1988), 21–22.
[131] Xiao Gongqin, "Chuantong wenhua duoxing dui Zhongguo xiandaihua de sanzhong zuzhang" (The Three Obstacles to Chinese Modernization in the Inertia of the Traditional Culture), in *XGQJ*, 338–43.
[132] Xiao Gongqin, "Ruxue de sanzhong lishi xingtai" (The Three Historical Forms of Confucianism), in *XGQJ*, 315–37.
[133] Xiao Gongqin, "Wenhua shifan yu xiandaihua de kun'e" (Cultural Anomie and the Conundrum of Modernization), in *XGQJ*, 344–49.
[134] Xiao, "Minzu zhuyi yu," 350–58.
[135] See Xiao, "Ruxue de sanzhong lishi xingtai," 315–37.

responsible for China's fate. In connection with the function of Confucianism in the modernization process, Xiao refers to Confucian adages, such as *weiren youji* (acting benevolent from within the self), *qiuren deren* (seek benevolence and receive benevolence), and *ziqiang buxi* (continuous self-renewal), as manifestations of moral autonomy.[136]

The claim that Confucianism contains moral autonomy is proposed by Thomas Metzger in his *Escape from Predicament*.[137] Metzger is responding to Max Weber's claim that Confucianism could not have the same function as Protestantism in the West with regard to the rise of the spirit of capitalism because Confucianism lacked moral autonomy. In Chinese intellectual circles, Metzger's argument about the moral autonomy of Confucianism has been utilized in debates on New Confucianism, as we shall see in Chapter 5. In this context, New Confucians subscribe to the Confucian value of benevolence (*ren*), a universal value that can be applied to tackle problems of modernization. Liberal Lin Yü-sheng, whose thesis on "totalistic antitraditionalism" has inspired mainland intellectuals, also refers to the moral autonomy of Confucianism in relation to his theory of the "creative transformation" of Chinese tradition.[138] He uses the theory to argue for the establishment of a liberal and democratic order.

Xiao Gongqin uses a different moral autonomy argument. He argues that it was moral autonomy that instilled the literati with a feeling of mission, an inner conscience, and a "crisis mentality" (*youhuan yishi*).[139] The problem with different manifestations of Confucianism is that moral autonomy was repressed. After the Han dynasty (206 BCE–220 CE), when Confucianism merged with the autocratic system and became "bureaucratized," the function of propriety (*li*) became more essential than that of benevolence. Scholars of the Song dynasty (907–1279) reacted against the ritualized Confucianism of the previous dynasties and developed *lixue* (Principle-centered Learning), which Xiao regards as a third form of Confucianism. This was an attempt to restore moral autonomy, but it failed because the content of the Heavenly Principles was still the feudal Confucian ethical code. Given this historical development, Xiao argues that the value rationality of benevolence can revive the repressed moral autonomy of Confucianism; it can provide intellectuals with a "feeling of mission." From this, we see that Xiao does not abandon a

---

[136] Ibid., 336; Xiao, "Minzu zhuyi yu," 356.
[137] Thomas A. Metzger, *Escape from Predicament: Neo-Confucianism and China's Evolving Political Culture* (New York: Columbia University Press, 1977). The book was translated as [Mo Zike], *Baituo kunjing: Xin ruxue yu Zhongguo zhengzhi wenhua de yanjin*, tr. Yan Shi'an, Gao Hua, and Huang Donglan (Nanjing: Jiangsu renmin chubanshe, 1995).
[138] Lin, "Reflections on the 'Creative Transformation of Chinese Tradition,'" 91–100.
[139] Xiao, "Ruxue de sanzhong lishi xingtai," 336.

definition of the Chinese intellectual as the moral savior of China after 1989—only intellectuals could help China modernize.

In brief, Xiao argues that traditional elements should function as "levers" in the modernization process, but he also refers to the vitality of benevolence, a term he adopts from the moral discourse of New Confucianism. Xiao's stress on benevolence and moral autonomy is in tension with his emphasis on historical particularity and experience based on Yan Fu's reading of tradition as a response to the challenges of the environment. From this reference to both Burkean particularity and the moral value of benevolence, it can be seen that Xiao, as an intellectual eager to perfect the modernization process, is torn between the reference to nationalism as a resource in his political theory and that part of Confucianism from which he draws to self-identify as an intellectual.

As we have seen, the Burke in Xiao is a Burke that was reinterpreted through the lens of Yan Fu's evolutionism and a liberalism in the spirit of Hayek and Popper. Even though this was a neoconservatism rooted in criticism of radicalism in modern Chinese history, especially the French "rationalist" type of radicalism, it nevertheless advocated preservation for the future. What is reminiscent of conservatism, however, is Xiao's emphasis on the social organism in Yan Fu. In 1992, other Chinese intellectuals also began to discuss Burke, but after Deng's Southern Tour the attention shifted to economic reform. In this situation, Chinese intellectuals advocated partial reform along liberal lines instead of invoking the social organism. A conservatism that envisioned a strong state, as that in Xiao's writings, gradually made room for views of conservatism as an ally of the market.

4   A Tale of Two Revolutions

> A state without the means of some change is without the means of its conservation.
>
> Edmund Burke, *Reflections on the Revolution in France*

"Research more problems, speak fewer '*-isms*'!" urged the famous liberal Hu Shi in *Meizhou pinglun* in July 1919.[1] In the debate that unfolded, Hu Shi, Lan Zhixian, and Li Dazhao discussed the relation between *-isms* and reality. Some seven decades later, the realistic revolutionaries of the early 1990s were generally critical of abstract ideals and advocated a return to "problems" through a more pragmatic, empirical, and gradual approach to change. Paradoxically, however, *-isms* continued to feature prominently in the debates on history and culture that followed the political intermezzo of 1989–91. In these debates, reflections (*fansi*) on the intellectual developments of the 1980s, which had ended with the Tiananmen tragedy, also included reflections on the May Fourth Movement and China's socialist path. With the dissolution of the Soviet Union in 1991 and the renewal of the economic reforms in 1992, the question of the future of socialism in China loomed especially large.

This chapter analyzes the public debates on radicalism and conservatism in modern Chinese history, which took off in the spring of 1992 in the pages of the Hong Kong-based scholarly journal *Ershiyi shiji* and thereafter continued in other prominent journals. Xu Jilin refers to *Ershiyi shiji* as "the most important magazine in the public realm of the Chinese intellectual community in the first half of the nineties."[2] It "offered a new kind of bridge between mainland and overseas intellectuals" as well as scholars based in Hong Kong and Taiwan.[3] Liu Qingfeng and Jin Guantao (b. 1947), two key figures in the cultural debates of the 1980s, established the journal in 1990 as a bimonthly

---

[1] Hu Shi, "Duo yanjiu xie wenti, shao tan xie 'zhuyi'" (Research More Problems, Speak Fewer "*-Isms*"), *Meizhou pinglun*, July 20, 1919, 1.

[2] Xu Jilin, "Contradictions within Enlightenment Ideas," tr. Adrian Thieret, in Cao Tianyu, Zhong Xueping, and Liao Kebin, eds., *Culture and Social Transformations in Reform Era China* (Leiden: Brill, 2010), 200.

[3] Wang, "Introduction: Minds of the Nineties," 16.

publication of the Institute of Chinese Studies at the Chinese University of Hong Kong. Chinese scholars based in the United States who had left China around 1949 and who argued for the continuity of Chinese tradition were instrumental in the discussions on twentieth-century radicalism. Their ideas became reinterpreted on mainland China following Deng Xiaoping's Southern Tour (*nanxun*) in early 1992 and its transformation to a "socialist market economy."

The debates addressed questions about the dominance of radicalism or conservatism in modern Chinese history and the evaluation of the May Fourth Movement. The debates were also part of an effort to rethink the political strategies of the 1980s and to redefine intellectual work. Discussions hence also revolved around reform and revolution, the differences between thought (*sixiang*) and learning (*xueshu*), and various theories of democracy.[4] Overall, the debates show that the core interest was in economic reform and the question of the legitimacy of the Chinese Revolution, as well as in fears about the place of Chinese intellectuals amid the rising commercialization and professionalization.

As Koselleck argues, in times of economic, political, and social change, old -*isms* change meaning and new -*isms* or neologisms emerge.[5] Whereas between 1989 and 1991 conservatism stood for a strong state and nationalism, after renewed reform in 1992, the meaning of conservatism began to shift toward a conservative liberalism. The French Revolution was synonymous with the socialist tradition, whereas the English model, inspired by the Glorious Revolution (1688–89) and based on Chinese interpretations of Burke, Hayek, de Tocqueville, and Popper, stood for gradual reform and a rejection of direct democracy. In addition, several participants in the debates began to argue for the primacy of the economic reforms, thus reflecting new confidence in the market.

In spite of the overall criticism of "radical" change and advocacy of realism, the debates also featured the very historical teleology that intellectuals sought to reject, not in the least because the debate was carried out through the framework of -*isms*. In twentieth-century China, following Koselleck, -*isms* were "concepts of movement" guided by a priori ideals.[6] The overemphasis on the role of ideas is indicative of the attempts by intellectuals to redefine their place politically, socially, and intellectually. Intent on casting aside the political engagement of the 1980s, intellectuals nevertheless continued to reveal

---

[4] Zheng Dahua and Jia Xiaoye, "Jiushi niandai yilai Zhongguo jindai sixiangshi yanjiu zhong de zhongda wenti zhenglun" (Discussions on Major Issues in Research on Modern Chinese Intellectual History since the 1990s), *Huaihua xueyuan xuebao* (Journal of Huaihua University) 24.3 (June 2005), 51–57; Wang, *China's New Order*, 80.
[5] Koselleck, *Futures Past*, 80, 83.   [6] Spira, *Conceptual History of Chinese -Isms*, 2.

traits of public intellectuals in their moral evaluations of history and in their quest for the most suitable reform formula. Hence, the debate is significant not only because it reflects a re-evaluation of the "conservative" trends after decades of revolutionary dominance but also because of what it reveals about the self-perception of Chinese intellectuals and the mode of Chinese intellectual discourse during this period.

Radicalism, the May Fourth Tradition, and a Century of Change

Following in the footsteps of the seventieth anniversary of the May Fourth Movement, the suppression of the student demonstrations in June 1989 left a deep impact on Chinese intellectuals. This event precipitated a need to rethink the cultural debates and strategies of the New Enlightenment Movement of the 1980s. Where had it gone wrong? To answer this question, we must first understand the organizational structure and mode of cultural discussions in the intellectual movement of the 1980s.

Critical to the formation of the movement in the 1980s was the establishment of several editorial committees, such as Zouxiang weilai (Toward the Future). The Zouxiang weilai committee was headed by Jin Guantao, who had originally been trained as a scientist but had been writing on history, philosophy, culture, and science since the late 1970s, and Bao Zunxin (1937–2007), then at the Institute of History of CASS. The editorial committees introduced to China works on both scientific methodologies and the philosophy of science.[7] The editorial committee of Wenhua: Zhongguo yu shijie (Culture: China and the World), which was based at CASS and Peking University, introduced Western thinkers from the humanities, philosophy, and the social sciences to Chinese audiences via two translation series.[8] The committee was led by Gan Yang (b. 1952), who had been sent to Heilongjiang during the Cultural Revolution, had obtained his doctorate from the Institute of Modern Western Philosophy at Peking University, and was then based at the Institute of Philosophy of CASS.

Academies, study societies, salons, and journals were prominent channels for the circulation of ideas during this period. In 1984, the Academy of Chinese Culture (Zhongguo Wenhua Shuyuan) was established. Under the guidance of Tang Yijie (1927–2014), professor in the Department of Philosophy of Peking University, the academy brought together a group of philosophers who were familiar with the works of Chinese scholars in the United

---

[7] Bao Zunxin was also the founder of the journal *Zhongguo zhexue* (Chinese Philosophy) (1978–1985) and deputy editor of *Dushu*. See Makeham, *Lost Soul*, 52. He was arrested after 1989 and in 1991 was sentenced to five years in prison, of which he served three and a half years.
[8] Xu, "Fate of an Enlightenment," 193.

States, such as Tu Wei-ming, Yü Ying-shih, and Lin Yü-sheng (to be further discussed below). Scholars in the academy also had a positive impression of the works of the philosopher and intellectual historian Li Zehou (b. 1930), then based in mainland China, and of historian and philosopher Qian Mu (1895–1990), who had left the mainland for Hong Kong in 1949 and later moved to Taiwan.[9] The journal *Xin Qimeng* (New Enlightenment), around which humanist Marxists gathered, was also influential, as was the editorial board of Ershi shiji wenku (Twentieth Century Book Series), which included scholars such as Chen Ziming (1952–2014), Li Zehou, and Liu Zaifu (b. 1941) and translated works from the social sciences.[10]

Through these channels, many Western works were introduced to Chinese audiences and a vibrant and optimistic atmosphere engulfed Chinese academia. The period was marked by several "fevers," such as the "root searching" fever and the fever about new methodologies.[11] However, the most well-known is the "culture fever," or the obsession with comparative research on the merits and demerits of Chinese and Western cultures in the form of debates, lectures, and newspaper articles. This culture fever culminated in the controversial documentary *Heshang*, first broadcast on television in June 1988.[12] Condemning China's "Sino-centrist peasant conservatism and the despotic nature of Chinese political culture," this six-part documentary urged viewers to exchange the inward-looking Yellow River for the outward-looking Blue Ocean, which represented seafaring industrialized societies. Intense intellectual and political debates surrounded the airing of the documentary because of its ardent criticism of Chinese culture and its pro-reform stance. After 1989, debates on *Heshang* became even more politicized and most of the participants in the writing of the documentary fled China.[13]

---

[9] Hua, *Scientism and Humanism*, 9; Xu, "Fate of an Enlightenment," 193–94.
[10] Xu Youyu, "Intellectual Discourses in Post-Mao China and Today," Independent Chinese PEN Center, www.chinesepen.org/english/xu-youyu:-intellectual-discourses-in-post-mao-china-and-today. Chen Ziming had contributed to the founding of the prodemocracy journal *Beijing Spring* in the late 1970s and was also the founder, together with Wang Juntao, of the Beijing Social and Economics Research Institute, an independent think tank in the 1980s.
[11] Wang, *High Culture Fever*, 38, 119.
[12] On *Heshang*, see Su Xiaokang and Wang Luxiang, *Heshang* (River Elegy) (Beijing: Xiandai chubanshe, 1988); Su Xiaokang and Wang Luxiang, *Deathsong of the River: A Reader's Guide to the Chinese TV Series Heshang* (Ithaca, NY: East Asia Program, Cornell University, 1991); Chen Fong-ching and Jin Guantao, *From Youthful Manuscripts to River Elegy: The Chinese Popular Cultural Movement and Political Transformation 1979–1989* (Hong Kong: Chinese University Press, 1997); Jing Wang, "Heshang and the Paradoxes of the Chinese Enlightenment," in Wang, *High Culture Fever*, 118–36.
[13] Alice De Jong, "The Demise of the Dragon: Backgrounds to the Chinese Film 'River Elegy,'" *China Information* 4.3 (1989), 28, 31–33. Su Xiaokang fled to France; Wang Luxiang was detained but released.

The climate of political repression that marked the years between 1989 and 1991 encouraged intellectuals to critically evaluate their engagement in the reform frenzy of the 1980s. At CASS, where some two thousand staff members were involved in the Tiananmen demonstrations, about 120 were subjected to disciplinary measures, including self-criticisms and/or imprisonment. In addition, ideological control measures were stepped up through the organization of party committees to monitor the research institutes.[14] Those based at universities were also subject to censorship. Consequently, many scholars opted for specialized academic research and exchanged the editorial committee structure for university offices and intellectual exchanges through academic journals.

During this time, reflections on the New Enlightenment Movement of the 1980s extended to debates on the May Fourth Movement. This movement comprised both the May 4, 1919, demonstrations, which were a response to the Shandong resolution of the Versailles Peace Treaty, and the broader New Culture Movement (1917–21), which advocated new thought and new literature. Different aspects of this movement had been criticized in the past, but now the rejections were more comprehensive as the movement came to be seen as one of several representations of a "radical" mode of thought that had been detrimental to China's development. This was, in fact, a reworking of non-liberal and non-Marxist interpretations of the movement, as further explored in the next chapter.

Even though 1989 was perceived to mark the end of the New Enlightenment spirit, this was not an absolute demarcation line.[15] Some of the reflections on May Fourth and radicalism had predated the events of 1989, but they spread after June Fourth. Zhu Xueqin compares this to the introduction of Marxism in China: although introduced before 1917, it did not spread until the "cannon shot" of the October Revolution. Similarly, the gunshots of June Fourth provided the backdrop for the spread of criticism of radicalism.[16]

During the early 1990s, these reflections on the 1980s and May Fourth extended to reflections on a century of modern Chinese history, going back to the 1898 Reform Movement. Intellectually, this return to the early reform movements also intersected with the rise of the modernization paradigm in historiography, as discussed in the previous chapter. As exposed in the account of Hu Sheng, historian and head of CASS (1985–98), the modernization

---

[14] Frenkiel, *Conditional Democracy*, 124.
[15] See, for example, Chen Xiaoming, "Fan jijin yu dangdai zhishi fenzi de lishi jingyu" (Anti-radicalism and the Historical Situation of Contemporary Intellectuals), in *ZFL*, 310; Chen Baiming, "Jinnian lai guonei dui wenhua jijin zhuyi de pipan zongshu" (Summary of Mainland Criticism of Cultural Radicalism in Recent Years), *Wenyi lilun yu piping* (Literature and Art Theory and Criticism), no. 1 (1997), 131.
[16] Zhu, "For a Chinese Liberalism," 102.

paradigm centered around modernization, top-down reform, and the contributions of the elite.[17] Consequently, a "reversal of verdicts" (*fan'an*) on historical figures emerged, with those previously denounced as villains now presented in a more positive light. A classic example is Zeng Guofan (1811–72), the general previously denounced as a traitor because he fought against the Taiping rebels who was now praised as a Confucian hero.[18] The debate was not merely a confirmation of reform against revolution, but both the modernization paradigm and the debate on radicalism highlighted economic reform and modernization and downgraded revolution.

Reflections from the Periphery

As noted, interactions with intellectual historians who had been born in China but who resided in the United States and who had been educated in Hong Kong, Taiwan, or the United States was one of the factors behind the antiradical trend on mainland China. Among them was Lin Yü-sheng, a historian based at the University of Wisconsin–Madison. Educated in Taiwan, where he studied with the liberal Yin Haiguang (1919–69), Lin pursued his graduate studies at the University of Chicago, where he studied under Friedrich Hayek and the sociologist Edward Shils, among others. Thereafter, Lin worked on Chinese intellectual history at Harvard University. Beginning in 1988, Lin became an adviser to Beijing's Academy of Chinese Culture, which had been a major vehicle of the culture fever of the mid- to late 1980s. Between 1988 and 1990, Lin was also a senior research fellow at the Institute of East Asian Philosophies in Singapore, which, as we will see in the next chapter, was crucial in the post-1980s' revival of Confucianism.[19]

A second intellectual whose writings figured in the antiradical trend on mainland China was Princeton-based historian Yü Ying-shih (b. 1930). Born in Tianjin, Yü studied at the newly established *Xinya shuyuan* (New Asia College) in Hong Kong, after which he pursued graduate studies at Harvard

---

[17] Hu Sheng, *Cong yapian zhanzheng dao wusi yundong* (From the Opium War to the May Fourth Movement), 2 vols. (Beijing: Renmin chubanshe, 1981); Huaiyin Li, *Reinventing Modern China: Imagination and Authenticity in Chinese Historical Writing* (Honolulu: University of Hawai'i Press, 2013).

[18] Ma, "Jindai lishi renwu yanjiu," 660. For an overview of the heroes and villains of the early 1990s, see Zhang Haipeng, "Jinnian lai Zhongguo jindaishi yanjiu zhong de ruogan yuanxing lunzheng" (Several Principal Debates in Research on Modern Chinese History in Recent Years), *Makesi zhuyi yanjiu* (Research on Marxism), no. 3 (1997), 14–22. On Zeng Guofan, see Yingjie Guo, "Rewriting National History: The Zeng Guofan Phenomenon," in Guo, *Cultural Nationalism*, 49–71.

[19] Lin lists Karl Polanyi, Friedrich Hayek, Hannah Arendt, Edward Shils, and Benjamin Schwartz as those who influenced him intellectually. Lin Yü-sheng, "Guanyu 'Zhongguo yishi de weiji': Da Sun Longji" (On "The Crisis of Chinese Consciousness": A response to Sun Longji), *Ershiyi shiji*, no. 3 (February 1991), 140.

University. After about a decade in the United States, Yü spent some years in Hong Kong as president of New Asia College and vice chancellor of the Chinese University of Hong Kong. He then returned to the United States, where he held professorships at Yale and Princeton.

Finally, Tu Wei-ming (b. 1940), who will be discussed in more detail in the next chapter, also instigated discussions on radicalism in modern Chinese history. Tu was born in China but was educated in Taiwan and later at Harvard. After graduation, he remained in the United States and taught at Princeton and Berkeley before returning to Harvard. In 1985 Tu was a visiting scholar in the Philosophy Department of Peking University and also lectured on Confucianism at several other universities in China.

First, Lin Yü-sheng criticized the "totalistic iconoclasm" behind the May Fourth Movement in his 1979 book *The Crisis of Chinese Consciousness*.[20] Unlike intellectuals of the previous generation (in the 1890s), such as translator Yan Fu and reformers Kang Youwei, Liang Qichao, and Tan Sitong (1864–98), who had never wholeheartedly rejected tradition, May Fourth intellectuals, such as Chen Duxiu (1879–1942), Hu Shi, and writer Lu Xun (1881–1936), negated tradition wholeheartedly. Lin ascribes this contrast between the first and second generations to the disintegration of the sociopolitical and cultural-moral orders that accompanied the collapse of the empire in 1911—the breakdown of the "universal kingship" link between the two orders. Politically, against the background of attempts by Yuan Shikai and Zhang Xun (1854–1923) to restore the monarchy, radical iconoclasts concluded that Confucianism was "predisposed to despotism."[21] This "totalistic antitraditionalism" was paradoxically the product of Confucian holist thinking. For Lin, "radical" refers to a "systematic" and inflexible ideology, which he describes as "totalistic iconoclasm."[22]

Chinese readers became familiar with Lin's work through the Chinese translation of *The Crisis of Chinese Consciousness*, which first appeared in 1986, and other writings by Lin that appeared on mainland China in the late 1980s.[23] In addition, Lin also took part in the debates in the Hong Kong journal *Ershiyi shiji* in the early 1990s. For example, in response to a critical review of *The Crisis of Chinese Consciousness*, Lin explained in detail his argument and methodology in the February 1991 issue of *Ershiyi shiji*.[24]

---

[20] Lin, *Crisis of Chinese Consciousness*. [21] Ibid., 24.
[22] Lin, "Reflections on the 'Creative Transformation of Chinese Tradition,'" 74.
[23] Lin Yü-sheng, *Zhongguo yishi de weiji: "Wusi" shiqi jilie de fan chuantong zhuyi* (The Crisis of Chinese Consciousness: Radical Antitraditionalism in the "May Fourth" Era) (Guiyang: Guizhou renmin chubanshe, 1986); Lin Yü-sheng, *Zhongguo chuantong de chuangzaoxing zhuanhua* (The Creative Transformation of Chinese Tradition) (Beijing: Shenghuo, dushu, xinzhi sanlian shudian, 1988).
[24] Lin, "Guanyu 'Zhongguo yishi de weiji.'"

Second, on the occasion of the twenty-fifth anniversary of the Chinese University of Hong Kong in 1988 Yü Ying-shih delivered a series of lectures at New Asia College. This was a highly symbolic venue. New Asia College, Yü's alma mater, had been established in 1949 by a group of intellectuals whose mission was "to represent, rejuvenate, promote, and sustain Chinese culture in Hong Kong while China was undergoing a phase of radical rejection of Chinese culture."[25] The college hence served as an institutional base to safeguard Chinese culture and Confucianism from Communist destruction. Among the founders of the college was Qian Mu (1895–1990), a historian who formerly had been at Peking University and later became Yü Ying-shih's teacher. In 1963, New Asia College was incorporated into the newly established Chinese University of Hong Kong. The mission of these cultural guardians had earlier attracted the attention of mainland scholars in the form of the New Confucian Movement, but they also became visible on the mainland during the 1980s and 1990s through lectures, translations, and publication of articles in academic journals, such as *Ershiyi shiji*.

One lecture that Yü delivered in Hong Kong that is included in the Chinese volume *Zhishi fenzi lichang: Jijin yu baoshou zhijian de dongdang*, but that first appeared in early 1990s' Chinese-language publications, is titled "Zhongguo jindai sixiangshi shang de jijin yu baoshou" (Radicalism and Conservatism in Modern Chinese Intellectual History).[26] Yü argues that modern China had not known conservatism, as opposed to what the authors in the volume *The Limits of Change*, as discussed in Chapter 1 of this volume, had maintained.[27] In the United States, conservatism and radicalism were relative to a liberal status quo—like "three legs of a *ding* vessel."[28] In modern China, in contrast, the status quo was changing continuously, and intellectual conflict centered around tradition versus modernity. This is reminiscent of Clinton Rossiter's argument that a conservatism that seeks to preserve the status quo is rare in rapidly modernizing societies.[29]

The destruction of Chinese tradition reached its peak under Marxism, when the CCP dismantled private property as well as intermediate groups, such as patriarchal clans, guilds, private schools, religious groups, and village

---

[25] Grace Ai-Ling Chou, *Confucianism, Colonialism, and the Cold War: Chinese Cultural Education at Hong Kong's New Asia College, 1949–1963* (Leiden: Brill, 2012), 2.
[26] Yü Ying-shih, "Zhongguo jindai sixiangshi shang de jijin yu baoshou: Xianggang Zhongwen daxue 25 zhounian jinian jiangzuo disi jiang" (Radicalism and Conservatism in Modern Chinese Intellectual History: Fourth Speech at the Commemoration of the 25th Anniversary of the Chinese University of Hong Kong), in *ZFL*, 1–29.
[27] See also Yü Ying-shih, "'Chuangxin' yu 'baoshou'" ("Renewal" and "Preservation"), in Yü Ying-shih, *Qian Mu yu Zhongguo wenhua* (Qian Mu and Chinese Culture) (Shanghai: Shanghai yuandong chubanshe, 1994), 288–95.
[28] Yü, "Zhongguo jindai sixiangshi shang de jijin yu baoshou," 1–3, 4.
[29] Rossiter, *Conservatism in America*, 219.

associations. Yü further criticized the 1980s' antitraditionalism on mainland China, which was outdated and several decades earlier had already been condemned in the West.[30] To bring the process of radicalization to a close, a strong middle class had to be created, but a tradition of democratic thought was equally imperative. Yü referred to Taiwan and to intellectuals such as Yin Haiguang, who had carried on the democratic tradition of the 1950s. Whereas previous generations of liberal intellectuals continued the antitraditionalism of May Fourth, liberals in Hong Kong and Taiwan were now sympathetic to Chinese culture.[31]

Of Chinese ancestry but based in the United States, Yü, Lin, and Tu had a foot in both the Sinophone and Anglophone discourses and hence were able to act as intermediaries between both worlds. In the Anglophone world, Yü's article "The Radicalization of China in the Twentieth Century" was published in a special issue of *Daedalus*, titled "On China in Transformation," for which Tu Wei-ming wrote the introduction.[32] China, Tu states in his introduction, was at an "ideological crossroads" after the end of the Cold War, the implosion of the Soviet Union, and the "Sinic world's unprecedented dynamism in democratization and marketization." The revolutionary ideology of the past now appeared to be "a form of unreflected first loyalty: passionate, naïve and dangerous."[33]

In the same issue, Yü Ying-shih boldly opens his essay as follows: "Since the turn of the century, a radical mode of thinking has dominated the Chinese mind."[34] In this essay, Yü identifies three stages of "radicalization," a process he attributes to both "the marginalization of China in the world" and "the marginalization of intellectuals in Chinese society." Until 1905, when the examination system was abolished, traditional scholars (*shi*) were still directly linked to state power. After 1905, however, the modern "intellectual" questioned the legitimacy of the traditional moral order. For Yü, the marginalization of China was not simply a political "Middle Kingdom complex" or a nationalist question; intellectuals wanted "to keep China from losing its status as a center of culture."[35]

---

[30] See Shmuel N. Eisenstadt, ed., *Multiple Modernities* (New Brunswick, NJ: Transaction, 2002); Edward Shils, *Tradition* (Chicago: University of Chicago Press, 1981).
[31] Yü, "Zhongguo jindai sixiangshi shang de jijin yu baoshou," 23–24.
[32] Tu Wei-ming, "Introduction: Cultural Perspectives," *Daedalus* 122.2 (Spring 1993), vii–xiv.
[33] Ibid., 8–9, 12.
[34] Yü Ying-shih, "The Radicalization of China in the Twentieth Century," *Daedalus* 122.2 (Spring 1993), 125.
[35] Ibid., 135, 142–43, 146. Historically, however, Yü traces the social marginalization of the scholar (*shi*) in relation to the merchant back to the sixteenth century or even earlier. See also Yü Ying-shih, "Zhongguo zhishi fenzi de bianyuanhua" (The Marginalization of Chinese Intellectuals), *Ershiyi shiji*, no. 6 (August 1991), 15–25.

According to Yü, the first stage of radicalization occurred between the 1890s and the 1911 Revolution. It was translator Yan Fu—according to Xiao Gongqin the first neoconservative modernizer—who initiated the process of radicalization by questioning the Confucian Way. Whereas Yan Fu's radicalism was still "tempered" with "evolutionary gradualism," Kang Youwei and Tan Sitong promoted both wholesale and immediate change.[36] Finally, the scholars around *Guocui xuebao* (1905–11) all drew on Western theories to study Chinese learning.[37] During the second stage of radicalization, intellectuals tried to bring China back to the center by importing the newest ideas, which Yü Ying-shih calls "a neoterist mentality" or "a mentality obsessed with change, with what is new."[38] May Fourth figures, such as Hu Shi and Chen Duxiu, developed an attitude of "iconoclastic antitraditionalism," which reminds us of Lin Yü-sheng's "totalistic antitraditionalism." The third and highest stage of radicalization began with the ideological confrontation between liberalism and Marxism, followed by the "Marxist radicalism" of Mao Zedong, whose masterpiece of destruction was the Cultural Revolution.

Third, Tu Wei-ming actively sought to bring Confucianism back from the "periphery" to the "center" by way of his theory of "Cultural China." Moving away from a narrow geopolitical lens of territory and ideology, Tu advocated a cultural definition of Chineseness, in which intellectuals from the three "symbolic universes" of mainland China, Taiwan, Hong Kong, Singapore, and Chinese overseas communities, and those of non-Chinese descent who made efforts to understand China, had a part to play.[39] Tu reveals his vision in a highly influential essay, also published in a special issue of *Daedalus*, titled "The Living Tree: The Changing Meaning of Being Chinese Today." In this issue, authors explore the relation between the center and Chinese communities on the periphery, with a view to answering the timely overarching question: "What does it mean to be Chinese?"[40] For Tu, the economic rise of Japan and the Four Mini Dragons challenged the belief of mainland intellectuals that tradition blocked modernization, as was declared in *River Elegy*. With the periphery "proudly marching toward an Asia-Pacific century" while the mainland was left behind, the mainland lost both the capacity and the power to set an agenda for a cultural debate.[41] In a 1990 article in the journal

---

[36] Yü, "Radicalization of China in the Twentieth Century," 129.
[37] The main figures included Chen Qubing, Deng Shi, Huang Jie, Liu Shipei, Ma Xulun, and Zhang Binglin. On the national essence movement, see Hon, *Revolution as Restoration*.
[38] Yü, "Radicalization of China in the Twentieth Century," 141.   [39] Tu, "'Cultural China.'"
[40] S.R.G., "Preface to the Issue 'The Living Tree: The Changing Meaning of Being Chinese Today,'" *Daedalus* 120.2 (Spring 1991), v–viii.
[41] Tu, "'Cultural China,'" 12, 27–28.

Jiushi niandai (The Nineties), Tu presents his vision of a "Cultural China" to Chinese audiences.[42]

The French and English Models and the 1992 Debate

In addition to the above works and interactions, Yü Ying-shih and Tu Wei-ming also published articles in *Ershiyi shiji*. For example, Yü Ying-shih's article "Picking Up the Pieces for a New Start" appeared in the December 1990 issue of *Ershiyi shiji*.[43] In a brief but bold statement, Yü condemns the twentieth century because throughout its chain of revolutions "the old had been destroyed in order to establish the new" (*pojiu lixin*).[44] In the same issue, Tu Wei-ming argues in favor of the dissolution of what he calls the "Enlightenment mentality."[45] This was a mentality of a rational spirit—as manifested in the values of science and democracy—but it was also exemplified by the instrumental rationality of scientism. Chinese tradition, Tu argues, could have a positive function in dealing with the negative aspects of such a mentality.

In the next issue of *Ershiyi shiji*, Gan Yang, formerly a major actor in the New Enlightenment Movement as editor in chief of the series Culture: China and the World, joined the debate. After the repression of the Tiananmen demonstrations, he had left for the United States, where he would spend the next decade at the Committee of Social Thought at the University of Chicago, before moving to Hong Kong and thereafter back to mainland China. In *Ershiyi shiji*, Gan was now expressing criticism of Enlightenment in the form of a denunciation of the French Revolution in favor of the Glorious Revolution.

Critical evaluations of the French Revolution were also common in international accounts published on the occasion of its two hundredth anniversary, and at about the same time comparative works on the French and American revolutions also began to appear in American scholarship.[46] However, for Chinese intellectuals after 1989 amid the decline of socialism, the French and Glorious revolutions served as symbolic models or counter-models, or

---

[42] Tu Wei-ming, "'Wenhua Zhongguo' chutan" (Probing "Cultural China"), *Jiushi niandai*, no. 6 (June 1990), 60–61. See also, for example, Tu Wei-ming, "'Wenhua Zhongguo yu huayi zhishi fenzi de 'ziwo yishi'" (Cultural China and Chinese Intellectuals' "Consciousness of Self"), *Shijie ribao* (World Journal), September 22, 1991.

[43] Yü Ying-shih, "Dai congtou, shoushi jiu shanhe" (Picking Up the Pieces for a New Start), *Ershiyi shiji*, no. 2 (December 1990), 5–7.

[44] Ibid., 6.

[45] Tu Wei-ming, "Huajie qimeng xintai" (Beyond the Enlightenment Mentality), *Ershiyi shiji*, no. 2 (December 1990), 12–13.

[46] See, for example, Simon Schama, *Citizens: A Chronicle of the French Revolution* (New York: Knopf, 1989); Patrice Higonnet, *Sister Republics: The Origins of French and American Republicanism* (Cambridge, MA: Harvard University Press, 1988).

"scripts" to be rewritten, rather than as comparative accounts of actual events.[47] The Glorious Revolution represented gradual and orderly transition. As discussed in the previous chapter, this interpretation was partially influenced by Friedrich Hayek, who, in his *Constitution of Liberty*, had also discarded the French model in favor of the English model.

According to Hayek, the French tradition of liberty was based on Cartesian rationalism and a belief in freedom as the goals of a grand collective purpose, whereas the British tradition was based on empiricism, cumulative growth, and a belief in freedom in the absence of coercion. Whereas change was enforced in the French tradition, change was realized through trial and error in the British tradition. Chinese intellectuals, as already noted, referred to Alexis de Tocqueville in their promotion of gradualism. This should not be surprising because, given de Tocqueville's argument that the French Revolution had failed to establish liberty, as revealed in his *Democracy in America* (1835–40) and *The Old Regime and the Revolution* (1856), it can be argued that he was closer to the British tradition than to the French tradition.[48]

In a 1991 article in *Ershiyi shiji*, Gan Yang argues that the May Fourth slogan of "democracy and science," which he associated with the French revolutionary model, should be questioned because actions based on this slogan had led to disastrous results.[49] Gan had already criticized this May Fourth slogan in a 1989 article in *Dushu*, written on the seventieth anniversary of the May Fourth Movement and based on a talk he had given for the occasion at Peking University.[50] Referring to Friedrich Hayek and the liberal philosopher and historian of ideas Isaiah Berlin, Gan Yang argues that the French revolutionary model did not know liberty, as opposed to the Anglo-American constitutional model of "liberty and order."

---

[47] Baker and Edelstein, "Introduction," 2.
[48] Hayek, "Freedom, Reason, and Tradition," 49–62. The "British" tradition included the Scottish philosophers David Hume, Adam Smith, and David Ferguson, and the English philosophers Josiah Tucker, Edmund Burke, and William Paley. The "French" tradition included the Encyclopedists and Rousseau, the Physiocrats and Condorcet. According to Hayek, de Tocqueville was closer to the British tradition.
[49] Gan Yang, "Yangqi 'minzhu yu kexue,' dianding 'ziyou yu zhixu'" (Discard "Democracy and Science," Establish "Liberty and Order"), *Ershiyi shiji*, no. 3 (February 1991), 7–10. In a response to Gan Yang, Gu Xin argues that the French model was not characterized by "democracy and science" but by rationalism. See Gu Xin, "Anggelu ziyou chuantong yu Falanxi langman jingshen" (On the Anglo-liberal Tradition and the French Romantic Spirit), *Ershiyi shiji*, no. 6 (August 1991), 138–40.
[50] See Gan Yang, "Ziyou de linian: Wusi chuantong zhi queshimian, wei 'wusi qishi zhounian er zou" (The Idea of Freedom: Loss of the May Fourth Tradition and the Making of the Seventieth Anniversary of the May Fourth Era), *Dushu*, no. 5 (1989), 11–19; Timothy Cheek, "Historians as Public Intellectuals in Contemporary China," in Gu and Goldman, eds., *Chinese Intellectuals between State and Market*, 212.

Gan also refers to Isaiah Berlin's famous essay "Two Concepts of Liberty"—he was reportedly the first person to introduce this essay to Chinese audiences—in which Berlin makes a distinction between positive and negative freedom, or the difference between having a chance to act and the absence of interference to act. Whereas the difference between positive and negative freedom had been the topic of extensive debate among political theorists, in China in the early 1990s positive freedom generally stood for a rejection of direct democracy due to the experience of the Cultural Revolution.[51] Like Berlin, Gan Yang repudiates the positive freedom of the French revolutionaries and Rousseau. Liberals in socialist countries had wrongly based themselves on the French Revolution because its legacy was the Communist Revolution.

Whereas these early criticisms of the French model were advanced after the seventieth anniversary of the May Fourth Movement and after June 1989, the main debate on conservatism versus radicalism began during the period following Deng Xiaoping's Southern Tour in early 1992. In addition to *Ershiyi shiji*, the discussion also took place in several leading mainland journals, such as *Dongfang, Zhexue yanjiu, Yuandao*, and *Dushu*.[52] The wider debate had outgrowths for many years after 1992, continuing well into the 2000s, but the debate peaked between 1989 and 1993.[53] Because the debate centered around revolution and reform, between the mid-1980s and the mid-1990s research on the 1911 Revolution also flourished.[54]

In the debate, most participants based in mainland China, including Lin Gang (b. 1957), Xu Jilin, and Fu Keng, referred to works such as Burke's *Reflections on the Revolution in France* (1790), de Tocqueville's *The Old Regime and the Revolution* (1856), Huntington's *Political Order in Changing Societies* (1968), and Popper's *The Open Society and Its Enemies* (1945). Contrasting the English model with the French model, they praised the Glorious Revolution as "bloodless" and gradual, and thus resembling a reform movement. The references to de Tocqueville and Huntington served as a reminder that revolution could also occur under reform; prosperity fueled

---

[51] Gan, "Ziyou de linian"; Gan Yang, "Ziyou de diren: Zhenshanmei tongyi shuo" (The Enemy of Freedom: The Unification of Truth, Goodness, and Beauty), *Dushu*, no. 6 (1989), 121–28; Lian Zhou, "The Debates in Contemporary Chinese Political Thought," in Fred Dallmayr and Zhao Tingyang, eds., *Contemporary Chinese Political Thought: Debates and Perspectives* (Lexington: University of Kentucky Press, 2012), 35; Isaiah Berlin, "Two Concepts of Liberty," in Berlin, *Four Essays on Liberty* (Oxford: Oxford University Press, 1969), 118–72.

[52] The main texts of the debate are collected in ZFL.

[53] See, for example, Zheng Dahua and Jia Xiaoye, "'Zhongguo jindai sixiangshi shang de baoshou yu jijin' xueshu taolun hui zongshu" (Summary of the Academic Symposium on "Conservatism and Radicalism in Modern Chinese Intellectual History"), *Jindaishi yanjiu*, no. 2 (February 2004), 291–301.

[54] Zheng and Jia, "Jiushi niandai yilai Zhongguo jindai sixiangshi yanjiu zhong de zhongda wenti zhenglun," 51–57; Interview with Ma Yong, Beijing, June 6, 2006.

revolution for de Tocqueville, and premature expansion of political participation fueled revolution for Huntington. Reform had to be introduced in a controlled manner and not through direct political participation.

Some Chinese scholars were very critical of Yü Ying-shih's thesis of "radicalization" and the central place it accorded to ideas. The most ardent attack on Yü's thesis came from the historian Jiang Yihua (b. 1939) at Fudan University. It is noteworthy that, in spite of his rejection of Yü's thesis, Jiang followed the same categorization scheme by arguing that modern China had witnessed too much rather than too little conservatism. In addition, in an interesting twist, the evaluation of the Cultural Revolution (1966–76) occurred in the form of references to Edmund Burke and Hugh Cecil, and their interpretations of conservatism. It is worthwhile to investigate the exchange between Yü and Jiang in more detail.

The Cultural Revolution through a Burkean Lens

In the April 1992 issue of *Ershiyi shiji*, Jiang Yihua challenges Yü Ying-shih's elitist account of modern Chinese history as a process of "radicalization" brought about by intellectuals.[55] Conservatism was not the preservation of the status quo, but, as in Hugh Cecil's 1912 *Conservatism* or in modern British conservatism, it was about the adherence to old familiar things, the safeguarding of religion and authority, and love for the greatness of one's country.[56] Change should occur "within the range of specific value orientations," such as respect for tradition, authority, and nationalism, and conservatism in modern China had been too strong rather than too weak.[57] For Jiang, "cultural conservatives" who advocated change while respecting tradition included intellectuals whom Yü Ying-shih had grouped as "radicals," such as Kang Youwei and the scholars around the journal *Guocui xuebao*. "Cultural conservatism" also included the spread of Confucian associations during Yuan Shikai's rule, Chiang Kai-shek's 1934 New Life Movement (*xin shenghuo yundong*), New Confucianism, and the resurgence of *guoxue* during the 1990s.[58]

Yet the focal point of Jiang Yihua's attack on Yü Ying-shih is Yü's characterization of the Cultural Revolution as radical. For Jiang, the defining

---

[55] Jiang Yihua, "Jijin yu baoshou: Yu Yü Ying-shih xiansheng shangque" (Radicalism and Conservatism: A Discussion with Yü Ying-shih), *Ershiyi shiji*, no. 10 (April 1992), 134–42.
[56] Hugh Cecil, *Conservatism* (London: Williams and Norgate, 1912), 244.
[57] Jiang, "Jijin yu baoshou," 135.
[58] Elsewhere, Jiang discusses eleven manifestations of "political conservatism" that appeared in opposition to democracy and liberalism. They include neo-authoritarianism between 1988 and 1989 and "new political conservatism" since 1990. See Jiang Yihua, "Ershi shiji Zhongguo sixiangshi shang de zhengzhi baoshou zhuyi" (Political Conservatism in Twentieth-Century Chinese Intellectual History), in *ZFL*, 57–73.

essence of the Cultural Revolution had been "all-round dictatorship" and political conservatism; it was a continuation of "the harmful tradition of feudal despotism in thought and politics."[59] On the Cultural Revolution, Jiang writes, "Its pan-moralism, its pan-politicism, its egalitarianism that only serves to spread poverty, its totemization, its religious idolatry and its individual arbitrariness are all deeply rooted in Chinese tradition."[60] Mao's thought was not "radical," but it contained elements of idealism, "thick populism," and rural socialism. Yü Ying-shih was unable to see this because he was an overseas intellectual who obtained his unnuanced views through the party journal *Hongqi* (Red Flag) and *Renmin ribao*. Jiang further objected to the radicalization thesis because it could be applied only to a few intellectuals and elites in coastal and urban areas. The majority of Chinese people remained poor and exploited. May Fourth was not characterized by wholesale antitraditionalism; rather, it was part of the reconstruction of Chinese culture.[61]

Because of the versatility of the terms "radical" and "conservative," Yü and Jiang use them to refer to intellectual and sociopolitical changes, respectively. In the same issue of *Ershiyi shiji*, Yü Ying-shih takes issue with Jiang Yihua's analysis of politics, society, and economics instead of intellectual radicalization.[62] In spite of this, Yü states that Jiang's argument reveals "the paradox of revolution": revolutionaries always end up employing the very traditional elements they are attempting to eradicate. In contrast, the "paradox of conservatism" implies that renewal is indispensable for preservation. As formulated by Edmund Burke in *Reflections on the Revolution in France*, "If a country does not have the ability to change, it can also not have the ability to preserve."[63] Instead of renewal, 1949 signified the beginning of the destruction of Chinese popular society (*minjian shehui*) through the eradication of private property rights. The CCP, in the words of Milovan Djilas, was a "New Class" of owners and exploiters, in the name of collective ownership, who had unlimited authority. As such, there was no continuity between Chinese tradition and China after 1949. China's new political system was based on Stalinism and Leninism, not China's "feudal" traditions.[64]

---

[59] Jiang, "Jijin yu baoshou," 137. [60] Ibid., 137–38.
[61] Interview with Jiang Yihua, Shanghai, August 8, 2006; Jiang Yihua and Chen Yan, "Jijin yu baoshou: Yiduan shangwei wanjie de duihua" (Conservative and Radical: An Unfinished Dialogue), in *ZFL*, 30–36, 32–33.
[62] Yü Ying-shih, "Zai lun Zhongguo xiandai sixiang zhong de jijin yu baoshou: Da Jiang Yihua xiansheng" (Further Thoughts on Radicalism and Conservatism in Modern Chinese History: A Response to Jiang Yihua), *Ershiyi shiji*, no. 10 (April 1992), 143–49.
[63] Ibid., 145. See Isaac Kramnick, ed., *The Portable Edmund Burke* (London: Penguin, 1999), 424.
[64] Yü, "Zai lun Zhongguo xiandai sixiang zhong de jijin yu baoshou," 147–48. Yü elaborates further on this point in "Zhongguo zhishi fenzi de bianyuanhua," 15–25; Milovan Djilas, *The New Class: An Analysis of the Communist System* (New York: Praeger, 1971 [1957]).

The exchange between Yü and Jiang reflects their different analyses of post-1949 China and its relation to Chinese tradition and how this was affected by their own trajectories. According to Jiang, Yü Ying-shih, as a Chinese intellectual based in the United States, had no real understanding of Chinese history. In addition, from a Marxist perspective, "conservatism" was a negative force and Yü's idealist approach ignored the true historical forces and the part of the masses. In contrast, according to Yü the CCP represented the highest stage of "radicalism" and the destruction of Chinese culture. Hence, this was very much a discussion about the nature of "China," the identity and place of Chinese intellectuals, and who had the right to speak on behalf of China.

Advocating Gradual Reform

Intellectuals based outside of mainland China who joined the debate often criticized the CCP and promoted the importance of a democratic tradition. Wang Rongzu (Wong Young-tsu, b. 1940), at the time a professor in the History Department of Virginia Polytechnic Institute and State University (Virginia Tech), argues in the June 1992 issue of *Ershiyi shiji* that radicalization was but a matter of perspective.[65] Wang was a historian who had published, in both English and Chinese, works on a number of major intellectual figures, such as Chen Yinke, Zhang Taiyan, Kang Youwei, and Chiang Kai-shek. Born in Shanghai, he had studied in the History Department of National Taiwan University and received his doctorate in history from the University of Washington.

Wang argues that Chinese culture and tradition in Taiwan had been marginalized, and the 1960s' movement for the revival of Chinese culture had been more significant politically than it had been culturally. Like Jiang Yihua, Wang notes the interactions between intellectual radicalization and conservative forces, such as the role of the gentry, land owners, and traders in the success of the 1911 Revolution. In addition, the success of Marxism-Leninism came about only after the military victory of the CCP, and whether or not it cut the "umbilical cord of tradition" is debatable.[66] Nevertheless, Wang argues that Deng Xiaoping's economic reform program was the perfect way to balance conservatism and radicalism; it was a "middle road" between the two.[67] Referring to the Taiwanese experience, Wang argues that a middle class and a tradition of liberty are crucial for the successful transition from

---

[65] Wang Rongzu, "Jijin yu baoshou zhuiyan" (Radicalism and Conservatism: Superfluous Words), *Ershiyi shiji*, no. 11 (June 1992), 133–36.
[66] Ibid., 133–35, 135.   [67] Ibid., 135.

economic to political reform. Although this tradition was missing in China, it still could be cultivated.[68]

Other intellectuals based outside of mainland China who took part in the 1992 debate launched an assault on the CCP. One of them was Sun Guodong (1922–2013), a historian of the Tang and Song dynasties at the Chinese University of Hong Kong. He had left China after 1949 and had been a student of Qian Mu at New Asia College in Hong Kong. Sun attacked Jiang Yihua's negative portrayal of conservatism, his views on the Cultural Revolution, and his praise of CCP policies.[69] Sun reproached Jiang for his uncritical application of both Edmund Burke and Hugh Cecil to China. As in the earlier criticism of the statist and nationalist traits of neoconservatism, American conservatism had taken issue with authority and contained no nationalist traits. Sun further criticizes Jiang's argument that the errors of the Cultural Revolution can be ascribed to Chinese tradition and questions Jiang's account of the positive achievements after 1949. A force to preserve social stability could not develop in China because the main members of this force, namely the intellectuals and the middle class, were the "most oppressed and wrecked" groups after 1949. This, Sun argues, was the crux of China's problems during the last decade.[70]

Wang Shaoguang, discussed in Chapter 2 as generally being associated with neoconservatism because of his defense of a centralized state, also argued in favor of gradual reform.[71] Also referring to Burke's admonition that change was necessary for preservation, Wang put forward that conservatism was not an attitude toward tradition, ultimate aims, the status quo, or the future, but "an attitude of people toward how to change their conditions."[72] Intellectual radicalization always interacted with social forces, and in this sense both Yü Ying-shih and Jiang Yihua were right. The debate was not about conservatism as a "systematic theory," which was rare in modern Chinese history, but rather about "conservative tendencies" and "conservative actions."[73] Because social change was a learning process, Wang pleads for social reform based on Popper's "piecemeal engineering" and Michael Oakeshott's concept of "practical knowledge," or knowledge obtained through practice.[74] Wang advocated gradual economic reform but also noted that neoconservatism opposed a

---

[68] On this point, see also Wang, "Ziyou zhuyi yu Zhongguo," 33–37.
[69] Sun Guodong, "Du Jiang Yihua 'jijin yu baoshou' shu hou" (After Reading Jiang Yihua's Writings on "Conservative and Radical"), *Ershiyi shiji*, no. 11 (June 1992), 141–43.
[70] Ibid., 143.
[71] Wang Shaoguang, "'Baoshou' yu 'baoshou zhuyi'" ("Conservative" and "Conservatism"), *Ershiyi shiji*, no. 12 (August 1992), 135–38.
[72] Ibid., 135.   [73] Ibid., 135, 136, 137.
[74] Michael Oakeshott coined this concept in his *Rationalism in Politics, and Other Essays* (London: Methuen, 1962), 12n53. Oakeshott contrasts "practical knowledge" with "technical knowledge," which is acquired through education and knowledge transmission.

radical pace and a radical strategy, but not radical aims, namely the establishment of political democracy and a market economy.[75]

In the same issue of *Ershiyi shiji*, Li Liangyu (b. 1951), a professor of history at Nanjing University who specializes in contemporary Chinese intellectual and cultural history, argues that conservatism and radicalism are relative to specific historical problems and attitudes.[76] True, changes in modern China had been too rapid and too intense, but it was only when advocates of cultural conservatism and radicalism were politically active or entangled with political power that violent revolution and civil war followed. Li argues that it is the task of modern intellectuals to counter intellectual polarization and to advocate tolerance. Precisely because modern Chinese intellectuals had failed to do this, many problems remained unresolved. Hence, for Li the problem is one of intellectual responsibility.

Other mainland intellectuals who joined the debate also supported gradual economic reform, but, like Gan Yang, they embedded their argument in a criticism of the French revolutionary model. The result was a conservative liberalism; contrary to the conservative defense of community, mainland intellectuals did not argue for the preservation of intermediary groups. In addition, they now conceived of radicalism as revolution and French-style liberalism, whereas they related English gradual liberalism to conservatism. For Yü Ying-shih, Marxists and liberals had both been "radicals." Conversely, in the context of the intensified economic reforms since 1992 and demonstrating the turn toward a Hayekian neoliberal consensus, mainland intellectuals separated the gradual forms of liberalism from the idea of radicalism.

However, this perceived link between liberalism and gradualism was not a strictly post-1992 phenomenon: in a February 1991 article in *Ershiyi shiji* on radicalism in modern Chinese history, Lin Gang, a graduate of the Chinese Department at Sun Yat-sen University and a researcher in the Institute of Literature of CASS, had already argued that liberalism was a form of gradualism. Radicalism, in contrast, drawing on Rousseau and the French Revolution, supported "basic solutions," rejected tradition, and advocated violence and revolution.[77] Liberalism was now associated with gradualism, and Popper's concept of "piecemeal engineering" was often invoked to support gradual reform.

One of the participants in the 1992 debate who associated liberalism with gradualism was Xu Jilin, a well-known liberal professor in the History

---

[75] Wang, "Qiubian paluan de xin baoshou sichao," 76–77.
[76] Li Liangyu, "Jijin, baoshou yu zhishi fenzi de zeren" (Radicalism, Conservatism, and the Responsibility of Intellectuals), *Ershiyi shiji*, no. 12 (August 1992), 132–34.
[77] Lin Gang, "Jijin zhuyi zai Zhongguo" (Radicalism in China), *Ershiyi shiji*, no. 3 (February 1991), 17–27.

Department of East China Normal University in Shanghai.[78] In the June 1992 issue of *Ershiyi shiji*, Xu Jilin argues that it is necessary to distinguish between cultural and political radicalism, and during the twentieth century cultural radicalism had alternated with a return to Chinese cultural values. This occurred in the 1920s and 1930s and again in the 1940s in Yan'an where Marxism-Leninism and popular culture had merged, but it also occurred beginning in the 1960s in Taiwan, and again in the years preceding the debate on mainland China.[79] Politically, in the absence of a status quo that could function as a coordinate, Popper's concepts of "piecemeal engineering" and "utopian engineering" replaced conservatism and radicalism as yardsticks to discuss modern Chinese history. Both radicalism and conservatism belonged to a type of "utopian social engineering" that lacked an open attitude in the cultural and academic realms. Chinese political conservatism was even more radical because it monopolized resources, used holism to solve problems, created "authoritative and self-contained ideological myths," and excluded the lower levels of society.[80] In twentieth-century China, both radicalism and conservatism had been too strong, whereas the "piecemeal social engineering" of liberalism had been too weak. In spite of Xu Jilin's embrace of gradualism, he did not support Hayekian liberalism because he felt it could not solve the problems of social inequality, whereas a liberalism that also incorporated John Rawls's agenda of social justice could.[81]

Other intellectuals who explicitly associated liberalism with conservatism included Fu Keng (b. 1959), a graduate of Fudan University's History Department and a researcher on the sociology of intellectuals at the Shanghai Academy of Social Sciences (SASS).[82] Fu Keng argues that Burke's *Reflections on the Revolution in France* was useful to think about the Cultural Revolution: it had suppressed Confucianism and witnessed dictatorship, harmed individual rights and property, and destroyed community organizations. Chinese intellectuals had wrongly supported the "idealist romantic political delusions" of the French Enlightenment thinkers.[83] Referring to Lin

---

[78] Xu Jilin, "Jijin yu baoshou de mihuo" (The Conundrum of Radicalism and Conservatism), *Ershiyi shiji*, no. 11 (June 1992), 137–40.
[79] Ibid., 138–39.   [80] Ibid., 139, 140.
[81] Ibid.; Interview with Xu Jilin, Shanghai, August 6, 2006. Xu Jilin contends that this form of liberalism was dominant during the May Fourth era, based on the influence of John Dewey, Hu Shi's teacher, and the English "social democracy" of the Fabianist Harold Laski. Xu Jilin, "Zhongguo zhishi fenzi de ziyou zhuyi chuantong" (The Tradition of Liberalism among Chinese Intellectuals), in *Xu Jilin zixuanji*, 98–109. On how Harold Laski inspired Chinese liberals beginning in the 1930s and how this differed from other "generations" of liberals, see Fung, *Intellectual Foundations of Chinese Modernity*, 128–58.
[82] Fu Keng, "Dalu zhishi fenzi de jijin zhuyi shenhua" (The Myth of the Radicalism of Mainland Intellectuals), *Ershiyi shiji*, no. 11 (June 1992), 144–47.
[83] Ibid., 145.

Yü-sheng, Fu laments the "spirit of utopian saviorism" that adhered to Max Weber's "ethic of ultimate ends": the radicals did not consider the effects of their actions.[84] The radicalism of the French Revolution and the socialist tradition had led to the persecution of intellectuals, and the "rationalist" belief in unlimited improvements, science, and progress should be exchanged for Hayek's "empirical" liberal tradition.[85]

Also in 1992, Hu Cheng (b. 1954), a graduate from and a lecturer in the History Department of Nanjing University, expressed a more nuanced view in *Ershiyi shiji*. Hu states that China had known only gradual reformism rather than true conservatism. However, gradual reformers had also pursued political progress and hence could also be radicals. Hu further rejects the ideology of violence (*baoli zhuyi*) that had obstructed the progress of modern Chinese history. Hu refers to the New Policies during the late Qing dynasty to argue that political and social reform on the basis of industrial and educational reforms looking for rapid returns could lead to chaos. Even though democratic reform was undoubtedly the path to eradicate violence, this should be pursued only in due course, the meaning of which he does not elaborate.[86]

Order, Liberty, and "Piecemeal Engineering"

From the above, we see that on mainland China Yü Ying-shih's radicalization thesis, in which a political liberalism is coupled with a defense of historical continuity and the preservation of intermediate organizations, was transformed into a confirmation of gradual reform. Other participants based outside of mainland China also defended gradual reform, but they concurrently criticized the CCP and argued for the cultivation of a liberal political culture. Some intellectuals, such as Xu Jilin, were skeptical about the use of *-isms* as yardsticks; they nevertheless underscored the need for gradual reform and the central part of the intellectual in reform. The process of radicalization was perceived of as a process of the marginalization of the Chinese intellectual, and unmaking radicalism also served to bring the intellectual back

---

[84] For Max Weber, the "ethic of ultimate ends" (*Gesinnungsethik*) did not take into account the possible effects of an action, unlike the "ethic of responsibility" (*Verantwortungsethik*). Weber declared in his lecture "Politics as a Vocation" (1919) that only a person who could combine the two was capable of a "vocation for politics." See Lin, *Zhongguo chuantong de chuangzaoxing zhuanhua*, 373–82.

[85] On this point and on Fu's support of "negative freedom," see Fu Keng, "Langman lixiang yu shigong jingshen: Ying Fa zhishi jieceng de chayi" (Romantic Ideals and the Spirit of Cause and Contribution: Differences between English and French Intellectuals), *Dushu*, no. 1 (1992), 30–37.

[86] Hu Cheng, "Jijin zhuyi yihuo shi baoli zhuyi" (Radicalism or Ideology of Violence), *Ershiyi shiji*, no. 13 (October 1992), 139–45.

to the center. Nevertheless, the following question remained: who was the Chinese intellectual, and who had the right to express his (or less often her) apprehensions?

A second point is the shift in meaning of the term "conservatism." Whereas criticism of "rationalism" as idealism originally went hand in hand with an advocacy for a strong state against the background of the legitimacy crisis, the present danger was now perceived to be French "rationalism" and the path from Rousseau to socialism. Hence, this was a *j'accuse* of socialist state power and a turn to the market as the creator of new individual space and order. Combining elements from Hayek, Burke, de Tocqueville, and Popper, the English model was one of conservative liberalism, which did not share the same "statist" and nationalist traits as neoconservatism. Its supporters did not invoke the social organism but instead brought in Popper to argue for piecemeal changes. Whereas the embrace of conservative liberalism did not become widespread until the mid-1990s, there was already a clear movement in this direction in the 1992 debate and even in some articles that appeared before this debate. Wang Hui describes the shift in the use of the term "conservatism" as a label as follows:

> In the mid-nineties, the group around Liu Junning argued publicly, claiming that true liberalism is a form of conservatism, because of its belief in order. This is a very revealing shift of terms, since in the eighties and early nineties conservatism was always used as a pejorative term to describe anyone who was regarded as insufficiently enthusiastic about the market, or too willing to envisage a positive role for the state—the label was applied to people like Hu Angang or Cui Zhiyuan.[87]

The advocacies of Liu Junning (b. 1961), a political scientist and liberal based at the Institute of Political Science at CASS, will be discussed further below. During the 1980s, the term "conservatives" (*baoshouzhe*) indeed did emerge as the negative counterpart of the term "reformers" (*gaigezhe*) in a political discourse that unfolded in relation to Zhao Ziyang's reform program.[88] The positive use of the term during the 1990s represented a drastic change from this earlier use. However, Wang Hui's point that this occurred in the mid-1990s requires some nuance because during the early 1990s, as revealed in the previous chapters, some intellectuals were already consciously using the term "conservatism" and interpreting it positively.

The negative connotation that was previously ascribed to conservatism was now reserved for radicalism, which was explicitly tied to socialism and revolution. However, some intellectuals' association of liberty and order was not without precedent in twentieth-century China. Edmund Fung argues that

---

[87] Wang, "New Criticism," 68.
[88] Schoenhals, *Doing Things with Words in Chinese Politics*, 119–20.

the alignment of liberty and order characterized Chinese liberalism during the Republican period. Li Dazhao, a central figure in the May Fourth Movement and one of the cofounders of the CCP, for example, referred to "orderly freedoms in a free order." In China, Fung argues, liberal thought foregrounded both personal freedom and service to society. Therefore, the nexus between the individual and society occupied a principal place in Chinese liberal thought during this earlier period.[89]

The repeated reference to Popper's "piecemeal engineering" that we find in Xu Jilin's and others' contributions to the discussion was in accordance with the pragmatism and realism of the official reform policy, as expressed in, for example, the slogan of "crossing the river by feeling for the stones." The "new era" (*xin shiqi*) that began with the policy of reform and opening up in 1978 was marked by the formation of what Xu Jilin refers to as a "secular socialism," which was intended to move away from the "idealism of utopian socialism" of the previous era.[90]

Popper had been introduced to Chinese audiences during the New Enlightenment of the mid- to late 1980s, but he became more popular during the early 1990s amid the renewal of reform.[91] In 1987, at a seminar on Popper organized in Wuhan, one participant considered Popper's "fallibilism" to be an "antidote to some eternal dogmas."[92] At the same conference, Fan Dainian, a researcher at CASS, argued that Chinese modernization should take place according to Popper's "piecemeal social engineering" and not according to "utopian social engineering":

In the past seven or eight years, Chinese Communists, having learned from the heavy losses caused by Utopian social engineering, have emphasized that we should be "practical and realistic" and "grope our own way" (through trial and error) from now on, that is, implement what Popper called piecemeal social engineering.[93]

Popper was especially appropriate for the debate on conservatism and radicalism because he too had used the term "radicalism" in reference to utopianism in his *Open Society and Its Enemies*. Utopianism was "the conviction that one

---

[89] Fung, *Intellectual Foundations of Chinese Modernity*, 154, 157.
[90] Xu, "Fate of an Enlightenment," 184.
[91] Some of Popper's works were translated into Chinese as early as 1986. See Karl Popper [Ka'er Bopu'er], *Caixiang yu fanbo* (Conjectures and Refutations), tr. Fu Jichong et al. (Shanghai: Shanghai yiwen chubanshe, 1986); Karl Popper [Ba Bo], *Kaifang shehui ji qi diren* (The Open Society and Its Enemies), tr. and ed. Li Yingming and Zhuang Wenrui (Taipei: Guiguan tushu gongsi, 1986).
[92] Ji Shu-li, "The Worlds of Cultures and World 3: A Discussion of Popper's Theory of Three Worlds," in W. H. Newton-Smith and Jiang Tianji, eds., *Popper in China* (London: Routledge, 1992), 111.
[93] Fan Dainian, "Science, Open Society and China," in Newton-Smith and Jiang Tianji, *Popper in China*, 19.

has to go to the very root of the social evil," which was "its uncompromising *radicalism*."[94] Contrary to the "utopian engineering" of ultimate ends and blueprints for the reform of society as a whole, Popper argued, "piecemeal engineering" was about reforming particular institutions based on reason instead of passion, thereby avoiding the lack of a rational method, a changing of the goals in the process, and the risk of dictatorship. Therefore, during the 1980s Popper was appropriate for the deconstruction of utopian socialism in China, but this became all the more apparent after the disillusionments of 1989.

Responses to Anti-radicalism: Apologetics or Heretics?

Not all Chinese intellectuals embraced the anti-radicalism framework. As we have seen, Xu Jilin argued against the resort to binary *-isms*, whereas Jiang Yihua challenged Yü Ying-shih's emphasis on ideas as an explanatory framework. Interestingly, Gan Yang, who had first defended the English model, later criticized his former position because, according to this thinking, mainland interpretations had become a denial of democracy and liberty. The discarding of radicalism in China implied a historical rejection of the revolutionary path, a cultural rejection of May Fourth, political conservatism disguised as liberalism, and economic liberalism.[95] Burke had missed out on the "universal significance" of the French Revolution because he adhered to "Old European aristocratic liberalism."[96] Gan reiterated that his criticism of science and democracy in favor of liberty and order was a necessity after the events of 1989, but in retrospect he questioned the "intellectual quality" and "ideological inclination" of this stance.[97]

For some Chinese critics based in mainland China, the rejection of radicalism and the theoretical musings surrounding it amounted to mere apologetics and a defense of the political status quo. The liberal Zhu Xueqin argued that Yü Ying-shih's goals were subject to a "pragmatic castration" on mainland China.[98] Wang Hui, who had taken part in the Tiananmen demonstrations, argued that "rethinking radicalism" was not an effective critique because it merely continued the discourse on liberation and freedom of the 1980s without

---

[94] Popper, *Open Society*, 1.164.
[95] Gan Yang, "Fan minzhu ziyou zhuyi haishi minzhu de ziyou zhuyi" (Anti-democratic Liberalism or Democratic Liberalism?), *Ershiyi shiji*, no. 39 (February 1997), 4–17; Gan Yang, "A Critique of Chinese Conservatism in the 1990s," tr. Zhang Xudong, *Social Text* 16.2 (Summer 1998), 45–66; Gan Yang, "Debating Liberalism and Democracy in China in the 1990s," in Zhang, ed., *Whither China?*, 79–101.
[96] Gan, "Debating Liberalism and Democracy," 85, 91. For his criticism of Burke, Gan Yang based himself on Isaiah Berlin, for whom Burke was a reactionary inspired by de Maistre.
[97] Gan, "Debating Liberalism and Democracy," 89. [98] Zhu, "For a Chinese Liberalism," 99.

realizing that China's problems were now deeply entwined with those of global capitalism. In addition, even liberals were now arguing that development of the market, without the discussion of specific mechanisms or the place of new interest groups in this process, would lead to democracy, thus rendering them no different from the neoconservatives or the neo-authoritarians.[99]

Chinese scholars in the United States also criticized the debate. Zhang Xudong (b. 1965), who was educated at Peking University and Duke University before becoming professor of comparative literature and East Asian studies at New York University, argued that mainland debates on Edmund Burke were debates on democracy in a "coded language," partly because of the political repression on the mainland but also because Western thought was used to claim legitimacy. Hence, paradoxically the radicalism of May Fourth was erased, and its liberal legacy became a neoliberal modernization ideology.[100] According to Xu Ben, a cultural critic who left China before 1989 and who has since been based at Saint Mary's College in California, the "conservatism/radicalism" pair is nothing but a "pseudo-binary." Radicalism, not liberalism, was chosen as a counter-concept because its meaning could be stretched, and it also gave the discourse an indigenous touch and enabled liberals to embrace conservative ideas.[101]

Both Leftist and liberal criticism accused reflections on radicalism of conforming to the status quo—for Leftists in the form of a blind affirmation of the market and for liberals in the form of not demanding political liberalization. First, even though the debate did indeed affirm economic reform and was highly philosophical, theoretical, and abstract, some of the nuances, as outlined in this chapter, are lost in these criticisms. The debate did away with the socialist rhetoric of reform by placing much more emphasis on liberal theory and the market, as explored further below. Second, by singling out the domestic situation of post-1989 China, critics such as Xu Ben ignore the fact that Chinese scholars abroad with liberal inclinations had first employed this framework. The choice of a conservatism/radicalism binary cannot be reduced to the climate on the mainland, but this climate was nevertheless crucial for a reinterpretation of the meaning of the terms.

Anti-radicalism also partially challenged the official ideology by its projection of the logic of reform into history. From the Marxist point of view, the embrace of gradualism and reform endangered the revolutionary narrative on which the legitimacy of the CCP was based. Here, we should also refer to a principal work that continued some of the advocacies in the 1992 debate but

---

[99] Wang, *China's New Order*, 78–84.
[100] Zhang Xudong, "Intellectual Politics in Post-Tiananmen China: An Introduction," *Social Text* 16.2 (Summer 1998), 5; Zhang, "Making of the Post-Tiananmen Intellectual Field," 31.
[101] Xu, *Disenchanted Democracy*, 182.

that explicitly rejected revolution. This was the controversial 1995 volume *Farewell to Revolution*, the account of a dialogue between philosopher Li Zehou and literary critic Liu Zaifu, the former head of the Institute of Literature at CASS.[102] Li Zehou had earlier taken issue with Mao Zedong's emphasis on the moral will instead of the mode of production. He had also explicitly argued that instead of revolution China needed reform and the 1911 Revolution had not been necessary.[103]

In their controversial 1995 volume, the authors part with class struggle, revolution, dialectical materialism, and the ideology of Lenin, Stalin, and Mao Zedong. Instead, they propose the economy as the basis, historical materialism, class cooperation, gradual reform, and the separation of society and government. For this purpose, Hayek and Popper had more to offer than Mao Zedong, whose politics of "you die, I live" had led to many "radical sentiments." The authors praise the "pragmatic rationality" of Deng Xiaoping's reforms, arguing that they did not conflict with classical Marxism. Similar to the primacy of economic reform in the 1992 debate, the authors conceive of political democracy as a four-stage process, namely economic development, individual liberty, social justice, and, finally, political democracy.[104]

The authors trace the origins of radicalism back to the late Qing intellectual Tan Sitong who had attacked the core of the Confucian order, namely the theory of the "three bonds" (*sangang*) between ruler and official, father and son, and husband and wife.[105] The constitutionalism of Kang Youwei and Liang Qichao that resembled the English model would have been preferable to the 1911 Revolution, which, resembling the French model, had led to warlordism and chaos. In a separate chapter, the authors discuss the Meiji Restoration (1868–1912) in light of the English model of the Glorious Revolution. Like Hayek, they equate the English and French models with two different traditions of individualism and liberty.[106] In a section on the

---

[102] Li and Liu, *Gaobie geming*. Both Li and Liu left China following the 1989 crackdown and have formally resided in Colorado since the early 1990s, but they have also taken up visiting positions abroad.

[103] Li Zehou, "Heping jinhua, fuxing Zhonghua: Tan 'yao gailiang bu yao geming'" (Peaceful Evolution, Reviving China: On "We Need Reform, Not Revolution"), *Zhongguo shibao zhoukan*, May 3–9, 1992, 42–45 and May 10–16, 1992, 44–47.

[104] Li and Liu, *Gaobie geming*, 10, 14–15, 18, 66. Some authors have criticized this four-staged approach as a return to the historical determinism that the authors sought to reject. Zou Dang [Tsou Tang], "Du 'Gaobie geming': Zhi Li Zehou, Liu Zaifu" (Reading *Farewell to Revolution*: To Li Zehou and Liu Zaifu), *Ershiyi shiji*, no. 33 (February 1996), 62–67; Chang Jiang, "Shehui zhuanxingqi de yizhong wenhua xianxiang: Ping *Gaobie geming*" (A Cultural Phenomenon in Societies at a Transitional Stage: On *Farewell to Revolution*), *Ershiyi shiji*, no. 33 (February 1996), 68–71.

[105] Li and Liu, *Gaobie geming*, 80–81.

[106] See the chapter "Geming yu gailiang: Shijixing de tongku xuanze" (Revolution and Reform: The Painful Choice of a Century), Li and Liu, *Gaobie geming*, 65–78, 141.

"philosophy of struggle," they disapprove of the revolutionary narrative of modern Chinese history. Marxist historians denounced the phenomenon of anti-radicalism, and *Farewell to Revolution* in particular, in official media such as *Guangming ribao*, *Renmin ribao*, *Beijing ribao* (Beijing Daily), and the party journal *Hongqi*. For example, a March 12, 1996, article in *Guangming ribao* on the "correct" assessment of modern Chinese history stated, "Without the armed revolution led by the CCP, there would be no talk of today's construction of socialist modernization."[107] The failure of the 1911 Revolution had to be ascribed to the historical conditions of imperialism and feudalism; the "soft reformism" of the English model had been based on violent struggle (such as the violent revolution of 1642–49) no less than the revolution itself had been. The claim that reform was better than revolution amounted to "historical idealism."

Criticism of anti-radicalism also appeared in journals such as *Qiushi* (Seeking Truth), *Gaoxiao lilun zhanxian* (Theoretical Front in Higher Education), *Zhexue yanjiu*, and *Wenyi lilun yu piping*.[108] In *Wenyi lilun yu piping*, Marxist Confucian Fang Keli argues that attacks on radicalism are part of a "cultural conservative trend" that denies revolution and Marxist ideology as part of an international attempt to bring down socialism after the Cold War.[109] Similarly, in studies of "cultural conservatism" in modern Chinese history, Marxist historians expounded upon dialectical materialism and denounced the "cultural view of history" (*wenhua shiguan*).[110] In the pages of several volumes that discuss crucial events in modern Chinese history, the "correct" view of modern Chinese history, namely dialectical materialism, is exposed.

Two famous volumes along these lines are *Lishi de huida* (History's Response) and *Zou shenme lu* (Which Way to Go), both of which deal with

---

[107] Ma Baozhu and Wei Zhaogai, eds., "Zhengque renshi Zhongguo jindaishi shang de geming yu gailiang" (Correctly Understanding Revolution and Reform in Modern Chinese History), *Guangming ribao*, March 12, 1996, 5.

[108] See, for example, Kong Lingzhao, "Ba lishi de neirong huangei lishi: Ping yizhong guannianlun de wenhua shiguan" (Returning the Content of History to History: Criticizing a Conceptual Cultural View of History), *Zhexue yanjiu*, no. 4 (1995), 3–7; Gong Shuduo, Li Wenhai, Zhang Haipeng, et al., "Wusi yundong yu ershi shiji Zhongguo de daolu" (The May Fourth Movement and the Road of Twentieth-Century China), *Gaoxiao lilun zhanxian*, no. 6 (1996), 16–25; Zhang Lin, Wang Yinhuan, Jing Jianbin, et al., "Qingnian xuesheng shiye zhong de jindai Zhongguo yilai de lishi daolu" (The Historical Road of China since Modern Times in the View of Young Students), *Gaoxiao lilun zhanxian*, no. 6 (1997), 31–40.

[109] Fang Keli, "Yao zhuyi yanjiu jiushi niandai chuxian de wenhua baoshou zhuyi sichao" (One Should Attentively Research the Cultural Conservative Trend That Appeared during the 1990s), *Wenyi lilun yu piping*, no. 3 (1996), 11–19.

[110] See, for example, Li Yi, *Zhongguo Makesi zhuyi yu dangdai wenhua baoshou zhuyi sichao yanjiu* (Research on Trends in Chinese Marxism and Contemporary Cultural Conservatism) (Tianjin: Tianjin shehui kexue chubanshe, 1998).

modern Chinese history in toto.[111] In the latter, Geng Yunzhi argues that each historical movement, be it the 1898 Reform Movement, the 1911 Revolution, or the May Fourth Movement, matters in liberating the people and reversing the old system. Hence radicalism had a historical part to play and was not the only intellectual trend of the times.[112] "Cultural conservatism" was also denounced in a number of other books, articles, or dissertations.[113] The edited volume *Zhishi fenzi lichang: Jijin yu baoshou zhijian de dongdang* also includes articles by Li Jinquan, Chen Xiaoya, and Jiang Yihua that criticize Li Zehou's interpretation of the 1911 Revolution.[114] For Zheng Dahua and Jia Xiaoye of the Modern Chinese History Research Institute of CASS, the debate manifested a "non-historicist" (*fei lishi zhuyi de*) tendency. Instead of starting from historical facts, the debate was primarily an exercise in counterfactual history (*ruguo shixue*).[115] It thus can be seen that, in spite of its theoretical nature, the debate did have serious political implications and was not simply an affirmation of the status quo.

The Influence of Conservative Liberalism

According to Marxist scholar Xie Wujun, "conservative liberalism" was the greatest challenge to socialism because those who adhered to it praised Edmund Burke's attack on the French Revolution as well as Friedrich Hayek's denial of socialism and the planned economy.[116] Xie's comment reveals the change in worldview exposed by the debate. The established link among liberalism, gradualism, and conservatism in the 1992 debate became more prominent in the form of advocacy of conservative liberalism in the second

---

[111] Gong, Jin, and Song, *Lishi de huida*; Sha Jiansun and Gong Shuduo, eds., *Zou shenme lu: Guanyu Zhongguo jinxiandai lishi shang de ruogan zhongda shifei wenti* (Which Way To Go: Some Major Disputes on Modern Chinese History) (Ji'nan: Shandong renmin chubanshe, 1997).
[112] Geng Yunzhi, "Yanjiu lishi yao kao lishi shishi" (In Researching History, One Must Rely on Historical Reality), in Sha and Gong, *Zou shenme lu*, 383. The sensitivity of the issue is reflected in the fact that, as one scholar informed me, the names of some of the younger mainland researchers are omitted from the volume.
[113] Jiang Xudong, "Lun dangdai Zhongguo wenhua baoshou zhuyi de jiazhi tezheng" (On the Value Characteristics of Contemporary Chinese Cultural Conservatism") (Ph.D. diss., Zhongguo renmin daxue, 2003); Li, *Zhongguo Makesi zhuyi*, 13–14.
[114] Li Jinquan, "Zhongguo jindaishi jige wenti pingjia de zai pingjia" (Re-evaluating the Assessments of Some Issues in Modern Chinese History), in *ZFL*, 84–92; Chen Xiaoya, "Shei yingdang dui Xinhai geming fuze" (Who Ought to be Responsible for the 1911 Revolution?), in *ZFL*, 93–102; Jiang and Chen, "Jijin yu baoshou," 30–36.
[115] Zheng and Jia, "Jiushi niandai yilai Zhongguo," 56.
[116] Xie Wujun, "Ping Zhongguo dangdai de baoshou zhuyi sichao" (Commenting on the Contemporary Chinese Conservative Trend), *Dangdai sichao*, no. 4 (2001), 13–29.

half of the 1990s, during which time selective repression of liberalism continued.[117] A clear example can be found in the works of Liu Junning, to whom Wang Hui refers above and one of the editors of the liberal journal *Gonggong luncong* (Res Publica).[118]

In a 1998 volume titled *Baoshou zhuyi* (Conservatism) Liu Junning argues that the "Burke of the Whigs is the Burke of liberty."[119] According to Liu, Chinese supporters of neoconservatism and neo-authoritarianism had distorted conservatism by subscribing to centralized power. Conservatism without liberalism led to political authoritarianism, whereas liberalism without conservatism brought about rationalism and radicalism driven by abstract ideals and wholesale change.[120] Modern China had not known a true Burkean conservatism that intended to preserve liberty through gradual change.[121] Liu further argues that "constructivist rationalist" liberalism, a term he borrows from Hayek—who applied it to describe the belief that man could shape the world according to his desires—was the farthest away from conservatism.[122] Liu is clearly following the interpretation that Hayek was a conservative liberal (although Hayek himself had stressed that he did not want to be related to conservatism).[123] Like the participants in the 1992 debate, Liu affirms the American and English revolutions as "realistic revolutions," whereas the French Revolution had been "utopian" in nature. With the economic reforms, Liu argues, political radicalism was denounced.[124]

---

[117] For example, Liu Junning was dismissed from his position in the Institute of Political Science of CASS following publication of a collection of texts on liberalism on the occasion of the one hundredth anniversary of Peking University in 1998. See Frenkiel, *Conditional Democracy*, 20.

[118] The other editors were Wang Yan, former editor of *Dushu*, and He Weifang, a liberal legal scholar. Xu, "Fate of an Enlightenment," 203n15.

[119] Liu Junning, *Baoshou zhuyi* (Conservatism) (Beijing: Zhongguo shehui kexue chubanshe, 1998), 9.

[120] Ibid., 14, 264.

[121] Ibid., 255–57. However, Liu Junning recognizes some "conservative elements" in the thoughts of Confucius, Laozi, and Yang Zhu. Furthermore, he mentions the thoughts of Yan Fu, Liang Qichao, Chen Yinke, Xu Fuguan, and Gu Zhun as examples of a "healthy conservatism." See Liu, *Baoshou zhuyi*, 263.

[122] Ibid., 27. Hayek, *Collected Works*, 8, 22, and 60–62.

[123] See Friedrich A. Hayek, "Postscript: Why I Am Not a Conservative," in *Constitution of Liberty*, 343–55. Anthony Giddens has separated "neoconservatism" from "neoliberalism" because of the latter's emphasis on economic individualism, which is incompatible with the conservative stress on community and social solidarity. Hence, for Giddens Hayek was by no means a "conservative liberal." See Anthony Giddens, *Beyond Left and Right: The Future of Radical Politics* (Stanford, CA: Stanford University Press, 1994), 39–41.

[124] Liu, *Baoshou zhuyi*, 49, 51, 70, 97, 263. See also Liu Junning, "Dang minzhu fang'ai ziyou de shihou" (When Democracy Obstructs Freedom), *Dushu*, no. 11 (1993), 74–80; Liu Junning, "Baoshou de Baike, Ziyou de Baike" (The Conservative Burke and the Liberal Burke), *Dushu*, no. 3 (1995), 77–85.

The embrace of conservative liberalism is also found in writings by other scholars in the humanities, especially during the second half of the 1990s. A case in point is Tao Dongfeng, a professor of literary studies in the Chinese Department of Capital Normal University in Beijing. Tao's article "Conservative Liberalism: The Third Choice for Chinese Cultural Construction," initially published in *Kaifang shidai* in 1997, was reprinted in *Zhishi fenzi lichang: Jijin yu baoshou zhijian de dongdang*.[125] Tao argues that thinkers such as Burke, de Tocqueville, and Hayek supported a conservative liberalism. In China, however, conservatism often joined hands with cultural nationalism, whereas liberalism merged with radicalism and antitraditionalism because Chinese intellectuals were affected by the tradition of radical individualism and the direct democracy of French liberalism. Conservative liberalism stands for continuity and gradual reform; it recognizes the limits of reason and envisions a union of order and liberty.[126]

The philosopher Li Zehou had already made the association between English liberalism and reform and between French liberalism and revolution in the late 1970s.[127] In a 1992 article, Li mentions John Locke, Karl Popper, Edmund Burke, Alexis de Tocqueville, and Friedrich Hayek as sources of inspiration.[128] Two years later, in two 1994 issues of *Dongfang*, Li explicitly links the reform practice of "crossing the river by feeling for the stones" to Hayek's opposition to an excessive belief in rationality and to Popper's "piecemeal engineering."[129] Li states that liberty is the product of the accumulation of experience and rule of law is a gradual process.

Why did Chinese intellectuals advance a gradualist liberalism at this point in time? Xu Jilin connects the rise of interest in gradual reform in China during the 1990s to several influential books and articles.[130] One is the above-mentioned 1989 article by Gan Yang on English and French liberalism.

---

[125] Tao Dongfeng, "Baoshou ziyou zhuyi: Zhongguo wenhua jiangou de di sanzhong xuanze" (Conservative Liberalism: The Third Choice for Chinese Cultural Construction), in *ZFL*, 475–85.
[126] Ibid. See also Tao Dongfeng, "Ershi shiji Zhongguo de baoshou zhuyi: Jianlun ziyou yu chuantong zhi guanxi" (The Conservatism of Twentieth-Century China: On the Relation between Liberty and Tradition), in *Wenhua yu meixue de shiye jiaorong: Tao Dongfeng xueshu zixuanji* (The Fusion of the Horizons of Culture and Aesthetics: Self-Selections of Tao Dongfeng's Academic Works) (Fuzhou: Fujian jiaoyu chubanshe, 2000), 217–61.
[127] See Li Zehou, *Zhongguo jindai sixiangshi lun* (On Modern Chinese Intellectual History) (Beijing: Renmin chubanshe, 1979). Li states that his division between the French and English models went back to 1978. See Li and Liu, *Gaobie geming*, 66.
[128] Li, "Heping jinhua, fuxing Zhonghua," 44.
[129] Li Zehou and Wang Desheng, "Guanyu wenhua xianzhuang, daode chongjian de duihua" (A Dialogue on the Cultural Status Quo and Moral Reconstruction), in *ZFL*, 74–83.
[130] Xu, "Fate of an Enlightenment," 198.

Another is Friedrich Hayek, who was first introduced to Chinese audiences during the 1980s and whose *The Road to Serfdom* and *The Constitution of Liberty* were translated into Chinese in 1997.[131] For the second half of the 1990s, we should also refer to the posthumous publication in 1994 of the collected works of Gu Zhun (1915–74), an accountant, economist, and CCP member who is often referred to as a liberal.[132] During the late 1950s and again during the 1960s, Gu Zhun had been labeled a Rightist and sent to labor camps.[133] Some of Gu Zhun's earlier arguments appealed to the intellectuals of the 1990s, such as that direct democracy was feasible only in the Greek city-state and that "ultimate ends" (*zhongji mudi*) would lead to dictatorship.[134] Gu Zhun was also praised for his individualism and independent spirit in the face of the tribulations of labor and thought reform, including hunger, illness, and isolation. He hence also symbolized the quest for independent scholarship of the 1990s.

According to Xu Youyu, another well-known liberal who specializes in philosophy at CASS and who has also published on the Cultural Revolution, Gu Zhun is representative of the re-engagement with the liberalism of the 1930s and 1940s. This includes the intellectual reassessment of figures such as Hu Shi and Yin Haiguang, both of whom had been widely criticized by the CCP. Yin Haiguang had been based in Taiwan, which now served as a model for some Chinese liberals because of its democratization.[135] By the late 1990s, liberalism was receiving further attention in the media. For example, in November 1997 the influential Guangzhou-based newspaper *Nanfang zhoumo* (Southern Weekend) dedicated an entire page to an obituary for Isaiah Berlin.[136] Advocacy of a strong role for the state had been replaced by an emphasis on the role of the market in the transition to democracy.

---

[131] Friedrich A. Hayek [Hayeke], *Tongxiang nuyi de daolu* (The Road to Serfdom) (Beijing: Shangwu yinshuguan, 1962). This book was first translated into Chinese during the 1960s, but with restricted circulation. Friedrich A. Hayek [Hayeke], *Ziyou zhixu yuanli* (The Constitution of Liberty), tr. Deng Zhenglai (Beijing: Shenghuo, dushu, xinzhi sanlian shudian, 1997); Xu, "Fate of an Enlightenment," 203n14.

[132] Davies, *Worrying about China*, 157. See Gu Zhun, *Gu Zhun wenji* (Collected Works of Gu Zhun) (Guiyang: Guizhou renmin chubanshe, 1994); Gu Zhun, *Gu Zhun riji* (Gu Zhun's Diaries), ed. Chen Minzhi and Ding Dong (Beijing: Jingji ribao chubanshe, 1997).

[133] After 1949, Gu Zhun headed the Shanghai Finance and Tax Bureau for several years. On his years as an accountant, see Wen-hsin Yeh, *Shanghai Splendor: Economic Sentiments and the Making of Modern China, 1843–1949* (Berkeley: University of California Press, 2007).

[134] Gu Zhun, *Gu Zhun wenji*, 370. On democracy in the Greek city-state, see his *Xila chengbang zhidu: Du Xilashi biji* (The Greek Polis System: Notes on Reading Greek History), 2nd ed. (Beijing: Zhongguo shehui kexue chubanshe, 1986).

[135] Xu Youyu, "The Debates between Liberalism and the New Left in China since the 1990s," *Contemporary Chinese Thought* 34.3 (Spring 2003), 6–17.

[136] He, *Dictionary of the Political Thought*, 692.

History and Linearity

For critics such as Wang Hui, one of the main problems of the debate was that it was ahistorical: instead of analyzing historical factors, social conditions, or the motivations of the actors, it approached radicalism and conservatism as strategies to be either confirmed or denied. The debate ignored discussion of the true social causes of the Tiananmen demonstrations and became an ideology of modernization. The rethinking of radicalism in the early 1990s was hence not unlike the engagement with the history of socialism since the late 1970s, in which the participants carried out "critiques of its consequences instead of conducting an historical analysis."[137]

It cannot be denied that participants in the discussion of radicalism in modern Chinese history did not primarily care about historical analysis. May Fourth ideas, multifarious and complex, cannot be reduced to adherence only to a French model, as Fung rightly notes. External events, such as the Russian Revolution, also greatly affected the transition to Marxism. Singling out the Glorious Revolution and the English model obscured the effect of the American liberalism of John Dewey or the Weimar Germany model on May Fourth scholars. Also, after May Fourth, as already noted, there was a move away from the "radical" ideas of May Fourth under the Nationalist government, which supported the New Life Movement and other movements that embraced Chinese culture.[138]

The reductionist discussion of a French or English model had a historical antecedent in China: in a 1902 essay on revolution, Liang Qichao had already set apart the Glorious and French revolutions. In Liang's view, only these revolutions had led to thorough change.[139] That the Russian Revolution was pushed to the sidelines of history during the 1990s can be explained by what we have already discussed in Chapter 2, namely that the Bolshevik Revolution as a source of legitimacy had dried up following the dissolution of the Soviet Union. It was understood that the French model involved a connection among the French, Russian, Communist, and Cultural revolutions. The two "models" erased many historical complexities and the "radicalism" narrative replaced multidirectionality and contingency with linearity. Here Zhu Xueqin's criticism of the discussion is relevant. He argues that Yü Ying-shih's radicalization

---

[137] Wang, *China's New Order*, 78–84, quotation on 110; Interview with Wang Hui, Beijing, July 27, 2006.

[138] Fung, *Intellectual Foundations of Chinese Modernity*, 136–37. For details on the conservative turn since the 1930s, see chap. 3, "The Politics of Modern Chinese Conservatism," in ibid., 96–127.

[139] Liang Qichao, "Shige" (Explaining Revolution), December 14, 1902, in *Yinbing shi heji* (Collected Works from the Ice Studio), 12 vols. (Beijing: Zhonghua shuju, 1989 [reprint]), vol. 1, pt. 9, 40–45. Cited in Yü, *Chinese History and Culture*, 222–23.

scheme, for all its criticism of radicalist idealism, amounted to a "historical teleology" à la Hegel:

The first question I would like to put to Yu Ying-shih is this: how far can we really attribute the social transformation of mainland China from 1919 to 1949 to shifts in intellectual thought, if we suspend value judgments and look only at the facts? ... A second question to Yu Ying-shih would be this: Was there really an intellectual train that ran directly from Tiananmen Square of 4 May 1919 to that of 1 October 1949?[140]

Zhu highlights the part that economic, political, social, and other factors have played in the course of modern Chinese history. In addition, it was education abroad that had led intellectuals to swing back and forth between conservative and radical positions. Zhu notes the continuity of the narrative of intellectual radicalization with the debates of the 1980s, in which radicalism presented another example of the "grand narrative of cultural history."[141] In the Guangzhou-based journal *Xiandai yu chuantong* (Modernity and Tradition), Zhu further argues that the radicalism narrative used a specialist perspective of intellectual history to explain history in its totality, inspired by the centrality of historiography in Chinese culture and by Continental thought.[142]

Zhu certainly has a point here. Even though scholars such as Yü Ying-shih intended to deconstruct "neoterism" and advocate historical continuity, they nevertheless did so in the form of a scheme that relied on "stages" of radicalism, linear development, and binary *-isms*. Yü's conception of a process of stages of radicalism hence contains traces of a modern linear interpretation of history that embraces revolution in the modern sense. As Koselleck notes, the word "revolution" originally involved the idea of a return or circulation. The term had a naturalistic and transhistorical connotation because it entered politics via astronomy, where it was applied to describe the "circular movement of celestial bodies" as expressed in the title of Copernicus's *De revolutionibus orbium coelestium* (1543). Since the time of the French Revolution, however, it was stripped of its connotation of return; revolution "led forward into an unknown future."[143] In China, *geming* had referred to dynastic change before the modern period. After 1898, through Japanese translation, the word came to denote revolution in the modern sense, as drastic change. The framework of *-isms* especially confirmed this linearity, teleology, and progressivism. Beginning in the late nineteenth century, neologisms had emerged, often through Japanese translations of Western concepts. Initially used to organize the new knowledge that had entered China since the late nineteenth century,

---

[140] Zhu, "For a Chinese Liberalism," 100. [141] Ibid., 101, 102.
[142] Zhu Xueqin, "Wusi sichao yu bashi niandai, jiushi niandai" (May Fourth Trends and the 1980s and 1990s), *Xiandai yu chuantong*, no. 1 (1995), 29–37.
[143] See Koselleck's chapter on "Historical Criteria of the Modern Concept of Revolution," in *Futures Past*, 43–57, 49.

after the May Fourth Movement these concepts became modern Chinese concepts carrying the remnants of their Western, Japanese, and original Chinese meanings.[144] These -*isms* became ideological and functioned as guiding principles to transform society. Radicalism had appeared during May Fourth at a time when the Leninist organization had also become influential, thus rendering radicalism highly ideological. As for conservatism, beginning with Yan Fu it had already been understood as preservation in the interest of progress.[145]

Here, it is worth mentioning an article by Ji Guangmao (b. 1963), a researcher of art and literature initially affiliated with Shandong Normal University and later affiliated with Beijing Normal University, that is critical of this linear concept of time. In his article, Ji argues that such a concept of time had led in China to an embrace of progressivism and "only-new-ism" (*weixin zhuyi*) or a belief that only new things are valuable.[146] According to progressivism, societies permanently move in ever-better directions, and positive value is placed on the future. Ji argues that in China, both "gradualism" (*jianjin zhuyi*) and radicalism were forms of progressivism: both adhered to a linear concept of time and a positive view of the future, but gradualists advocated orderly and slow change. Conservatism envisioned historical continuity, but in China it did not discard the linearity of radicalism. Its goal remained Chinese development, progress, and prosperity. This is reminiscent of Koselleck's notion of "futures past" (*Vergangene Zukunft*): even though visions of the future by past generations were reclaimed, the present continued to be trapped in a modernization fever and attempts to design better futures. In China of the early 1990s, the point was to demonstrate that conservatives were also modernizers.

History and Morality

In spite of the embrace of linearity, history in debates of the early 1990s was also closely intertwined with morality and the place of the intellectual in Chinese society. Benjamin Schwartz has coined the concept of "unhistorical history," with Chinese history functioning as a storehouse of moral examples in historiographical practice.[147] In dynastic China, history, morality, and

---

[144] Jin and Liu, *Guannianshi yanjiu*, 7–14.
[145] Spira, *Conceptual History of Chinese -Isms*, 4–9, 160–62.
[146] Ji Guangmao, "Nanyuan yu beizhe zhijian: Cong liangpian wenzhang lüekui baoshou zhuyi yu jijin zhuyi de xunxi" (In between Opposite Directions: Taking a Quick Peek at the Message of Conservatism and Radicalism from Two Texts), *Wenyi zhengming* (Debates on Literature and Art), no. 4 (1995), 12–20.
[147] Benjamin Schwartz, "History in Chinese Culture: Some Comparative Reflections." *History and Theory* 35.4 (December 1996), 23.

culture were entwined; history was a manifestation of the *Dao*. History in this setting was not only moral, but also cyclical, as reflected in the idea of the Mandate of Heaven (*tianming*) that connected the mandate to rule to moral legitimacy and a cycle of the rise and fall of dynasties.[148] By rewriting history, it was believed that the ideal *Dao* would again become visible and the Confucian order could be restored.[149] In addition, morality and politics were connected through the Confucian examination system that had been the entry point to officialdom for centuries.

In the 1992 debate, we see traces of this connection among history, value, and culture. By organizing ideas and trends as "conservative" or "radical," it was believed that moral and cultural reconstruction could be achieved. This rewriting of history as a moral exercise also permeated the mode of historical inquiry among Chinese intellectuals abroad. Yü Ying-shih's criticism of the CCP and his liberal political sympathies are moral criticisms rather than calls for political action. The foundation of Yü's political stand is what Michael Quirin calls *Machtferne* (distance from power), or a discrepancy between his utopian political desires and his limited interest in mechanisms and institutions that could crystallize these political hopes. Yü approaches political responsibility in the form of a moral call.[150] He argues for the restoration of the cultural authority of Chinese intellectuals, which had been obliterated due to their identification with Western culture.[151]

Similarly, Lin Yü-sheng's criticism of radicalism is a moral criticism and an attempt to "reconstruct" Chinese tradition. Drawing on the American anthropologist Clifford Geertz, Lin coined the concept of the "creative transformation" of Chinese tradition, which denotes both a continuation of the May Fourth spirit and aims, such as science, democracy, and liberty, and a reinvestigation of its relation with Chinese tradition.[152] Specifically, it refers to the reorganization and reconstruction of "selected indigenous Chinese symbols, ideas, values, and modes of behavior," which will lead these elements to gain "a clear sense of cultural identity."[153] Lin sought to transform Confucian

---

[148] Luke S. W. Kwong, "The Rise of the Linear Perspective on History and Time in Late Qing China c. 1860–1911," *Past and Present* 173.1 (November 2001), 157–90.
[149] See Schneider, "Between *Dao* and History."
[150] Michael Quirin, "Yü Yingshi, das Politische und die Politik" (Yü Ying-shih, the Political, and Politics), *Minima Sinica: Zeitschrift zum Chinesischen Geist* (Minima Sinica: Journal for the Chinese Mind) 6.1 (1994), 60–64.
[151] Yü Ying-shih, "Zixu" (Preface), in Yü, *Qian Mu yu Zhongguo wenhua*, 1–6.
[152] Lin, *Zhongguo chuantong de chuangzaoxing zhuanhua*; Lin, "Reflections on the 'Creative Transformation of Chinese Tradition,'" 73–114.
[153] Lin Yü-sheng, "Radical Iconoclasm in the May Fourth Period and the Future of Chinese Liberalism," in Benjamin Schwartz, ed., *Reflections on the May Fourth Movement: A Symposium* (Cambridge, MA: East Asian Research Center, Harvard University, 1972), 23–58; Lin, "Reflections on the 'Creative Transformation of Chinese Tradition,'" 78.

humanism by uniting it with Western liberal humanism. This is a rather abstract moral explanation of the reconstruction of Chinese culture and an elitist intellectual undertaking. According to Lin, however, this cultural reconstruction involves elements other than culture and hence goes beyond the cultural determinism of the May Fourth intellectuals whom he criticizes in his book *The Crisis of Chinese Consciousness*.[154]

Mainland Chinese intellectuals also pursued a moral call in their rejection of radicalism. They distanced themselves from the "radical" cultural discourse of the 1980s and the Enlightenment tradition as part of cultural reconstruction and moral self-positioning efforts after 1989. The rigid distinction that intellectuals made between a cultural and political conservatism should be understood in this light. Cultural conservatism includes, among others, national studies, New Confucianism, and advocacies of postcolonialism and postmodernism, which will be discussed in Chapter 5 and Chapter 6, respectively.[155] This was part of an attempt of self-identification as scholars rather than intellectuals during the early 1990s. As the popularity of the 1995 book *Chen Yinke de zuihou ershi nian* (Chen Yinke's Last Twenty Years) reveals, the scholarship of figures such as Chen Yinke came to be preferred to the political engagement of Lu Xun.[156] Yü Ying-shih also motivated part of this mainland trend of scholarship on Chen Yinke through his own research on Chen during the 1980s.[157]

Chen Yinke de zuihou ershi nian contains a letter written by Chen Yinke in which he explains why he could not take up the position of director of the Second Historical Research Office that had been established in Beijing in 1954. In research, Chen posits, one should have "a free will and an independent spirit" (*ziyou de yizhi he duli de jingshen*). A predetermined Marxist-Leninist framework prevents independent research. In his letter, Chen also refers back to the obituary he had written for Wang Guowei. Wang, a scholar of Chinese history and literature who had been affiliated with the *Xueheng* journal, had committed suicide in 1927. Chen attributed his suicide not to

---

[154] Lin, "Guanyu 'Zhongguo yishi de weiji,'" 146–47.
[155] See, for example, Yang Chunshi, "Xin baoshou zhuyi yu xin lixing zhuyi: Jiushi niandai renwen sichao pipan" (Neoconservatism and Neorationalism: A Critique of Trends in the Humanities in the 1990s), in *ZFL*, 486–92; Meng Fanhua, "Wenhua bengkui shidai de taowang yu guiyi: Jiushi niandai wenhua de xin baoshou zhuyi jingshen" (The Exile and Conversion of the Era of Cultural Collapse: The Neoconservative Spirit of the Culture of the 1990s), in *ZFL*, 287–92; Ye Wen, "Ying qubie zhengzhi de baoshou zhuyi he wenhua de baoshou zhuyi" (One Should Distinguish between Political Conservatism and Cultural Conservatism), *Ershiyi shiji*, no. 40 (April 1997), 136–367.
[156] Lu, *Chen Yinke de zuihou ershi nian*.
[157] In 1983 and 1984, Yü published a series of articles on Chen Yinke (incorporated into a book published in 1984) that triggered official responses from mainland China. See Josephine Chiu-Duke and Michael S. Duke, "Editorial Note," in Yü, *Chinese History and Culture*, xxin12.

Wang's loyalty to the imperial house or to his conflict with Luo Zhenyu, as was widely assumed, but to Wang's struggle for independent scholarship.[158]

Intellectual repositioning also involved the re-establishment of academic norms and scholarship, and the debate on radicalism and conservatism should also be read through this lens. New academic journals, such as *Xueren* and *Yuandao*, both established in the early 1990s and often designated as "conservative" journals, reflected this new attention to scholarship.[159] The title of *Yuandao*, edited by Chen Ming of the Institute of World Religions of CASS and established in October 1994, refers to an essay with the same title by the Tang philosopher Han Yu (768–824), a critic of Buddhism and Daoism and a defender of orthodox Confucianism. The reference to Han Yu's essay was hence intended to identify with his mission of restoring the Confucian Way. The opening sentence of the first issue reads, "Shi shang zhi, zhi yu dao. Jintian de dao shi shenme" (The scholar values ideals, ideals are in the *dao*. What is today's *dao?*).[160]

The book series *Xueren* (1991–2000), edited by Chen Pingyuan, Wang Hui, and Wang Shouchang, also set out to "retrieve the history of modern Chinese scholarship."[161] In journals such as *Xueren* and the Hong Kong journal *Zhongguo shehui kexue jikan*, scholars debated the question of "academic standardization" in response to the sociopolitical orientation in the cultural discussions of the 1980s.[162] Those who rejected radicalism and its "romanticist" epistemology argued for a "sympathetic understanding" of a cultural conservative attitude, with a rift emerging between those advocating continued public engagement of "thought" and those advocating specialized research or "scholarship."[163] For example, Wang Yuanhua argues that thought and scholarship should not be separated but should enrich each other.[164] Zhu Xueqin

---

[158] Lu, *Chen Yinke de zuihou ershi nian*, 111–12. On the letter and Chen's obituary for Wang Guowei, see also Schneider, "Bridging the Gap," 139–40 and 137n56.

[159] Davies, "Self-Made Maps," 19. Wang Hui argues against calling all those associated with *Xueren* "conservatives." See Wang, *China's New Order*, 202n35.

[160] *Yuandao* 1 (October 1994) (Beijing: Zhongguo shehui kexue chubanshe), 1.

[161] Wang, "Introduction: Minds of the Nineties," 17. See Chen Pingyuan, Wang Hui, and Wang Shouchang, eds., *Xueren*, no. 1 (1991).

[162] Tang, "Some Reflections on New Confucianism," 125.

[163] Xu, "Fate of an Enlightenment," 195. For some of the main articles in this discussion, see *Xiandai yu chuantong*, no. 6 (1995) and no. 7 (1995); *Zhongguo shuping* (China Book Review), no. 5 (1995) and *Dushu*, no. 6 (1997). See also Deng Zhenglai, ed., *Zhongguo xueshu guifanhua taolun wenxuan* (Selections from the Debate on Chinese Academic Standardization) (Beijing: Falü chubanshe, 2004).

[164] Wang Yuanhua, "Guanyu jinnian de fansi dawen" (Answering Questions about Reflections in Recent Years), *Xueshu jilin* (Academic Collection), no. 3 (Shanghai: Shanghai yuandong chubanshe, 1998).

also criticizes the negation of the 1980s due to the importance of scholarship, as opposed to thought, during the 1990s.[165]

The discussants also disagreed about the meanings of "scholarship" and "modern Chinese scholarship," about which works should be included in the "modern scholarship classics," and how thought, scholarship, and learning (*xuewen*) related to one another. Could Lu Xun's *The True Story of Ah Q* be included in scholarship?[166] The debate revisited previous debates of Han versus Song learning during the Qing dynasty and among different schools of Neo-Confucianism during the Song dynasty, but it also reflected differences among contemporary intellectuals regarding "their views on continuing tradition and walking toward the world, seeking knowledge or expressing concepts, and appreciating history or worrying about the present."[167]

At this juncture, the 1992 debate was not, and could not, be a critical engagement with Chinese modernity, but it nevertheless exposed the contradictions in the official ideology and paved the way for later discussions that went beyond procedural matters. Because it was conducted in a binary framework of *-isms*, which were programmatic "concepts of movement" in a Chinese context, a linear view of history still prevailed in the debate. However, due to the effect of the market, the debate included a positive re-evaluation of conservatism in relation to liberalism after renewed reform—Burke had befriended Hayek. Rather than dismissing the debate as ahistorical, we should read it as an attempt by Chinese intellectuals to come to terms with 1989 and 1992 and to re-establish academic norms. In the words of Zhu Xueqin, in order to forget in the present, intellectuals produced a "narrative of forgetting" in the past that overemphasized the role of ideas.[168] This overemphasis on ideas, intellectuals, and morality came to exist in an uneasy relation with an increasingly commercialized society, to which we will turn next.

---

[165] Zhu, "Wusi sichao yu bashi niandai, jiushi niandai," 35–36. This division regarding the role of the scholar was also present in the "new *guoxue*": those who engaged in scholarship on Wu Mi and Mei Guangdi, for example, did not refer to Chen Yinke and his advocacy of scholarship detached from politics. See Schneider, "Bridging the Gap," 138–41.

[166] Zheng and Jia, "Jiushi niandai yilai Zhongguo," 55–56.

[167] Ge Zhaoguang, *An Intellectual History of China: Volume One*, tr. Michael S. Duke and Josephine Chiu-Duke (Leiden: Brill, 2014), 16.

[168] Zhu, "Wusi sichao yu bashi niandai, jiushi niandai," 29–37.

5 Chen Lai and the Max Weber Dilemma

> The Chinese in all probability would be quite capable, probably more capable than the Japanese, of assimilating capitalism.
>
> Max Weber, *The Religion of China*

During the 1980s, in debates on neo-authoritarianism Chinese scholars were already referring to the so-called Four Mini Dragons as a model for China's economic, political, and cultural trajectory. The capitalist development of Japan, as well as of other East Asian countries in the 1970s, all of which had Confucian heritages, led sociologists, philosophers, scholars of religion, and area specialists to debate questions related to an East Asian development model. Drawn to these international debates on the relation between Confucianism and capitalism, and amid China's ongoing economic reforms, beginning in the 1980s Chinese scholars began to discuss the place of Confucianism in modern society.

On mainland China, this renewed interest in Confucianism, referred to as "*ruxue* fever" (*ruxue re*),[1] intersected with the rejection of the cultural radicalism of the May Fourth Movement following the seventieth anniversary of May Fourth in May 1989 and the crackdown on the Tiananmen demonstrations in June 1989. Intellectually, the "culture fever" of the 1980s, as covered in the previous chapter, facilitated debates on Confucianism and Chinese culture.[2] Especially noteworthy was the Academy of Chinese Culture that was established in the early 1980s by scholars affiliated with Peking University. As Xu Jilin notes, "Their efforts [i.e., by the academy] provided the bedrock on which the 'craze for national learning' of the 1990s developed."[3] After the 1992 renewal of the reforms, the matter of the place of Confucianism

---

[1] For the distinction between the Chinese terms *ru, rujia, rujiao,* and *ruxue,* see Makeham, *Lost Soul.*

[2] Hon, "Introduction." On the "culture fever" and New Confucianism, see Song Xianlin, "Reconstructing the Confucian Ideal in 1980s China: The 'Culture Craze' and New Confucianism," in John Makeham, ed. *New Confucianism: A Critical Examination* (Houndmills: Palgrave Macmillan, 2003), 81–104.

[3] Xu, "Fate of an Enlightenment," 194.

in an increasingly commercialized and individualist society came to the fore.[4] Once more, foreign thinkers introduced to China during the culture fever of the 1980s figured prominently in the Chinese discussions on Confucianism, but this time the emphasis was not on Edmund Burke or Friedrich Hayek but rather on the German sociologist and philosopher Max Weber. A "Weber fever" facilitated discussion on the connection between Confucianism and capitalist development and its implications for socialist modernization and East Asia.

The key figure in this chapter is Chen Lai (b. 1952), a philosopher based in the Philosophy Department of Peking University at the time. Chen's writings discuss May Fourth radicalism and the place of Confucianism in a rapidly modernizing China. Chen had studied with Confucian philosopher Zhang Dainian (1909–2004), who supported the relevance of traditional Chinese philosophy under Marxism. Under Zhang's supervision at Peking University, Chen Lai wrote a dissertation on the Neo–Confucian philosopher Zhu Xi (1130–1200).[5] However, Chen also studied with Tu Wei-ming and regarded Tu as a major intellectual influence. Hence, Chen's writings reflect the growing intellectual exchanges between scholars in mainland China and China-born scholars in the United States.

Central to this chapter are the themes of Chen Lai's place in the broader discourse on New Confucianism and May Fourth radicalism, how interactions with Tu Wei-ming shaped this discussion, and Chen's reading of May Fourth debates through a Weberian lens. The chapter argues that Chen's plea for Confucian values in response to May Fourth's "cultural radicalism" was based not only on their inherent values but also on the positive part they could play in Chinese modernization. Like Tu Wei-ming, Chen saw Confucianism both as an antidote to the ills of modernization and as compatible with modernization. The modernization (or "Weberization") of Confucianism was hence another manifestation of Koselleck's "futures past," or the projection of change into the future.

Accompanying the rise of the so-called "new *guoxue*," Chen Lai re-evaluated "conservative" Republican scholars such as Zhang Junmai, Du Yaquan, and Liang Qichao, and argued that they had been moderns with a global and cosmopolitan outlook. They too had been modernizers exposed to transnational knowledge flows. In addition, Chen's "cultural conservatism" and his moral interpretation of Confucianism are also connected to his normative

---

[4] In addition to these factors, Makeham also mentions the movement for the "Sinicization of sociology" in Hong Kong and Taiwan during the early 1980s as a factor contributing to the Confucian revival. See Makeham, *Lost Soul*, 42–46.

[5] Frédéric Wang, "Le confucianisme et la Chine actuelle: l'héritage de Zhang Dainian (1909–2004)" (Confucianism and China Today: The Legacy of Zhang Dainian (1909–2004))," *Histoire et Missions Chrétiennes* (History and Christian Missions), no. 2 (2011), 69–87, www.cairn.info/revue-histoire-monde-et-cultures-religieuses1-2011-2-page-69.htm.

reading of the meaning of "intellectual" as a scholar devoid of political and commercial interests. In fact, Chen's reading of Weber was also very much entangled with the question of intellectual independence: Chen's criticism of "instrumental rationality" was a criticism of the politicization of culture.

Confucianism, New *Guoxue*, and Socialism

Before we move on to the so-called New Confucianism that flourished in 1980s and 1990s China, we first need to outline the rehabilitation of Confucianism and the rise of "new *guoxue*" in reform China. The Confucian revival during the reform period is part of a wider phenomenon that includes the official rehabilitation and commercialization of Confucianism as well as academic discussions on the topic.[6] Although some aspects of this rehabilitation suited the economic reform project on mainland China, as with neoconservatism, it also existed in tension with socialism.

Since the late 1970s, the reassessment of Confucianism occurred through media endorsements and new forms of institutionalization, including transnational organizations and conferences. As early as August 12, 1978, the word "Confucius" was, for the first time, mentioned positively in the official *Guangming ribao* and said to be in need of reassessment.[7] In 1980 the Kongzi Yanjiu Zhongxin (Confucius Research Center) was established in Qufu. This was followed by a number of conferences and celebrations of the rites occurring throughout the 1980s. Some significant developments include a 1985 symposium on Confucius held in Beijing, the same year that Tu Wei-ming was a visiting scholar at Peking University and when the Zhonghua Kongzi Yanjiusuo (China Confucius Research Institute) was established. Also noteworthy are the 1987 joint Sino-Singaporean international conference on Confucianism and East Asian development and the 1989 national symposium on Confucianism that coincided with the 2,540th anniversary of the birth of the sage.[8] Singapore featured prominently in bringing together scholars and publishing relevant works through its Institute of East Asian Philosophies, which, during the 1980s, served to promote Confucianism. Journals in Taiwan and the United

---

[6] Daniel Bell, *China's New Confucianism: Politics and Everyday Life in a Changing Society* (Princeton, NJ: Princeton University Press, 2008); Sébastien Billioud and Joël Thoraval, *The Sage and the People: The Confucian Revival in China* (Oxford: Oxford University Press, 2015); Kenneth J. Hammond and Jeffrey L. Richey, eds., *The Sage Returns: Confucian Revival in Contemporary China* (Albany: State University of New York Press, 2015); Guy Alitto, ed., *Contemporary Confucianism in Thought and Action* (Berlin: Springer, 2015).
[7] Wang, *High Culture Fever*, 68.
[8] Edward L. Davis, ed., *Encyclopedia of Contemporary Chinese Culture* (London: Routledge, 2005), 426.

States as well as academies and foundations in China also helped to shape new forms of collaboration.[9]

Such new forms of institutionalized interactions continued during the 1990s. In 1994, the Guoji Ruxue Lianhehui (International Confucian Association [ICA]) was established. This association included members from mainland China, Taiwan, Hong Kong, Singapore, Korea, Japan, the United States, and elsewhere. Gu Mu, vice chairman of the Chinese People's Political Consultative Conference and former vice premier of the State Council, was its president, with Singapore's former prime minister, Lee Kuan Yew, serving as honorary president. Scholars such as Tu Wei-ming, Tang Yijie, and Li Zehou were among its board members, and it received funding from Hong Kong business magnates.[10] In the same year, the opening ceremony of the conference that marked the 2,545th birthday of Confucius was attended by, among others, high officials such as Gu Mu and Li Ruihuan as well as Lee Kuan Yew.[11] This official endorsement was part of an effort to construct a socialist spiritual civilization that involved a re-evaluation of traditional Chinese culture.

For the early 1990s, we need to single out the promotion of "national learning" or *guoxue*. On August 16, 1993, an article was published in *Renmin ribao* on the occasion of the publication of the first volume of "national learning research" by the Traditional Chinese Culture Research Center of Peking University that had been established in 1992.[12] This was remarkable because it was the first long article in *Renmin ribao* to report on Peking University since the crackdown on the Tiananmen uprising.[13] In this article, national learning is praised as part of the construction of a socialist spiritual civilization. Two days later, the *Renmin ribao* devoted a front-page article to the topic.[14] In 1994, a third long article on the same topic also appeared in *Renmin ribao*.[15] In addition to other articles in official newspapers, several

---

[9] Makeham, *Lost Soul*, 26–27, 42. The Institute of East Asian Philosophies was active between 1983 and 1989. In 1992, it was replaced by the Institute of East Asian Political Economy (and later the East Asian Institute, or EAI).

[10] Sheldon Hsiao-peng Lu, "Global POSTmodernIZATION: The Intellectual, the Artist, and China's Condition," in Arif Dirlik and Zhang Xudong, eds., *Postmodernism and China* (Durham, NC: Duke University Press, 2000), 150, 173 fn11.

[11] Wm. Theodore de Bary, "The New Confucianism in Beijing," *American Scholar* 64.2 (January 1995), 175.

[12] Bi Quanzhong, "Guoxue, zai yanyuan you qiaoran xingqi: Beijing daxue Zhongguo chuantong wenhua yanjiu sanji" (The Quiet Rise of National Studies on the Old Campus: Random Notes on Chinese Traditional Culture Research at Peking University), *Renmin ribao*, August 16, 1993, 3.

[13] Liu Qingfeng, "The Topography of Intellectual Culture in 1990s Mainland China: A Survey," tr. Gloria Davies, in Davies, ed., *Voicing Concerns*, 54.

[14] Wenzhe, "Jiuyuan le, guoxue!" (National Studies, It Has Been a Long Time!), *Renmin ribao*, August 18, 1993, 1.

[15] Ji Xianlin, Liu Junning, and Pang Pu, "Zouchu chuantong yanjiu chuantong" (Out of the Traditional Research Tradition), *Renmin ribao*, December 6, 1994, 1.

Beijing broadcasting stations aired special programs on national learning, leading to the term "national learning fever" (*guoxue re*).[16] According to Chen Lai, however, this represented a mere "talking about national studies fever" (*shuo guoxue re de re*).[17]

The official endorsement of national learning was possible because it was not clearly delineated in terms of either intellectual stance or academic trend. Instead, it was marked by a revival of interest in the non-Marxist and non-liberal approaches of academics and journalists of the Republican period. This new *guoxue* included research on national essence scholars, on the debates on Eastern and Western cultures and the 1923 debate on Science and Metaphysics, on Yan Fu and Liang Qichao, on the *Xueheng* group, and on New Confucianism between the 1920s and 1940s.[18] Especially the 1990s witnessed the reassessment of these "conservative" Republican scholars.

Historically, *guoxue* had been preceded by the Japanese *Kokugaku*, which emerged during the Tokugawa period (1603–1867) and peaked during the Meiji Restoration (1868–1912). It was "a mode of scholarship, an epistemology, a textual tradition, a repository of native learning, a guardian of national spirit, an inquiry into a complicated past shaped by forces both local and global."[19] *Guoxue* reflects the entanglement of history, scholarship, culture, philosophy, and morality in a Chinese framework, which does not lend itself to neat disciplinary distinctions.[20] The journal *Yuandao*, for example, established in 1994 and linked to national studies, promoted traditional Chinese culture by publishing primarily on *ruxue*. Other newly founded journals that published on *ruxue* include *Guoxue yanjiu* (National Studies Research), *Zhongguo wenhua* (Chinese Culture), *Xueren*, and *Yuanxue*.[21] Here, commercial interests intersected with scholarly enterprises in the form of financial support from businesses for research projects, journals, and conferences. For example, the journal *Zhongguo wenhua* received two hundred thousand yuan per year from entrepreneur Xie Yongjian and *Yuandao* was funded by a Hainan business.[22]

---

[16] Chen Lai notes that, apart from publications in leading newspapers, students at Peking University also organized events such as National Learning Month. Broadcasting stations featured items on the topic as well, sometimes inviting Peking University professors to answer questions from the audience. Interview with Chen Lai, Beijing, August 10, 2005.

[17] Chen Lai, "'Guoxue re' yu chuantong wenhua yanjiu de wenti" (The "National Studies Craze" and the Problem of Research on Traditional Culture), *Kongzi yanjiu* (Confucius Research), no. 2 (1995), 4–6, 5.

[18] Schneider, "Bridging the Gap," 129–44.

[19] Arif Dirlik, "Guest Editor's Introduction," *China Perspectives*, no. 1 (2011), 2.

[20] This is also why, according to Dirlik, the development of modern academic disciplines may have been detrimental to the development of *guoxue*. See Dirlik, *Culture and History in Postrevolutionary China*, 263–65.

[21] Makeham, *Lost Soul*, 67.   [22] Tang, "Some Reflections on New Confucianism," 128.

Although promotion of traditional Chinese culture suited official efforts to construct a socialist spiritual civilization, it was also subject to criticism because, as a value system, it could pose a threat to socialism. *Guoxue* was also a nod to "conservative" scholars of the Republican period, and debates on the topic, as discussed in the introduction, could also involve the defense of intellectual autonomy. Especially some scholars associated with the journal *Xueheng* (Critical Review, 1922–33) represented ideals of independent scholarship in early 1990s China. For these reasons, *guoxue* could both be an opportunity and a threat from an official perspective. In June 1994, for example, articles criticizing "national studies" and the move away from socialism appeared in the journal *Zhexue yanjiu*. Also in 1994, Hu Sheng, Marxist scholar and head of CASS, expressed approval of such criticism in the journal *Liaowang* (Outlook), which led to further debates between supporters and opponents of such criticism.[23] In spite of these tensions, however, the emergence of new foundations and associations that facilitated scholarly interaction and the rehabilitation of Confucianism and Republican scholars created a favorable climate for research on Confucianism beginning in the 1980s. The latter would be transformed into New Confucianism on mainland China during the second half of the 1980s.

New Confucianism and the Role of "Cultural China"

At roundtables and conferences, overseas Chinese scholars and scholars from Singapore, Hong Kong, Taiwan, and the United States exchanged ideas. In this climate, publications by New Confucians of the so-called second generation, which will be explained below, became popular.[24] The deaths of New Confucians Tang Junyi (1909–78) and Xu Fuguan (1903–82) also fueled renewed interest in New Confucianism.[25] In addition to such transnational interactions, official support for major Chinese research projects and publications on New Confucianism since the mid-1980s were crucial to create conditions for academic debates on the topic.[26] In 1986, New Confucianism was selected as one of seventy-five "national research topics." This proved to be crucial to the transformation of Confucianism into New Confucianism on mainland China.[27]

---

[23] Ibid., 127.
[24] On New Confucianism, see, for example, Umberto Bresciani, *Reinventing Confucianism: The New Confucian Movement* (Taipei: Taipei Ricci Institute for Chinese Studies, 2001); Makeham, *New Confucianism*; Makeham, *Lost Soul*; N. Serena Chan, *The Thought of Mou Zongsan* (Leiden: Brill, 2011); Sébastien Billioud, *Thinking through Confucian Modernity: A Study of Mou Zongsan's Moral Metaphysics* (Leiden: Brill, 2012).
[25] Makeham, "The Retrospective Creation of New Confucianism," in Makeham, *New Confucianism*, 33–34.
[26] Ibid.; Hon, "Introduction," xi–xxix.
[27] Song, "Reconstructing the Confucian Ideal in 1980s China," 86.

New Confucianism (*xiandai xin rujia, dangdai xin rujia*, or *dangdai xin ruxue*) is a reinterpretation of the Neo-Confucianism that flourished during the Song (907–1279) and Ming (1368–1644) dynasties. Although some advocates trace the movement back to the early twentieth century, Makeham argues that the movement did not become a distinct school of thought until the late 1970s.[28] Whereas Chen Lai does not belong to this group, many of Chen's arguments reflect the core pursuits of the New Confucians.[29] The two main schools in Song and Ming Neo-Confucianism are, first, the "heart-mind centered learning" (*xinxue*) of Lu Xiangshan (1139–92) and Wang Yangming (1472–1529) and, second, the "Principle-centered Learning" (*lixue*) of Cheng Yi (1033–1107) and Zhu Xi (1130–1200). According to the Lu-Wang school, the universe is identical to the mind, and the unity between man and heaven is realized through the development of innate knowledge of the good. According to the Cheng-Zhu school, the principles of the universe must be grasped through an "investigation of things," which in turn enables realization of one's good nature. In spite of the differences between the two schools, they are both about ethical cultivation.

This is the Confucianism that twentieth-century scholars, drawing on readings of Kant and Hegel, reinterpreted. A core concept from Neo-Confucianism that twentieth-century New Confucians elaborated upon is the so-called doctrine of "learning of the mind and nature" (*xinxing zhi xue*). As Chang Hao explains, for the New Confucians nature (*xing*) must be understood in a metaphysical sense; it implies a belief in inner transcendence. This inner transcendence is connected with the outer transcendence of heaven (*tian*), and together they constitute the "unity between man and heaven" (*tianren heyi*). Another critical concept is *ren* (benevolence, humaneness), which is actualized through self-cultivation. Having become an "inner sage" (*neisheng*), one must rise above this moral cultivation by taking part in the outer world and by becoming an "outer king" (*waiwang*).[30]

Tu Wei-ming, as discussed in the previous chapter because of his rejection of the "Enlightenment mentality," was influential in the New Confucian revival on mainland China. Tu had studied under Mou Zongsan (1909–95) and was one of the main exponents of New Confucianism in North America, sometimes referred to as "Boston Confucianism."[31] He spent six months as a

---

[28] See Makeham, *Lost Soul*, 25–53. On the New Confucian lineage and the notion of *daotong* (the interconnecting thread of the Way), see his "The New Daotong," in *Lost Soul*, 55–78.
[29] Makeham, *Lost Soul*, 68.
[30] Chang, "New Confucianism and the Intellectual Crisis," 289–96. For the development of Neo-Confucianism and different views on the nature of Song learning, see Yü, Chinese *History and Culture*, 1–39.
[31] Bresciani, *Reinventing Confucianism*, 411. Tu sometimes describes himself as a promotor of Confucianism rather than as a New Confucian. See Makeham, "Retrospective Creation of New

lecturer in the Philosophy Department of Peking University in 1985. During his time in China, Tu lectured throughout the country on what he called "the third epoch of Confucianism," an idea that some consider to have triggered the New Confucian revival in China.[32] Following Mou Zongsan, the first epoch was that of Confucius, Mencius, and Xunzi, and the second epoch of Confucianism referred to the Neo-Confucianism of the Song and Ming dynasties. The third epoch was contemporary Confucianism. Tu Wei-ming expanded this theory to a model of development for humanity as a whole: it was the revival of Confucianism at the periphery that would restore the damage done to Confucianism on mainland China.[33]

This was in accordance with his idea of a "Cultural China," in which scholars outside mainland China played a vital part in the reconceptualization of Chinese cultural identity. According to Tu, a relevant meeting was the 1988 International Symposium on *Ruxue*, held at the Institute of East Asian Philosophies in Singapore. In addition to overseas scholars such as Tu Wei-ming and Lin Yü-sheng, mainland scholars included, among others, Chen Lai, Bao Zunxin, Gan Yang, Fang Keli, Jin Guantao, and Tang Yijie. Even though the "Cultural China" movement was unsuccessful at this point in time, Tu Wei-ming's ideas about Confucianism resonated with scholars in China.[34]

Many of the discussions among scholars of New Confucianism were directed at identifying who could be considered a New Confucian. In a broad sense, New Confucianism included those twentieth-century Chinese intellectuals who supported the Confucian tradition. Tu Wei-ming makes a distinction among three "generations" of New Confucians, including Liang Shuming (1893–1988), Ma Yifu (1883–1967), Xiong Shili (1885–1968), Zhang Junmai (Carson Zhang, 1887–1969), Feng Youlan (1895–1990), He Lin (1902–92), and Qian Mu (1895–1990) as members of the first generation from 1921 to 1949. The second generation, from 1950 to 1979, includes Fang Dongmei (Thomé H. Fang, 1899–1977), Tang Junyi, Xu Fuguan, and Mou Zongsan. Finally, the third generation, from 1980 to the present, consists of Cheng Zhongying (b. 1935), Liu Shu-hsien (b. 1934), Tu Wei-ming, and Yü Ying-shih, of whom only Liu Shu-hsien and Tu Wei-ming belong to the Xiong Shili lineage.[35]

Confucianism," 41. On "Boston Confucianism," see Robert Cummings Neville, *Boston Confucianism: Portable Tradition in the Late-Modern World* (Albany: State University of New York Press, 2000).

[32] Bresciani, *Reinventing Confucianism*, 423. Tu Wei-ming had already visited China in 1978; in 1980, he spent nine months at Beijing Normal University. See Makeham, *Lost Soul*, 43.

[33] See Tu Wei-ming, *Ruxue disanqi fazhan de qianjing wenti: Dalu jiangxue, wennan, he taolun* (Prospective Issues in the Third Epoch of Confucianism: Mainland Lectures, Questions, and Discussions) (Taipei: Lianjing chuban shiye gongsi, 1989).

[34] Makeham, *Lost Soul*, 22–23, 40.   [35] Bresciani, *Reinventing Confucianism*, 23.

However, Yü Ying-shih has famously stated that his teacher Qian Mu was not a New Confucian because he did not reinterpret Confucianism and was a historian instead of a philosopher.[36] In a narrow sense, New Confucianism refers to the philosophical school of Xiong Shili and his students, Tang Junyi, Xu Fuguan, and Mou Zongsan.[37] Yü Ying-shih employs a three-tiered distinction, with those who have offered new interpretations of Confucianism as a middle layer in between the broad and narrow definitions.[38]

Vital for discussions on Confucianism in the mainland during the 1980s is the fact that the ideas of the New Confucians of the 1950s and 1960s, who had left mainland China and were based in Hong Kong and Taiwan, regained prominence in China only during the reform era. Both Tang Junyi and Qian Mu, the latter Yü Ying-shih's teacher, were involved in the 1949 establishment of New Asia College in Hong Kong. During the 1960s and 1970s, Mou Zongsan and Xu Fuguan also taught at New Asia College. Yü Ying-shih's lecture on radicalism and conservatism that was delivered at New Asia College represented a symbolic nod to the movement to preserve Chinese culture outside of Communist China before the period of reform and opening up.

In a 1958 document that has generally been regarded as the "manifesto" of New Confucianism, the "Declaration on Behalf of Chinese Culture Respectfully Announced to the People of the World," authors Mou Zongsan, Tang Junyi, Xu Fuguan, and Zhang Junmai argue that the core of Chinese culture is the doctrine of *xinxing*, or the "conformity of heaven and man in virtue."[39] They reject the use of external standards to evaluate Chinese culture and criticize the "feverish pursuit of progress" in the West.[40] The authors envision a modernization that includes science and democracy as well as Confucian ethics. Some have interpreted the manifesto to be a continuation of the 1934 movement for "cultural construction on a Chinese basis" (*Zhongguo benwei de wenhua jianshe*) because they both issue a plea for the continued importance of Chinese culture in the modern world.[41] In reform China, this mid-twentieth-century re-evaluation of Chinese culture gained new meaning as

---

[36] See Yü Ying-shih, "Qian Mu yu xin rujia" (Quan Mu and the New Confucians), in Yü, *Qian Mu yu Zhongguo wenhua*, 30–90. See also Makeham, "Retrospective Creation of New Confucianism," 36.

[37] Bresciani, *Reinventing Confucianism*, iv–v. For contestations regarding who should be regarded as a New Confucian, see Makeham, "Retrospective Creation of New Confucianism," 34–36.

[38] Makeham, "Retrospective Creation of New Confucianism," 38–39.

[39] For an English version of the manifesto, see Zhang Junmai, "A Manifesto for a Re-appraisal of Sinology and Reconstruction of Chinese Culture," in Carsun Chang [Zhang Junmai], *The Development of Neo-Confucian Thought*, 2 vols. (New York: Bookman Associates, 1957–62), 2.455–83, 2.464. The manifesto was published in the 1958 New Year issues of the journals *Zaisheng* (Renaissance) and *Minzhu pinglun* (Democratic Tribune).

[40] Chang, *The Development of Neo-Confucian Thought*, 2.476.

[41] Davis, *Encyclopedia of Contemporary Chinese Culture*, 425.

mainland scholars reflected on the relation between tradition and modernity. One of the most prominent scholars in this regard is philosopher Chen Lai, then based at Peking University.

Chen Lai is not a New Confucian in the sense that Tu Wei-ming is. He belongs to a different generation of scholars and his teachers are not all considered New Confucians. In addition, compared to Tu Wei-ming, he is much less publicly involved in the New Confucian project. However, like the New Confucians, Chen Lai is convinced that core Confucian values can foster community in an environment of increased social rationalization. Chen Lai thinks of himself as being intellectually influenced by Tu Wei-ming, to whom mainland New Confucians attribute a key part in the revival of Confucianism in China. Chen Lai was at Peking University during the same time that Tu Wei-ming was a visiting scholar there in 1985. Between 1986 and 1988, Chen Lai was a visiting scholar at Harvard University, where Tu Wei-ming was a professor in the Department of East Asian Languages and Civilizations.[42]

Chen Lai, Confucianism, and May Fourth

This chapter draws on Chen Lai's writings from the late 1980s and early 1990s, published in the main intellectual journals. Many of these writings were collected in the 2006 volume *Chuantong yu xiandai: Renwen zhuyi de shijie* (Tradition and Modernity: The Scope of Humanism).[43] Central themes in Chen's articles include the autonomy versus politicization of culture, the historical continuity of Chinese tradition, and the particularity versus universality of Confucian values. The term "humanism" in the book's title must be understood in relation to Chen Lai's interpretation of Confucianism as "a human way rather than a way of the spirits."[44] According to Chen, since ancient times *rujia* culture has undergone a process of "humanization" and "rationalization," in which magic and religious elements have been replaced by the cultivation of spirituality in education and rites.[45] The term "humanism" also refers to the New Confucian interpretation of Confucianism as an ethical system in which the core aspect is, in the words of Tu Wei-ming, "how we learn to be human."[46] For Tu Wei-ming, Confucianism is a "religio-philosophy" and its core element is *ren*, which Tu translates as "human-relatedness."[47]

---

[42] Chen Lai was also at Harvard in 1997 and 2006–7, when Tu Wei-ming was director of the Harvard-Yenching Institute (1996–2008).
[43] Chen Lai, *Chuantong yu xiandai: Renwen zhuyi de shijie* (Tradition and Modernity: The Scope of Humanism) (Beijing: Beijing daxue chubanshe, 2006) (hereafter cited as *CYX*).
[44] Makeham, *Lost Soul*, 335.   [45] Ibid., 286–87.
[46] Tu Wei-ming, *Confucian Ethics Today: The Singapore Challenge* (Singapore: Curriculum Development Institute of Singapore, Federal Publications, 1984), 4.
[47] Neville, *Boston Confucianism*, 56–57; Makeham, *Lost Soul*, 280.

Chen Lai uses the term "humanity" in response to what he perceives as "cultural radicalism"; the original title of his book even contained the subtitle "A Critique of Cultural Radicalism."[48]

Relevant for our purposes is Chen's criticism of "cultural radicalism" with respect to the May Fourth Movement and how this intersected with the reassessment of Confucianism on mainland China. To grasp the implications of criticism of May Fourth "radicalism," we must first understand how it relates to earlier interpretations of the movement. In a well-known 1986 piece, Li Zehou addresses the relationship between the "Enlightenment" (*qimeng*) agenda of the so-called New Culture Movement (*xin wenhua yundong*) that began in 1917 and the patriotic anti-imperialist movement, seeking to "save the nation" (*jiuguo*), that culminated in the protests of May Fourth. Li Zehou argues that the national crisis repressed the pursuit of liberty, democracy, equality, and human rights; because of this crisis, the revolutionary struggle of "basic solutions" was substituted for gradual action.[49] Hence Li Zehou highlights the tensions between "Enlightenment" and nationalism, which were also present in earlier interpretations.

Chinese liberals such as Hu Shi considered the May Fourth Movement to be a Renaissance similar to that in Europe because of its promotion of new literature, freedom, reason, and humanist values. Others interpreted it as a "Chinese version of the French Enlightenment" because of currents such as rationalism and naturalism.[50] However, in the official Chinese interpretation, as put forward by Mao Zedong, May Fourth was an anti-imperialist and antifeudalist patriotic movement that paved the way for the birth of the CCP and the beginning of "new democracy."[51] Even though the CCP referred to May Fourth, it always preserved a clear separation between the "'correct' Communist line" that arose out of the movement and the "bourgeois 'deviations'" among those who joined the KMT ranks. During the 1990s, however, following the emphasis on patriotic education and nationalism, this separation was somewhat downgraded.[52] International scholarship on May Fourth had been mindful of these tensions among its various agendas. In his classic account of the May Fourth Movement, Tse-tsung Chow outlines both the

---

[48] In Chinese: *Wenhua jijin zhuyi pipan*. Interview with Chen Lai, Beijing, August 10, 2005.
[49] Li Zehou, "Qimeng yu jiuwang," 36.
[50] Chow, *May Fourth Movement*, 339, 341. Whereas Chow associates both "Renaissance" and "Enlightenment" with liberal positions, Yü argues that Marxists first applied the term "Enlightenment" to May Fourth to launch a "New Enlightenment Movement." For Yü, the term "Enlightenment" refers to the Marxist project. See Yü, *Chinese History and Culture*, 200–206, and 214–15n1.
[51] Ibid., 2.347–55. See Mao Zedong, "The May Fourth Movement," May 1939, in *Selected Works of Mao Zedong* (Peking: Foreign Languages Press, 1965), 2.237–40.
[52] Edward Vickers, "Museums and Nationalism in Contemporary China," *Compare* 37.3 (2007), 370–71.

intellectual and sociopolitical aspects of the movement as well as its complexity.[53] Questioning the coherence of the movement, Vera Schwarcz, like Li Zehou, notes the tensions between nationalism and Enlightenment during May Fourth.[54] Other studies on the main intellectual figures, including, for example, that by Jerome Grieder on Hu Shi and the liberal aspects of the movement, depict its failure as an intellectual revolution.[55]

Chinese reflections on May Fourth in the 1990s criticized the movement due to its underlying attitude toward Chinese tradition generally and toward Confucianism specifically. The criticism of "Enlightenment" as antitraditionalism did, however, not represent a mere return to a nationalist or traditionalist interpretation of the movement, as was the case under the conservative KMT wing. Chiang Kai-shek, for example, embraced the nationalist aspects of the movement, but he rejected its criticism of tradition and acceptance of foreign ideas.[56] During the late 1980s and 1990s, Chinese scholars criticized the antitraditional agenda of the May Fourth Movement, but at the same time they highlighted the key function of intellectual exchanges in the formation of May Fourth ideas. Conservatives of the May Fourth period, they argued, were also progressives with a worldly outlook. In this sense, the debate moved beyond earlier interpretations that highlighted either Enlightenment or nationalism and argued instead that both conservatives and radicals were preoccupied with modernization and had been exposed to foreign ideas. In addition, criticism of the political radicalism of the May Fourth intellectuals served to promote intellectual independence after 1989 and 1992, as we have seen in the broader debate on radicalism and conservatism in modern Chinese history.

During the first several months of 1989, with the approaching seventieth anniversary of the May Fourth Movement, intellectuals thoroughly examined its legacy. In 1990, on the occasion of the anniversary of May Fourth Peking University Press published a collection of articles that addressed questions such as the following: What constituted the essence or spirit of the May Fourth Movement? Could it be defined as wholesale antitraditionalism? How should one conceive of the relation between tradition and modernity?[57] Similarly, in volumes that appeared in Hong Kong and Taiwan, scholars such as Lin Yü-sheng engaged in dialogues with Wang Yuanhua, Chen Lai, Gan Yang,

---

[53] Chow, *May Fourth Movement*.
[54] Vera Schwarcz, *The Chinese Enlightenment: Intellectuals and the Legacy of the May Fourth Movement of 1919* (Berkeley: University of California Press, 1986).
[55] Jerome Grieder, *Hu Shih and the Chinese Renaissance: Liberalism in the Chinese Revolution, 1917–1937* (Cambridge, MA: Harvard University Press, 1970).
[56] Chow, *May Fourth Movement*, 342–44.
[57] Beijing daxue shehui kexuechu (Peking University Social Sciences Department), ed., *Beijing daxue jinian wusi yundong qishi zhounian lunwenji* (Collection of Articles on the Occasion of Peking University's Commemoration of the Seventieth Anniversary of the May Fourth Movement) (Beijing: Beijing daxue chubanshe, 1989).

and others about the legacy of May Fourth. The questions that were addressed included wholesale antitraditionalism, wholesale Westernization, the relation between Enlightenment and nationalism, and the break with the past.[58]

In addition to these collections of articles on May Fourth, intellectuals also debated the topic in academic journals such as *Dongfang*, *Wenxue pinglun* (Literary Review), *Xueren*, and *Yuandao*. In the January 1994 issue of *Yuandao*, for example, Wang Shuren and Han Demin both discuss the cultural crisis, the "cultural nihilism," and the thorough antitraditionalism that had resulted from May Fourth.[59] In particular, articles that appeared in the literary journal *Wenxue pinglun* in 1993 and 1994 discuss the literary revolution of 1917, a topic to be discussed in the following chapter. Chen Lai's article on "cultural radicalism" appeared in the first issue of *Dongfang* in 1993. One year later in the same journal, Liu Dong (b. 1955), professor of comparative literature at Peking University, criticized the May Fourth Movement. He noted the tolerant, liberal spirit of May Fourth in the intellectual sphere but the negative consequences of "cultural radicalism" and "political radicalism" with regard to modernization, morality, and culture.[60]

As in other debates on radicalism, not all mainland scholars embraced the views of their overseas counterparts. In an edited volume on May Fourth, Wang Yuanhua (1920–2008), former professor at Fudan University who had also been a proponent of "socialist humanism" during the early 1980s, rejects Lin Yü-sheng's notion of "totalistic antitraditionalism" and its association with other movements, the extremism of which was based on resentment rather than evidence.[61] Overseas scholars, in the view of Wang Yuanhua, did not understand the nature of mainland Chinese cultural discourse and merely echoed this

---

[58] Some of the main volumes include Zhou Yangshan, ed., *Cong wusi dao xin wusi* (From May Fourth to the New May Fourth) (Taipei: Shibao wenhua chuban qiye youxian gongsi, 1989); Tang Yijie, ed., *Lun chuantong yu fan chuantong: Wusi qishi zhounian jinian wenxuan* (On Tradition and Anti-Tradition: Selected Works on the Commemoration of the Seventieth Anniversary of May Fourth) (Taipei: Lianjing chuban shiye gongsi, 1989); Lin et al., *Wusi: Duoyuan de fansi*; Li Zehou and Lin Yü-sheng, *Wusi: Duoyuan de fansi* (May Fourth: Multiple Reflections) (Taipei: Fengyun shidai chuban gongsi, 1989); Liu Guisheng and Zhang Buzhou, eds., *Tai Gang ji haiwai wusi yanjiu lunzhu xieyao* (Selection of Essential Taiwan, Hong Kong, and Overseas Research Works on May Fourth) (Beijing: Jiaoyu kexue chubanshe, 1989); Ding Xiaoqiang and Xu Zi, eds., *Wusi yu xiandai Zhongguo: Wusi xinlun* (May Fourth and Modern China: New Views on May Fourth) (Taiyuan: Shanxi renmin chubanshe, 1989).

[59] Wang Shuren, "Wenhua de weiji, ronghe yu chongjian" (The Crisis, Reconciliation, and Reconstruction of Culture), *Yuandao* 1 (1994), 95–114; Han Demin, "Chuantong wenhua de weiji yu ershi shiji fan wenhua sichao" (The Crisis of Traditional Culture and Twentieth-Century Anti-culture Trends), *Yuandao* 1 (1994), 311–40.

[60] Liu Dong, "Beida xuetong yu 'wusi' chuantong: Lishi de ling yizhong kenengxing" (The Tradition of Learning at Peking University and the "May Fourth" Tradition: Another Possibility in History), in *ZFL*, 241–51.

[61] Together with Wang Ruoshui, Wang Yuanhua had drafted Zhou Yang's speech on the occasion of the centenary of Karl Marx's death in 1983. See Xu, "Fate of an Enlightenment," 186.

criticism under the sway of the spread of New Confucianism.[62] However, in 1994, after having read the works of Du Yaquan (1873–1933)—the founder and editor of the journal *Dongfang zazhi* (Eastern Miscellany)—Wang Yuanhua criticized the "intention ethics" (*yitu lunli*) of thought that was driven by the willpower, utilitarianism, radical mood, and evolutionism of the May Fourth spirit. Wang now argued that the attitude of extreme belief in human power and the rationality of Enlightenment thinkers such as Rousseau were attractive to Chinese thinkers because it was difficult for them to embrace the idea of human limits. Since the late nineteenth century, each generation had increasingly identified with radicalism.[63]

Against May Fourth Radicalism: Modernizers and Independent Scholars

A chapter that appears in an edited Taiwan-published volume on May Fourth is also noteworthy for a discussion on the scholars who congregated around the journal *Xueheng zazhi*. Its author is Yue Daiyun (b. 1931), who was based in the Contemporary Chinese Literature and Comparative Literature Department of Peking University.[64] Yue Daiyun was married to the head of the Academy of Chinese Culture, Peking University philosophy professor Tang Yijie, who was the son of *Xueheng* scholar Tang Yongtong. In her memoir *To the Storm*, Yue narrates the eminent couple's experiences as intellectuals in Mao's China, with both facing persecution.[65] Not unlike the chapters in the 1976 volume *The Limits of Change*, in the above-mentioned volume on May Fourth Yue reconsiders the widely held belief that those around the journal *Xueheng* opposed the New Culture Movement. She argues that all intellectuals during that period sought answers to the question of modernization and engaged in intellectual exchanges. Yue Daiyun ascribes her early revision of conservative figures to her 1980s' experience as a visiting scholar in Harvard University's Comparative Literature Department, where many *Xueheng* scholars had

---

[62] Wang Yuanhua, "Wei 'wusi' jingshen yi bian" (In Defense of the "May Fourth" Spirit), in Lin et al., *Wusi: Duoyuan de fansi*, 1–27.
[63] See Wang Yuanhua and Li Hui, "Duiyu 'wusi' de zai renshi da kewen" (Answering Questions on the Re-acknowledgment of "May Fourth"), in *ZFL*, 271–86.
[64] Yue Daiyun, "Chonggu 'xueheng': Jianlun xiandai baoshou zhuyi" (Re-evaluating *Xueheng* and Concurrently Discussing Modern Conservatism), in Tang, *Lun chuantong yu fan chuantong*, 415–28. The article was also published in mainland China in the same year in the journal *Zhongguo wenhua*. See also Yue Daiyun, "Shijie wenhua duihua zhong de Zhongguo xiandai baoshou zhuyi: Jianlun 'Xueheng' zazhi" (Modern Chinese Conservatism in the Global Cultural Dialogues: On the *Xueheng* Journal), in Beijing daxue shehui kexuechu, *Beijing daxue jinian wusi yundong qishi zhounian lunwenji*, 56–67. For responses to Yue Daiyun's text and further debate on *Xueheng*, see Schneider, "Bridging the Gap."
[65] Yue Daiyun and Carolyn Wakeman, *To the Storm: The Odyssey of a Revolutionary Chinese Woman* (Berkeley: University of California Press, 1987).

studied under Irving Babbitt (1865–1933), who is known for developing New Humanism at the turn of the century. In addition, Yue states that debates on neoconservatism that were popular in the United States at the time also left an imprint on her thinking.[66] During the 1980s, Yue's intellectual journey also included visits to the University of California, Berkeley, Italy, and Tunis.[67]

In a similar vein, in an article on the May Fourth debates in Eastern and Western cultures, published in a volume titled *Beijing daxue jinian wusi yundong* (Peking University Remembers the May Fourth Movement), Chen Lai presents the "conservatives" of the May Fourth era as modernizers.[68] He had initially written an article on "cultural radicalism" for a February 1991 conference in Hawai'i that included Yü Ying-shih, Lin Yü-sheng, and Tu Weiming as participants. However, an extended version of this article appeared in 1993 in the journal *Dongfang*.[69] In the later article, Chen Lai singles out three "cultural movements" in twentieth-century China, namely, the May Fourth Movement, the Cultural Revolution, and the culture fever of the 1980s, all of which were characterized by radicalism, or a totalistic denial of tradition. The basic thought of radicalism is what Chen Lai calls "overcorrection" (*jiaowang guozheng*), or going to extremes to rectify perceived wrongs. In brief, the three "movements of cultural criticism" exceeded by far the "movement for the reconfiguration of Confucianism" (*ruxue chonggou yundong*), as Jiang Yihua argued in his debate with Yü Ying-shih.[70]

In the *Dongfang* article, Chen Lai first argues that those who were active in the May Fourth Movement had reduced the political problems since the 1898 Reforms to cultural problems; he calls this "culturalism directed at political action" (*zhixiang zhengzhi xingwei de wenhua zhuyi*) or "pan-politicism" (*fan zhengzhi zhuyi*), an attitude that can be traced to the impact of the political orientation of traditional scholars.[71] Second, May Fourth intellectuals wanted to make China rich and strong after a history of humiliation, as a result of which they resorted to utilitarianism. Finally, they were obsessed with science and democracy; these values were mistakenly used as a yardstick to judge all other values. The Cultural Revolution continued the resolute separation of the new

---

[66] Interview with Yue Daiyun, Beijing, July 12, 2006.   [67] Ibid.
[68] Chen Lai, "'Wusi' Dong Xi wenhua lunzheng de fansi" (Reflections on the May Fourth Debates on Eastern and Western Cultures), in Beijing daxue shehui kexuechu, *Beijing daxue jinian wusi yundong qishi zhounian lunwenji,* 157–74.
[69] Chen Lai, "Ershi shiji wenhua yundong zhong de jijin zhuyi" (Radicalism in Twentieth-Century Cultural Movements), in *ZFL*, 293–308, and in *CYX*, 68–83. See also Chen Lai's writings on "cultural radicalism," in Feng, *Chongxin renshi bainian Zhongguo,* 2.451–66.
[70] See Jiang Yihua, "Ershi shiji ruxue zai Zhongguo de chonggou" (The Reconfiguration of Twentieth-Century Confucianism in China), *Ershiyi shiji,* no. 1 (October 1990), 28–35; Chen, "Ershi shiji wenhua yundong zhong de jijin zhuyi," in *ZFL,* 295.
[71] Ibid., 305, 307.

and old of the May Fourth era, as epitomized in slogans such as "there is no making without breaking" and "destroy the old in order to establish the new."

The third radical cultural movement occurred in the 1980s, during which time the lack of democracy was criticized by attacking Confucianism and scientism flourished in the form of the popularity of systems theory, information theory, and cybernetics, as well as through interest in scientific methods and the philosophy of science. During the 1980s, the politicization of culture and the adoration of science were prominent, but modernization was the core topic in the debate. Like Lin Yü-sheng, Chen Lai believes that the antitraditionalism of the May Fourth intellectuals had been wholesale; he describes his critique of radicalism as "anti-antitraditionalism" (*fan fan chuantong zhuyi*). Following Lin Yü-sheng, Chen ascribes this totalism to a traditional mode of thinking.[72]

In response to Chen's argument, as in the debate on radicalism in modern Chinese history, critics questioned the similarities among the three movements and argued for the inclusion of sociopolitical factors in the analysis. The May Fourth Movement, they argued, disapproved of the feudal despotism and the superstition that the Cultural Revolution had embodied. The disasters of the Cultural Revolution were ascribed to its sociopolitical ideals rather than to its "cultural radicalism."[73] Several scholars also objected to a total rejection of tradition, to which the critics of May Fourth radicalism, including Chen Lai, ascribed. For example, Yan Jiayan argued that the criticism of tradition in the New Culture Movement involved only the "three bonds" (*sangang*) in Confucianism and ignored the nonmainstream elements in Confucianism. In addition, extremism was not a main characteristic of the New Culture Movement. Yuan Weishi argued that the term "tradition" was not accurate because the New Culture Movement involved only cultural discussions that had commenced prior to this period and that was a time when culture was flourishing.[74]

Chen's critique of radicalism was not about historical analysis, but it served to support his overall argument that morality in general, and Confucianism in particular, was very much needed in modern society. Since the late 1980s, Chen Lai had addressed the issue of the crisis of Confucianism—which he conceived of both as a cultural crisis and as a crisis of the belief in values—in a

---

[72] Ibid. See Chen Lai, "Zhongguo jindai sixiang de huigu yu qianzhan" (Retrospect and Prospects for Modern Chinese Thought), in *CYX*, 13–30.

[73] Yan Jiayan, "Ping wusi, wenge yu chuantong wenhua de lunzheng" (On the Debate about May Fourth, the Cultural Revolution, and Traditional Culture), *Ershiyi shiji*, no. 42 (August 1997), 134; Chen Shaoming, "Didiao yixie: Xiang wenhua baoshou zhuyi jiangyan" (Tone Down a Little: Advice to Cultural Conservatism), in *ZFL*, 507–13, 509.

[74] Yan Jiayan, "Wusi, wenge, chuantong wenhua" (May Fourth, the Cultural Revolution, and Traditional Culture), in *ZFL*, 231–40; Yuan Weishi, "Xin wenhua yundong yu 'jijin zhuyi'" (The New Culture Movement and "Radicalism"), in *ZFL*, 252–70.

number of articles that featured prominently in intellectual dialogues, one of which appeared in the Taiwan journal *Zhongguo luntan*.[75] In another article on the topic, Chen Lai argues that prior to May Fourth, even though Confucianism had been eradicated from politics and education, it still stood firm in the ethical and spiritual realms. This changed after May Fourth. In spite of this, *rujia* values continued to matter in society, for example during the New Life Movement (1934), during the Anti-Japanese War (1937–45), and even during the 1950s and 1960s. Since 1949, however, the position of Confucianism was seriously damaged, this time not by liberals but by dogmatism and "extreme leftist false Marxism."[76] In brief, it had been eradicated institutionally, but spiritually it continued to exist as part of Chinese culture and part of daily life.[77] In his article "A Propitious New Start," written for *Ershiyi shiji* in 1992, Chen Lai describes how, after decades of denial, a shift had taken place: "Confucianism has already passed its hardest time; it has already left the low ebb."[78]

Like the realistic revolutionaries in the previous chapters, Chen Lai argued for a gradual approach to change and condemned the totalistic attitude of the May Fourth generation. In addition, he maintained that conservatives and radicals both advocated modernization. Like the self-proclaimed scholars of the 1990s, Chen also criticized the politicization of Confucianism and defended scholarship disconnected from politics. However, even though Chen Lai's advocacy of Confucian values was based on his belief in their inherent value, his attempt to attach importance to Confucianism in reform-era China turned out to be a double-edged sword. We will explore this further in an analysis of how Chen Lai read the May Fourth debates on Chinese culture through the lens of Max Weber's distinction between value rationality and instrumental rationality.

Through the Lens of Max Weber: Value Rationality

Unlike those who connected radicalism with socialism and revolution, Chen Lai reinterpreted radicalism based on a Weberian framework. This also provides us with insights into the reception of Max Weber, and sociology more

---

[75] Chen Lai, "Duoyuan wenhua jiegou zhong de ruxue ji qi dingwei" (Confucianism and Its Place in Multicultural Structures), *Zhongguo luntan* 27.1 (1988), 21–23. Taiwanese scholars who engaged in the debate on Confucianism include Cai Renhou, Wei Zhengtong, Liu Shuxian, and Li Minghui. Chou, *Confucianism, Colonialism, and the Cold War*, 9n16.
[76] Chen Lai, "Ershi shiji Zhongguo wenhua zhong de ruxue kunjing" (The Predicament of Confucianism in Twentieth-Century Chinese Culture), *Zhejiang shehui kexue* (Zhejiang Social Sciences), no. 3 (May 1988), 31.
[77] Makeham, *Lost Soul*, 116–17.
[78] Chen Lai, "Zhenxia qiyuan" (A Propitious New Start), *Ershiyi shiji*, no. 10 (April 1992), 10–11.

broadly, in China during the reform era. Since the early 1980s, courses on Weber had been offered at some Chinese universities with the 1979 reintroduction of the discipline of sociology, after being banned during the 1950s because of its alleged bourgeois nature. Weber also appears in the translation series of the editorial committee Culture: China and the World. In 1988, the journal *Dushu* organized a symposium on Max Weber to introduce him to Chinese audiences. Weber was also instrumentalized in a quest for cultural modernization. In spite of more critical approaches, this continued during the 1990s.[79]

In an article on radicalism in twentieth-century cultural movements that was published in *Dongfang* in 1993, Chen Lai resorts to Weber to discuss the "cultural radicalism" (*wenhua jijin zhuyi*) of the May Fourth era, the Cultural Revolution, and the "New Enlightenment" of the 1980s.[80] Chen associates Weber's "value rationality" (*jiazhi lixing*) with the "cultural conservatives" of the May Fourth era. He sees this as advocacy of traditional values based on a belief in their inherent worth. "Cultural radicals," in contrast, rejected these values based on "instrumental rationality" (*gongju lixing*), or a reliance on external standards of economic or political usefulness.[81] "Value rationality" (*Wertrationalität*) and "instrumental rationality" (*Zweckrationalität*) are the two types of social action that Weber outlines in his *Economy and Society*.[82]

For Weber, instrumental rationality is a type of rational action in which the actor calculates how to reach a certain end. This type of action is present in modern capitalism and in the bureaucracy. Value rationality, in contrast, refers to an action that is not a means to an end but one that is "determined by a conscious belief in value for its own sake," as for example a religious calling or some higher cause.[83] Weber adds that these ideal types are heuristic devices;

---

[79] Angie Baecker, "Max Weber in Twentieth-Century China" (unpublished conference paper, AAS-in-Asia, Taipei, June 23, 2015). On the development of the social sciences in China, see Arif Dirlik, "Zhongguohua: Worlding China: The Case of Sociology and Anthropology in Twentieth-Century China," in Dirlik, *Culture and History in Postrevolutionary China*, 197–240.

[80] Chen, "Ershi shiji wenhua yundong zhong de jijin zhuyi."

[81] Chen also uses the term "functional rationality" (*gongyong lixing*) instead of "instrumental rationality" (*gongju lixing*). See, for example, Chen Lai, "Huajie 'chuantong' yu 'xiandai' de jinzhang: 'Wusi' wenhua sichao de fansi" (Dissolving the Tensions between "Tradition" and "Modernity": Reflections on "May Fourth" Cultural Trends), in Chen Lai, *Chen Lai zixuanji* (Self-Selected Works of Chen Lai) (Guilin: Guangxi shifan daxue chubanshe, 1997), 373–98, esp. 377. In other articles, Chen Lai also uses the terms "jiazhi helixing" and "gongju helixing" as well as "shizhi lixing" (essence rationality) and "xingshi lixing" (form rationality). See, for example, Chen Lai, "Xin luxue yu xiandaixing siwei de fansi" (New Rational Philosophy and Reflections on Modernity Thought), in *CYX*, 174.

[82] Also translated as "substantive-value rationality" or "formal-procedural rationality."

[83] Max Weber, *Economy and Society: An Outline of Interpretive Sociology*, ed. Günther Roth and Claus Wittich (Berkeley: University of California Press, 1978), 24–25. Weber discerns two other types of action, namely "affectual" and "traditional" action. See ibid., 4–5.

in practice, it is difficult to find action that can be reduced to only one type of rational action. It is relevant to note that Weber's distinction between the types of rationality, as discussed in his *Economy and Society*, formed part of his critique of modernity as a process of rationalization, alienation, and dehumanization.

Chen Lai, however, reads Weber to criticize the politicization and rejection of culture during the May Fourth period. In a chapter published in a 1989 collection on May Fourth, edited by Lin Yü-sheng, Chen Lai explains the distinction between the two types of rationality: "The standard of functional rationality refers to taking the efficiency of politics or economics of a certain society as a starting point. The standard of value rationality is taking ethical and cultural values as a yardstick."[84] In Chen Lai's view, the main representative of this "radical utilitarianism" (*jijin gongli zhuyi*) was Chen Duxiu. His articles in *Xin qingnian* (New Youth) were particularly typical of this trend. For example, Chen Duxiu discerns a contrast between value rationality and "scientific and technological rationality" (*keji lixing*) in an article in which he praises the French for giving mankind the ideals of liberty, equality, and fraternity, whereas by contrast the Germans were oriented toward technological inventions and strengthening the state.[85]

The radicalism in *Xin Qingnian* was countered by what Chen Lai refers to as the "cultural conservatism" of *Dongfang zazhi* contributors, who employ value rationality as a yardstick to judge values. Against the backdrop of World War One, the success of the Russian Revolution, and the Marxist critique of capitalism, "cultural conservatives" such as Zhang Junmai were critical of Western modernity and demanded a continuity with Chinese tradition. Hence, Chinese conservatism was more than merely a reaction to May Fourth thought; it was "created by complex dynamics in the global political-cultural process."[86] Both groups shared the same views on political progress and economic reform.[87] In addition, contrary to the "cultural radicals," such as Chen Duxiu, for whom old and new were irreconcilable opposites, the "cultural conservatives," such as Zhang Shizhao (1881–1973), Du Yaquan, and Liang Qichao, rejected instrumental rationality.[88]

---

[84] Chen, "Huajie 'chuantong' yu 'xiandai' de jinzhang," 373–98, 377.
[85] Chen Lai refers to Chen Duxiu in "Falanxi yu jindai wenming" (The French and Modern Civilizations), *Xin qingnian* 1.1 (September 1915), 1–4.
[86] Chen Lai, "Dui xin wenhua yundong de zai sikao: Cong 'wusi' houqi de Liang Shuming shuoqi" (Reconsidering the New Culture Movement: On Liang Shuming in the Post-"May Fourth" Era), *Nanchang daxue xuebao* (Nanchang University Journal) 31.1 (January 2000), 1–5, 3. On Chinese conservatism and Western criticism of capitalism, see also Tao, "Baoshou ziyou zhuyi," 478–80.
[87] Chen Lai, "Bayu: Shiji zhi jiao hua chuantong" (Afterword: On Tradition at the End of the Century), in *CYX*, 288.
[88] Chen, "Huajie 'chuantong' yu 'xiandai' de jinzhang," 380–81.

Reminiscent of Benjamin Schwartz's argument that modern China did not know Burkean conservatism in defense of the sociopolitical status quo, Chen argues that cultural conservatives in China were modernizers.[89] Chen attempts to give conservatism a positive meaning and to rescue it from the burden of history. In the Chinese environment, Chen Lai explains, the word "conservative" has a negative connotation, which is why Western China scholars avoid the term and instead rely on terms such as "maintaining the achievements of one's predecessors" (*shoucheng*), as demonstrated in, for example, Guy Alitto's work on the topic.[90] To support the point that conservatives were not necessarily against change, Chen also refers to the criticism by American neoconservative Daniel Bell of late industrial societies in his *Cultural Contradictions of Capitalism* (1976), where he makes a distinction among the economic, political, and social realms in modern society. He argues that tensions existed between the economic need for productivity and self-restraint, on the one hand, and consumerism in the cultural sphere, on the other hand. Furthermore, the demand that the state be involved in both realms led to a mounting crisis. Chen Lai relies on Bell's above distinction to argue that cultural conservatism in China can be combined with a variety of economic and political advocacies: conservatives were both reformers and revolutionaries. Conservatism in China did not necessarily entail a "farewell to revolution," as Li Zehou and Liu Zaifu would have us think.

For Chen Lai, cultural conservatism is a moral conservatism (*daode baoshou zhuyi*).[91] Cultural conservatives believed that science, democracy, or the market economy could not automatically create public virtue or an ethical order; they were convinced that the individualism and utilitarianism of modern society hurt community life.[92] Relying on Max Weber, Daniel Bell also argues that in the postindustrial era, capitalism eroded those virtues that are so central to the spirit of capitalism, such as self-discipline, restraint, and frugality. Chen Lai asserts that this criticism can also be applied to China because it addresses the question of "how to establish a humanist environment suited to the modernization project [of late twentieth-century China]."[93] In addition to "anti-antitraditionalism," Chen Lai also describes "cultural conservatism" as "anti-pan-utilitarianism" (*fan pangongli zhuyi*).[94] Values were very much needed, especially amid the commercialization and marketization of the reform era.

---

[89] See Schwartz, "Notes on Conservatism," 3–21.
[90] Alitto [Ai Kai], *Shijie fanwei nei de fan xiandaihua sichao*, 4–5.
[91] Chen Lai, "Renwen zhuyi de shijie" (The Scope of Humanism), *Dongfang wenhua* (Eastern Culture) 18.1 (1997), 14–20, 18.
[92] Chen, "Ershi shiji Zhongguo wenhua zhong de ruxue kunjing," 31.
[93] Chen, "Renwen zhuyi de shijie," 16. See Daniel Bell, *The Cultural Contradictions of Capitalism* (New York: Basic Books, 1978), xi.
[94] Chen, "Renwen zhuyi de shijie," 16.

In his promotion of value rationality under modernization, Chen Lai refers to the Chinese philosopher Liang Shuming (1893–1988), who is most famous for his 1921 book *Dong Xi wenhua ji qi zhexue* (Eastern and Western Cultures and Their Philosophies).[95] Liang Shuming, often identified as a New Confucian by mainland scholars, came under attack during the Mao period, but by the end of the 1970s he was again being treated positively.[96] Although the "Westernizers" often presented Liang as a conservative who resisted modernization, following Alitto's interpretation in *The Last Confucian*, Chen Lai depicts Liang as a modernizer who nevertheless accorded value to tradition.[97] More specifically, here, Chen Lai invokes Liang Shuming's concept of *lixing*. Alitto argues that for Liang *lixing* was "the normative sense that directs moral action ... the sense of right and wrong which makes man human."[98] For Chen Lai, in some respects Liang Shuming's concept of *lixing* resembles Habermas's concept of "communicative rationality" because it is a "manner of interaction," a "mutual understanding," or a "mentality of mutual connection." This, Chen Lai notes, is similar to benevolence.[99] Whereas Habermas's theory of "communicative rationality" accords a central place to communication in the establishment of rationality, Chen Lai interprets this communication as a moral concept that connects people and offers normative guidance; that is, communication is essential to the formation of a community.

Here we see how Chen Lai's interactions with Tu Wei-ming shaped his thinking on the matter. Tu also indicates the importance of communicative rationality instead of instrumental rationality in the Confucian education system, and especially in the *Analects*.[100] Core aspects of interest for Tu are the Mencian tradition of humaneness, personal cultivation, and the universality of Confucian values. He argues that Confucian morality enables the creation of a "fiduciary community," a community that not only is an aggregate of individuals but also is based on a relation of mutual trust.[101] Similarly, he

---

[95] Liang Shuming, *Dong Xi wenhua ji qi zhexue* (Eastern and Western Cultures and Their Philosophies), ed. Chen Zheng and Luo Changpei (Shanghai: Shangwu yinshuguan, 1922).
[96] Makeham, "Retrospective Creation of New Confucianism," 30. During the Cultural Revolution Liang Shuming's books were burned and Liang had to make a formal self-criticism and was subject to re-education.
[97] Chen Lai, "Liang Shuming zaoqi de Dong Xi wenhuaguan" (Liang Shuming's Early Views of Eastern and Western Cultures), in *CYX*, 97–129. See also Chen, "Dui xin wenhua yundong de zai sikao," 3–4; Alitto, *Last Confucian*.
[98] Alitto, *Last Confucian*, 184.
[99] Chen Lai, "Rujia sixiang yu xiandai Dong Ya shijie" (Confucian Thought and the Modern East Asian World), in *CYX*, 186.
[100] Tu Wei-ming, Milan Hejtmanek, Alan Wachman, et al., eds., *The Confucian World Observed: A Contemporary Discussion of Confucian Humanism in East Asia* (Honolulu: East-West Center, University of Hawai'i, 1992), 65.
[101] Neville, *Boston Confucianism*, 91.

underscores the function of communication in Confucianism because of its "philosophy of mutuality."[102]

We also find traces of Tu in Chen's reading of Confucianism. Like Tu Wei-ming, Chen makes a clear distinction between Confucianism as a system of thought and orthodox state Confucianism. Chen Lai's interpretation of value rationality and his defense of the autonomy of values must be understood in relation to his conception of Confucianism as a moral system detached from social referents or institutions. This view differs from the view of scholars such as Lin Yü-sheng and Yü Ying-shih, for whom Confucianism is tied to concrete social referents and is very much intertwined with social institutions.[103] For Yü in particular, preservation of intermediate organizations is driven by the fact that these institutions are embodiments of a living Confucian culture. For Chen Lai, conversely, Confucianism can be equated with its social amalgamations, as the latter destroy its transcendental values.[104]

Therefore, Chen's moral conservatism upholds Weber's value rationality in that it defends values on the basis of their inherent value. This is in accordance with the argument of Tu Wei-ming and other New Confucians that Confucianism can be a moral cure against the erosion of meaning and community in a modernized world. Thus, both Chen and Tu frame their Confucian project as a critique of modernity, defending the free-spirited value rationality against the instrumental rationality of modern industrial society. For Chen, the virtues that make man human are benevolence (*ren*) and harmony (*he*), values that Tu Wei-ming also identifies as a kernel of Confucianism. Harmony, Chen argues, can serve as an antidote to the problems of modernity, such as man's exploitation of nature and individualism. As Chen Lai puts it, "One can say that '*ren*' is the representation of Confucian value rationality and the concentrated manifestation of substantive tradition."[105]

Chen Lai opposes instrumental rationality in the realm of culture, but his own advocacy of Confucianism is not free from instrumental streaks. To demonstrate that Confucianism matters in modern society, its advocates also became involved in the discussion on the relation between Confucianism and capitalism. This debate, as noted earlier, was triggered by the economic rise of Japan and the Four Mini Dragons, which led scholars to revise their view that Confucianism hindered modernization. This debate was based on the other side of Weber's theory, namely the thesis, as outlined in his *The Protestant*

---

[102] Tu, *Confucian Ethics Today*, 9.
[103] See Lin, *Crisis of Chinese Consciousness*; Yü, "Radicalization of China in the Twentieth Century."
[104] Chen Lai, "'Wusi' sichao yu xiandaixing" (The "May Fourth" Trend and Modernity), in *CYX*, 60–67, 62–63.
[105] Chen Lai, "Rujia sixiang yu xiandai Dong Ya shijie," 179–87 at 186.

Ethic and the Spirit of Capitalism, that Protestant values contributed to the development of capitalism. This side of the debate supported an argument about instrumental rationality, to which we now turn.

The Other Side of Weber: Instrumental Rationality

Ironically, it was Tu Wei-ming who was also notable in bringing the debate on the relation between Confucianism and capitalism to Chinese audiences. Tu Wei-ming had picked up the Confucian capitalism thesis during the late 1970s' discussions in the United States, where the successes of the East Asian economies were widely debated. Tu also connected the question of the role of Confucian values in the modern world to criticism of the May Fourth Movement for being too radical. In order to understand the reassessment of Weber in East Asia, we should first look at Weber's views on Confucianism and capitalism and how these views relate to his famous Protestantism thesis.

In *The Protestant Ethic and the Spirit of Capitalism*, Weber holds that the Calvinist doctrine of predestination affected the formation of capitalism because mystical contemplation was exchanged for ascetic and this-worldly action. Ascetic Protestantism provided a "systematic rational ordering of moral life as a whole."[106] It was this spirit of rational conduct, duty, and discipline on the basis of the idea of a calling that gave rise to modern rational capitalism. In his *The Religion of China: Confucianism and Taoism*, Weber further asserts that "Protestant rationalism" was marked by its "disenchantment" with the world; there was a tension between the rational ethical imperatives of Protestantism and this-worldly irrationalities.[107]

For Weber, Confucianism did not benefit the development of capitalism in China because it differed from Protestantism in three critical respects. First, the tensions between the ethical demands of Confucianism and this-worldly realities were minimal. For Confucians, "the world was the best of all possible worlds; human nature was disposed to the ethically good."[108] Confucianism aimed at the moral perfection of the "man of the world," whereas the goal of Protestantism was to enable man to be attentive to the will of God.[109] Furthermore, Confucians were not ascetics, and although they were

---

[106] Max Weber, *The Protestant Ethic and the Spirit of Capitalism*, tr. Talcott Parsons (New York: Scribner, 1958), 126.
[107] Max Weber, *The Religion of China: Confucianism and Taoism*, tr. Hans Gerth (New York: The Free Press, 1968), 226–27.
[108] Ibid., 227. Elsewhere, Weber formulates it as follows: "Completely absent in Confucian ethic was any tension between nature and deity, between ethical demand and human shortcoming, consciousness of sin and need for salvation, conduct on earth and compensation in the beyond, religious duty and sociopolitical reality." Ibid., 235–36.
[109] Ibid., 240.

sober and thrifty, they invested their savings in education, not business.[110] Finally, relations among people were not rationalized but based on tradition, custom, and personal favors.[111]

During the 1970s and 1980s, American scholars of China had already criticized Weber's argument that there are no tensions between Confucianism and reality and that Confucianism was "this-worldly" because it was characterized by adjustment to the world.[112] The 1980s witnessed an upsurge in debates on the place of Confucianism in the modern world against the background of the rise of Japan and the Four Mini Dragons. Some Japan scholars were referring to Confucianism in their analyses of Japan's economic success. In 1978, economist Michio Morishima employed the term "Confucian capitalism"; one year later, Japan scholar Ezra Vogel, in his *Japan as Number One*, and sociologist Herman Kahn, in his *World Economic Development*, tied Confucianism to Japan's economic rise.[113] Shortly thereafter, scholars also began to apply the concept of Confucian capitalism to a broader context. For example, in 1980 China scholar Roderick MacFarquhar wrote about a "Post-Confucian challenge." The East Asian development thesis, with Peter Berger as a supporter, thus began to become popular in the United States.[114]

Ironically, the very same "ideational factors" that were designated as an obstacle to development in the 1950s and 1960s were now thought to contribute to economic success. For instance, John King Fairbank, operating in the milieu of post-World War Two modernization theories, famously argued that China had failed to respond to the impact of the West precisely because of its Confucian worldview "of China as central, superior, and self-sufficient."[115]

---

[110] Ibid., 242, 247. [111] Ibid., 229, 236–37, 241.

[112] See Metzger, *Escape from Predicament*. See also "Review Symposium: Thomas A. Metzger's Escape from Predicament," *Journal of Asian Studies* 39.2 (February 1980), 237–90; Shmuel N. Eisenstadt, "This-Worldly Transcendentalism and the Structuring of the World: Weber's 'Religion of China' and the Format of Chinese History and Civilization," *Journal of Developing Societies* 1.2 (1985), 168–86.

[113] Michio Morishima, "The Power of Confucian Capitalism," *Observer* (London), June 1978; Ezra F. Vogel, *Japan as Number One: Lessons for America* (Cambridge, MA: Harvard University Press, 1979). See also his later work, *The Four Little Dragons: The Spread of Industrialization in East Asia* (Cambridge, MA: Harvard University Press, 1991). The Japan scholar Robert Bellah (b. 1927), a student of Talcott Parsons, in the 1950s had already applied the Weber thesis to Japan. See Robert N. Bellah, *Tokugawa Religion: The Values of Preindustrial Japan* (Glencoe, IL: Free Press, 1957). Another early Weberian approach to Japanese thought is Maruyama Masao's *Nihon seiji shisōshi kenkyū* (Studies on the History of Japanese Political Thought) (Tōkyō: Tōkyō Daigaku Shuppankai, 1952); Herman Kahn, *World Economic Development: 1979 and Beyond* (Boulder: CO: Westview, 1979).

[114] Roderick MacFarquhar, "The Post-Confucian Challenge," *Economist*, February 9, 1980, 67–72; Peter L. Berger, "An East Asian Development Model?," in Berger and Hsin-Huang Michael Hsiao, eds., *In Search of an East Asian Development Model* (New Brunswick, NJ: Transaction, 1988), 3–11.

[115] Harriet T. Zurndorfer, "Confusing Confucianism with Capitalism: Culture as Impediment and/or Stimulus to Chinese Economic Development" (paper, Third Global Economic History

In the field of intellectual history, Joseph Levenson similarly exposed the rupture between Confucianism and modern society in his well-known trilogy *Confucian China and Its Modern Fate*.[116]

Despite the irony, scholars and advocates of Confucianism joined economists, area studies specialists, and sociologists to discuss the role of Confucianism in the modernization process.[117] Here, Tu Wei-ming and Yü Ying-shih served as intermediaries between the Anglophone and Sinophone discourses. In 1985 Yü Ying-shih expanded application of the Weber thesis to China by arguing that Confucian ethics, altered through interactions with Buddhism and Daoism, functioned similarly to the Protestant ethic in the development of Ming dynasty commerce.[118] Contemporaneously, Tu Wei-ming entered the debate by editing several conference volumes on Confucianism and East Asia.[119] Yü and Tu were also involved in the development of a Confucian ethics curriculum in Singapore to promote "Asian values" through moral and religious education in the city-state, partly in response to the perceived dangers of Western counterculture.[120]

Of the many publications at that time, the 1991 conference volume *The Confucian World Observed: A Contemporary Discussion of Confucian Humanism in East Asia* clearly shows the relationship between Confucianism and capitalism.[121] Conference participants pointed out that in order to solve

---

Network Meeting, Konstanz, Germany, June 3–5, 2004), 5, 7, www.researchgate.net/publication/237385777_Confusing_Confucianism_With_Capitalism_Culture_As_Impediment_And_Or_Stimulus_To_Chinese_Economic_Development.

[116] Joseph R. Levenson, *Confucian China and Its Modern Fate: A Trilogy* (Berkeley: University of California Press, 1968).

[117] For an overview of the different positions in the debate, see Dirlik, *Culture and History in Postrevolutionary China*, 121–26.

[118] See Yü Ying-shih, *Zhongguo jinshi zongjiao lunli yu shangren jingshen* (The Modern Chinese Religious Ethic and the Mercantile Spirit) (Taipei: Lianjing chuban shiye gongsi, 1987). This was first published in 1985 in the Taiwan journal *Zhishi fenzi*.

[119] These conferences were held in the United States, China, Taiwan, Hong Kong, and Singapore. See Dirlik, *Culture and History in Postrevolutionary China*, 109. See also, for example, Tu et al., *Confucian World Observed*; Tu Wei-ming, ed., *The Triadic Chord: Confucian Ethics, Industrial East Asia, and Max Weber: Proceedings of the 1987 Singapore Conference on Confucian Ethics and the Modernisation of Industrial East Asia* (Singapore: Institute of East Asian Philosophies, 1991); Tu Wei-ming, ed., *Confucian Traditions in East Asian Modernity: Moral Education and Economic Culture in Japan and the Four Mini-Dragons* (Cambridge, MA: Harvard University Press, 1996).

[120] For a detailed overview of this experiment in Singapore, see John Makeham, "The Singapore Experiment and *Rujia* Capitalism," in Makeham, *Lost Soul*, 21–41. See also Tu, *Confucian Ethics Today*. The "Asian values" debate, which became internationally visible during the 1990s, centers around political Confucianism, the paternalistic state, the family, and a cultural relativism that rejected universal human rights. It was mostly advocated by political leaders such as Senior Minister of Singapore Lee Kuan Yew and Prime Minister Mahathir of Malaysia. Michael D. Barr, "Lee Kuan Yew and the 'Asian Values' Debate," *Asian Studies Review* 24.3 (2000), 309–34.

[121] Tu et al., *Confucian World Observed*, 75.

the tensions between Confucianism and capitalism, scholars in the past had attempted to legitimate profit making in Confucianism as a way to improve the conditions of the people. In the West, the tensions between ethics and profit making were similarly resolved by referring to Adam Smith's invisible hand: profit making was justified as being part of a larger goal.[122] As such, as Tze-ki Hon notes, Tu Wei-ming's contribution is that he connected the discourse on the East Asian development model among sociologists and economists in the United States with the discourse on New Confucianism in overseas Chinese communities. He did this through the figure of Max Weber and his *Protestant Ethic*.[123]

In addition to Tu's writings in English on Confucianism and East Asia, his writings and lectures on the "third epoch of Confucianism" were published in China, and he also contributed articles to *Ershiyi shiji*. Other works by Tu also became available on mainland China during the late 1980s.[124] During the mid-1980s, many mainland intellectuals went to the United States, where the writings of both Max Weber and Talcott Parsons (1902–79), with whom Tu Wei-ming had studied at Harvard, were in vogue. Against this background, mainland Chinese scholars again began to contemplate the relationship between Confucianism and modernization. In 1985, as Chen Lai recalls, a doctoral dissertation on Weber was completed in China.[125] After Chinese interest in Weber peaked in 1986, the year when *The Protestant Ethic and the Spirit of Capitalism* was translated into Chinese, the New Confucian discourse evolved from a reappraisal of Confucianism in China to a debate on the existence of an East Asian development model.[126] By applying Weber's Protestantism thesis to Confucianism, Chinese scholars refuted his verdict on Confucianism in *The Religion of China*.

Chen Lai's writings on the topic also form part of this discussion that was inspired by Max Weber's thesis on the relationship between Protestantism and capitalism. Like Tu Wei-ming, Chen Lai held that the economic miracle of East Asia represented a serious challenge to Weber's theories on Confucianism. Chen Lai further argued that the debate on Confucian ethics and East Asian modernization focused not on the "coming into being" (*chansheng*) of capitalism but rather on the "assimilation" (*tonghua*) of capitalism.[127]

---

[122] Ibid.   [123] Hon, "Introduction," xv.
[124] See, for example, Tu Wei-ming, *Renxing yu ziwo xiuyang* (Humanity and Self-Cultivation) (Beijing: Zhongguo heping chubanshe, 1988).
[125] Interview with Chen Lai, Beijing, August 10, 2005.
[126] Wang, *High Culture Fever*, 66, 68; Interview with Chen Lai, Beijing, August 10, 2005.
[127] According to Chen Lai, Jin Yaoji [Ambrose King] opened the Weber debate in China in 1983; in 1986, Fu Yongjian presented the difference between "inner development" (*neifa*) and "outside learning" (*waixue*); in 1988, Lao Siguang reiterated the division between "coming into being" (*chuangsheng*) and "imitation" (*moni*). See Chen Lai, "Rujia lunli yu Zhongguo xiandaihua" (Confucian Ethics and Chinese Modernization), in *CYX*, 188–206.

Following Tu Wei-ming, Chen Lai argued that Weber makes a distinction between creation and assimilation. In his last chapter of *The Religion of China* Weber states that "the Chinese in all probability would be quite capable, probably more capable than the Japanese, of assimilating capitalism."[128] Although Weber does not specify whether Confucian ethics could contribute to this assimilation, for Chen Lai they clearly could, at least at the initial stage.

Here, Chen Lai refers to the term of Boston University sociologist Peter Berger—"vulgar Confucianism" (*shisuhua de rujia lunli*).[129] Whereas Weber discusses the ethics of Chinese imperial ideology, Berger analyzes the daily ethics of commoners. He concludes that daily ethics indeed contribute to economic development, and this is confirmed by the existence of an East Asian development model in the Four Mini Dragons.[130] Berger's argument, Chen Lai posits elsewhere, addresses an inconsistency in Weber, who looks at ethical beliefs and attitudes in daily life in the case of Protestantism, but who analyzes religion instead of ethical beliefs and attitudes in daily life in the case of Confucianism.[131] This is again reminiscent of Tu Wei-ming's distinction between orthodox Confucianism and classical Confucianism—both Chen Lai and Tu Wei-ming advocate Confucian ethics as distinct from the imperial ideology.

At times, Chen Lai admits that a cultural explanation of East Asian development is too simplistic. Modernization cannot be reduced to economic function, and even if Confucian values are unrelated to the coming into being and assimilation of capitalism, this does not make them lose value in a modern society. Precisely because Confucianism, as a system of thought, cares about more than the economy, Confucian values can exist in creative tension with the instrumental rationality of modern society. Chen Lai therefore distinguishes between Confucian values as a critique of modern society and the sociopolitical debate on Asian values, in which these values are transformed into instrumental rationality to boost industrial production.[132] In a further attempt to justify his participation in both debates, Chen adds that political scientists, not New Confucians, first raised the issue of the role of Confucian values in East Asian capitalism.[133]

Chen Lai's advocacy of value rationality is clearly in tension with the Confucian capitalism that he and Tu Wei-ming explain in broader terms as

---

[128] Weber, *Religion of China*, 248. Tu Wei-ming also refers to this statement by Weber in his "Introduction" to Tu, *Confucian Traditions in East Asian Modernity*, 4.
[129] Chen, "Rujia lunli yu Zhongguo xiandaihua," 188–206.
[130] See Berger, "East Asian Development Model?," 3–11.
[131] Chen Lai, "Rujia lunli yu Zhongguo xiandaihua," 195.
[132] Chen, "Rujia sixiang yu xiandai Dong Ya shijie," 179–87; Interview with Chen Lai, Beijing, August 10, 2005.
[133] Chen, "Rujia lunli yu Zhongguo xiandaihua," 188–206.

being about the relation between tradition and modernity.[134] At a 1982 seminar at the National University of Singapore, for example, Tu discussed the link between East Asian capitalism and "Confucian ethics."[135] From this, we find that in the interpretation of advocates of New Confucianism, such as Tu Wei-ming, the tension between Confucian values as an antidote to capitalism and the question of whether Confucian values benefited capitalism were not at all problematic. Instead, they considered the matter of the function of Confucian values in the modern world to be an extension of that of the relation between Confucian values and capitalism—both are about the relation between tradition and modernity.

The Max Weber Dilemma

We can refer to this double role of Confucianism as both a spiritual antidote and a facilitator of capitalism as the "Max Weber dilemma" because we find the same ambiguity in Max Weber. On the one hand, Weber offers a critique of the "iron cage" of modern rationality, as expressed in his *Economy and Society*. On the other hand, Weber investigates the relation between ideas, primarily those of ascetic Calvinism, and this rationalization in the form of capitalism in his *Protestant Ethic*. He seeks to demonstrate the force of ideas in the rationalization process, a process that is at the same time detrimental to these ideas, as later exposed by sociologist Daniel Bell. Weber's "rationalization" has multiple meanings: it refers to "disenchantment" (*Entzauberung*) with the world as well as to rationality to attain both practical and ethical goals.[136]

In mainland China, however, this two-sided nature of Weber has not been at the forefront of discussions precisely because Chinese intellectuals turned to how to improve the Chinese modernization process.[137] Even after 1989, as can be seen in Chen's article on cultural radicalism, rather than questioning modernity, its Chinese antitraditional manifestation is targeted in order to create a modernization inclusive of a tradition reinvented for the global era. As noted, Chen Lai argues that early twentieth-century conservatives were also modernizers with a global point of view. Following the existing discourses of

---

[134] Tu Wei-ming, "Introduction," in Tu, *Confucian Traditions in East Asian Modernity*, 2.
[135] See Makeham, *Lost Soul*, 30, 34–37.
[136] Anthony Giddens, *Politics and Sociology in the Thought of Max Weber* (London: Macmillan, 1972), 44.
[137] Angie Baecker notes that Chinese intellectuals relied on Talcott Parsons's "universal" interpretation of Weber rather than the "German" Weber who notes the contradictions inherent in modernization. Chinese scholars of Weber, however, including Su Guoxun and Gan Yang, wanted to rescue Weber from this Parsonian interpretation. Baecker, "Max Weber in Twentieth-Century China."

the time, Chen Lai promoted historical continuity through reliance on a model of "critical inheritance" (*pipan de jicheng*) derived from New Confucianism. This model was mainly promoted by Fang Keli (b. 1938), a Confucian Marxist philosopher based at Renmin University and later at Nankai University, who headed the officially supported New Confucianism research project.[138]

Chen Lai had already outlined a Hegelian model of "dialectical denial" in an article written for a symposium to commemorate the seventieth anniversary of May Fourth in April 1989.[139] This Hegelian framework of "dialectical denial" not only was acceptable to a Marxist audience but also reflected the popularity of Hegel at the time. Between 1987 and 1992, between 3,500 and 3,800 translations and other works on Western philosophy were published in China, half of which dealt with German idealism.[140] In his commemorative article, Chen Lai expresses support for the "dialectical attitudes" of "critical inheritance," "creative development" (*chuangzao de fazhan*), "developing what is useful and discarding what is not" (*yangqi*), and "transformation" (*zhuanhua*), all of which did not carve up historical continuity.[141]

Chen Lai also developed an advocacy for cultural inheritance drawing on the philosopher Feng Youlan (1895–1990), whom mainland scholars often identify as a New Confucian.[142] Like Liang Shuming, as a Confucian thinker Feng Youlan was the subject of criticism, and some of his works were banned under Mao Zedong.[143] Feng had studied at Columbia University between 1920 and 1923 and is most famous for his *Zhongguo zhexueshi* (History of Chinese Philosophy, 1934). Chen Lai draws on Feng Youlan's discussion of the relation between "particulars" and "universals," which constituted the basis of Feng's later work *Xin lixue* (A New Philosophy of Principle).[144] New Confucians on mainland China used Feng's distinction between specific and abstract values to advocate cultural inheritance in a manner that was consistent with Marxist advocacies. The concept of "abstract inheritance"

---

[138] Makeham, *Lost Soul*, 245–52. On this research project, see Tze-ki Hon, "Global Capitalism with Chinese Characteristics: Fang Keli's New Confucian Research Project (1986–1995)," in Hon and Stapleton, *Confucianism for the Contemporary World*, 3–18.

[139] Chen, "Huajie 'chuantong' yu 'xiandai' de jinzhang," 151–85.

[140] Meissner, "New Intellectual Currents," 7.

[141] Chen, "Huajie 'chuantong' yu 'xiandai' de jinzhang," 393.

[142] Makeham, "Retrospective Creation of New Confucianism," 30. Whether Feng Youlan was a New Confucian remains highly debated. Zheng Jiadong, a mainland scholar of New Confucianism, identifies him as such, but Lauren Pfister argues against this. See Lauren F. Pfister, "A Modern Chinese Philosophy Built upon Critically Received Traditions: Feng Youlan's New Principle-Centered Learning and the Question of Its Relationship to Contemporary New Ruist ('Confucian') Philosophies," in Makeham, *New Confucianism*, 165–84.

[143] Feng Youlan had to write over one hundred self-criticisms and his *Xin lixue* was banned on the mainland during the 1950s.

[144] See Feng Youlan, *The Hall of Three Pines: An Account of My Life*, tr. Denis C. Mair (Honolulu: University of Hawai'i Press, 2000), 255.

(*chouxiang jicheng*), Makeham states, is "another variation of 'developing what is positive and discarding what is negative.'"[145] Chen Lai refers to Feng Youlan to argue that the dilemma between "native culture" and "wholesale Westernization" can be resolved if advocates of both groups concentrate on industrialization.[146] In addition, Chen argues, traditional Chinese culture also included the principles of general societies—it was a "concrete universal" (*yi juti de gongxiang*).[147] By treating societies primarily as universals, the value rationality of tradition could be included in modern society.

The duality of the New Confucian position in which values are perceived of as an antidote to the ills of capitalism but are also supportive of capitalism has been noted. Leftist critics have attacked Confucianism as an unreflective confirmation of a capitalist system. One of the fiercest critics of the Confucian revival has been Arif Dirlik, who argues that Tu Wei-ming and other Confucian scholars merely confirm the utility of Confucianism for capitalism; their goal is to "modernize tradition." The final result is that "Confucius has been moved from the museum to the theme park."[148] In the same vein, Timothy Brook observes the irony of Confucianism being used both as an antidote against the ills of capitalism and as a driving force behind capitalism.[149] Similarly, Zhang Xudong maintains that the resort to culture by the New Confucians is simply a way to revive national politics against the backdrop of the universalism of global capital.[150] Liu Kang adds "regional anti-communism" to "global capitalism" as the ideological and political implications of New Confucianism.[151]

If we look beyond the "global capitalism" criticism, a more fundamental contradiction is clearly at work, namely the tension between value rationality and instrumental rationality that extends back to Max Weber. Gan Yang, who is more familiar with Weber's works, had already noted this by arguing that the attempt to prove how Confucian values suited modernization contradicted the essence of the value rationality upheld by Confucians. Does it not, he asks, harm the basic Confucian principle of "learning for oneself" (*weiji zhixue*)?[152]

---

[145] Makeham, *Lost Soul*, 243–44.
[146] Chen Lai, "Feng Youlan wenhuaguan de jianli yu fazhan" (The Foundation and Development of Feng Youlan's Cultural Perspective), in *CYX*, 143–44.
[147] Chen, "Xin lixue yu xiandaixing siwei de fansi," 163–79, 165; Chen, "Feng Youlan wenhuaguan de jianli yu fazhan," 155.
[148] Arif Dirlik, "Confucius in the Borderlands: Global Capitalism and the Reinvention of Confucianism," *Boundary 2* 22.3 (Fall 1995), 267, 273.
[149] Timothy Brook, "Profit and Righteousness in Chinese Economic Culture," in Brook and Hy V. Luong, eds., *Culture and Economy: The Shaping of Capitalism in Eastern Asia* (Ann Arbor: University of Michigan Press, 1997), 44.
[150] Zhang, "Making of the Post-Tiananmen Intellectual Field," 44.
[151] Liu Kang, "Is There an Alternative to (Capitalist) Globalization? The Debate about Modernity in China," *Boundary 2* 23.3 (1996), 206.
[152] Makeham, *Lost Soul*, 38.

Jing Wang similarly argues that the alliance between Confucianism and capitalism delegitimated the claim of value rationality because "Confucianism is no less susceptible to instrumental reason and materialistic motivation on which capitalism is based than capitalism itself."[153] Instrumentalist appropriations of Confucian values in the service of modernization, be they in the form of an East Asian development model or in the form of the socialist modernization project in mainland China, have challenged the moral project of Confucianism in its search for "authentic existence." Mainland scholars of Confucianism all seek to demonstrate the contemporary relevance of *ruxue* to China's modernization.[154]

On mainland China, the critique of modernity in the writings of the "German" Weber received less attention at the time. Given the limited familiarity with original works by Weber and relying on introductions or English translations, the discussion revolved around the Weberian thesis about the relation between Protestantism and capitalism. Amid the modernization craze of the 1980s, the question on the minds of most Chinese intellectuals was how to create a better modern. Even though the 1990s were marked by less optimism than the 1980s, the period after 1989 did not immediately witness a shift to an engagement with the inherent contradictions of modernity, as revealed by the debate on radicalism. We should also note that, in spite of the more open climate of the reform era, resistance to Marxist theories that did not support the base-superstructure scheme remained. Advocacies of humanist Marxism and the argument that alienation could occur under the socialism of the 1980s were subjected to criticism. The Frankfurt School, which developed the side of Weber that is critical of modernity, Chinese critics argue, turned revolution into a mere psychological revolution of individual liberation rather than a social revolution that altered the relations of production.[155] In this environment, Weber was incorporated into the modernization narrative.

Historical Radicalism and the *Ruxue* Solution

As an advocate of Confucianism, Chen Lai's agenda was vastly different from that of some of the historians involved in the 1992 debate on modern Chinese history, yet he was no less a realistic revolutionary. Chen Lai criticized cultural radicalism during May Fourth, the Cultural Revolution, and the 1980s' cultural movement and instead argued in favor of cultural continuity and gradual progress—for "making without breaking." His solution to the cultural radicalism of twentieth-century China was, however, prescriptive and abstract. Like other intellectuals, he categorized movements in a dualist scheme reminiscent

---

[153] Wang, *High Culture Fever*, 66, 67.   [154] Makeham, *Lost Soul*, 62–63.
[155] See Brugger and Kelly, *Chinese Marxism in the Post-Mao Era*, 45–49.

of Confucian efforts at "rectifying names," but also with a Marxist interpretation of the struggle between opposites, now revived in a Hegelian form and through the lens of Max Weber's distinction between value rationality and instrumental rationality.

As we have seen, Yü Ying-shih saw Confucianism as being tied to institutions and intermediate social groups—he criticized the advocacy of Confucian values without these references as a "wandering soul" (*youhun*) and emphasized Confucianism as a lived experience.[156] Even though he acknowledged the cultural development of Confucianism, Chen Lai still identified certain abstract values as an antidote to China's illness. Chen Lai's position, in Makeham's words, hints at "a compromise between the Marxist's historical determinism and the New Confucian's transcendent idealism." Chen Lai considers *rujia* to have undergone a cultural development during the period of the Three Dynasties, thereby linking thought to culture, but he also criticizes the institutionalization of Confucianism.[157]

These tensions between abstract universal values and the cultural development of Confucianism mean that a "cultural nationalism" interpretation of New Confucianism, for example in the work of Guo Yingjie, is too simplistic.[158] Makeham has developed the concept of "*ruxue*-centered Chinese cultural nationalism" to refer to the discourse on New Confucianism, which he describes as "a movement based on the ideological conviction that *ruxue* is a cultural formation fundamental to the consciousness of identity of the Chinese (*Zhonghua*) nation."[159] This concept, he argues, avoids the problems related to the distinction between culturalism and nationalism, as in the works of historian Joseph Levenson, for whom culture as the locus of loyalty made room for nationalism only under the impact of Western imperialism.[160]

Makeham nevertheless also recognizes, for several reasons, the limits of "*ruxue*-centered cultural nationalism" as a framework for the New Confucian discourse because not all discussants backed the re-creation of Chinese civilization. Although Li Zehou's thesis that *ruxue* is a "cultural-psychological formation" (*wenhua xinli jiegou*), sedimentation (*jidian*), or deep structure (*shenceng jiegou*) is very influential, he does not insist that *ruxue* should be promoted. It is also unclear whether New Confucianism is a cultural or a

---

[156] Makeham, *Lost Soul*, 1–2. See Yü Ying-shih, *Xiandai ruxue lun* (Essays on Contemporary Confucianism) (Shanghai: Shanghai renmin chubanshe, 1998).
[157] Makeham, *Lost Soul*, 108–9.   [158] See Guo, *Cultural Nationalism*, 19, 72–90.
[159] Makeham, *Lost Soul*, 15.
[160] See Levenson, *Confucian China and Its Modern Fate,* in particular 1.98–104. Both Prasenjit Duara and James Townsend have taken issue with Levenson's "culturalism-to-nationalism thesis." See James Townsend, "Chinese Nationalism," in Jonathan Unger, ed., *Chinese Nationalism* (Armonk, NY: M.E. Sharpe, 1996), 1–30; Prasenjit Duara, "De-constructing the Chinese Nation," in Unger, *Chinese Nationalism,* 31–55.

philosophical movement; even the 1958 declaration was about the "spiritual vitality" of "China's cultural history." In addition, scholars such as Tu Weiming endeavored to revive only the Confucian tradition, not Confucian society as such. Finally, the existence of terms such as "East Asian *ruxue*" and "Han cultural circles" identified with a cultural sphere that exceeded the scope of the nation.[161]

Chen Lai's writings demonstrate the validity of these concerns: Chen did not seek to revive Confucian civilization; in addition, his imagined Confucian culture was highly elitist and belonged to the domain of intellectuals. As in Chang Hao's argument, China's cultural crisis was a crisis of intellectual identity, in response to which Chen called for pure scholarship, a *guoxue* devoid of political and commercial interference. The overemphasis on culture and "culturalism" as a narrative was a way to underline the relevance of intellectuals for China's modernization process. Nor was Chen Lai's Confucianism tied to the Chinese nation—it was caught up between Chinese socialist modernization, East Asian capitalism, and abstract universalism. As such, it was not able to offer an answer to the history of cultural radicalism that Chen Lai had condemned.

Chen Lai's criticism of radicalism could be limited only amid a modernization frenzy and an intellectual discourse that remained restrained by the fetters of Marxism. In spite of his criticism of instrumental rationality, Chen did not reject the Confucianism/capitalism thesis and continued to subscribe to the agenda of the socialist modernization project with which New Confucianism had become aligned on mainland China. However, Chen's writings are significant in that he reinterprets May Fourth conservatives as modern global thinkers. Furthermore, he condemns the politicization of culture and, like other scholars of the early 1990s, advocates an independent scholarship through Max Weber's value rationality. Chen's defense of moral conservatism and abstract Confucian values, such as *ren* and *he*, however, would come under attack as debates on postmodernism accompanied globalization.

---

[161] Makeham, "Retrospective Creation of New Confucianism," 32–33; Makeham, *Lost Soul*, 16, 118–25.

6 Of Post-*Isms* and May Fourth

> How can one love without a heart?
> Zheng Min, on the simplified Chinese character for "love,"
> Interview with Zheng Min, Beijing, July 6, 2006

> Always historicize!
> Fredric Jameson, *The Political Unconscious: Narrative as a Socially Symbolic Act*

As China was becoming increasingly integrated into the world economy after 1992, nationalism and Chinese cultural identity turned into topics of interest. In the debates on the East Asian development model, Chinese intellectuals had already asked whether being modern and Chinese could mean something other than subscribing to universal liberal or socialist models of development. Hence, the Chinese criticism of May Fourth amid globalization not only was a rejection of Chinese liberal and socialist modernity, but also challenged the singular modernity represented by the West. Increasing commercialization, academic specialization, and professionalization raised further questions about the place of Chinese intellectuals in society and the nature of knowledge production.

Amid these transformations, the matter of what it means to be Chinese also took the form of discussions on Chinese language and modernity. "Translingual practice," as noted, was central to Chinese modernity because, at the turn of the century and during the May Fourth era, the Western *-isms* had been translated into Chinese and brought to China, often through Japan.[1] *-Isms*, as "concepts of movement," were the carriers of the newly imagined futures of the May Fourth youth.[2] For Hu Shi, the creation of a new literature in the vernacular was one of the aspects that rendered May Fourth akin to the European Renaissance. The new intelligentsia of the May Fourth generation relied on a new language to reorganize knowledge, but what did this signify in terms of their social and cultural identities? In the climate of the early 1990s, some intellectuals argued that the 1917 New Literature Movement

---

[1] Liu, *Translingual Practice*.   [2] Spira, *Conceptual History of Chinese -Isms*, 2.

(*Xin wenxue yundong*), during which Chen Duxiu and Hu Shi advocated a vernacular language as a vehicle for the modern thought and culture of the May Fourth era, was detrimental to Chinese language and cultural identity. Following the sociohistorical and philosophical questions addressed earlier, the debate on the literary revolution heralded discussions that took a "linguistic turn."[3]

In a seemingly unusual twist, the debate on the literary revolution, which took off in 1993, became intertwined with debates on postmodernism and postcolonialism. As some areas of China began to assume characteristics of a capitalist society, a theory about the stages of capitalism found an audience among those familiar with Marxism. In addition, with its rejection of grand narratives, the theory also supported the quest for an alternative Chinese modern in the face of a Marxism in crisis and criticism of the May Fourth spirit. The rejection of universalism and opposition to the grand designs of twentieth-century socialism and liberalism rallied anti-radicalism and postmodernism behind a common goal. As elsewhere, however, because of an enduring interest in modernization, postmodernism was co-opted by the modernization discourse. In addition, the preoccupation with cultural identity and language served to restore the cultural authority of Chinese intellectuals vis-à-vis the mass culture of post-1992 China. Chinese theorists of postmodernism and postcolonialism, in spite of their embrace of the market, engaged in a restoration of the perceived lost authenticity under Western dominance.

This chapter investigates how criticism of May Fourth in China became entangled with post-theories against the backdrop of the post-1992 commercialization. I argue that anti-radicalism and postmodernism became natural allies in China, in opposition to the perceived universal Western knowledge models and the post-1989 and 1992 teleology of the nation-state. As such, reading this discussion as a confirmation of the political status quo on mainland China neglects the revisionist aspect of its criticism of May Fourth and socialism. However, like anti-radicalism, postmodernism in China was also incorporated into a search for a better modern and for a dialogue about what it means to be an intellectual in this new climate.

In this discussion, in spite of the growing socioeconomic contradictions from the reforms, the debate continued to revolve around abstract ideas of culture to reimagine China's modernization process, but now reinvented as Chineseness. In this sense, the postmodernists, although they rejected the grand narratives, were realistic revolutionaries no less so than the neoconservatives. The debate once again reflected the changing meaning of the

---

[3] Davies, *Worrying about China*, 138.

"neoconservatism" label amid the growing commercialism. It also reveals the transnationalization of the Chinese intellectual and the resistance to this development.

Postmodernism and China

Postmodernism, as a set of methodologies, including poststructuralism, postcolonialism, and deconstruction, reached China during the culture fever and against the background of a modernist literary revival during the 1980s. The latter had originally flourished in China during the 1920s, but subsequently waned under the dominance of Marxism before being revived after 1978.[4] A notable vehicle for the introduction of postmodern theories, in which Zhang Yiwu, a student of Fredric Jameson, and Chen Xiaoming were key figures, was the series Culture: China and the World, which featured articles on Michel Foucault, Jacques Derrida, Fredric Jameson, and others.[5] This was followed by Chinese translations of leading theorists, including Jürgen Habermas, Ihab Hassan, Jean-François Lyotard, Linda Hutcheon, William Spanos, Douwe Fokkema, and Hans Bertens. These translations appeared in literary and cultural journals such as *Zhongguo shehui kexue* (Social Sciences in China), *Dushu*, *Wenyi yanjiu* (Studies on Literature and Art), *Wenxue pinglun*, *Zhongshan* (Purple Mountain), and others.[6]

In addition to translations, lecture tours by foreign experts and international conferences further spurred the circulation of foreign theories during the second half of the 1980s and the early 1990s. Fredric Jameson delivered a series of lectures on postmodernism at Peking University and Shenzhen University in 1985, and then again in Shanghai and Beijing in May 1993. His lectures were also published in Chinese in both mainland China and Taiwan during the late 1980s, thereby becoming a major vehicle for discussions on postmodernism.[7] Douwe Fokkema spoke in Nanjing and Beijing in 1987 and 1993. Furthermore, in 1993 the International Conference on Postmodernism and Contemporary Chinese Literature was held in Beijing, with a keynote address delivered by Hans Bertens. At the 1995 International Conference on

---

[4] Wang Ning, "The Mapping of Chinese Postmodernity," in Dirlik and Zhang, *Postmodernism and China*, 25.

[5] Wang, "New Criticism," 71; Xu, "Fate of an Enlightenment," 193.

[6] Arif Dirlik and Zhang Xudong, "Introduction: Postmodernism and China," in Dirlik and Zhang, *Postmodernism and China,* 1; Wang, "Mapping of Chinese Postmodernity," 26, 38n17; Douwe Fokkema and Hans Bertens, *Approaching Postmodernism* (Amsterdam: J. Benjamins, 1986) was translated into Chinese as *Zouxiang houxiandai zhuyi*, tr. Wang Ning et al. (Beijing: Beijing daxue chubanshe, 1991; Taipei: Taiwan shuxin chubanshe, 1993).

[7] Wang, "Mapping of Chinese Postmodernity," 38n17; Dirlik and Zhang, "Introduction," 16n1. Jameson's lectures appeared under the title Fredric Jameson [Zhan Mingxin], *Houxiandai zhuyi yu wenhua lilun* (Postmodernism and Cultural Theory), tr. Tang Xiaobing, 3rd rev. ed. (Taipei: Hezhi wenhua shiye gufen youxian gongsi, 1980).

Cultural Studies: China and the West, held in Dalian, Terry Eagleton and Jonathan Arac served as keynote speakers.[8]

Even though postmodernism was introduced to China during the 1980s, it did not become part of Chinese discourse until the early 1990s when the effects of Deng's Southern Tour became clear. For Jameson, postmodernism was a manifestation of the "cultural logic" of "late capitalism" or "multinational capitalism." The division of labor on an international scale and the new media landscape were characteristics of this new stage of capitalism. David Harvey similarly connected postmodernism to new developments in capitalism, whereas Daniel Bell linked postmodern culture to what he termed "post-industrial society." Lyotard and others associated it with new forms of communication and representation, such as "spectacle or image society" or "media capitalism."[9] Jameson noted that in the case of China, global capital, hi-tech developments, and consumer culture explained the rise of an interest in postmodernism. Several Chinese theorists have ascribed Chinese acceptance and popularity of postmodernism to the climate of commercialization, with the rise of mass media and popular culture in the form of TV series, advertising, and the entry of market forces in journalism and the film industry.[10]

However, in spite of the visible effects of reform, modernism was not exhausted and Chinese modernization was not completed in the 1990s, which led one critic to argue that it was still "too early" for postmodernism in China.[11] Also, because economic development was uneven, with tensions between city and countryside and the coastal and interior areas, theorists invoked Ernst Bloch's concept of "the synchronicity of the nonsynchronous," or the coexistence of the premodern, the modern, and the postmodern, to justify use of the theory in a Chinese environment.[12] Dirlik and Zhang argue that it is precisely this "temporal desynchronization," together with "spatial fracturing," that justifies the use of postmodernism in reform China, a claim

---

[8] Wang, "Mapping of Chinese Postmodernity," 38n18.
[9] Fredric Jameson, *Postmodernism; or, The Cultural Logic of Late Capitalism* (Durham, NC: Duke University Press, 1991), 49. Fredric Jameson's stages of capitalism draw on Mandel's theory of the stages of "classical capitalism," "monopoly capitalism" (Lenin's imperialist stage), and "late capitalism" or "multinational capitalism"; David Harvey, *The Condition of Postmodernity: An Enquiry into the Origins of Cultural Change* (Oxford: Blackwell, 1990); Bell, *Cultural Contradictions of Capitalism*; Jean-François Lyotard, *The Postmodern Condition: A Report on Knowledge,* tr. Geoff Bennington (Minneapolis: University of Minnesota Press, 2010).
[10] Wang, "Mapping of Chinese Postmodernity," 33, 38n19; Fan Xing, "Fulu: Jiushi niandai de sixiang liebian" (Addendum: Thought Fission of the 1990s), in Fan Xing, *Shijimo wenhua sichaoshi* (History of Cultural Trends at the End of the Century) (Wuhan: Hubei jiaoyu chubanshe, 1999), 282.
[11] Interview with Tao Dongfeng, Beijing, June 28, 2006.
[12] Jameson, *Postmodernism,* 307. See Ernst Bloch, "Nonsynchronism and Dialectics," *New German Critique,* no. 11 (Spring 1977), 22–38.

echoed by Chinese theorists.[13] According to Wang Yuechuan, postmodernism in China was conceived in relation to abrupt political, economic, and cultural transitions; the Chinese postmodern was a "problem aggregate" rather than an *-ism*, a faction, or a fad.[14] Instead of challenging Truth, Chinese critical discourse concentrated on the application of Western theories to resolve Chinese problems.[15] Zhang Yiwu (b. 1962), a postmodernist critic based at Peking University, has noted the reciprocity of the process: Chinese postmodernists applied theory to explain reality, and if the theory did not suit the reality, then the reality was utilized to reflect on the theory.[16]

In addition to the socioeconomic transformations that accompanied the 1992 renewal of reform, such as changes in information technology and the mobility of capital and labor, postmodernism gained ground after the 1989 repression of the student demonstrations. Bringing an end to the New Enlightenment Movement of the 1980s, 1989 also signified the end of the grand May Fourth narratives about modernity, progress, and the nation-state. With the international decline of socialism, the master narratives of revolution and socialism lost credibility. As such, the theory functioned as a window into the tensions between the realities of the economic reform and the revolution on which CCP legitimacy is based.[17] In the framework of the "disjuncture" between economic liberalization and pragmatics and political control, a core task was to "reposition" the intellectual.[18]

The Linguistic Turn: Debating May Fourth through Post-theories

Against the backdrop of the spread of post-theories—postmodernism, poststructuralism, and postcolonialism—in 1990s China scholars used them to reflect on twentieth-century radicalism and on the New Literature Movement. Because debates on radicalism also revisited Chinese modernity in its May Fourth and socialist forms, there was some common ground among the debates. Both the conservative criticism of May Fourth and postmodernism raised the question of whether Chinese modernity betrayed Chineseness because of its reliance on Western models. Literature had been central to the creation of a modern Chinese cultural identity during the period of imperial decline and military defeat after the late nineteenth century, exchanging

---

[13] Dirlik and Zhang, "Introduction," 3; Lu, "Global POSTmodernIZATION," 146.
[14] Wang Yuechuan, "Xuyan" (Preface), in Wang, *Zhongguo houxiandai huayu* (The Chinese Postmodernism Discourse) (Guangzhou: Zhongshan daxue chubanshe, 2004), 1–3, 6–8.
[15] Gloria Davies, "Anticipating Community, Producing Dissent: The Politics of Recent Chinese Intellectual Praxis," *China Review* 2.2 (Fall 2002), 3, emphasis original.
[16] Interview with Zhang Yiwu, Beijing, July 26, 2006.
[17] Dirlik and Zhang, "Introduction," 7.   [18] Lu, "Global POSTmodernIZATION," 146–47.

Sino-centric pretensions with the realization that China was but one nation among many. This was translated into a literary "rhetorical mode of overcoming and regeneration" that sought to renew the people and the "national character."[19] Literature in China thus served as a vehicle for the creation of a modern Chinese nation.

During the literary revolution, liberal Hu Shi and Chen Duxiu, who would later become a cofounder of the CCP, promoted a "living language expressed in a free form" to replace "the dead language bound by classical poetry and prose."[20] This living language was the vernacular language (*baihua*), which they felt should replace the "dead" classical Chinese (*wenyan*). In the article "Some Tentative Suggestions for the Reform of Chinese Literature," published in *Xin qingnian* in January 1917, Hu Shi proposes eight principles as a basis for the reform of literature, such as avoidance of classical phrases and constructions, use of the vernacular language, and rejection of the classical form in favor of substance.[21] Even though Hu Shi does not use the word "revolution" in this article, the term is present in drafts and was already circulating before and after January 1917.[22] In February 1917, Chen Duxiu praised European revolutions for having realized a radical break between the old and the new, whereas in his *Xin qingnian* article "On the Literary Revolution," he writes that Chinese revolutions were never thoroughly carried out. A true revolution, Chen Duxiu claims, should target not only the political realm but also the realms of ethics, literature, and the arts.[23]

Discussions about the literary revolution by intellectuals have centered on, among others, the artistic value versus the social engagement of works, and the

---

[19] Jing Tsu, *Failure, Nationalism, and Literature: The Making of Modern Chinese Identity, 1895–1937* (Stanford, CA: Stanford University Press, 2005), 7–8.

[20] Michelle Yeh, *Modern Chinese Poetry: Theory and Practice since 1917* (New Haven, CT: Yale University Press, 1991), 11. On the literary revolution, see Tse-tsung Chow, "The Literary Revolution," in Chow, *May Fourth Movement*, 269–88; David Der-Wei Wang, "Chinese Literature from 1841 to 1937," in Kang-I Sun Chang and Stephen Owen, eds., *The Cambridge History of Chinese Literature, Volume II: From 1375* (Cambridge: Cambridge University Press, 2010), 413–564; Leo Ou-fan Lee, "Literary Trends: The Quest for Modernity, 1895–1927," in Merle Goldman and Leo Ou-Fan Lee, eds., *An Intellectual History of Modern China* (Cambridge: Cambridge University Press, 2002), 142–95.

[21] Chow, *May Fourth Movement*, 274. See Hu Shi, "Wenxue gailiang chuyi" (Some Tentative Suggestions for the Reform of Chinese Literature), reprinted in Chen Duxiu, Wang Zhongjiang, and Yuan Shuya, *Xin qingnian: Minzhu yu kexue de huhuan* (New Youth: The Call of Democracy and Science) (Zhengzhou: Zhongzhou guji chubanshe, 1999), 146–55.

[22] Michelle Yeh, "Chinese Postmodernism and the Cultural Politics of Modern Chinese Poetry," in Wen-hsin Yeh, ed., *Cross-Cultural Readings of Chineseness: Narratives, Images, and Interpretations of the 1990s* (Berkeley: Institute of East Asian Studies, University of California, 2000), 100.

[23] Chow, *May Fourth Movement*, 275. See Chen Duxiu, "Wenxue geminglun" (On the Literary Revolution), reprinted in Chen, Wang, and Yuan, *Xin qingnian*, 164–67.

question of whether the movement was a product of domestic developments or of foreign influence. Overall, it is agreed that both elements were present, but under discussion is the extent to which each was present. According to the so-called Czech School, "the May Fourth writers were conscious iconoclasts in their rejection of traditional conventions and modes of writing, but in practice their rejection was far from total."[24] During the early 1990s, similar to the question of "totalistic iconoclasm" with regard to May Fourth, Chinese debates included questions about whether there were historical continuities or discontinuities in the New Literature Movement.

It was the poetess Zheng Min (b. 1920), formerly a professor in the Foreign Language and Literature Department of Beijing Normal University, who, in 1993, questioned the merits of the literary revolution. Zheng Min had gained fame during the 1940s as a modernist poetess who belonged to the so-called Nine Leaves poets (*Jiuye shipai*), a group of nine poets associated with journals such as *Shi chuangzao* (Poetry Creation) and *Zhongguo xinshi* (Chinese New Poetry). These modernists dealt with the theme of alienation under industrial modernity, and they deployed avant-garde techniques and psychoanalytical critiques in their poetry.[25] Zheng Min later graduated in English literature from Brown University in 1952, after which she became a researcher in the Institute of Literature of CASS.[26] During the 1980s, along with the revival of modernism, interest in Zheng Min's poetry boomed.[27] Given her reputation as a modernist and avant-garde poetess, perhaps it came as a surprise that in 1993 Zheng Min fulminated against the protagonists of the 1917 New Literature Movement.

In an article that appeared in the literary journal *Wenxue pinglun* in 1993 and that is also included in the collection of articles *Zhishi fenzi lichang: Jijin yu baoshou zhijian de dongdang* on the conservatism/radicalism debate, Zheng Min began her inquiry into modern Chinese poetry with a question that had been raised in "international Sinological circles": Why was it that contemporary Chinese literature, with its history of several millennia of poetry, had not

---

[24] See Merle Goldman, ed., *Modern Chinese Literature in the May Fourth Era* (Cambridge, MA: Harvard University Press, 1977), 7–8, 8.

[25] Gregory B. Lee, *Troubadours, Trumpeters, Troubled Makers: Lyricism, Nationalism, and Hybridity in China and Its Others* (London: Hurst, 1996), 65n4. During the 1940s, the "Nine Leaves poets" were based at National Southwestern Associated University (Xi'nan Lianhe Daxue), from which Zheng Min had graduated in 1943 from the Philosophy Department. Other poets who belonged to this group include Chen Jingrong, Du Yunxie, Mu Dan, and Xin Di.

[26] Zhongwai mingren yanjiu zhongxin (Research Center on Chinese and Foreign Eminent Persons), ed., *Zhongguo dangdai mingrenlu* (Record of Contemporary Chinese Eminent Persons) (Shanghai: Shanghai renmin chubanshe, 1991), 612.

[27] Wilt Idema and Lloyd Haft, *Chinese letterkunde: Een inleiding* (Chinese Literature: An Introduction) (Amsterdam: Amsterdam University Press, 1996), 285.

produced any internationally recognized masterpieces or renowned poets?[28] Michelle Yeh suggests that the "international Sinological circles" to which Zheng Min is referring include William Jenner of the Australian National University and Stephen Owen of Harvard University. Several years earlier, both had disparaged modern Chinese poetry in their review articles of Bei Dao's *The August Sleepwalker*: there was no great modern poetry in Chinese, and modern Chinese poetry manifested a lack of Chineseness.[29]

According to Zheng Min, the reason why this had occurred was because of Chen Duxiu and Hu Shi, the architects of the 1917 New Literature Movement. Chen Duxiu and Hu Shi had applied the "logic of dual oppositions" with respect to language—namely, renewal versus preservation of tradition, vernacular versus literary Chinese, and colloquial versus written Chinese—and had attempted to construct a "new" language based on a rational design. In sum, they had "denied continuity" with ancient literature, from its language to its content, by taking *baihua* novels from the Yuan dynasty (1260–1368) as the point of departure for language reform.[30] Both Hu Shi and Chen Duxiu ignored the fact that theory comes from practice, and they discarded the accumulated cultural essence in the Chinese language. Whereas seven centuries separated Chaucer's *Canterbury Tales* from twentieth-century modernism, a modern language was created in China overnight.

Following other intellectuals at the time who rejected cultural radicalism, Zheng Min further condemned the mode of thought of "over-straightening the crooked," or the excessive correction of perceived wrongdoings. Whereas Chen Lai targeted the politicization of Confucianism, Zheng Min criticized the politicization of art and literature during both the May Fourth era and the Mao era. Similar to other critics of radicalism, Zheng Min equated the radicalism of May Fourth with that of the Mao period, including the Cultural Revolution. During both periods, decisions about language reform were based not on the value of the language but rather on political efficacy. Between 1950 and 1979, an entire new *baihua* language was created, and although the clarity of the language peaked, its richness declined. It was only after 1979, when young poets came across works dating from prior 1949, that the

---

[28] Zheng Min, "Shijimo de huigu: Hanyu yuyan bianhe yu xinshi chuangzao" (Retrospect at the End of the Century: The Chinese Language Reform and the Creation of New Chinese Poetry), in *ZFL*, 158–86.

[29] Yeh, "Chinese Postmodernism and the Cultural Politics of Modern Chinese Poetry," 115–17. See William J. F. Jenner, "Review of *The August Sleepwalker*," *Australian Journal of Chinese Affairs*, no. 23 (January 1990), 193–95; Stephen Owen, "What Is World Poetry?," *New Republic* 203.21 (November 19, 1990), 28–32. On China and international recognition, see also Julia Lovell, *The Politics of Cultural Capital: China's Quest for a Nobel Prize in Literature* (Honolulu: University of Hawai'i Press, 2006).

[30] Zheng, "Shijimo de huigu," 158.

language was reformed amid the rediscovery of tradition and practice became the origin of change.[31]

What is unusual in Zheng Min's advocacy of historical continuity is her resort to structuralism and poststructuralism. With respect to structuralism, Zheng Min invoked the theories of Swiss linguist Ferdinand de Saussure, according to whom meaning is created by the contrast between "signifiers," and the relationship between the "signifier" and the "signified" is arbitrary and merely based on convention.[32] Zheng Min used de Saussure's theory to argue that language is not only the product of the individual; the individual is also the product of the language. Consequently, a language cannot be selected because it always inherits elements from a previous historical stage. Drawing then on the theories of Lacan and Derrida, Zheng Min argued that no new language could ever be created ex nihilo. For Lacan, there is always a gap between the signifier and the signified, Derrida conceived of language as an unlimited exchange of "traces." For Zheng Min, the theories of both Derrida and Lacan were evidence that the design of a clear vernacular language—which was expressed in May Fourth slogans such as "my hand writes what my mouth says"—was but an illusion.[33]

Moreover, for Zheng Min the classical Chinese language contained the characteristics of what de Saussure defines as a "mother tongue": it is a social action in which all the members of the community participate. In this respect, May Fourth intellectuals had "killed their own mother."[34] Zheng Min gave a special twist to de Saussure's argument that linguistics should concentrate not on actual speech (*parole*) but rather on the objective structure of signs and with language as a system (*langue*) by equating the vernacular language pressed for in the literary revolution with de Saussure's *parole*. The advocacies of the protagonists in the literary revolution showed signs of "vernacular centralism" and "phonocentrism," or a preoccupation with the colloquial instead of the written language.[35] Although Anglo-American modernist poetry found inspiration from Chinese characters—Zheng Min refers to Ernest Fenollosa, Ezra

---

[31] Ibid., 173–77.
[32] Terry Eagleton, *Literary Theory: An Introduction*, 2nd ed. (Cambridge, MA: Blackwell, 1996 [1983]), 84.
[33] Huang Zunxian (1848–1905), who is often considered the predecessor of the modern poetry movement, coined the slogan "My hand writes what my mouth says, how can antiquity restrain me?" (*Wo shou xie wu kou. Gu qi neng ju qian*). At the same time, intellectuals such as Tan Sitong and Liang Qichao launched a "revolution in poetry" (*shijie geming*).
[34] Interview with Zheng Min, Beijing, July 6, 2006.
[35] According to poststructuralists, Western philosophy is generally "phonocentric" because it prefers the colloquial over the written language. Western philosophy is also "logocentric" because it believes in, as Eagleton puts it, "some ultimate 'word,' presence, essence, truth or reality which will act as the foundation of all our thought, language and experience." See Eagleton, *Literary Theory*, 113.

Pound, and T. S. Eliot—modernism was disputed when it reached China in the 1930s and the 1940s.[36]

Discussants primarily engaged with the claims that Zheng Min put forward about the nature of the Chinese vernacular and its relation to classical Chinese. The question of whether or not May Fourth is radical was now conducted through the medium of postmodernism. In 1994, also in the pages of *Wenxue pinglun*, Fan Qinlin, an associate professor in the Chinese Department of Nanjing University, refutes Zheng Min's accusation of "logocentrism" in the vernacular language; since the Song (907–1279) and Yuan (1260–1368) dynasties, both written literary Chinese (*wenyanwen*) and written vernacular Chinese (*baihuawen*) had existed.[37] Moreover, Fan Qinlin claims that the true "mother tongue" in a de Saussurian sense is the vernacular: "Only the vernacular is the sole social action in which all social members participate, and only the vernacular can fully identify with social life."[38] Zheng Min simply misunderstood what Hu Shi and Chen Duxiu meant by vernacular language; their modern vernacular was based on vernacular language in the written form (*baihua shumianyu*), to which elements from the vernacular language in the colloquial form (*baihua kouyu*) and from classical Chinese are added. Nevertheless, Fan Qinlin argues, a transition to the vernacular language was necessary from the perspective of the modernization of Chinese culture.

In her rejoinder to Fan Qinlin, Zheng Min reiterates that for her, both vernacular Chinese and literary Chinese were the "mother tongue" of China—her point was to overcome the "logic of dual oppositions" and to demonstrate that they were complementary.[39] Whereas written Chinese is closer to the "subtext," colloquial Chinese is closer to life. Colloquial language provides the written language with vitality; the written language provides the colloquial language with depth. Zheng Min further declares that language is the expression of a historical spirit, and in this respect the Chinese language is superior. Referring to Heidegger's views on language as the "home of Being," Zheng Min claims that language symbolizes the existence of a country and its people. Since the superiority of the Chinese language is situated in its pictographs, it was all the more necessary to move away from the "phonocentrism" that Hu Shi and Chen Duxiu recommended.

---

[36] On imagism in China, see Guiyou Huang, *Whitmanism, Imagism, and Modernism in China and America* (Selinsgrove, PA: Susquehanna University Press, 1997).

[37] Fan Qinlin, "Ruhe pingjia 'wusi' baihuawen yundong? Yu Zheng Min xiansheng shangque" (How to Evaluate the "May Fourth" Vernacular Language Movement? A Discussion with Zheng Min), in *ZFL*, 187–97.

[38] Ibid., 188.

[39] Zheng Min, "Guanyu 'Ruhe pingjia "wusi" baihuawen yundong?' Shangque zhi shangque" (A Rejoinder to the Rejoinder: "How to Evaluate the 'May Fourth' Vernacular Language Movement?"), in *ZFL*, 198–206.

In scholarship on Zheng Min's article and the ensuing debate, critics questioned Zheng Min's account of the nature of the literary revolution and the Chinese vernacular as well as her reception of postmodernism. Michelle Yeh, a specialist on Chinese poetry based at the University of California, Davis, takes issue with what she perceives to be a set of intellectual flaws in Zheng Min's article. These include Zheng Min's equating of the literary revolution with the political revolution of 1949 and her understanding of Hu Shi and Chen Duxiu's extremism as a praxis rather than as a form of "strategic iconoclasm."[40] Hu Shi knew very well that the modern remained branded by tradition, as demonstrated by mockery of his own poetry as "bound feet unbound."[41] In addition, Zheng Min's equating of the vernacular with colloquial language was mistaken: the vernacular to which Hu Shi was referring included not only the spoken language but also vernacular poetry and prose.[42]

A second point that Michelle Yeh takes issue with is Zheng Min's uncritical and simplistic reading of the theories of de Saussure, Lacan, and Derrida. A case in point is Zheng Min's reference to Lacan's theory of the gap between the signified and the signifier; Lacan's point by no means indicates that no meaning can ever be reached. In addition, Zheng Min's reference to Derrida's traces leads to a contradiction; if there are indeed traces of classical Chinese in the vernacular, then "why worry about classical Chinese not being part of modern Chinese if it is always already there?"[43] Instead of deconstructing the "logocentrism" she so criticized, Zheng Min upholds it and merely supplants modern Chinese with classical Chinese. As Michelle Yeh puts it, "Tradition—with a capital T—is upheld as if it were a self-contained, stable, unchanging entity."[44] Zheng Min envisioned a return to tradition to solve the problem of the lack of Chineseness in modern Chinese poetry, but since tradition had been cut off from modern poetry, her argument creates a vicious cycle. Paradoxically, Zheng Min's attempt to deconstruct dual oppositions ends up reinforcing Chineseness in a kind of reversed Orientalist tour de force.

Other criticisms of Zheng Min's article reiterated her failure to deconstruct binaries and instead confirm Chinese tradition as well as her uncritical use of poststructuralism. Writing about the reception of critical theory in China, Gloria Davies refers to Zheng Min's article as "arguably the most strident *J'accuse* of the modern Chinese vernacular" in which deconstruction becomes "deconstructionism" (*jiegou zhuyi*): it was perceived of as a methodology and a theory.[45] Guo Yingjie reads Zheng Min's goal of the "rediscovery of cultural authenticity" and the "activation of the historical community" as a manifestation of cultural nationalism.[46] In this respect, Guo refers to Herder and Fichte

---

[40] Yeh, "Chinese Postmodernism and the Cultural Politics of Modern Chinese Poetry," 108.
[41] Ibid., 107.   [42] Ibid., 110.   [43] Ibid., 112.   [44] Ibid.
[45] Davies, *Worrying about China*, 22, 52–53.   [46] Guo, *Cultural Nationalism*, 133.

as well as to Stalin and Sun Yat-sen because they all regarded language as an essential element of the nation.

Such engagements with Zheng Min's argument already touched upon the broader problem of Chinese modernity and concern with the recovery of Chineseness amid the anxieties brought about by globalization. As discussed, it was amid globalization that postmodernism gained ground in China. However, Zheng Min's revisiting of the literary revolution was also very much part of a broader debate on cultural radicalism and May Fourth that took place in the early 1990s. Along with other articles, her article is included in the volume *Zhishi fenzi lichang: Jijin yu baoshou zhijian de dongdang* that retrospectively organized the debate. Not only does Zheng Min rely on postmodernism to make a conservative argument, but mainland Chinese postmodernists responded to her article by engaging in a broader discussion on Chinese modernity.

Whereas existing interpretations emphasize Zheng Min's "simplistic" reading of postmodernism or Chinese postmodernists' "uncritical" confirmation of the status quo, this chapter looks at how postmodernism overlapped with the conservative criticisms of May Fourth in opposition to the Enlightenment narratives. Even though part of the criticism served nationalist concerns and the official discourse, the common anti-Enlightenment position in both theories represented a questioning of the grand liberal and socialist narratives of Chinese modernity. In addition, both debates revolved around Chinese identity and the place of Chinese intellectuals in post-1989 and post-1992 society. Hence, this chapter approaches the debate on the literary revolution as a manifestation of anti-radicalism that paradoxically relied on postmodern theories to make a conservative argument but that also became entwined with discussions on postmodernism in China. This debate furthermore reveals how, in the mid-1990s, the debate on modernization (*xiandaihua*) became transformed into a debate on modernity (*xiandaixing*).

Zheng Min and Mainland Postmodernists: The Continued Debate

Zheng Min's text provoked a debate on the literary revolution in the pages of the literary journal *Wenxue pinglun* in which the terms "radical" (*jijin*) and "neoconservatism" resurfaced. In general, this debate was about the relation between language and modernity, the nature of Chinese modernity, China's cultural identity, and the place of Chinese intellectuals in a society undergoing transition. Behind the debate were the ruptures of Tiananmen of 1989 and the consumer revolution of 1992, both of which raised the indirect question of the legitimacy of the Chinese Revolution. Globalization and transnational market forces challenged the teleology of the nation-state, and the intellectuals who had pursued Enlightenment during the 1980s made room for those proposing a Chinese model of knowledge and cultural identity against the backdrop of China's changing global economic presence and the cultural pluralism brought about by marketization.

In the discussion between Zheng Min and theorists of postmodernism, Chinese intellectuals discussed both postmodernism and postcolonialism. Wang Hui notes that this development occurred when Edward Said's *Orientalism* reached Chinese audiences in 1993. The background against which this occurred, according to Wang, was the perceived hypocrisy of American approval when Boris Yeltsin stormed the Russian parliament after being ousted in the fall of 1993. Additionally, 1993 was when the *Yinhe* incident took place and when the 2000 Olympics were awarded to Sydney instead of Beijing. Later, opposition to China's bid to enter GATT and the Taiwan Straits crisis of 1995–96 offered fruitful ground for the reception of Said's theories.[47] The situation of new economic pride and a perception of American hostility toward China therefore paved the way for the reception of the theories of postmodernism and postcolonialism in the Chinese quest for international recognition and the reclaiming of subjectivity.

Samuel Huntington's 1993 article "The Clash of Civilizations?" also triggered debates on Chinese cultural identity vis-à-vis the West. Between 1994 and 1995, Huntington's article provoked debates on postcolonialism, nationalism, and globalization in journals such as *Dushu* and *Tianya*. Additionally, special issues on Huntington appeared in *Ershiyi shiji* and *Zhanlüe yu guanli*.[48] In this environment, Chinese theorists connected postmodernism with the "'decolonization' of Asian indigenous cultures and literary discourses" or with "the question of Chineseness in relation to the Eurocentric narrative of history, modernization, and capital."[49] In Yue Daiyun's view, postcolonialism became entangled with a debate on cultural identity, in which race, language, and history formed the basis of "cultural clusters."[50] It needs to be noted, though, that these clusters still very much represented the dominant group—the Han Chinese—and that the reclaiming was that of a Chinese

---

[47] Wang, *China's New Order*, 190n10. See Edward Said, *Orientalism* (New York: Pantheon Books, 1978). For discussions on Edward Said, see *Dushu*, no. 9 (1993), *Dushu*, no. 10 (1994), *Tianya*, no. 2 (1996), *Tianya*, no. 4 (1996), and *Dushu*, no. 8 (1996). Although interest in Said did not become widespread until 1993, there had earlier been some discussion on the concept of Orientalism. For example, the concept appeared in a text by Zhang Jingyuan in the first issue of *Wenxue pinglun* in 1990. See Fan, "Fulu: Jiushi niandai de sixiang liebian," 297–98.

[48] Wang, *China's New Order*, 94; Wang, "New Criticism," 70. See Samuel P. Huntington, "The Clash of Civilizations?," *Foreign Affairs* 72.3 (Summer 1993), 22–49; for the Chinese debates, see, for example, the October and December 1993 issues of *Ershiyi shiji*.

[49] Wang, "Mapping of Chinese Postmodernity," 34; Lu, "Global POSTmodernIZATION," 151.

[50] Yue Daiyun, "On Western Literary Theory in China," tr. Gloria Davies, in Davies, ed., *Voicing Concerns*, 114.

subjectivity from Western hegemony, leaving the reclaiming of other subjectivities within China untouched. This was the background against which the conservative criticism of May Fourth and postmodernism became entangled in the reclaiming of a Chinese modern.

Also in *Wenxue pinglin* in 1994, Xu Ming, a researcher in literature at CASS, asserted that the crux of the discussion between Zheng Min and Fan Qinlin concerned the question of "cultural radicalism."[51] Whereas Zheng Min treated cultural radicalism as problematic, Fan Qinlin considered it as a progressive force for Chinese modernization. Xu Ming lined up with Fan Qinlin—the movement in support of vernacular Chinese was not the concoction of some intellectuals, it was a rational choice of history. Within the broader framework of cultural radicalism, the language reforms were valuable because they constituted but one aspect of a larger process of ideological change. Xu Ming also engaged with Zheng Min's language theories and argued that Zheng Min confused some radical slogans with reality. In practice, the writing style of the May Fourth intellectuals was still immersed with traditional elements.

Later that year, two other authors, Chen Feng and Zhi Zhong, engaged with Zheng Min's criticism of May Fourth in *Wenxue pinglun*.[52] They not only disapproved of Zheng Min's siding with traditional culture but also accused her of a lack of originality in her treatment of May Fourth. A decade earlier, the authors A Cheng and Zheng Yi had also raised the question of why Chinese literature had not been able to reach the ranks of first-class world literature. A Cheng attributed this to the cultural nihilism of May Fourth, which had caused a rupture with traditional culture.[53] Chen Feng and Zhi Zhong also discerned in Zheng Min's argument traces of Lin Yü-sheng's book *The Crisis of Chinese Consciousness* (discussed in Chapter 4), which links the debate to discussions on radicalism and the "totalistic iconoclasm" of May Fourth.

Zheng Min's reading of an "absolute denial" of tradition, so the authors claimed, was reminiscent of Lin Yü-sheng's "totalistic antitraditionalism," and, like Lin Yü-sheng, Zheng Min drew an imaginary line between May Fourth and the Cultural Revolution. However, for Chen Feng and Zhi Zhong neither point was valid: May Fourth was not aimed at a total destruction of traditional culture, and the Cultural Revolution and the May Fourth Movement could by no means be linked. Whereas May Fourth stood for science,

---

[51] Xu Ming, "Wenhua jijin zhuyi de lishi weidu: Cong Zheng Min, Fan Qinlin de zhenglun shuokai qu" (The Historical Dimension of Cultural Radicalism: Explaining the Debate between Zheng Min and Fan Qinlin), in *ZFL*, 207–18.
[52] Chen Feng and Zhi Zhong, "Kua shiji zhi jiao: Wenxue de kunhuo yu xuanze" (Stepping into a New Century: Literature's Puzzlement and Options), in *ZFL*, 219–30.
[53] The authors quoted from A Cheng, "Wenhua zhiyuezhe renlei" (Culture Conditions Humanity), *Wenyibao* (Literary Gazette) July 9, 1985.

democracy, and liberty, the Cultural Revolution represented feudal despotism, hierarchy, and traditional virtues.[54] (We have already encountered similar criticism of the perceived link between the two movements in Chapter 5.)

Postmodernism theorists joined the discussion on Zheng Min's article in the pages of *Wenxue pinglun*. One such theorist is Zhang Yiwu, a literary critic from Peking University and a former student of Fredric Jameson, who has been dubbed "post-master Zhang" (*Zhang houzhu*) for being one of the main post-theorists on mainland China. In a 1994 article, Zhang sees the discussion as a debate on Chinese culture since May Fourth, or, more generally, as a debate on modernity. The creation of a modern Chinese language, Zhang Yiwu maintains, was a core topic in the creation of a modern Chinese nation and a modern Chinese identity.[55] Zhang insists that the relationship between literary and vernacular Chinese had already been discussed during the 1930s, 1940s, and 1950s. Zheng Min's deconstructionist approach was novel, but it did not enable her to look at the issue in a broader cultural setting—the black-and-white approach of the debate was a mere reproduction of the binary opposition that was under attack.

Zhang Yiwu claims that his new point of departure, modernity, allowed him to understand the replacement of classical language with vernacular language as the replacement of the classical with modernity.[56] Zhang explains that his interpretation of modernity was indebted to Habermas's interpretation of the term as unlimited progress in the field of knowledge and to Lyotard's definition of modernity as a master narrative of rationality. Modernity in this sense had been the goal of the vernacular movement because the latter was clearly aimed at Enlightenment, education, liberty, subjectivity, and knowledge transformation. The May Fourth intellectuals faced the dilemma that a radical denial of the native culture—what Zhang calls "Otherization" (*tazhehua*)—could fail because it could bring about the obliteration of all traces of subjectivity, whereas preservation of too many traditional elements could blunt the meaning of modernity and prevent the development of tradition.

In a nod to postcolonial criticism, which he uses to denounce Euro-American hegemony, Zhang argues that Third World intellectuals were often caught up in this dilemma of Otherization. The binary opposition of the classical and vernacular language was a characteristic of this dilemma. Although Zheng Min believed that this dichotomy had been abolished, she actually confirms one side of it—tradition—and hence it still was prone to

---

[54] Chen and Zhi, "Kua shiji zhi jiao," 224.
[55] Zhang Yiwu, "Chonggu 'xiandaixing' yu Hanyu shumianyu lunzheng" (A Re-evaluation of "Modernity" and the Debate on Written Chinese), *Wenxue pinglun*, no. 4 (1994), 107–13, 120; Interview with Zhang Yiwu, Beijing, July 26, 2006.
[56] Zhang, "Chonggu 'xiandaixing,'" 109.

Otherization. To overcome this, Zhang Yiwu argues for a dialogue among multiple cultural and language fields and for the creation of what he calls a "post-vernacular," which would dialectically unite the classical and the vernacular and would enable the "double continuation and double transcendence of the binary opposition of the classical and the vernacular."[57]

Rejecting Otherization also meant rewriting Chinese modernity as a narrative that transcends a Western universal account. In an article that Zhang Yiwu coauthored with Zhang Fa and Wang Yichuan in the literary journal *Wenyi zhengming* in 1994 that puts forward the thesis that China had moved from modernity to Chineseness (*Zhonghuaxing*), the authors refer to Zheng Min's argument.[58] They define modernity as a Chinese "knowledge model" used for self-definition since the 1840s. Ever since the end of the First Opium War, China had made attempts to reconstruct its central location, but it always used a Western reference system. The process of "self-discovery" was at the same time a process of "self-loss."[59]

This process of the loss of subjectivity ended after 1989 with the growing internationalization and marketization of mainland culture. In the cultural realm, the authors claim that the "new era" made room for a "post–new era," an era of new discourse methods and cultural practices that were represented by challenge, revolt, and transcendence. The new knowledge model of Chineseness that the authors propose does not deny modernity, but rather continues both classicism and modernity. Additionally, it does not adhere to a Western linear view of development, but argues in favor of multiple differences: each nation can follow its own road of development. In the model of Chineseness, the question of "Sinification" versus "Westernization," or whether the "essence" (*ti*) and "function" (*yong*) are Chinese or Western, does not exist. In this rewriting of Zheng Min's argument about cultural continuity, the elitist position of the intellectual is exchanged for a celebration of popular culture.

In the final part of the article, the authors propose the establishment of a "Chinese Culture Rim" (*Zhonghua wenhuajuan*), which, in addition to East Asia, might also include Southeast Asia. China would most probably be at the center, not only because of its size and cohesive force but also, and most importantly, because its profound traditional culture could function as a centripetal force. The authors also reiterate the prediction of economists that the twenty-first century would be the "Pacific century," which implies the possible rise of a particular cultural-economic rim. The cultural rim would suit

---

[57] Ibid., 113.
[58] Zhang Fa, Zhang Yiwu, and Wang Yichuan, "Cong 'xiandaixing' dao 'Zhonghuaxing': Xin zhishixing de tanxun" (From "Modernity" to "Chineseness": Explorations into a New Knowledge Model), *Wenyi zhengming*, no. 2 (1994), 10–20.
[59] Ibid., 10–14; Interview with Zhang Yiwu, Beijing, July 26, 2006.

both Chineseness and variety, but the authors nevertheless perceive of China as the center.[60] In a fashion reminiscent of Tu Wei-ming's "Cultural China" theory, the authors identify four different layers in this rim. Mainland China is the core, followed by Taiwan, Hong Kong, and Macao. The third and fourth layers consist of Chinese based outside of China and the countries of East Asia and Southeast Asia that had been influenced by China. When the authors discuss the need for a new vernacular language as part of a new identity pattern, they invoke Zheng Min because "the Chinese language can best reflect the national spirit of the Chinese nation."[61]

Anti-radicalism and Postmodernism: Unlikely Allies?

Critics have interpreted Zhang Yiwu's quest for pluralism as a disguised essentialism. Tang Xiaobing refers to this issue as the "unwieldy new language of universal significance" only serving to "prolong and fortify" the old contradictions.[62] Guo Yingjie insists that the relativism on behalf of which postcolonialists argued was a "defense tactic rather than a genuine conviction"; for them, Chinese culture was unique, but at the same time it was absolute and universal.[63] Moreover, because theorists such as Zhang Yiwu maintained that Chinese culture was superior, critics declared that this "latent Greater China complex" and "Sinocentrism" could set in motion a new "self-imposed isolation" that would prevent all forms of dialogue.[64] In her discussion of Zhang Yiwu, Michelle Yeh notes the tensions between the empowerment behind postmodernism as a theory of resistance and the "logic of reductionism" that equates a critique of modernization with a critique of the West.[65]

According to Gunter Schubert, postmodernism in China challenged a unilinear Western modernity, and this is how it was connected with the "nationalist conservatism" of the 1990s.[66] Other critics have also related postmodernism to a neoconservatism that was understood as anti-Westernism and nationalism.[67] Some authors have also made this argument with respect to Chinese conservatism: Chinese conservatism was not only a criticism of Enlightenment or modernity as a general construct but also a criticism of a Western modernity. As Haun Saussy points out, Chinese postmodernists denounced

---

[60] Zhang, Zhang, and Wang, "Cong 'xiandaixing' dao 'Zhonghuaxing,'" 14–20.   [61] Ibid., 19.
[62] Tang Xiaobing, "The Function of New Theory: What Does It Mean to Talk about Postmodernism in China?" in Liu Kang and Tang, eds., *Politics, Ideology, and Literary Discourse in Modern China: Theoretical Interventions and Cultural Critique* (Durham, NC: Duke University Press, 1993), 281.
[63] Guo, *Cultural Nationalism*, 110.   [64] Ibid., 115.
[65] Yeh, "Chinese Postmodernism and the Cultural Politics of Modern Chinese Poetry," 124.
[66] Schubert, "Was Ist Neokonservativismus?," 67.
[67] See Yang, "Xin baoshou zhuyi yu xin lixing zhuyi," 487.

"modernist, *cosmopolitan* legitimation-devices"; "the rejection of existing modes of legitimation is doubled with the identification of these modes as specifically Western."[68]

Even though this is relevant—as noted, becoming modern in China was also perceived of as overcoming the West—singling out the anti-Western elements in conservatism and postmodernism obscures the extent to which the debate on postmodernism was also a response to a liberal and socialist Chinese past. This explains why the discussion on postmodernism became entangled with the debate on radicalism and the reassessment of the May Fourth Movement; after the failure of the "second Enlightenment" in 1989, intellectuals turned to new modes of discourse. A new element in this debate that distinguishes it from other rejections of radicalism is globalization. Zhang Yiwu notes that the distinction between the cultural stance of the 1990s and the cultural conservatism since May Fourth is that the former revolved around the question of globalization, whereas the latter revolved around the topic of modernity.[69] The merger of the two debates reflects a rethinking of the question of how to modernize under the impact of globalization.

Wang Hui identifies the response to 1989 as one of the four characteristics of postmodernism in a Chinese context, the others being a lack of interest in the theory as used elsewhere, the fact that it was not restricted to mainland China, and the absence of a consensus on what it entailed.[70] Xu Jilin also argues that after 1989, which he compares to 1968 in the West, the main discourse on Enlightenment and modernization was exchanged for historical reflections. Criticism of the 1980s occurred in the form of a sociohistorical debate on conservatism and radicalism as well as in the form of postmodernism, which was directed against the "master narratives" of modernity.[71] Xu elsewhere states that the theories of Karl Popper and Thomas Kuhn might serve as a basis for the "critical falsification" of the "myth of truth" put forward in these metanarratives.[72] As Liu Kang, who was Jameson's interpreter in 1993, puts it, postmodernist critics accused the intellectuals of the 1980s of "blindly subscribing to the Western Enlightenment discourse of the 'grand narratives' about 'modernity' and 'nation-state.'"[73]

---

[68] Haun Saussy, "Postmodernism in China: A Sketch and Some Queries," in Wen-Hsin Yeh, ed., *Cross-Cultural Readings of Chineseness: Narratives, Images and Interpretations of the 1990s* (Berkeley: Institute of East Asian Studies, University of California, 2000), 130, 131.
[69] Interview with Zhang Yiwu, Beijing, July 26, 2006.
[70] Anfeng Sheng, "Traveling Theory, or, Transforming Theory: Metamorphosis of Postcolonialism in China," *Neohelicon* 34.2 (2007), 122–23.
[71] Ibid., 130–32.   [72] Xu, "Fate of an Enlightenment," 193.
[73] Liu, "Is There an Alternative to (Capitalist) Globalization?," 212; Davies, *Worrying about China*, 174.

Although postmodernism engaged with the perceived universal liberal modernity of the 1980s, it also engaged with the decline of socialism and the commercialization of Chinese society after 1992. As Dirlik and Zhang note, postmodern also means "postsocialist" and "postrevolutionary." Since the "post" in postmodernism involves inheritance of and a connection with modernity, when it is applied to China, postmodernism is both antirevolutionary and the heir of socialism. Consequently, "postmodernity may serve as a site of struggle between the legacy of the past and the forces of the present."[74] Zhang Yiwu does not call postmodernism "antirevolutionary," but instead he applies the term "de-revolution" (*jie geming*). He further contends that Chinese postmodernists use the theory to reflect on Chinese modernity as a whole; revolution and socialism constitute a core aspect of this whole.[75]

In China, postmodernism did not direct itself wholly against capitalism, as it did in Jameson's account. Against the backdrop of Chinese socialism, postmodernist culture was perceived of as a "new space of popular freedom."[76] After the ideological rigidity of the Cultural Revolution, new approaches such as deconstruction were welcomed. For some, the characteristics of relativism and the language games of postmodernism resembled the Daoism of Laozi and Zhuangzi.[77] The global market challenged the socialist state. Both Dirlik and Pickowicz make use of the term "postsocialism" in relation to postmodernism. Whereas Dirlik applies the term to refer to the official policy of "socialism with Chinese characteristics," Pickowicz understands it as a loss of faith in socialism on behalf of the masses.[78] According to Pickowicz, "Postsocialism involves a perception among ordinary people at the bottom that socialism has failed, that it is not the solution to what ails society, but rather the very cause."[79]

In relation to May Fourth and socialism, postmodernism was also a manifestation of a realistic revolution against the path of Chinese modernity. The events of 1989 and 1992 challenged not only the validity of universal models of development but also the teleology of the Chinese nation-state and

---

[74] Dirlik and Zhang, "Introduction," 7–8.
[75] Interview with Zhang Yiwu, Beijing, July 26, 2006.
[76] Wang, "Introduction: Minds of the Nineties," 21.
[77] Yue, "On Western Literary Theory in China." In an interview discussing intellectual influences, Zheng Min mentions Derrida, Laozi, and Zhuangzi in the same breath. Interview with Zheng Min, Beijing, July 6, 2006; Interview with Yue Daiyun, Beijing, July 12, 2006.
[78] Arif Dirlik first used the term in "Postsocialism? Reflections on 'Socialism with Chinese Characteristics,'" in Dirlik and Maurice Meisner, eds., *Marxism and the Chinese Experience: Issues in Contemporary Chinese Socialism* (Armonk, NY: M.E. Sharpe, 1989), 361–84. Pickowicz applies the term to analyze films by director Huang Jianxin. See Paul G. Pickowicz, "Huang Jianxin and the Notion of Postsocialism," in Nick Browne et al., *New Chinese Cinemas: Forms, Identities, Politics* (Cambridge: Cambridge University Press, 1994), 57–87.
[79] Pickowicz, "Huang Jianxin and the Notion of Postsocialism," 63.

its twentieth-century trajectory. As Saussy notes, dismissing "post-*isms*" in China as a confirmation of the status quo overlooks the "revisionary force" of anti-radicalism and postmodernism.[80] Postmodernism in China is not only an uncritical confirmation of commercialism but also an expression of "de-revolution." As argued above, claiming the May Fourth legacy did not necessarily serve official interests and postmodern also meant postrevolutionary. Even though the practice of reform was a form of de-revolution, as argued in Chapter 2, official justifications of economic reform still placed the revolution firmly in the past. Officially, capitalism was necessary because China, as noted in 1987, was still only at the "primary stage of socialism." Therefore, the grand narrative of socialism and the nation-state persisted in the official ideology.

From a Marxist perspective, postmodernism was utterly antirevolutionary. For Terry Eagleton, a "radical epistemology" resulted in "conservative politics" because postmodernists engaged in discourses that had no direct political results.[81] Or, in the words of David Harvey, "The rhetoric of postmodernism is dangerous for it avoids confronting the realities of political economy and the circumstances of global power."[82] Fredric Jameson notes that under postmodernism both cultural criticism and political resistance seemed to have become "secretly disarmed and reabsorbed by a system of which they themselves might well be considered a part, since they can achieve no distance from it."[83] For Arif Dirlik, postcolonial criticism is all but radical. The "post" in postcolonialism relegates both colonialism and its structures to the past, thus concealing not only its origins but also the struggles against it. Targeting Eurocentrism instead of capitalism, it ends up embracing the latter.[84]

Because critics of radicalism and postmodernists both did away with the teleology of a Chinese modernity, be it liberal or socialist, that had been detrimental to China's cultural and historical continuity, they shared common ground. Chinese rejections of radicalism in the 1990s were directed at change based on an abstract design rather than that based on experience and gradual reform. Postmodern critics similarly revisited Chinese modernity from the perspective of how adoration of Western models had led to a detachment from China's cultural identity. In the words of Wang Ning, as a philosophical trend postmodernism in China was "a sort of post-Enlightenment phenomenon characterized by the crisis of legitimation and representation."[85]

---

[80] Saussy, "Postmodernism in China," 138.
[81] Terry Eagleton, *The Illusions of Postmodernism* (Cambridge, MA: Blackwell, 1996), 14.
[82] Harvey, *Condition of Postmodernity*, 117.   [83] Jameson, *Postmodernism*, 48–49.
[84] Arif Dirlik, "Reversals, Ironies, Hegemonies: Notes on the Contemporary Historiography of Modern China," *Modern China* 22.3 (July 1996), 274–75.
[85] Wang, "Mapping of Chinese Postmodernity," 23.

The merger of conservatism and postmodernism in post-1989 China is not necessarily an anomaly or merely a product of circumstance. Philosophically, conservatism and postmodernism both oppose the universalism and abstract design of Enlightenment progressivism. Jürgen Habermas held that both neoconservatives and postmodernists abandoned the "tradition of reason in which European modernity once understood itself."[86] Conservatism and postmodernism share a common enemy, that is, Enlightenment rationalism. In postmodernism, the attack on Cartesian rationalism and its "blueprint aspirations" manifested itself in what Lyotard calls the "incredulity towards metanarratives": the relative and the contingent are preferred to the absolute and the universal. Conservative critics, beginning with Edmund Burke, also attacked the Cartesian subject as the architect of an ideal society, thereby ignoring the limits of man's reason and his moral imperfections. Because of this theoretical affinity, one could argue that it is paradoxical that in practice postmodernism and conservatism denounced each other.[87] Guy Alitto, the author of the book on Liang Shuming discussed in the previous chapter, contends that postmodernism and conservatism were both antimodernity theories. After World War Two, criticism of the Enlightenment spirit of rationalization that conservatives had been expressing since the eighteenth century was continued in the form of postmodernism.[88]

In China, in the words of Yü Ying-shih, "the postmodern rage against Enlightenment rationality" also began "to cast a shadow on the May Fourth Project."[89] In the Chinese setting of the early 1990s, however, reflections on Chinese modernity became strident quests for an alternative modern given that modernization had not yet been completed. Paradoxically, postmodernism became integrated in the search for a better modern. In this sense, postmodern critiques were not dissimilar from conservative critiques; in an effort to move away from the teleology of a liberal or socialist modernity, they remained trapped in narratives of modernization and discussions about the relation between tradition and modernity. Now, however, the latter were accompanied by discourses on globalization and consumerism. In the words of Jason McGrath, "In the importance of the *future* to the ideology of postsocialist China, we find yet another justification for insisting on postsocialist *modernity*."[90]

---

[86] Jürgen Habermas, *The Philosophical Discourse of Modernity: Twelve Lectures*, tr. Frederick Lawrence (Cambridge, MA: MIT Press, 1987), 4.
[87] Bruce Pilbeam, "Conservatism and Postmodernism: Consanguineous Relations or 'Different' Voices?," *Journal of Political Ideologies* 6.1 (2001), 42–43.
[88] Guy Alitto, "Postmodernism" (lecture, Peking University, June 27, 2006).
[89] Yü, *Chinese History and Culture*, 198.
[90] Jason McGrath, *Postsocialist Modernity: Chinese Cinema, Literature, and Criticism in the Market Age* (Stanford, CA: Stanford University Press, 2008), 204.

The Chinese Intellectual: The Right to Represent "China"

The debate among Zheng Min and the postmodernism theorists was also a debate among those who advocated a continuation of the role of the Chinese intellectual as responsible for the fate of the Chinese nation, and those who lauded the popular culture of the 1990s that signified the death knell of the elitist humanist and Enlightenment culture of the 1980s. However, even those who lauded the arrival of the market continued their search for new knowledge models and a Chinese modern.

We should situate this preoccupation with the place of the intellectual in Chinese society within the broader setting of the debates about reform in the early 1990s. As Wang Hui notes, a shift in "political vocabulary" occurred around 1993 following Deng Xiaoping's Southern Tour. Both Cui Zhiyuan, then a political scientist at MIT, and Gan Yang, then also in the United States, who were later referred to as New Leftists, criticized the economic reforms.[91] At the same time, a debate on the "humanist spirit" was taking place, led by scholars in Shanghai where the effects of commercialization were most visible. This debate on the "loss of the humanist spirit" was carried out in journals such as *Shanghai wenxue* (Shanghai Literature) and *Dushu* in 1993 and 1994.[92] In the debate, one group of intellectuals, whose main representatives were literary historian Wang Xiaoming and literary scholar Chen Sihe, asserted that the 1990s had witnessed the loss of what they called the "humanist spirit" (*renwen jingshen*) or the embrace of "ultimate concerns" (*zhongji guanhuai*).[93]

Wang Xiaoming summarizes the debate as a cultural crisis and a loss of existential meaning; advocacy of the humanist spirit or ultimate concerns was thus nothing less than "the self-saving action of intellectuals."[94] These intellectuals opposed the commercialization of society and argued in favor of a continuation of the ultimate ideals of the 1980s. Works by the "two Zhangs," author Zhang Wei, whose writings on China's social change contain romantic elements, and author Zhang Chengzhi, known for his writings on rural

---

[91] Wang, "New Criticism," 58–59. See Cui Zhiyuan, "Zhidu chuangxin yu di'erci sixiang jiefang" (Institutional Innovation and a Second Liberation of Thought), *Ershiyi shiji*, no. 24 (August 1994), 5–16; Gan Yang, "Xiangtu Zhongguo chongjian yu Zhongguo wenhua qianjing" (The Future of Chinese Culture in Relation to Rural Reconstruction), *Ershiyi shiji*, no. 16 (April 1993), 5.

[92] The key journals in the "humanist spirit" debate also included *Dongfang*, *Shanghai wenhua* (Shanghai Culture), *Tansuo yu zhengming*, *Xiandai yu chuantong*, and *Wenyi zhengming*. See Wang Xiaoming, ed., *Renwen jingshen xunsi lu* (Collection of Reflections on the Humanist Spirit) (Shanghai: Wenhui chubanshe, 1996). For an analysis of the debate, see Barmé, *In the Red*, 283–86, 296–97; McGrath, *Postsocialist Modernity*, 25–58; Giorgio Strafella, *Intellectual Discourse in Reform Era China: The Debate on the Spirit of the Humanities in the 1990s* (London: Routledge, 2017).

[93] Barmé, *In the Red*, 284.   [94] Wang, *Renwen jingshen xunsi lu*, 272, 273.

Mongolia and Sufism, are read as expressions of this preoccupation with the humanist spirit, although neither of them took part in the debate in *Dushu*.[95] The opposing position in the debate, that of an embrace of the liberating effects of the market and mass culture, is reflected in the works of the "two Wangs," former minister of culture and writer Wang Meng and novelist Wang Shuo.[96] For these intellectuals, consumer society meant a departure from the political authoritarianism of the Mao era; it was also a move toward economic prosperity and cultural pluralism. Works by Wang Shuo showed characteristics of cynicism, criticism of authoritarianism, and repudiation of ideology and ideals; the flawless exemplary figures of the revolutionary era were exchanged for *liumang*, a term that includes "everything from hooligans to alienated youth, individualists, and unscrupulous entrepreneurs."[97]

The debate on the humanist spirit shared some communalities with the debate on the literary revolution. McGrath notes that in the debate on the humanist spirit, Chinese intellectuals linked a crisis in Chinese literature to a crisis in spirituality. This connection can be traced back to Liang Qichao at the start of the twentieth century, but it can also be traced to advocates of the literary revolution, such as Hu Shi and Chen Duxiu.[98] In the debate on the humanist spirit as well as that on the revision of the literary revolution, the perceived spiritual crisis served as a point of entry to discuss cultural identity. In addition, both the debate on the humanist spirit and the humanism advocated by the New Confucians addressed challenges to the place of intellectuals in a consumer society and under conditions of specialization and professionalization.[99]

This is the backdrop against which discussions on mainland postmodernism continued in the pages of *Ershiyi shiji* in 1995. The term "neoconservatism" entered the debate when Chinese scholars based and sometimes also educated at universities in Europe and the United States used it as a label for mainland appropriations of postmodernism, poststructuralism, and postcolonialism. Whereas previously the neoconservatism label had been applied to advocates of a strong state, it now stood for an uncritical embrace of the market, consumer culture, and the lack of higher ideals. Articles on the continuing

---

[95] Both Zhang Wei and Zhang Chengzhi have been identified as proponents of a "cultural conservatism," which in this case signifies moral idealism and aesthetic romanticism. Lan Aiguo, "Shijimo wenxue: Wenhua baoshou zhuyi sichao" (End of the Century Literature: The Cultural Conservative Trend), *Wenyi zhengming*, no. 6 (1994), 34–37.

[96] Wang Meng, "Duobi chonggao" (Shunning the Sublime), *Dushu*, no. 1 (1993), 10–17. On Wang Shuo, see Barmé, *In the Red*, 287–96.

[97] Barmé, *In the Red*, 63–98, 73.   [98] McGrath, *Postsocialist Modernity*, 28–29.

[99] Chen Pingyuan, "Jin bainian Zhongguo jingying wenhua de shiluo" (The Decline of High Culture in China during the Last One Hundred Years), *Ershiyi shiji*, no. 17 (June 1993), 11–22. This was a response both to Wang Meng's "Duobi chonggao" and to Yü Ying-shih's "Zhishi fenzi de bianyuanhua." See Wang, "Introduction: Minds of the Nineties," 20n21.

debate on postmodernism also featured in the volume *Zhishi fenzi lichang: Jijin yu baoshou zhijian de dongdang*, not only because of the appearance of the term "neoconservatism" but also because the heart of the discussion in the post-1992 climate centered on a redefinition of the position of intellectuals.

The transnational element that figured in the formation and development of the debates on radicalism was also present as Chinese scholars outside of mainland China joined the conversation in 1995. The consequent rift that formed between these scholars and scholars based on mainland China reveals that, under the effect of commercialization and mobility, the definition of a Chinese intellectual had become fluid. Who had the right to speak on behalf of Chinese intellectuals? Furthermore, should they still, as Gloria Davies calls it, "worry about China" given the impact of transnational market forces?[100] Ironically, in their accusation of mainland uses of postmodernism for being a political neoconservatism in support of the status quo, several Chinese scholars based abroad upheld the traditional conception of the Chinese intellectual as the guardian of culture and the moral conscience of the people.[101]

Post-Isms and Neoconservatism

One such overseas critic is Zhao Yiheng (b. 1943), also known as Henry Y. H. Zhao, a scholar of modern Chinese literature at the School of Oriental and African Studies (SOAS) at the University of London. In the February 1995 issue of *Ershiyi shiji*, he launched an assault on the paradox of "post-isms" (*houxue*)—postcolonialism, postmodernism, and poststructuralism—in the service of what he calls the "neoconservative trend" in Chinese intellectual circles.[102] Zhao Yiheng also presented his argument in Dalian at the 1995 International Conference on Cultural Studies: China and the West, which included participants such as Terry Eagleton and Jonathan Arac.[103] In his 1995 article, Zhao asks, was the neoconservative appropriation of postmodernism a theory considered radical in the West a product of the mainland Chinese situation,

---

[100] See Davies, *Worrying about China*.
[101] The main texts in the debate are collected in Wang Hui and Yu Guoliang, eds., *Jiushi niandai de "houxue" lunzheng* (The Debates in the 1990s on "Post-*Isms*") (Hong Kong: Chinese University of Hong Kong Press, 1998).
[102] Zhao Yiheng, "'Houxue' yu Zhongguo xin baoshou zhuyi" ("Post-*Isms*" and Chinese Neoconservatism), *Ershiyi shiji*, no. 27 (February 1995), 4–15. A slightly different version of the article appears in ZFL, 343–56, titled "'Houxue,' xin baoshou zhuyi yu wenhua pipan" ("Post-*Isms*," Neoconservatism, and Cultural Criticism). Dirlik and Zhang translate "houxue" as "postology" and note that it can also mean "postscholarship" or "late-born learning." Dirlik and Zhang, "Introduction," 13.
[103] The papers presented at the conference also appear in *New Literary History* 28.1 (Winter 1997). For Zhao Yiheng's paper, see Henry Y. H. Zhao, "Post-*Ism* and Chinese New Conservatism," *New Literary History* 28.1 (1997), 31–44.

or was it due to the very nature of the theory?[104] In his condemnation of neoconservatism, Zhao Yiheng targets Zheng Min for making use of "new theories" to strengthen an "old perspective on an old problem," namely conservative criticism of May Fourth.[105] Zhao also considers "national studies," as discussed in the previous chapter, and the affirmation of popular commercial culture by mainland intellectuals to be aspects of a political "neoconservative trend."[106]

Zhao Yiheng uses the label "neoconservatism" to indicate the opposite of "critique" (*pipan*).[107] Mainland intellectuals' abandonment of their elitist stance and the responsibilities it entailed—concern for the state, the nation, and humanity—Zhao claims, constitutes the main characteristic of neoconservatism. For Zhao, elite culture is a progressive and "radical," or "critical," force, whereas the embrace of mass culture signifies the decline of culture.[108] Amid criticism of commercialization and praise of the elitist position of intellectuals in the 1980s, Zhao Yiheng also refers to the debate on the "loss of the humanist spirit," noted earlier. In another article in *Ershiyi shiji*, Zhao Yiheng elaborates on the conformist and noncritical aspects of postmodernism, preferring quantity over quality and confirming contemporary culture.[109] Elsewhere, Zhao explains that for him poststructuralism signifies the end of the 1980s' narrative.[110]

Another overseas Chinese critic of mainland uses of postmodernism is Xu Ben, associate professor of English at Saint Mary's College in California. In the same issue of *Ershiyi shiji* in which Zhao Yiheng launches his attack on "post-*isms*," Xu Ben finds fault with what he calls "Chinese style 'third world criticism.'" For Xu Ben, the reason why cultural criticism on mainland China after 1989 became "conservative" can be found in the Chinese situation.[111] After 1989, Xu Ben claims, literary criticism on mainland China lost its political character; intellectuals only disapproved of "safe" objects, such as commodity culture, the "loss of the humanist spirit," or the "Orientalism" of Western culture. Xu Ben attributes this depoliticization of literary criticism to

---

[104] Zhao, "'Houxue' yu Zhongguo xin baoshou zhuyi," 5.   [105] Ibid., 5.
[106] See the conversation among Chen Xiaoming, Zhang Yiwu, Dai Jinhua, and Zhu Wei, "Dongfang zhuyi he houzhimin zhuyi" (Orientalism and Postcolonialism), *Zhongshan* 88.1 (1994), 126–48.
[107] Zhao Yiheng, "'Houxue,' xin baoshou zhuyi yu wenhua pipan," 344.
[108] Davies, *Worrying about China*, 97–98.
[109] Zhao Yiheng, "Wenhua pipan yu houxiandai zhuyi lilun" (Cultural Criticism and Postmodernism Theory), *Ershiyi shiji*, no. 31 (October 1995), 147–51, esp. 149.
[110] Zhao Yiheng, "Ruhe miandui dangjin Zhongguo wenhua xianzhuang: Haineiwai dalu xuezhe de yichang bianlun" (How to Confront the Status Quo in the Present Chinese Culture: A Debate among Mainland and Overseas Scholars), in *ZFL*, 357–67, esp. 359–61.
[111] Xu Ben, "'Di san shijie piping' zai dangjin Zhongguo de chujing" (The Predicament of "Third World Criticism" in Present-Day China), *Ershiyi shiji*, no. 27 (February 1995), 16–27.

the state of political control, the spread of a commodity economy, and the instrumental use of nationalism by the authorities. Unlike postcolonial criticism in the West, which is an oppositional discourse that is aligned with social movements, the theories of Zhang Yiwu and others were characterized by "nativism." Consequently, the battle against oppression became the "discursive oppression of the First World against the Third World," thus implying that Chinese intellectuals avoided dealing with the oppression in Chinese society. In brief, Chinese "Third World criticism" was marked by a tendency to "reject what is near and seek what is far away" (*shejin qiuyuan*) and to "dwell on the abstract and avoid real issues" (*bishi jiuxu*).[112] Elsewhere, Xu Ben calls "Chinese nativist post-ist theory" "a prima facie unlikely union of Western postmodern, postcolonial theories and Chinese concerns about national authenticity and identity."[113] Because intellectuals were very careful about their attitudes toward the official nationalist discourse, mainland cultural criticism and official nationalism could coexist peacefully.

Other Chinese intellectuals based outside of mainland China joined in this condemnation of mainland cultural criticism. They include Zhang Longxi, a scholar of cross-cultural studies educated at Peking University and Harvard University who first taught in the United States and later in Hong Kong. In an article that appeared in the February 1996 issue of *Ershiyi shiji*, Zhang Longxi praises Zhao Yiheng's analysis for being "modern" and "rational," for being rooted in modern Western democracy and science, and for continuing the "critical tradition" of May Fourth.[114] In contrast, the use of postmodernism on mainland China in the service of the promotion of tradition, national interest, and the status quo in part could be attributed to historical and cultural factors but primarily to the Chinese political system. Zhang Longxi further condemns the self-contradictory move to apply Western theories to attack the West as well as the fact that mainland Chinese intellectuals saw overseas Chinese academics as part of the Western academic system.[115]

Responses from Mainland China: Targeting Outsiders

As in the broader debate on radicalism, it is too simplistic to say that the division was primarily between mainland scholars and those based outside of mainland China. Since those who criticized the postmodern abandonment of the Enlightenment ideals were liberal intellectuals, some mainland liberals equally criticized mainland theorists of postmodernism. One such example is

---

[112] Ibid., 17, 27. [113] Xu, *Disenchanted Democracy*, 178.
[114] Zhang Longxi, "Duoyuan shehui zhong de wenhua piping" (Cultural Criticism in Pluralistic Societies), *Ershiyi shiji*, no. 33 (February 1996), 18–25, 19.
[115] Ibid., 22, 24, 25.

Lei Yi, who worked in the Institute of Modern Chinese History of CASS. In 1995, Lei Yi criticized Zhang Yiwu and others for "gulping down uncritically" a foreign theory without exploring its concrete background.[116] The theories of Foucault and others had truly been revolutionary in the West because they stood up to a monolithic discourse. However, because this discourse was only marginal in China, both the spearhead and the revolutionary character of the theory disappeared in the Chinese setting. For this reason, Lei Yi spoke of a "feeling of 'dislocation'" with regard to postmodernism and postcolonialism in China.[117]

Other mainland Chinese scholars also objected to the nationalist turn of mainland postmodernism. According to Wang Yuechuan, postcolonialism should reflect on modernity instead of becoming an "oppositional ideology" of East and West, which could create an outmoded "Cold War consciousness." Nationalism often led to new problems in China—could the postcolonial and the postmodern truly provide a new value choice to face the cultural hegemony of the West?[118] Tao Dongfeng argues that the quest for Chineseness in Chinese postcolonialism obscured its cultural-political quest for liberal democracy.[119] For Wang Hui, it is paradoxical that Chinese post-theorists used the postmodernist attack on Eurocentrism to argue on behalf of Chineseness. In its original milieu, postmodernism challenged the mainstream culture, whereas in China, after its merger with nationalism, postmodernism strengthened the mainstream culture.[120]

Still other mainland Chinese intellectuals refuted use of the "neoconservatism" label and, reminiscent of Jiang Yihua's attack on Yü Ying-shih, accused overseas Chinese intellectuals of a lack of familiarity with Chinese intellectual practices. Liu Dong (b. 1955), then a researcher at the Institute of Foreign Literature of CASS, accused overseas scholars of "pidgin scholarship," a scholarship "produced by deliberate acts of misreading."[121] Liu refers to overseas intellectuals' use of the neoconservatism label as "a strategy of

---

[116] Lei Yi, "Beijing yu cuowei: Ye tan Zhongguo de 'houzhimin' yu 'houxiandai'" (Background and Dislocation: Also on China's "Postcolonialism" and "Postmodernism"), *Dushu*, no. 4 (1995), 16–20, 18.
[117] Ibid., 17–18. [118] Wang, "Xuyan," 7–8.
[119] Tao, "Ershi shiji Zhongguo de baoshou zhuyi," 253–61.
[120] Wang, *China's New Order*, 170; Wang Hui and Zhang Tianwei, "Wenhua pipan lilun yu dangdai Zhongguo minzu zhuyi wenti" (Cultural Criticism Theory and the Issue of Contemporary Chinese Nationalism), *Zhanlüe yu guanli*, no. 4 (1994), 17–20.
[121] Liu Dong, "Revisiting the Perils of 'Designer Pidgin Scholarship,'" tr. in Davies, ed., *Voicing Concerns*, 87–108, 102. Liu Dong's article was first published in December 1995 in *Ershiyi shiji*, together with responses from Lei Yi, Cui Zhiyuan, and Gan Yang. See Liu Dong, "Jingti renwei de 'yangjingbing xuefeng'" (Beware of "Designer Pidgin Scholarship"), *Ershiyi shiji*, no. 32 (December 1995), 5–13.

calling things by dramatic names to mislead and whip up overseas public opinion."[122] Those who engaged in Chinese studies abroad lacked "in-depth cultural awareness"; they failed to make sense of the "problematic consciousness" of Chinese people; and they suffered from a "novelty-seeking" syndrome.[123] For Liu Dong, those who had emigrated from mainland China had lost their identity and, consequently, their sense of mission.[124]

In a more moderate rebuttal, in the June 1995 issue of *Ershiyi shiji* liberal Xu Jilin contends that mainland postmodernism cannot be labeled neoconservative, as Zhao Yiheng would have it, because it differs from national studies; in all instances it also cannot be linked to popular culture. Xu distinguishes between the discourse on postmodernism, consisting of theoretical research and cultural critique, and the phenomenon of postmodernism. The latter consists of avant-garde literature and art as well as mass and commercial popular works. As in the debate on conservatism versus radicalism, Xu Jilin claims, the problem is that critics such as Zhao Yiheng do not clarify what yardstick they are applying to measure neoconservatism.[125]

Those mainland intellectuals targeted by overseas accusations of neoconservatism fought back. In her response to Zhao Yiheng in the June 1995 issue of *Ershiyi shiji*, Zheng Min accuses Zhao of being unfamiliar with the cultural reflections on mainland China and of manifesting signs of "Western centralism." Zhao Yiheng's views represent the traditional view of the politically revolutionary character of the May Fourth Movement that Zheng Min wants to discard. In this view, culture is but a byproduct of politics; language is but a tool. For Zheng Min, in contrast, based on the language theories of Heidegger and Derrida, language is an infinite system that carries traces of history, culture, and tradition.[126] Zhao Yiheng's use of the "neoconservatism" label, according to Zheng Min, contained a negative political connotation, similar to that contained by conservatism during the May Fourth era.[127] Her concern, she reiterates, is the future of Chinese culture during the period of transition and during its appearance on the world stage. She asks, is that conservative?

Zheng Min also takes issue with Zhao Yiheng's definition of poststructuralism as a radical theory in a Western setting because it wrongly assumes that poststructuralism seeks total destruction. In fact, Zheng Min claims,

---

[122] Liu, "Revisiting the Perils of 'Designer Pidgin Scholarship,'" 103.   [123] Ibid.
[124] Michelle Yeh, "International Theory and the Transnational Critic: China in the Age of Multiculturalism," in Rey Chow, ed., *Modern Chinese Literary and Cultural Studies in the Age of Theory: Reimagining a Field* (Durham, NC: Duke University Press, 2000), 264.
[125] Xu Jilin, "Bi piping geng zhongyao de shi lijie" (What Is More Important Than Criticizing Is Understanding), *Ershiyi shiji*, no. 29 (June 1995), 130–36.
[126] Zheng Min, "Wenhua, zhengzhi, yuyan sanzhe guanxi zhi wo jian" (My Views on the Relationship among Culture, Politics, and Language), *Ershiyi shiji*, no. 29 (June 1995), 122.
[127] Zheng Min, "Hewei 'dalu xin baoshou zhuyi'?," (What Is "Mainland Neoconservatism"?), *Wenyi zhengming*, no. 5 (1995), 40–48.

Derrida had demonstrated that language and culture could not be created; rather they were always linked to tradition. She asks, was that radical? For Zheng Min, a return to tradition and adoration of Western ideas were signs of centralism. Instead, she argues, one should, in a hermeneutical fashion, reread and reconstruct Chinese tradition. The "flesh and blood of the cultural heritage" should be transformed into "tomorrow's living and new-born cultural tradition."[128] This cannot be realized only through the vernacular language because the mother tongue is the "true carrier" of Chinese culture.[129] Here we see echoes of the hermeneutic exercise by other Chinese intellectuals, both in mainland China and abroad, to reconstruct Chinese tradition for the modern era.

The logic of a demarcation between mainland and overseas scholars as representatives of a Western system also runs through Zhang Yiwu's response to Xu Ben, as Zhang notes that it is only for overseas critics that postmodernism becomes a "political problem."[130] The attempts by Zhao Yiheng and Xu Ben are manifestations of what Zhang Yiwu calls an "anxiety to interpret China," which can be attributed to China's complex state after undergoing rapid social changes, the end of the Cold War, and increased commercialization, which rendered defunct both past explanations through either Chinese culture or the West.[131] Both authors seek new explanatory models to make sense of this changed situation and, in their treatment of post-trends as manifestations of nationalism or neoconservatism, turn China into an Other. They also both criticize mainland theories for pursuing "particularity," which is but a repetition of the cultural conservatism that existed during May Fourth. In contrast, Zhang Yiwu argues that postmodernism and postcolonialism attempt to reach "the Other of the Other." The denouncement by Zhao Yiheng and Xu Ben of Western cultural hegemony is not tantamount to a conservative and absolute nativist position; they once again grasp the environment of hybridity of China.[132] Zhang Yiwu also contends that the political reductionism in overseas analyses is mistaken because China had already become part of the global capitalist system and this had affected its cultural production.[133]

---

[128] Zheng, "Wenhua, zhengzhi, yuyan," 123. [129] Ibid.

[130] Zhang Yiwu, "Chanshi 'Zhongguo' de jiaolü" (The Anxiety of Interpreting "China"), *Ershiyi shiji*, no. 28 (April 1995), 128–35. For Xu Ben's response, see Xu Ben, "Zai tan Zhongguo 'houxue' de zhengzhixing he lishi yishi" (Again on the Political Nature and Historical Consciousness of Chinese "Post-*Isms*"), *Ershiyi shiji*, no. 39 (February 1997), 132–37.

[131] The phrase "chanshi Zhongguo de jiaolü" can be translated as "interpreting China's anxiety" or as "the anxiety of interpreting China." Zhang Yiwu uses the latter. See Tao Dongfeng and Jin Yuanpu, *Chanshi Zhongguo de jiaolü: Zhuanxing shidai de wenhua jiedu* (The Anxiety of Interpreting China/Interpreting China's Anxiety: Cultural Interpretations of the Transitional Era) (Beijing: Zhongguo guoji guangbo chubanshe, 1999).

[132] Zhang Yiwu, "Chanshi 'Zhongguo' de jiaolü," 129, 132, 133–35.

[133] Interview with Zhang Yiwu, Beijing, July 26, 2006.

In spite of the centrality of China, Zhang Yiwu's model, in his reference to "Greater China" and the contributions of Chinese outside of mainland China, reflects an acknowledgment of changing global structures and transnational forces. Because of these forces, the intellectual can no longer be a public intellectual who serves the nation-state, as he or she had in the May Fourth tradition. Postmodernist theorists advocate a position for the intellectual that is diametrically opposed to that of the 1980s' Enlightenment intellectual who could rescue China. In addition, this position also acknowledges the fragmentation of the intellectual landscape due to the forces of the market and mobility, although it still held on to the simplistic dichotomy of a Chinese and Western knowledge system.

Nevertheless, overseas critics were right in noting that some overlap did exist between the debates on postmodernism and certain official discourses at the time. The postcolonialists' argument that the concepts of democracy, freedom, and human rights had to be denounced because they were part of a Western ideological framework suited the government's criticism of "peaceful evolution" and spiritual pollution.[134] In spite of this, however, there were also tensions between the cultural nationalism of the postmodernists and the official nationalism in that, as Guo Yingjie notes, "what constitutes Chineseness in the cultural nationalists' imagination generally excludes socialist ideas and practices."[135] Moreover, whereas the official propaganda's critique of colonial culture can be traced to Mao Zedong, the attack on imperialism in the postcolonial discourse relies on Western postcolonial theories. Also, the official propaganda is especially concerned about the negative effects of colonialism, whereas the attack on imperialism in the postcolonial discourse first and foremost interprets colonialism as a discursive practice.[136] As already noted, in spite of certain parallels between official and intellectual discourse, the relation between intellectual practice and official policy during the 1990s could be depicted neither as a relation of complicity nor as a relation of dual opposition between official and unofficial voices. This was due to the commercialization, the rise of popular culture, or the concomitant development of a private sphere.[137]

Paradoxically, in spite of the transnationalization of the debate and the redefinition of Chineseness in cultural terms, mainland intellectuals made a distinction between Chinese and Western knowledge systems, and they believed that Chinese intellectuals outside of mainland China belonged to the Western knowledge system. Similarly, those Chinese intellectuals based in Europe or the United States, even though their presence abroad reflected

---

[134] Yue, "On Western Literary Theory," 114. [135] Guo, *Cultural Nationalism*, 109. [136] Ibid., 111. [137] Yeh, "International Theory," 259, 274.

the fluidity of the term "Chinese intellectual," reduced mainland Chinese intellectuals to spokespersons for the political status quo. In this battle between mainland and overseas intellectuals, the physical location of the intellectuals became a key factor to judge the authenticity of their concerns.[138] Hence, this spatial turn in the intellectual discourse became a discourse about who had the right to represent China. This was also apparent in other debates in the early 1990s, such as the discourse on New Confucianism, in which scholars from mainland China, Hong Kong, and Taiwan contested the meaning of what it meant to be a New Confucian and who could be designated as such.

United in their common anti-universalist stance, conservative criticisms of the May Fourth Movement and postmodernist theories in China were equally united in their inability to genuinely overcome modernity. It was the background of the rapid transition that led to the spread of postmodernism; amid economic, political, and cultural ruptures, concern with modernization remained paramount. Both conservative and postmodern critiques were aligned in their re-creation of "futures past." This is apparent not only in Zheng Min's attempts to create a more perfect Chinese culture by reinvigorating the language as its perceived essence but also in the postmodernists' design of improved knowledge models. Just as the search for future perfection was utterly incompatible with the belief in fallibility that marks conservatism, the search for future narratives and authentic modes of development was utterly incompatible with the postmodern embrace of relativism and pluralism. As McGrath argues, the 1990s' Chinese postmodernism was a "postmodern utopianism" that was theoretical in nature merely because the modernist utopias had already been shattered.[139]

The difference between Zheng Min and Zhang Yiwu, or between overseas critics of postmodernism and mainland theorists of postmodernism, is that the overseas critics upheld the idea of the intellectual as the guardian of Chinese culture against the threat of the market and the professionalization of knowledge. In the words of Zheng Min, it was the mission of the intellectuals to rescue a buried cultural tradition.[140] Those intellectuals who upheld the humanist and May Fourth Enlightenment traditions considered themselves to be endowed with the moral authority to judge the past and with the cultural capital to enable them to lead others out of the predicament of cultural radicalism. The realism of those in favor of mass culture, however, did not indicate that they had completely abandoned the revolutionary idealism that existed before the "post-new era." They, too, remained concerned with China's future path.

---

[138] Davies, *Worrying about China*, 99.   [139] McGrath, *Postsocialist Modernity*, 40.
[140] Zheng, "Wenhua, zhengzhi, yuyan," 123.

In these models, however, the nation-state made at least some room for a more globalized understanding of Chineseness, one that acknowledged the impact of transnational capital, the influence of Chinese based outside of mainland China, and the rise of East Asia. Because of the prominence of transnational capital, advocates of postmodernism were no longer establishment intellectuals. Here, apart from the ideology of modernization, the ideologies of commercialization and globalization shaped the debate, with nationalism existing in tension with these teleologies. Anti-radicalism had moved from its post-Tiananmen defense of a strong state and the crisis of socialism to an embrace of gradual reform, and finally it became embroiled with the anxieties caused by the socioeconomic and cultural consequences of China's entry into the global capitalist system.

7 The Double Nature of Realistic Revolution

> Revolutions are always verbose.
> Leon Trotsky, *The History of the Russian Revolution*

The phenomenon of the unmaking of twentieth-century radicalism in China in the early 1990s is highly significant. To some extent, engagement with the May Fourth Movement and twentieth-century Chinese socialism continued reflections on the socialist legacy that commenced after the end of the Cultural Revolution, but it also changed shape after June Fourth, the end of the Cold War, and the second round of reform in 1992. This was not merely a discussion about modernization; it was also about modernization amid globalization and commercialization. Though still theoretical and philosophical, the debate touched upon issues such as the legitimacy of the CCP, the nature of Chinese modernity, the role of the state in reform, the formation of civil society, how to realize democracy, and the position of Chinese intellectuals in modern Chinese history and contemporary Chinese society.

This was a realistic revolution in a number ways. First, as argued throughout this volume, the turn to pragmatism and realism, in both official and academic discourse, and against the background of utopian socialism, was revolutionary. Academic discussions on radicalism also represented a realistic revolution in that they exposed the contradictions in the official justification of reform. The official strategy was to preserve the past status of the revolution by separating the excesses of the Cultural Revolution from China's revolutionary path. The symbolic trial of the Gang of Four and the 1981 Resolution on the History of Our Party served as transitional moments toward taking a more rational path, in which reform was presented as a second revolution. In academic discussions, however, beneath the seemingly conformist explorations of China's historical and cultural pasts lay the following question: Would China have been better off without the decades of revolution and the all-permeating radical change? After the Soviet coup of 1991, the document "Realistic Responses and Strategic Options for China after the Soviet Upheaval" had already urged for a turn to nationalism because the other source of CCP legitimacy, namely the Bolshevik Revolution, had dried up. This also exposed the limits of the rhetorical acrobatics in the official justifications of reform. Instead of using the official strategy of reinterpreting the present in light of the past, intellectuals in the early 1990s reinterpreted the past in light of the present.

Second, in this environment realistic revolution also refers to the model of the Glorious Revolution, which Chinese intellectuals contrasted positively with the radical French Revolution. The reductionist interpretation of the French and English models, to which some intellectuals had already resorted before the 1990s, was inspired by writings by liberal scholars such as Friedrich Hayek and Karl Popper, but the interpretation took on new meaning in China. The two models, like the binaries of radicalism and conservatism in the discussions, were ideal types that did not conform to the historical reality. Using Koselleck's terms, the French Revolution functioned as a counter-model, analogous to the counter-concept of radicalism; it was presented so as to induce identification with the English model of gradual and sensible reform.

Throughout this volume the term "realistic revolution" refers to three sets of tensions. The first is the tensions in radicalism, as a criticism of change in China that was put forward in the service of modernization and that remained oriented toward the future. The second is the tensions in the post-1980s' quest for a more objective and rational scholarship, of which the anti-radicalism debate was a manifestation, and the continued moralistic trends in the debate. Here, the moral function of history in traditional China and the continuity of this view of historiography should be noted. Therefore, the rewriting of history in China in the 1990s was also a way of establishing new moral standards. At the same time, however, the ideas of stages, linear development, and the conflict between opposite forces also reveal the persistence of modern views on evolution and linearity, as also expressed in Marxist historiography. Finally, this reorganization of knowledge is connected to the tensions in the self-identification of intellectuals as scholars during the early 1990s, but also reflects the intellectuals' continued concern with China's future. Below I provide more detail about these three sets of tensions and evaluate their main strengths and weaknesses in the unmaking of radicalism.

Conservatism in the Service of Modernization

For Edmund Burke, change had to be limited because institutions are the result of a long process of historical growth. In addition, institutions had to be preserved because they represent accumulated past wisdom. Since there are limits to man's reason and morality, institutions are also required to keep man in check. In the 1990s, however, Chinese intellectuals reiterated Burke's dictum that change is necessary for preservation, but they omitted the accompanying emphasis on the preservation of institutions or the limits of reason that are so central to Burke. Following changes in political and socioeconomic context, conservatism could take the guise of statism, economic liberalism, morality, or Chineseness, but the *jin* (advancement) in *jijin* (radicalism) was never abandoned. Does this, we should ask, confirm Clinton Rossiter's argument that there is no conservatism in rapidly modernizing societies?[1] Even though criticisms of radicalism as "French rationalism" or "antitraditionalism" may be reminiscent of some traits in Mannheim's definition of conservatism as a "style of thought" against Enlightenment rationalism, Chinese intellectuals applied this procedural criticism in support of progress. As one Chinese intellectual puts it, "The two attitudes of radicalism and conservativism were without exception intellectual trends that praised and promoted modernization."[2] Indeed, the point was precisely to show that conservatives, earlier denounced as "bitterly opposed to change" (*wangu*), were *also* modernizers. Even though the argument that Chinese conservatives were moderns had already been put forward in the volume *Limits of Change* during the 1970s, in the 1990s the argument became aligned with the agenda for modernization in mainland China.

Rather than informed by "limits of change," to recall Furth's reference to conservatism in Republican China, intellectuals remained driven by future possibilities. They reclaimed the idealistic futures that had been imagined under liberalism and socialism, with the May Fourth Movement serving as a weighty symbol in the quest for abstract ideals, such as science and modernity. However, they still rewrote past narratives from the vantage point of the modern, and with a modern time consciousness of future "horizons of expectations" that left the "accelerated time" that accompanied modernity unquestioned.[3] In this setting, the critique of rationalism was only partial—even though the discussants favored empiricism over abstract designs—because their criticism was procedural instead of substantive. Paradoxically, this epistemological critique was a moral critique rather than a critique of the omnipotence of reason. It was part of the re-establishment of academic norms in response to the dramatic outcome of the New Enlightenment Movement of the 1980s.

We can understand this advocacy of conservatism in the service of modernization from a historical perspective. According to Chang Hao, it was the preoccupation with China's wealth and power (*fuqiang*) and the "crisis

---

[1] Rossiter, *Conservatism in America*, 219.
[2] Zheng Dahua, He Xiaoming, and Yu Zuhua, "Guanyu 'Zhongguo jindaishi shang de jijin yu baoshou' de duihua" (Dialogue on "Radicalism and Conservatism in Modern Chinese History"), in Zheng Dahua and Zou Xiaozhan, eds., *Zhongguo jindaishi shang de jijin yu baoshou* (Radicalism and Conservatism in Modern Chinese History) (Beijing: Shehui kexue wenxian chubanshe, 2011), 2.
[3] Tribe, "Introduction," x–xi; Koselleck, *Futures Past*, 10, 79, 258.

consciousness" of Chinese intellectuals that since the late nineteenth century led to both a critique of modernity in its Western manifestation and an embrace of modernity at another level.[4] Thomas Metzger argues that Chinese criticism of modernity addressed its societal aspects but not its epistemological tenets. For Metzger, this "epistemological optimism" accounts for the difference between Chinese and Western critiques of modernity—whereas the latter attacked reason, the former did not question it.[5] In his article on contemporary Chinese thought, Wang Hui describes Chinese thought since the late Qing as an "antimodern theory of modernization" (*fan xiandai de xiandai zhuyi*).[6] As in Wang's succinct summary, "Indeed, in China's historical situation, the struggle for modernization and the rejection of rationalization have proceeded together, something that has produced profound historical contradictions."[7] Because the discourse was framed within the binaries of China/West and tradition/modernity, the problems were situated in Western modernity or in Chinese tradition instead of being regarded as produced by the modernization process itself.[8] After 1989 and 1992, amid the setbacks and transitions, intellectuals remained consumed by completing an unfinished project. In this setting, in the words of Jia Xiaoye, the problem of modernity remained the problem of "how to *realize* modernity" (*zenme shixian xiandaixing*).[9]

In spite of these contradictions, we cannot simply reduce Chinese advocacies of conservatism during the 1990s to manifestations of cultural nationalism. References to conservatism in the 1990s, as we have seen, were not necessarily about the preservation of culture or about imagining China along cultural lines. After the Maoist period, conservatism also referred to advocacy of a strong state, as in neoconservatism, and after that to advocacy of conservative liberal interpretations of partial reform. The prominence of the state was not unique to conservatism: Chinese liberalism had also known a variant that defended a strong state and elitism, while containing socialist traits.[10] In these manifestations of conservatism, the nation was not imagined culturally in

---

[4] Chang, "New Confucianism and the Intellectual Crisis." On the interest in "wealth and power" among Chinese intellectuals, see Orville Schell and John Delury, *Wealth and Power: China's Long March to the Twenty-First Century* (London: Little, Brown, 2013).
[5] Thomas A. Metzger, *A Cloud across the Pacific: Essays on the Clash between Chinese and Western Political Theories Today* (Hong Kong: Chinese University of Hong Kong Press, 2005), 50–51, 53, 142–43.
[6] See Wang Hui, "Dangdai Zhongguo de sixiang zhuangkuang yu xiandaixing wenti," originally published in *Tianya*, no. 5 (1997): 133–50. A translation by Rebecca Karl appears in Wang, *China's New Order*, 139–87, titled "Contemporary Chinese Thought and the Question of Modernity." See also Viren Murthy, "Modernity against Modernity: Wang Hui's Critical History of Chinese Thought," *Modern Intellectual History* 3.1 (April 2006), 137–65.
[7] Wang, "Contemporary Chinese Thought," 150.   [8] Ibid., 145.
[9] Interview with Jia Xiaoye, Beijing, June 18, 2014.
[10] Fung, *Intellectual Foundations of Chinese Modernity*, 5, 14, 23; Interview with Xu Jilin, Shanghai, August 6, 2006.

opposition to the nation-state, but rather culture served to strengthen social stability and state building.

In addition, when Chinese intellectuals singled out the preservation and continuity of Chinese culture, their advocacy was not necessarily a form of cultural nationalism. Rather than promoting a cultural particularism, Chinese intellectuals defended an abstract moralism far removed from Burke's attention to historical particularity. Here we can refer to Makeham's term of "*ruxue*-centered Chinese cultural nationalism," which prevents a clear distinction between "culturalist" and "nationalist" advocacies. In this sense, Chinese culture was treated not only as a particularity but also as a representative of a global culture in which elements from both Chinese and Western culture could be integrated. For those who identified with conservatism as a value position, the exercise was about making Chinese culture matter in the modern world.

The cultural renewal that Chinese intellectuals advocated was also highly elitist—the nation was primarily an academic nation—and they promoted a moral call rather than an actual program. Therefore, critics such as Dirlik denounced this cultural solution as an essentialized culturalism. This depoliticized and dehistoricized moral idealism was far removed from the contemporary society that Chinese intellectuals inhabited.[11] Other scholars such as Ien Ang targeted the perceived essentialism of the exercise and rejected Tu Weiming's Chineseness as a failed effort to break with standard definitions of what it means to be Chinese, such as "belonging to the Han race, being born in China proper, speaking Mandarin, and observing the 'patriotic' code of ethics." Tu's re-envisioned Chineseness ended up confirming essentialism, for the goal of the periphery was to become a new center, a "Cultural China."[12]

As discussed in previous chapters, some intellectuals certainly understood culture in terms of abstract moral values, but it was not always clear how this could serve the cultural continuity that they envisioned. There was, however, no consensus among Chinese intellectuals regarding what was entailed in cultural construction or how it was to be realized. We should also note that scholars now accentuated the place of cultural exchange in the development of Chinese culture, for example in the debates on a re-evaluation of *Xueheng* or May Fourth, moving beyond the more simplistic cultural dichotomies that were constructed in the 1980s. Nonetheless, intellectuals still perceived of culture as a solution to China's problems and accorded Confucianism a central part in their interpretation of culture, in spite of references to a global cultural dialogue. In this sense, it is questionable to what extent Chinese intellectuals managed to free themselves from the "cultural-intellectualistic approach" or

---

[11] Dirlik, *Culture and History in Postrevolutionary China*, 61–62, 135.
[12] S.R.G., "Preface to the Issue," viii. Quoted in Ien Ang, "Can One Say No to Chineseness? Pushing the Limits of the Diasporic Paradigm," in Chow, *Modern Chinese Literary and Cultural Studies in the Age of Theory*, 285, 288.

the priority of cultural and intellectual change over economic, political, and social change that Lin Yü-sheng identifies as one of the roots of radicalism.[13]

Chinese intellectuals' distinction between cultural conservatism (*wenhua baoshou zhuyi*) and political conservatism (*zhengzhi baoshou zhuyi*), inspired partly by Charlotte Furth's volume on Republican conservatism and by Daniel Bell's separation of economic, political, and cultural spheres, was a mode of self-identification. It served to distance intellectuals from the political engagement of the 1980s and to redefine their position in Chinese society after 1989 and 1992. Cultural conservatism, as Schwartz rightly notes, was not about a Burkean preservation of the sociopolitical order as a whole. However, it was part of the call for a reconstruction of culture as intellectual culture first and foremost. Hence, Chinese intellectuals referred to conservatism to advocate various forms of historical continuity in the face of modernization-cum-globalization. It was an uneasy struggle to move beyond the century-old discussions about Chinese tradition and modernity and the relation between China and the West, but nevertheless there was some acknowledgment that it also involved a global reinvention of tradition.

Objectivity, Morality, and History

The second tension is that between the search for a more objective scholarship and the very moralistic nature of the discussions on radicalism. Behind the abstract concepts there were value judgments about how society should be organized. These value judgments stood in the way of the envisioned rational knowledge production. According to Xu Jilin, in the late 1970s "scientism" replaced the "political/moral didacticism of Maoism" in intellectual discourse.[14] Therefore, Chinese discourse in the early 1990s reflected a continued attempt to move away from such "didacticism." However, the binary form of discussion that categorized thinkers, trends, and movements as either radical or conservative evoked the Maoist-inspired black-and-white (*heibai*), yes-no (*shifei*), or all-or-nothing (*nisi wohuo*) approach to history.

"Moral didacticism" was not restricted to the Mao era; it also was a core feature of Confucianism. As Benjamin Elman notes, the intellectual history of modern China is mostly a "narrative history" that demonstrates the weight of the Confucian tradition of "praising and blaming" (*baobian*). This leads us to question whether Chinese intellectual history is merely the reversal of historical verdicts, and, given the centrality of Confucianism in this process, a "referendum on Confucianism."[15] Here, it is useful to refer to Ge Zhaoguang's reflections on Chinese intellectual history as a "roll of honor" or a "progress report":

---

[13] Lin, *Crisis of Chinese Consciousness*, 26.   [14] Xu, "Fate of an Enlightenment," 187.
[15] Elman, "Failures of Contemporary Chinese Intellectual History," 372.

In the minds of many intellectual historians, intellectual history is not just a narrative of history, but also an evaluation of history. For them, history is like a roll of honor: not just anyone can easily be included on that list, and the standard for inclusion cannot be lowered. Although this is a respectable way of writing, on the one hand it turns intellectual history into a progress report—if one does not represent progress, one is not eligible for inclusion on the list; and on the other hand, it brings the traditional Chinese praise and blame principle in through the back door.[16]

Reflections on radicalism in the early 1990s, in spite of a reversal in meanings, continued this tradition of praising and blaming. The debate was highly evaluative and marked by an absence of clear standards of inclusion or exclusion. Davies treats the taxonomy of conservatism versus radicalism as an example of the Confucian practice of rectifying names, which Michael Schoenhals also refers to in his study of language in Chinese politics. According to this belief, as expressed in the *Analects*, calling things by their right name is essential for successful government.[17] As Davies argues, the use of binaries was therefore more about the correct way of understanding and self-reflection than it was about clear-cut theories.[18]

Some intellectuals, however, were highly self-reflective and aware of the limits of the discussion. Xu Jilin, for example, argues that the terms "conservatism" and "radicalism" should not be applied as yardsticks because of this lack of a clear-cut definition. He also warns against the either/or demarcation in favor of a middle course. Historian Ma Yong is also critical of the mushrooming of reversals of verdicts on historical figures, which accompanied the modernization paradigm during the 1990s because they turned into a mere "research method of the denial of denial."[19] Ge Zhaoguang also notes that even though verdicts were reversed, the idea of a "linear social evolution" in Chinese intellectual history continued nevertheless.[20]

In addition to the binary structure of the discourse, the resort to *-isms* as a basis for discussion reflects a continued fixation on future changes and ideological demarcations. As other *-isms* that reached China through Japan during the early twentieth century, radicalism and conservatism were "concepts of movement" that denoted ideals or programs yet to be realized in the age of revolution and nationalism. In the words of Spira, "All too easily, the uniform organization of knowledge morphed into the uniform organization of society. In this process the 'new man' became synonymous with the 'ismatic man,' who had no choice but to submit to collective ideology."[21] During the early 1990s, *-isms* remained symbols connected to programs to shape society.

---

[16] Ge, *Intellectual History of China*, 47.
[17] Davies, *Worrying about China*, 127; Schoenhals, *Doing Things with Words in Chinese Politics*, 2.
[18] Davies, "Self-Made Maps," 26. [19] Ma, "Jindai lishi renwu yanjiu," 683.
[20] Ge, *Intellectual History of China*, 50. [21] Spira, *Conceptual History of Chinese -Isms*, 286.

As such, unwriting the past in the framework of -*isms* was, at the very least, a paradoxical way of advocating a more empiricist, realist, and rational approach to change.

We should also note the conflicting function of history in discussions on radicalism. In dynastic China, history had been the *magister vitae*—the teacher of life—to the Chinese literati.[22] In traditional Chinese historiography, the historical process also involved the rise and fall of an ideal moral order. History reflecting "cosmic-human interconnectedness" was cyclical and contained moral purpose.[23] To express the relevance of this historical consciousness so tied to morality and the unity of empire, Kun Qian uses the term "imperial-time-order," a "deep structure of Chinese intellectual thinking that encompasses time, unity, morality, and collectivism as its central concepts."[24] In Chinese historiography, the image of a mirror has often been invoked to refer to the relationship between past and present, or, by extension, past and future—it was believed that one could "know the future in the mirror of the past" (*jianwang zhilai*). Well known in this regard is the *Zizhi tongjian* (A General Mirror to Aid to Government), a historiography of sixteen dynasties compiled by Sima Guang and others during the Northern Song dynasty (960–1127). As Axel Schneider puts it, "It was by writing history that the *dao* was made visible to the present." Since it was believed that the ideal moral order had been realized in history—namely during the Three Dynasties—history was, so to speak, a channel to Truth.[25] With the rise of modern historiography in China at the turn of the twentieth century, dynastic history made room for a national history marked by linearity, development—rooted in the Western Judeo-Christian tradition of Destiny—and scientific methods. However, this pursuit of objectivity continued to exist in tension with the moralizing function of traditional Chinese historiography that was so central to Confucian culture.[26]

Rewriting modern Chinese history as the history of radicalism contains traces of both the traditional meaning of historiography as tied to a moral order and a modern historiography marked by linearity and the pursuit of

---

[22] On-cho Ng and Q. Edward Wang, "Prologue," in Ng and Wang, *Mirroring the Past: The Writing and Use of History in Imperial China* (Honolulu: University of Hawai'i Press, 2005), viii.

[23] Schwartz, "History in Chinese Culture," 23; Kwong, "Rise of the Linear Perspective on History and Time," 161.

[24] Kun Qian, *Imperial-Time-Order: Literature, Intellectual History, and China's Road to Empire* (Leiden: Brill, 2016), 11.

[25] Schneider, "Between *Dao* and History," 55. The Three Dynasties include the Xia dynasty (ca. 2000–ca. 1600 BCE), the Shang dynasty (ca. 1600–ca. 1100 BCE), and the Zhou dynasty (ca. 1100–249 BCE).

[26] Yü, *Chinese History and Culture*, 294–95, 303.

objectivity. History served as a space to reconstruct the "humanistic ideals" of intellectuals and included the task of cultural reconstruction.[27] "Ethical behavior was upheld as the key to historical assessment."[28] As such, rejections of radicalism were also about the moral reconstruction of a lost order, the place of Chinese intellectuals in this order, and a humanist culture that we need to broadly understand as a concern with history, culture, and scholarship. This traditional analysis of history existed in uneasy tension with the quest for objective scholarship, the demarcation of stages in historical development, and the rigorous categorization of thinkers and intellectual currents within a binary scheme that is reminiscent of Marxist and Hegelian historiography.

Knowledge Organization and the Scholar-Intellectuals

A third and final tension is that between the self-identification of Chinese intellectuals of the 1990s as scholars pursuing specialist knowledge and the continuation of their role as intellectuals concerned about China's future. The discussion on radicalism reflects the state of mind of Chinese intellectuals at the time as well as their efforts to come to terms with the effects of not only de-revolution but also transnational mobility. Facing these changes, they sought a rehabilitation of status during the early 1990s through a reconstruction of Chinese culture and a reorganization of knowledge. Epistemologically, this was reflected in rejections of radicalism because knowledge was to be based on empiricism rather than ideals, abstract designs, desired outcomes, or, as inspired by Max Weber, "ultimate ends." This stress on gradualism, empiricism, and an English model, as contrasted with the rationalism and blueprint ideals of a French model, was part of an attempt to reconstruct a nonpoliticized, nonromanticized, and more "rational" (*lixing*) scholarship.

In this context, the starting point of the 1999 book *Zhishi fenzi lichang: Jijin yu baoshou zhijian de dongdang* reflects a continued concern with knowledge organization in the form of edited volumes and conferences.[29] As noted, it includes texts on anti-radicalism in relation to debates on neoconservatism, the May Fourth Movement, New Confucianism, and the literary revolution—some of which were published after the peak of the debate.[30] Rather than further developing the debate, this later period finally came to terms with the debate. After 1995, according to Jia Xiaoye of CASS, "everyone had already reached a

---

[27] Chen, "Antiradicalism and the Historical Situation of Contemporary Chinese Intellectuals," 39.
[28] Kwong, "Rise of the Linear Perspective on History and Time," 164. [29] ZFL.
[30] For example, the volume includes an article by Chang Hao titled "Zhongguo jin bainian lai de geming sixiang daolu" (The Revolutionary Road of China during the Past One Hundred Years), in *ZFL*, 42–56.

consensus that radical and conservative were not absolute."[31] Nevertheless, after the mid-1990s the articles also represented an attempt to further delineate the norms for knowledge organization and construction. The mode of criticism in the debate, it was acknowledged, was to be replaced by more empirical research.[32]

Zheng Dahua and Jia Xiaoye, both at the Intellectual History Research Unit of the Modern History Research Institute of CASS in Beijing, were key figures in the organization and analysis of the debates on radicalism, and they also convened conferences on the topic.[33] In their own words, "systematically sorting out" (*xitong shuli*) the reflections on radicalism was helpful to "correctly understand" (*zhengque lijie*) conservatism and radicalism in modern Chinese history. It was also useful for "correctly dealing with the relation between conservatism and radicalism in today's cultural construction."[34] In the 2000s, the Intellectual History Research Unit of the Modern History Research Institute of CASS also organized several conferences on the topic.[35] Therefore, organization of the debates became part of the "correct" interpretation of radicalism and conservatism and continued the earlier categorization efforts to reconstruct culture.

However, because the reorganization of knowledge was driven by concerns about morality, status, and responsibility, the epistemological facets remained subservient to the moral and evaluative concerns. According to the well-known intellectual historian Ge Zhaoguang, the project of "re-writing" intellectual history from the 1980s onward was "an emotional expression of a reassessment of values."[36] In the words of liberal Zhu Xueqin, discussions on radicalism were intended to be a criticism of historical teleology, but they were also an "articulation of frustration" following the Tiananmen demonstrations.[37] Even though "concepts" (*guannian*) and "trends" (*sichao*) constituted the main form of discussion, as the title of the collection of articles in

---

[31] Interview with Jia Xiaoye, Beijing, June 18, 2014. However, Ma Yong argues that the problem became more urgent during the second half of the 1990s as calls for a re-evaluation of modern Chinese history continued. Interview with Ma Yong, Beijing, September 1, 2005.
[32] For an overview of relevant articles in the debate after the mid-1990s, see Zheng and Zou, *Zhongguo jindaishi shang de jijin yu baoshou*.
[33] See, for example, Zheng and Jia, "Ershi shiji jiushi niandai yilai," 289–314; Zheng and Zou, *Zhongguo jindaishi shang de jijin yu baoshou*.
[34] Zheng and Jia, "Ershi shiji jiushi niandai yilai," 289.
[35] For example, in November 2003 it co-organized a conference with the History Department of Capital Normal University in Beijing and the History Department of Hunan Normal University on "Conservative and Radical in Modern Chinese Intellectual History." See Zheng and Jia, "'Zhongguo jindai sixiangshi shang de baoshou yu jijin' xueshu taolun hui zongshu," 291–301. It also co-organized other conferences on the topic, such as a conference with Luoyang Normal University, Capital Normal University, and other institutions on "Radical and Conservative in Modern Chinese History," held in Luoyang in August 2010.
[36] Ge, *Intellectual History of China*, 9. [37] Zhu, "For a Chinese Liberalism," 104.

Zhishi fenzi lichang: Jijin yu baoshou zhijian de dongdang reveals, the underlying preoccupation was with "intellectual positions" and the restoration of these positions after 1989. There was, however, no consensus among the authors as to how the intellectual should reposition himself (or, unfortunately, only rarely, herself) in Chinese society, and not all were convinced that intellectuals should become scholars.

According to historian Ma Yong, a "major issue" of the 1990s was the "public intellectuals" (*gonggong zhishi fenzi*) who, while turning toward their specializations, also continued to discuss public matters.[38] For example, Xiao Gongqin repeatedly referred to the "crisis consciousness" of Chinese intellectuals. Writing about history, he was interested in China's economic and political transition. In the 1992 debate, nonspecialists engaged in a debate about modern Chinese history and pondered the future of the Chinese reforms. Chen Lai called for a pure scholarship devoid of political or commercial interference, but his concerns became entangled with a discussion on the relation between Confucianism and capitalism. Postmodernists had bid farewell to elitist culture, but they nevertheless engaged in reconstructions of Chinese modernity and the reclaiming of Chinese subjectivity. In this sense, mainland intellectuals followed Yü Ying-shih's call for a continuation of the tradition of the "public-mindedness" (*gong*) of the Confucian scholar, according to which the scholar "must take the whole world as his own responsibility."[39] When asked about his position in the debate on Chinese culture, one intellectual replied that it was a "Chinese position" (*Zhongguo lichang*)—he was a "Chinese intellectual" (*Zhongguo zhishi fenzi*).[40] In spite of their call for scholarship, Chinese intellectuals were still obsessed with China's future.

Criticism of the Reforms and Shifting Labels

To fully grasp the meaning of the debates of the early 1990s, we also need to relate them to developments of the late 1990s and 2000s. Beginning in the mid-1990s, the realistic revolution that had marked early 1990s China faced serious challenges as the complexities of the economic reforms became more apparent. The elitist vision of top-down gradual economic reforms, order, and stability under the guidance of traditional elements made room for a more critical evaluation of the market reforms. Some argued that the state, which had been central in the creation of the market in the first place, should also act to

---

[38] Interview with Ma Yong, Beijing, August 8, 2005.
[39] Yü, "Radicalization of China in the Twentieth Century," 145–46. This is one of two mottoes attributed to Fan Zhongyan (989–1052).
[40] Interview with Wang Yuechuan, Beijing, June 21, 2006.

mitigate the social effects of the reforms. Although there was a consensus about the reforms, the following question became more pressing: Who was to benefit from the reforms? In the mid-1990s, some were already voicing criticism of the reforms and arguing that China should move away from Western models and market dominance and draw on its own experience.[41] Chinese scholars in the United States also began to use neo-Marxist theories to criticize the reforms.[42]

As the question of state intervention in the reforms became dominant, the meaning of political labels shifted once again. In the second half of the 1990s, some of those who had been associated with neoconservatism because of their defense of political centralization joined the ranks of the so-called New Left or became designated as such. This group also came to include Gan Yang, one of the key figures in the New Enlightenment Movement of the 1980s and in the discussion on radicalism. The emergence of a rift between a camp of liberals and a camp of New Leftists was, according to Xu Jilin, one of the three major rifts in the 1990s; the other two, as discussed in the previous chapters, were that between thought and scholarship and that between humanist and common concerns.[43] Members of the New Left assumed many of the concerns of the humanist scholars because of their critical stance toward the market.[44]

The gradual embrace of liberalism as a positive force developed further in the late 1990s, when a true "Hayek craze" took off. Whereas during the 1980s "bourgeois liberalization" referred to morally unacceptable behavior, in the late 1990s liberalism achieved a "cultural cachet previously enjoyed by such terms as democracy and science."[45] During the mid- to late 1990s, however, advocacy of classical liberalism à la Locke, Smith, and Hayek, as promoted by Liu Junning and others, came to coexist with advocacies of social democracy, in the works of Qin Hui, an agrarian historian at Tsinghua University, and Zhu Xueqin, among others.[46]

Wang Hui, who is considered a leading voice among the New Left in China, cites 1997, the year of the global financial crisis, as a turning point in the Chinese intellectual world. This was also the year that Wang's article "Contemporary Chinese Thought and the Question of Modernity" was published in

---

[41] Wang, "Introduction: Minds of the Nineties," 23–24; Wang, "New Criticism," 59. See Cui, "Zhidu chuangxin yu di'erci sixiang jiefang," 5–16. See also the debate that followed in *Ershiyi shiji* (December 1994, February 1995, April 1995, February 1996, April 1996, and August 1996).
[42] Xu, "Fate of an Enlightenment," 197–98.   [43] Ibid., 195–99.
[44] McGrath, *Postsocialist Modernity*, 28.
[45] Cheek, "Historians as Public Intellectuals in Contemporary China," 206. Cheek cites Barmé, "Revolution of Resistance," 210.
[46] On the history of liberalism and social democracy in China, see Fung, *Intellectual Foundations of Chinese Modernity*, 128–58 and 191–223.

Tianya, even though it had been written earlier.[47] In the media in 1996, Cui Zhiyuan, Gan Yang, Wang Shaoguang, and Wang Hui were labeled New Leftists, a label that Wang Hui rejects in favor of critical intellectuals.[48] Gan Yang uses the term "liberal Left" rather than "New Left" to describe his position, but he also traces the origin of the New Left back to Wang Shaoguang's early 1990s' writings on "state capacity" in which he questions unbridled marketism.[49] Whereas arguing for a strong state earned a "conservative" label during the early 1990s, following the retreat of the state that intensified after 1992, advocacy of a strong state represented resistance to neoliberal reform. For the New Left, the state was paramount because the market monopolized assets. Liberals, in contrast, supported rule of law and political reform. In the words of liberal Zhu Xueqin, the problem was that the "visible foot" of the state stamped on the "invisible hand" of the market; if the hand was "dirty," it was because the foot was "violent."[50]

Chinese intellectuals had previously used postmodern theories to defend historical continuity and nationalism amid anxieties about globalization, as in the example of the debate on the literary revolution and Chinese modernity. Now the New Left was relying on both Leftist and postmodernist theories to criticize neoliberalism. Therefore, postmodernism began to flourish in its Marxist form after the mid-1990s following the growing criticism of rising social inequalities, as in the works of Zhang Xudong, a student of Fredric Jameson based in the United States.[51] During the late 1990s, instead of advocating "goodbye to revolution," as Li Zehou and Liu Zaifu had famously declared in 1995, the New Left mourned the decline of revolution. For Wang Hui, the problem was the "mass depoliticization" in contemporary China that the postmodernists had earlier welcomed.[52] In addition, whereas Chinese intellectuals inspired by Friedrich Hayek and Isaiah Berlin had embraced

---

[47] Wang Hui, "Dangdai Zhongguo de sixiang zhuangkuang yu xiandaixing wenti," *Tianya*, no. 5 (1997), 133–50.

[48] Wang, "New Criticism," 62. On the New Left, see Fewsmith, *China since Tiananmen*; Leslie Hook, "The Rise of China's New Left," *Far Eastern Economic Review* 170.3 (April 2007), 8–14.

[49] Gan Yang, "Zhongguo ziyou zuopai de youlai" (The Origins of China's Liberal Left)," in Gong Yang, ed., *Sichao: Zhongguo "xin zuopai" ji qi yingxiang* (Trend of Thought: China's "New Left" and Its Influence) (Beijing: Zhongguo shehui kexue chubanshe, 2003), 111. Cited in He Li, "Debating China's Economic Reform: New Leftists vs. Liberals," *Journal of Chinese Political Science* 15.1 (2010), 5, 7.

[50] Xu, "Debates between Liberalism and the New Left"; Zhu, "For a Chinese Liberalism," 107.

[51] Wang, "Introduction: Minds of the Nineties," 22. See, for example, Zhang Xudong, "Houxiandai zhuyi yu Zhongguo xiandaixing" (Postmodernism and Chinese Modernity), *Dushu*, no. 12 (1999), 12–20. For an outline of Zhang Xudong's position, see his "Making of the Post-Tiananmen Intellectual Field."

[52] Wang Hui, *The End of the Revolution: China and the Limits of Modernity* (London: Verso, 2009).

negative freedom in the post-Tiananmen setting, the New Left now argued that the problem was precisely the opposite: the majority of Chinese people had been excluded from political participation.

In the early 2000s, Gan Yang began introducing to Chinese audiences the works of Leo Strauss, a critic of modern liberalism who is considered to be the intellectual godfather of the neoconservative movement in the United States.[53] After writing a lengthy introduction to a Chinese translation of Leo Strauss's 1953 work *Natural Right and History*, Gan was labeled a conservative.[54] To Gan, Strauss upheld "all-round criticism and examination of Western modernity and liberalism from a Western classical perspective."[55] Xu Jilin refers to the popularity of Strauss in the 2000s as the "fourth attitude" toward modernity among Chinese intellectuals, following the 1990s' three main attitudes, which included universalist liberalism, pluralist modernity critical of American and Eurocentric models, and a postmodernist rejection of modernity. The turn to Strauss therefore represented a resort to absolute morality in response to the relativism inherent in some of the earlier models. As such, in spite of Gan Yang's criticism of the conservative liberalism he had first embraced, he now espoused a new cultural conservatism, this time universalist rather than Burkean.[56]

Gan Yang also called for integrating the so-called "three traditions" (*tong santong*), namely, the tradition of the market, liberty, and rights that had developed during the reform era; the tradition of equality and justice that had developed during the Republican period and the Mao era; and China's civilizational tradition (*wenming chuantong*). Gan Yang argued that Deng Xiaoping, Mao Zedong, and Confucius all belonged to the same continuous tradition. In a 2007 article, "The Chinese Way: Thirty Years and Sixty Years," Gan Yang further coined the term "Confucian Socialist Republic."[57]

---

[53] After spending a decade at the University of Chicago, in the late 1990s Gan Yang became affiliated with the Chinese University of Hong Kong. In 2008, he accepted a professorship at Sun Yat-sen University in Guangzhou. Another central figure in introducing Strauss to China was Liu Xiaofeng (b. 1956), a theologian and specialist on German philosophy at Renmin University in the 2000s. Liu also played a role in introducing the Western classics to China through translation series and journal articles.

[54] See Gan Yang, "Zhengzhi zheren Shitelaosi: Gudian baoshou zhuyi zhengzhi zhexue de fuxing" (Political Philosopher Leo Strauss: The Revival of Classical Conservative Political Philosophy), in *Ziran quanli yu lishi* (Natural Right and History), tr. Peng Gang (Taipei: Zuo'an wenhua, 2005), 5–86; Zhou, "Debates in Contemporary Chinese Political Thought," 34.

[55] Gan, "Zhengzhi zheren Shitelaosi," 6.

[56] Xu, "Contradictions within Enlightenment Ideas," 126–27.

[57] He called for integrating the three traditions in a 2004 interview and in a lecture at Tsinghua University in 2005. See Gan Yang, *Tong santong*, 5; Zhou, "Debates in Contemporary Chinese Political Thought," 35–36.

Therefore, during the 2000s there emerged a more defined tripartite intellectual space in which those referred to as New Left, liberal, and conservative could coexist. Because the latter had lost its cachet to liberalism and because advocates of a strong state were now referred to as New Leftists, conservatism, as earlier, came to stand for the promotion of tradition, which here mainly referred to New Confucianism.[58] By the late 2000s, even the main theorist of neoconservatism, Xiao Gongqin, refrained from using the term, reverting back to neo-authoritarianism and "middle-of-the-road rationality" (*zhongdao lixing*). In Xiao Gongqin's view, conservatism was once again associated with opposing reform or being synonymous with Mao Zedong Thought, whereas there was already a consensus in contemporary China about stability and reform.[59]

Institutionalizing "Cultural China" and Redefining Reform

The new millennium also witnessed the popularization, commercialization, and institutionalization of research on Chinese cultural traditions. For example, 2004 was declared "Cultural Conservatism Year," highlighted by the "Cultural Summit Forum of 2004" at the Great Hall of the People in Beijing. During the closing ceremony, a "Cultural Manifesto of 2004," sponsored by high-ranking scholars, was announced. This was followed by the establishment of national studies institutes at several universities, including Renmin University and Wuhan University.[60]

In 2009, the Tsinghua Academy of National Learning (Qinghua Daxue Guoxue Yanjiuyuan) was formally re-established. Philosopher Chen Lai, who is discussed in Chapter 5, was appointed dean of the academy, assisted by Liu Dong, formerly a professor in Peking University's Literature Department and also one of the participants in the debates on anti-radicalism. This re-establishment of the academy represented a nod to the national studies scholars of the Republican period. The academy had first been established in 1925, under the management of prominent scholars such as Liang Qichao, Wang Guowei, Chen Yinke, and Zhao Yuanren (1892–1982).[61] The re-established academy published a

---

[58] For English translations of some of the recent writings by well-known liberals, New Leftists, and New Confucians, see the Reading the China Dream website. www.readingthechinadream.com.
[59] Interview with Xiao Gongqin, Shanghai, June 9, 2014; Xiao Gongqin, *Chaoyue zuoyou jijin zhuyi: Zouchu Zhongguo zhuanxing de kunjing* (Beyond Left and Right Radicalism: Moving Away from the Predicament of China's Transformation) (Hangzhou: Zhejiang daxue chubanshe, 2012).
[60] Xu, "Intellectual Discourses in Post-Mao China and Today."
[61] Tsinghua University website, www.tsinghua.edu.cn/publish/shssen/4590/2010/20101216141022433824265/20101216141022433824265_.html.

number of academic journals, the titles of which are reminiscent of the journals in the early 1990s, such as *Zhongguo xueshu* (Chinese Scholarship) and *Guoxue wenzhai* (Digest on Chinese Learning). One of the purposes of this Chinese scholarship was to strengthen "the cohesion of 'Cultural China.'"[62]

Meanwhile, at Peking University the cultural reimagining of China and the place of Confucianism in this process were institutionalized at the Institute for Advanced Humanistic Studies (IAHS), which was symbolically inaugurated on Confucius's birthday on September 28, 2010. Tu Wei-ming, famous for his "Cultural China" thesis and his promotion of Confucianism both inside and outside of China, became the director of the Institute.[63] "Cultural China," Tu announced, would become the focal point of one of the research centers, with the other centers concentrating on "dialogue between civilizations" and "world religion and universal ethics."[64] Almost three decades after his initial tour to China when he promoted the "third epoch" of Confucianism based on his criticism of the "Enlightenment mentality," Tu's vision was reinstated at one of China's top educational institutions.

That the early 1990s' emphasis on culture was insufficient to cure the ills of modernization, as Leftist critics asserted, became apparent in the new millennium with the increasing nervousness about social inequality. Under Hu Jintao, the concepts of "harmonious society" and "scientific development" reflected an emphasis on state welfare, health, education, sustainable development, and improvements in the rural areas.[65] During this period, political stability centered on redefining reform. Hence, when references to Alexis de Tocqueville's *The Old Regime and the Revolution*, widely cited as an example of the type of gradual reform that China needed during the early 1990s, resurfaced in the 2010s, they reflected new anxieties about social inequality threatening social stability. Chinese leaders were urged to read de Tocqueville because China would not "modernize all that smoothly."[66] In a 2013 article in *Renmin ribao*, the French Revolution is described as "pursuing social equality,

---

[62] Ibid. Peking University renamed its Research Centre of Traditional Chinese Culture, founded in 1992, the Research Institute for National Studies (Guoxue Yanjiuyuan) in 2001. Davis, *Encyclopedia of Contemporary Chinese Culture*, 510.
[63] "Beijing daxue gaodeng renwen yanjiuyuan juxing jiepai dianli" (Peking University Institute for Advanced Humanistic Studies Holds Inauguration Ceremony), http://pkunews.pku.edu.cn/xwzh/2010-09/29/content_184568.htm.
[64] Ibid.   [65] Li, "Debating China's Economic Reform," 18–19.
[66] Joseph Fewsmith, "De Tocqueville in Beijing," *China Leadership Monitor*, no. 39 (Fall 2012), 1, http://media.hoover.org/sites/default/files/documents/CLM39JF.pdf.

while not sacrificing liberty and order."[67] Gone was the belief of the early 1990s that economic reform would bring inclusive wealth and democracy.

Meanwhile, the CCP engaged in its own realistic revolution as the reinterpretation of socialism came ever closer to the spirit of capitalism. With Jiang Zemin's "Three Represents," or the idea that the CCP represents the advanced social productive forces, the progressive course of China's advanced culture, and the fundamental interests of the majority, intellectuals, entrepreneurs, and managers were able to join the ranks of the party. Furthermore, class struggle was no longer the driving force behind the CCP regime.[68] Whereas in the past Marxism had been presented as a "double emancipation"—emancipation from foreign imperialism and emancipation from the shackles of a tradition that was considered partly responsible for China's loss of its position as the Middle Kingdom—this stance was now softened.[69]

The musical epic *Fuxing zhi lu* (Road to Revival), performed in the Great Hall of the People in Beijing on the occasion of the sixtieth anniversary of the CCP, represented a shift in both the narrative of the CCP's history and modern Chinese history.[70] Moving beyond the linear narrative of revolution and the centrality of modernization, *Fuxing zhi lu* refers to the "depoliticized politics" that Wang Hui denounced and a call for the "farewell to revolution" of the 1990s through a nationalist narrative and mention of China's own achievements rather than external reference points, such as the Soviet Union or Western civilization. Instead of characterizing the reform period as a new phase, as it had been in the 1980s, now the continuity between the 1949–79 period and the 1979–2009 period was underscored in the formula of the two "thirty years."[71]

During the latest stage under Xi Jinping, the reinterpretation of socialism has come to include the "rejuvenation" of the Chinese nation, the envisioning of a new "Chinese dream," and the spatial imaginings of a former Middle Kingdom. Combining Communism with elements of nationalism and Leninism, Xi has attempted to bolster legitimacy in the face of stalled economic reforms, corruption, mounting social inequalities, and environmental pollution.[72] The new emphasis on Marxism and anticorruption reflects an even more profound

---

[67] Zhang Guangzhao, "Wang Qishan weihe tuijian *Jiu zhidu yu da geming*?" (Why Does Wang Qishan Recommend *The Old Regime and the Revolution*?), *Renmin ribao haiwaiban* (Overseas Edition of People's Daily), January 18, 2013, 11.
[68] Cheek, *Living with Reform*, 44. [69] Ci, *Dialectic of the Chinese Revolution*, 39, 41.
[70] Xiaoping Cong, "Road to Revival: A New Move in the Making of Legitimacy for the Ruling Party in China," *Journal of Contemporary China* 22.83 (2013), 905–22. *Road to Revival* was also the title of a documentary and of the permanent exhibition in the National Museum of China, which opened in 2011.
[71] Ibid., 908, 910–11, 915, 918.
[72] Suisheng Zhao, "The Ideological Campaign in Xi's China: Rebuilding Regime Legitimacy," *Asian Survey* 56.6 (2016), 1168–93.

legitimacy crisis than that in 1989–91 and a revived looming specter of a Soviet scenario. After the alliance between intellectuals and the state ended in 1989, few could have imagined that decades later, and a century after May Fourth, when intellectuals had called for science and democracy, the unfinished project of modernity would receive ever greater blows. Similarly, those calling for a sensible Glorious Revolution during the early 1990s could not have expected that their calls would be overshadowed by echoes for a French-style rationalist revolution.

"Rationality Against Rationality"

In light of these developments, what was the meaning of discussions of the early 1990s? Looking back, even though reflections on radicalism did not lead to a genuine questioning of the less desirable traits of the modern at this stage—such as scientism, progressivism, individualism, or materialism—as had been the case during the May Fourth era, they did question the pervasive belief that change had to come at the cost of violence and radical breaks with the past. As noted, during the 1980s Chinese scholars had already rewritten modern Chinese history from the perspective of modernization, a paradigm that was popular in China during the Republican era.[73] As we have seen, some of the research on reform during the late Qing that was part of the discussion on radicalism took place within the framework of research on the history of modernization. Therefore, we need to understand the interest in the ideals of the Republican-era scholars as part of the wider reassessment of the Republican period that accompanied the official emphasis on reform and the appeal to nationalism after the Tiananmen crackdown. Like anti-radicalism, however, the official re-evaluation of the Republican period also turned out to be a double-edged sword because of its perceived free intellectual climate.[74]

In the debates on radicalism, non-Marxist and nonliberal intellectuals who had been repressed and criticized during the Mao era for distorting the revolutionary paradigm, such as those around the *Xueheng* journal, and May Fourth critics, such as Du Yaquan and philosopher Liang Shuming, became the subjects of renewed interest, discussion, and research. As Schwartz rightly notes, the neglect of scholars who were associated with an interest in Chinese tradition during the Mao era was "based on the premise that its presumed defeat in 1949 renders its ideas completely uninteresting."[75] Furthermore, China in the 1990s has been compared to the China in the 1930s that promoted

---

[73] Li, "From Revolution to Modernization."
[74] Zhang and Weatherley, "Rise of 'Republican Fever.'"
[75] Benjamin Schwartz, "Themes in Intellectual History: May Fourth and After," in Goldman and Lee, *Intellectual History of Modern China*, 437.

state Confucianism, nativist ideas, development of national studies, and a reinterpretation of Confucianism in a form that would later be identified as New Confucianism. This 1930s nativist moment, like that in the 1990s, was a response to the cosmopolitan movement of the 1920s that parallels the New Enlightenment Movement of the 1980s, and the nativism was equally inspired by foreign theories.[76] In spite of the many differences between the two decades, both were marked by a renewed sense of historical continuity.

Even though conservatives were drawn into the modernization framework during the 1990s, criticism of the dichotomy between conservatives and modernization allowed for a broader interpretation of the May Fourth Movement that paid more attention to transnational intellectual dimensions. As noted by Yü Ying-shih, if we understand it as a movement of "cultural borrowing," those who were earlier branded "conservatives" or "enemies" of May Fourth, such as the *Xueheng* scholar Mei Guangdi or the "last Confucian" Liang Shuming, also made their arguments based on Western theories.[77] Yü denounced May Fourth's "iconoclastic anti-traditionalism," but he also argued for a new reading of May Fourth "including every active member of the May Fourth intellectual world as a participant of the New Culture movement."[78] This reading became more common among mainland Chinese intellectuals. The latter also acknowledged that, regardless of their cultural positions, May Fourth intellectuals all constituted part of a larger process of intellectual exchange. The limitation of this reinterpretation of May Fourth was evidently that May Fourth itself remained very much at the center of Chinese modernity. Anglophone scholarship on the Chinese modern, in contrast, had attempted to "decenter" May Fourth by paying attention to a variety of other movements and by seeking to move beyond elite culture.[79] On mainland China, if there was any move beyond May Fourth it was one that reaffirmed elitism by an emphasis on modernization and top-down reform.

This was nevertheless a drastic change as compared to the Maoist period. The impact of the cultural vision of Chinese intellectuals outside of China reflects the growing interconnection of the economies and societies of East Asia and the redefinition of being Chinese along the economic and cultural lines of "Greater China" and "Cultural China." I argue that a conceptual history approach allows for a better analysis of the depth of this change. For decades, under the sway of the May Fourth and socialist traditions, radicalism

---

[76] See the introduction to this volume. The terms "nativism" and "cosmopolitanism" are taken from Dirlik's description of the development of *guoxue* in China. See Dirlik, *Culture and History in Postrevolutionary China*, 247–50.
[77] Yü, *Chinese History and Culture*, 206–7.   [78] Ibid., 209, 224.
[79] Hung-Yok Ip, Tze-ki Hon, and Chiu-Chun Lee, "The Plurality of Chinese Modernity: A Review of Recent Scholarship on the May Fourth Movement," *Modern China* 29.4 (October 2003), 490–509.

reflected the underlying belief that there was "no making without breaking." Conservatism was a label imposed on "feudal" or "backward" opponents of progress. Conservatives were diehard defenders of tradition who obstructed modernization. In the 1980s, as exemplified in the documentary *Heshang*, this perception was still extremely powerful. Now, however, conservatism was considered a "rational" and healthy mode of modernization that enabled historical continuity with the past. Progress (*jin*), it came to be believed, could be achieved without violence (*ji*).

In addition, we should also consider what the debate contributes in terms of knowledge production, intellectual inquiry, and modes of theorizing. Wang Hui calls the debate "unhistorical" because the participants did not conduct a historical analysis, were fixated on the consequences of events, and shunned sociopolitical realities.[80] Also criticizing the debate from the perspective of historiography, Zhu Xueqin notes the paradox of the overemphasis on the role of intellectual currents in the development of modern Chinese history as a strategy to justify the new role of intellectuals in the present.[81] Rather than dismissing the debate because of its alleged shortcomings in terms of historical inquiry or methodology based on "scientific standards," we can argue that it was remarkable that the debate revealed the above tensions, thereby integrating "modern" historiographical modes of inquiry as analysis and argumentation with century-old practices of debate as very much connected to moral rectification and political order.

Therefore, the conservatism that was defended was both rational and moral, local and global, and it intended to integrate past wisdom in a forward-looking manner. History was the vector and the object of the discussion, but it was also a transcendent moral guide in the discussion and allowed for debate on sensitive issues in the present, offering lessons on a better way forward. In this mode of inquiry, history and morality were very much intertwined. Similarly, there was no rigid disciplinary distinction, with participants from backgrounds as diverse as history, political science, literature, and philosophy all taking part in the discussion. In addition, seeking both objectivity and specialization at the same time, the debate was highly prescriptive. Rather than reading the discussion based on "modern" or "Western" interpretations of historiography or academic discourse, this study has attempted to investigate the use of concepts in the Chinese intellectuals' process of making sense. Here I am inspired by Leigh Jenco's efforts to move away from seeking "equivalence" in the study of political thought or concepts and to think about how Chinese theory can contribute to global theory. To do this, it is fruitful to

---

[80] Wang, *China's New Order*, 78–84.   [81] Zhu, "For a Chinese Liberalism," 103.

explore the conditions of knowledge production and to approach thought from within the intellectual discourse that we are investigating.[82]

However, there remains one caveat. Returning to Jenco's ambitious project that asks how we can reverse the "historical directional arrow" of the one-directional flow of theory in the modern era, are there any traces of a "reversal" of this flow in the account of the travels of theory during the early 1990s?[83] Or, in the words of Peter Burke, do intellectuals in exile truly contribute to a process of intellectual "deprovincialization"?[84] In the early 1990s, Tu Wei-ming argued that whereas in previous decades those in the "third symbolic universe" (Sinologists in North America, Japan, Europe, and Australia) had the power to set the agenda for discourse, now this power was moving toward other universes, namely those of mainland China, Taiwan, Hong Kong, and Singapore and those of global Chinese communities.[85] Even though this study shows that to some extent this is true, we also wonder if the resultant discourse is any different.

Tu Wei-ming's advocacy of a "Cultural China," the debate on Confucianism and capitalism, and the idea of a Pacific Rim were all strongly shaped by debates mostly held at elite universities in the United States. As for discussions on conservatism, Chinese scholars remained inspired by translated works by Sinologists and American scholars. In addition, Yü's revision of modernization theory drew on earlier American sociologists such as Eisenstadt and Shils. We should also add that works by scholars such as Max Weber had already been mediated through American interpretations when they were reinterpreted in China. Thus, were Tu Wei-ming, Lin Yü-sheng, and Yü Ying-shih agenda setters or cultural brokers who facilitated translingual practices inspired by American ideologies, infusing one discourse with the agenda of another? This, as Zhu Xueqin argues, is also a question that stymied a true academic discussion during the early 1990s because many mainland scholars merely singled out Yü's anti-Communist and liberal views and the ideological nature of the debate. Paradoxically, after the "end of history," history could be discussed only through the lens of ideology.

Nevertheless, Chinese uses of conservatism during the early 1990s encourage us to move beyond the search for "equivalent" conceptual counterparts and to rethink existing notions of conservatism based on Eurocentric definitions and Eurocentric interpretations of modernity. The Mannheimian definition of conservatism that criticizes Enlightenment rationality places it firmly in an eighteenth-century European framework. It does not take into account

---

[82] Leigh Jenco, "Introduction: On the Possibility of Chinese Thought as Global Theory," in Jenco, ed., *Chinese Thought as Global Theory: Diversifying Knowledge Production in the Social Sciences and Humanities* (Albany: State University of New York Press, 2016), 2.
[83] Ibid., 4.   [84] Burke, *Exiles and Expatriates*, 16.
[85] Tu, "'Cultural China,'" 12–13, 27–28.

manifestations of conservatism in places where Western-based assumptions of what it meant to be modern were imposed from outside. In addition, as this volume has demonstrated, a Eurocentric *Begriffsgeschichte* in which the meaning of concepts remains tied to the nation-state needs to make room for a *Begriffsgeschichte* that looks at how meaning is contested across borders and among multiple "universes" and communities of discourse. This is not to say that the nation-state becomes redundant, but that it exists in dialogue with exchanges at multiple levels—local, regional, global—and that these exchanges matter in how concepts obtain meaning.

During the early 1990s, members of several Chinese communities contested the meaning of China, thus revealing the importance of studying how ideas travel not only across nation-states, but also within communities of discourse. Across these Chinese communities, in spite of disagreements, intellectuals pondered how Chinese culture could simultaneously be Chinese, modern, Asian, and universal. Discourses on conservatism, for them, like discourses on nationalism, were always already transnational in outlook. We can argue, as Chinese in the 1990s did, that this was also true for Chinese conservatism during the early twentieth century. Behind the seemingly simplistic binaries of matter and spirit or the preservation of Chinese tradition versus wholesale Westernization lay complex advocacies in which Chinese tradition was reimagined as both particular and universal, while making selective use of Western philosophical traditions.

Whereas after World War One much of the criticism had been directed at the ills of modernity in its Western manifestation—scientism, progress, materialism, and individualism—in China in the 1990s the return to conservative alternatives was a response both to the universalism of the 1980s' "New Enlightenment" as well as to China's twentieth-century trajectory. After the Cultural Revolution, Chinese intellectuals acknowledged the limits of collectivism and Rousseauan romanticism rather than those of individual reason and Enlightenment rationalism. *Pace* Burke or Mannheim, it was not reason as such that needed to be limited – a different mode of knowing was required altogether. The destructive rationality behind blueprint designs that had typified utopian socialism and liberalism was to be replaced by constructive reason. As such, just as modern Chinese thought had been an instance of "modernity against modernity,"[86] rather than opposing Enlightenment rationality, the references to conservatism in the 1990s were an instance of "rationality against rationality." Following decades of revolution and utopia, conservatism was a steady, gradual, constructive, and "rational" path toward the future. This was a conservatism *after* revolution, a post-conservatism for a post-new era.

---

[86] See Murthy, "Modernity against Modernity."

Biographies of Prominent Intellectuals

Chen Lai 陈来 (b. 1952)
A renowned philosopher and scholar of Neo-Confucianism during the Song, Yuan, Ming, and Qing dynasties and of New Confucianism, Chen Lai received his Ph.D. from Peking University, where he studied with Zhang Dainian. Chen was a professor in the Philosophy Department of Peking University before moving to the Philosophy Department of Tsinghua University in 2009, where he is also dean of the Tsinghua Academy of Chinese Learning.

Gan Yang 甘阳 (b. 1952)
After spending eight years in Heilongjiang province during the Cultural Revolution, Gan Yang graduated from Peking University with a major in Western philosophy. Gan was a central figure in the culture movement of the 1980s due to his role on the editorial committee of Culture: China and the World. In 1989, he went to the United States and enrolled in a Ph.D. program at the University of Chicago. In the late 1990s, Gan moved to Hong Kong, where he became affiliated with the Chinese University of Hong Kong and later with Sun Yat-sen University in Guangzhou. During the 1990s, Gan was associated with the New Left, but he is also known for introducing the works of Leo Strauss to China in the 2000s. In September 2017, Gan became head of Xinya College at Tsinghua University.

He Xin 何新 (b. 1949)
A prolific researcher in fields that vary from politics and economics to history and language, He Xin was admitted to university in Heilongjiang after the college entrance examinations were resumed in 1977, but he did not complete his studies. As a result of a number of influential papers, he attracted the attention of academia and joined CASS. During the late 1980s, he advocated neoconservatism and nationalism, among others, through a rejuvenation of Chinese culture. However, he is also known for opposing rapid economic liberalization and for supporting the Tiananmen crackdown.

Hu Angang 胡鞍钢 (b. 1953)
An influential scholar and economic and policy adviser to senior politicians, Hu Angang spent seven years in Heilongjiang during the Cultural Revolution and then received his Ph.D. in engineering from CASS. From 1991 to 1992 he was a postdoctoral researcher in economics at Yale University, where he was familiar with Wang Shaoguang. He later became affiliated with Tsinghua

Biographies of Prominent Intellectuals 219

University, where he is currently professor of economics and director of the Institute for Contemporary China Studies. In 1993, he coauthored, with Wang Shaoguang, the "Report on China's State Capacity." His advocacy of a strong state led him to be associated with neoconservatism during the early 1990s and later with New Leftism.

Jia Xiaoye 贾小叶 **(b. 1974)**
Jia Xiaoye obtained her Ph.D. from Beijing Normal University and is currently a researcher in the Modern Intellectual History Unit of the Institute of Modern History of CASS. She conducts research on late Qing intellectual and cultural history, but she has also published on the 1990s' discussions on radicalism and conservatism.

Jiang Yihua 姜义华 **(b. 1939)**
Jiang Yihua is professor of history at Fudan University, where he also obtained his Ph.D. His research interests include modern intellectual and cultural history, theories of history, history of Sino-foreign relations, and Chinese modernization theory and practice. He engaged in a discussion with Yü Ying-shih on the nature of modern Chinese history in the journal *Ershiyi shiji* in 1992.

Jin Guantao 金观涛 **(b. 1947)**
Originally trained as a scientist, Jin was coeditor of the Towards the Future book series that was central in the "culture fever" of the 1980s. He is also known, together with his wife Liu Qingfeng, for the theory of the "ultrastable structure" in traditional Chinese society. After 1989, Jin and Liu Qingfeng left mainland China for the Chinese University of Hong Kong, where they launched the renowned journal *Ershiyi shiji* that was instrumental in the cross-fertilization of thought and the formation of the major discussions of the 1990s.

Li Zehou 李泽厚 **(b. 1930)**
Li is a distinguished philosopher who graduated from Peking University. He is known for his expertise on Kant and for combining Confucianism with Marxism in a reconfiguration of the subject referred to as "subjectality" (*zhutixing*). During the New Enlightenment of the 1980s, Li argued that nationalism had repressed China's Enlightenment agenda. After 1989 Li was the target of official criticism, and in 1992 he left China for the University of Colorado at Boulder, where he has since formally resided. Together with Liu Zaifu, Li coauthored the controversial volume *Gaobie geming* (Farewell to Revolution), which was published in Hong Kong in 1995.

Lin Yü-sheng 林毓生 **(b. 1934)**
Lin, a well-known liberal and intellectual historian who criticized the "totalistic iconoclasm" of May Fourth intellectuals, originates from Liaoning province. He obtained his undergraduate degree in history from National Taiwan University, where he studied with liberal Yin Haiguang (1919–69). He later earned his Ph.D. from the Committee of Social Thought at the University of Chicago, where his intellectual influences included Friedrich Hayek and Edward Shils. After developing an interest in Chinese intellectual

history while a researcher at Harvard University, Lin moved to the University of Wisconsin–Madison. In 2004, he became professor emeritus of history. Since 2005, Lin has also been affiliated with the Academia Sinica in Taiwan.

Liu Dong 刘东 (b. 1955)
Liu Dong, a cultural critic, graduated from Nanjing University, where he majored in philosophy. After pursuing graduate studies at CASS under Li Zehou, specializing in Chinese aesthetics, he became professor of literature at Peking University. During the 1980s, Liu was also a member of the editorial committee of Culture: China and the World. During the early 1990s, he was an advocate of independent scholarship. He is currently professor of philosophy at Tsinghua University and vice dean of the Academy of Chinese Learning at Tsinghua University.

Liu Junning 刘军宁 (b. 1961)
Liu, a political scientist and liberal scholar trained at Peking University, was formerly based at the Institute of Political Science of CASS. In the mid-1990s, Liu launched the liberal journal *Gonggong luncong* (Res Publica). He has also written on conservatism. Liu was dismissed from his post because of his advocacy of political reform in the late 1990s and is currently a researcher at the Institute of Chinese Culture under the Ministry of Culture.

Liu Qingfeng 刘青峰 (b. 1949)
Liu graduated from Peking University and was active in the cultural discussions of the 1980s as coeditor of the Towards the Future book series and then writing on the theory of ultrastability during the 1980s and 1990s. Following the 1989 crackdown, together with her husband Jin Guantao, Liu left China for the Chinese University of Hong Kong. She was the chief editor of the prominent journal *Ershiyi shiji*. Liu and Jin have led several research projects on conceptual history (*guannianshi*) in China.

Liu Zaifu 刘再复 (b. 1941)
A literary and cultural critic, Liu graduated from Xiamen University and was director of the Chinese Literature Research Institute of CASS. Liu was targeted during the political campaigns of the 1980s for his writings on aesthetic subjectivity, and he left China after the Tiananmen demonstrations. Like Li Zehou, he has since formally resided in Boulder, Colorado, but he has also taken several positions outside of the United States.

Ma Yong 马勇 (b. 1956)
After Ma, a recognized Chinese historian, graduated from the History Department of Fudan University, he joined the Modern History Institute of CASS. He has published widely on modern Chinese intellectual and cultural history, on the history of modernization, as well as on premodern Chinese intellectual history.

Sheng Hong 盛洪 (b. 1954)
Sheng Hong obtained his Ph.D. in economics from CASS. During the late 1980s, Sheng introduced and translated scholarship on new institutional economics, which was used to reject "romantic" reform and the "shock

therapy" of the Soviet Union. Sheng is also known for his nationalist writings. Together with other economists, Sheng founded the Unirule Institute of Economics (*Tianze*), a think tank based in Beijing, in 1993.

Tang Yijie 汤一介 (1927–2014)
Tang, specializing in Chinese philosophy, was a graduate of Peking University. He was a professor at Peking University and was married to the scholar of comparative literature Yue Daiyun. Persecuted during the 1950s and during the Cultural Revolution, Tang was rehabilitated in the late 1970s. During the 1980s, he supported the Academy of Chinese Culture. In 2010 Tang became head of the newly established Confucius Research Institute at Peking University.

Tao Dongfeng 陶东风 (b. 1959)
Tao graduated from Beijing Normal University, where he received his Ph.D. in Chinese literature. He is a professor in the Chinese Department at Capital Normal University, specializing in cultural studies and art and literature in contemporary China. Tao also introduced cultural studies in China to Western audiences.

Tu Wei-ming 杜维明 (b. 1940)
Tu is a philosopher, an expert on Confucianism and Neo-Confucianism, and an advocate of the idea of "Cultural China," an effort to redefine what it means to be Chinese in a global setting. Tu was born on mainland China, and his family relocated in 1949 to Taiwan, where he studied at Tunghai University. Tu later pursued graduate studies in history and East Asian languages at Harvard University. He taught at Princeton and the University of California, Berkeley, before returning in 1981 to Harvard, where he served as director of the Harvard-Yenching Institute from 1996 to 2008. In 2010, Tu became director of the Institute for Advanced Humanistic Studies at Peking University.

Wang Hui 汪晖 (b. 1959)
One of China's most influential scholars, both within China and internationally, Wang Hui received his Ph.D. from CASS and is currently a professor in the Department of Chinese Language and Literature at Tsinghua University. Even though he is a scholar of intellectual and literary history and is renowned for his research on Lu Xun (1881–1936), Wang is also known for his writings on Chinese political economy and as a New Leftist, a label he himself rejects. Wang cofounded the series *Xueren* in 1991, and from 1996 to 2007 he served as coeditor (with Huang Ping) of the influential journal *Dushu*.

Wang Shaoguang 王绍光 (b. 1954)
Wang received his Ph.D. in political science from Cornell University in 1990. He taught at Yale University from 1990 to 2000. He is currently professor emeritus in the Department of Government and Public Administration at the Chinese University of Hong Kong. Wang has written extensively on political economy, fiscal and comparative politics, and democratization processes, as well as on the Cultural Revolution. In 1993, he coauthored, with Hu Angang,

the "Report on China's State Capacity," which led him to be associated with neoconservatism.

Wang Xiaodong 王小东 (pseudonym Shi Zhong) (b. 1955)
Wang Xiaodong, who researches politics, economics, and international relations, graduated from Peking University and Tokyo Institute of Technology. He published a number of articles on nationalism during the 1990s (under the pseudonym Shi Zhong) and was also editor of the journal *Zhanlüe yu guanli*.

Wang Yuanhua 王元化 (1920–2008)
A literary theorist, critic, writer, and professor at East China Normal University, Wang suffered political persecution during the Hu Feng incident in the 1950s and was not rehabilitated until the 1980s. Involved in the "New Enlightenment" of the 1980s, he edited the publication *Xin qimeng* (New Enlightenment). However, he was critical of May Fourth and advocated a rethinking of its main tenets. In his criticism of May Fourth, Wang drew on his research on Jean-Jacques Rousseau and his criticism of Rousseau's concept of the "General Will."

Wang Yuechuan 王岳川 (b. 1955)
Educated in the Chinese Department at Sichuan University and at Peking University, Wang specializes in literary theory and aesthetics as well as cultural criticism. He is a professor in the Department of Chinese Language and Literature at Peking University. His publications include works on cultural developments and post-theories in China in the 1990s. Wang is also a well-known calligrapher.

Xiao Gongqin 萧功秦 (b. 1946)
Having spent twelve years as a factory worker during the Cultural Revolution, Xiao graduated from the History Department of Nanjing University. A historian and political theorist, Xiao was a key advocate of the theories of neo-authoritarianism and neoconservatism during the late 1980s and 1990s. He is currently a professor in the History Department of Shanghai Normal University and professor of political science at Shanghai Jiaotong University. Xiao has written on the problems of Chinese modernization, modern Chinese history, and reform.

Xu Jilin 许纪霖 (b. 1957)
Xu is an esteemed liberal public intellectual and historian based at East China Normal University in Shanghai, where he is also head of the Contemporary Chinese Thought and Culture Research Institute. His work concentrates on Chinese intellectuals and modern Chinese thought. In the debates between liberals and the "New Left," Xu advocates a "third way."

Yü Ying-shih 余英时 (b. 1930)
Yü, an eminent scholar of Chinese studies, is broadly interested in intellectual discourse, and values in Chinese civilization and their fate in the modern world. His writings on the "radicalization" of China during the twentieth century triggered an influential debate among Chinese intellectuals. Born in Tianjin, Yü left mainland China for Hong Kong in 1950 to study at the newly founded New Asia College. He then went to the United States and obtained

his Ph.D. from Harvard University in 1962. He later returned to Hong Kong, where he served as president of New Asia College and pro vice chancellor of the Chinese University of Hong Kong (1973–75). Subsequently, he held professorships at Yale and Princeton University, where he became professor emeritus of East Asian studies and history in 2001.

Yue Daiyun 乐黛云 (b. 1931)
Yue majored in Chinese at Peking University and is a professor in the Chinese Contemporary Literature and Comparative Literature Division of Peking University. She also spent time at Harvard and Berkeley as well as in Italy and Tunis. Labeled a Rightist during the 1950s, Yue was important in mainland China's re-evaluation of the *Xueheng* scholars in the late 1980s. She is also known for her memoir, titled *To the Storm*. She was married to philosopher Tang Yijie.

Zhang Xudong 张旭东 (b. 1965)
Zhang received his Ph.D. in literature from Duke University in 1995 and is professor of comparative literature and East Asian studies at New York University. Zhang is also affiliated with Peking University and East China Normal University and publishes in both English and Chinese on topics related to critical theory, political philosophy, and twentieth-century Chinese literature and culture.

Zhang Yiwu 张颐武 (b. 1962)
A postmodernist critic, Zhang is a graduate of Peking University, where he is also a professor in the Chinese Department. Zhang has reinterpreted the cultural changes of the 1990s in relation to global capitalism and has embraced the arrival of mass culture as a positive development. His writings discuss the place of culture in China's transition from modernity to postmodernity.

Zhao Yiheng 赵毅衡 (Henry Y. H. Zhao) (b. 1945)
A well-known literary scholar, Zhao Yiheng received his M.A. from CASS and his Ph.D. from the University of California, Berkeley. He was based at the School of Oriental and African Studies at the University of London until 2006, when he became professor of comparative literature at Sichuan University.

Zheng Dahua 郑大华 (b. 1956)
Zheng obtained his Ph.D. in history from Beijing Normal University and specializes in modern Chinese political, intellectual, and cultural history. He has published on modern Chinese cultural conservatism (especially on Liang Shuming and Zhang Junmai) and on cultural thought during the Republican era. He has also conducted research on cultural conservatism in China in the 1990s. He is head of the Modern Intellectual History Research Unit of the Modern History Institute of CASS and a specially appointed professor at Hunan Normal University.

Zheng Min 郑敏 (b. 1920)
A revered poetess and member of the Nine Leaves school of poetry, Zheng studied philosophy at National Southwestern Associated University (Xi'nan Lianda). She became a poet during the Sino-Japanese War (1937–45) and

later obtained her M.A. in English literature from Brown University and then taught in the Foreign Languages and Literature Department of Beijing Normal University. In 1993, Zheng triggered a debate after she wrote an article that criticized modernist New Poetry and the literary revolution.

Zhu Xueqin 朱学勤 **(b. 1952)**
Zhu received his Ph.D. in history from Fudan University in 1992. He is a major proponent of liberalism, a scholar of Jean-Jacques Rousseau, and professor of history at Shanghai University.

Glossary

baihua	vernacular language
baihua kouyu	vernacular language in the colloquial form
baihua shumianyu	vernacular language in the written form
baihuawen	written vernacular Chinese
banjiquan	semiauthoritarian
baobian	praising and blaming
baoli zhuyi	ideology of violence
baoshou (保守)	conservative; conservatism
baoshouzhe	conservative (noun)
bishi jiuxu	to dwell on the abstract and avoid real issues
Bu'erzhaweike zhuyi	Bolshevism
bupo buli	there is no making without breaking
chansheng	come into being
chouxiang jicheng	abstract inheritance
chuangzao de fazhan	creative development
dagemingshi de weili zhuyi de jijin zhuyi	French Revolution-style rationalist radicalism
dangdai xin rujia	New Confucianism
dangdai xin ruxue	New Confucianism
danwei	work unit
danxiang yinjin	single import
daode baoshou zhuyi	moral conservatism
daode zizhuxing	moral autonomy
dongluan	counterrevolutionary disturbance; turmoil
Faguo dagemingshi de lixiang zhuyi	French Revolution-style idealism
Faguo dagemingshi de weili zhuyi de jijin zhuyi	French Revolution-style rationalist radicalism
fan'an	reversal of verdicts
fan fan chuantong zhuyi	anti-antitraditionalism
fangquan rangli	devolving authority and granting benefits
fan pangongli zhuyi	anti-pan-utilitarianism

fansi	reflections
fan xiandai de xiandai zhuyi	antimodern theory of modernization
fan zhengzhi zhuyi	pan-politicism
fei jiaowang bu zuyi guozheng	overcorrection
fei lishi zhuyi de	nonhistoricist
fei lixing zhuyi	irrationalism
fuqiang	wealth and power
gaigezhe	reformer (noun)
gemingdang	revolutionary party
glasnost	opening
gong	public mindedness
gonggong zhishi fenzi	public intellectual
gongju lixing	instrumental rationality
guannian	concepts
guannianshi	conceptual history
guocui	national essence
Guoji Ruxue Lianhehui	International Confucian Association
guoji zhuyi	radicalism
guojia zhuyi	statism
guoqing	national conditions
guoxing	national character
guoxue	national learning; national studies
guoxue re	national learning fever
he	harmony
heibai	black-and-white
heli	rational
houxue	post-*isms*
ji	violence
ji (激)	to dash, to arouse, fierce, and violent
jianjin zhuyi	gradualism
jianjin zhuyi de baoshou zhuyi	gradualist conservatism
jianjin zhuyi de xiandaihua	incrementalist modernization
jianwang zhilai	know the future in the mirror of the past
jiaolügan de jijin zhuyi	feeling-of-anxiety radicalism
jiaowang guozheng	overcorrection, "over-straightening the crooked"
jiazhi lixing	value rationality
jidian	sedimentation
jie geming	de-revolution

jiegou zhuyi	deconstructionism
jieji liyi	personal interests
jieti	ladder
jijin (激进)	radical (economic and political reform)
jijin (急进)	to advance, far-reaching, thorough, radical (youth)
jijin de gaigeguan	radical reform view
jijin fan chuantong zhuyi	radical antitraditionalism
jijin gongli zhuyi	radical utilitarianism
jijin zhuyi	radicalism
jin (进)	to advance, to enter, to receive
jin	progress (noun)
jinbu	to progress (verb)
jindaishi yanjiu	research on modern history
jingyan zhuyi	empiricism
jingyan zhuyi leixing de zhuyi	empiricist-type *-isms*
jisu qianjin	to advance rapidly
jiti jingyan	collective experience
jiuguo	save the nation
jiuwang	salvation
Jiuye shipai	Nine Leaves poets
keji lixing	scientific and technological rationality
kongxiang shehui zhuyi	utopian socialism
kongxiang ziben zhuyi	utopian capitalism
Kongzi Yanjiu Zhongxin	Confucius Research Center
langman zhuyi gaigeguan	romantic reform view
li	propriety
liangban	two semis
linian chongbai	adoration of ideas
linian juedinglun	ideas determinism
liumang	hooligans, alienated youth, individualists, or unscrupulous entrepreneurs
lixing	rational, reason
lixing zhuyi	rationalism
lixue	Principle-centered Learning
minjian shehui	popular society
minzu de liyi	national interests
minzu texing	national particularity
mozhe shitou guohe	crossing the river by feeling for the stones
nanxun	Southern Tour
neisheng	inner sage

228 Glossary

nisi wohuo	"you die, I live," all-or-nothing
perestroika	restructuring
pipan	critique
pipan de jicheng	critical inheritance
pojiu lixin	destroy the old in order to establish the new
qianlima	winged steed
qimeng	Enlightenment
Qinghua Daxue Guoxue Yanjiuyuan	Tsinghua Academy of National Learning
qiuren deren	seek benevolence and receive benevolence
quanpan Xihualun	wholesale Westernization theories
quanxiang yinjin	wholesale import
qun	grouping
re	fever
ren	benevolence, humaneness
renwen jingshen	humanist spirit
ruguo shixue	counterfactual history
ruxue chonggou yundong	movement for the reconfiguration of Confucianism
ruxue re	Confucianism fever
sangang	three bonds
shehui	society
shehui youjilun	theory of the social organism
shejin qiuyuan	reject what is near and seek what is far away
shenceng jiegou	deep structure
shi	literati, traditional scholars
shifan	anomy
shifei	yes-no
shijian shi jianyan zhenli de weiyi biaozhun	practice as the sole criterion of truth
shisuhua de rujia lunli	vulgar Confucianism
shoucheng	maintaining the achievements of one's predecessors
shouti	receptor
shuo guoxue re de re	talking about national studies fever
sichao	trend
sige xiandaihua	Four Modernizations
sixiang	thought
sixiangjia danchu, xueshujia tuxian	thinkers fade out, scholars protrude
taizidang	princelings
tazhehua	Otherization

Glossary

teshu de guoqing	particular national conditions
ti	essence
tian	heaven
tianming	Mandate of Heaven
tianren heyi	unity between man and heaven
tianxia zhuyi	cosmopolitanism; all-under-heaven-ism
tiaojianlun	circumstance theory
tiyong	borrowing foreign technology for application, but relying on Chinese learning for the essence
tiyong bukeli lun	essence and function cannot be separated from each other
tonghua	assimilation
Tongmenghui	Revolutionary Alliance
tong santong	unifying the three traditions
waiwang	outer king
wangu	bitterly opposed to change
wanmei zhuyi	perfectionism
weiji zhixue	learning for oneself
weili zhuyi	rationalism, rationality
weili zhuyi leixing de zhuyi	rationalist-type *-isms*
weiren youji	acting benevolent from within the self
weixin zhuyi	only-new-*ism*
wenhua baoshou zhuyi	cultural conservatism
wenhua jijin zhuyi	cultural radicalism
wenhua linghun	cultural soul
wenhua re	culture fever
wenhua shiguan	cultural view of history
wenhua xinli jiegou	cultural-psychological formation
wenjin zhuyi	gradualism
wenming chuantong	civilizational tradition
wenshixing zhidu	greenhouse model system
wenti yu zhuyi	problems and *-isms*
wenyan	classical Chinese
wenyanwen	classical Chinese writing
wuxu bianfa	Hundred Days Reform Movement
xiandaihua	modernization
xiandaihua lishi yanjiu	early modernization history research
xiandaixing	modernity
xiandai xin rujia	New Confucianism
xianshi zhuyi	realism
Xi'nan Lianhe Daxue	National Southwestern Associated University

xin baoshou zhuyi	neoconservatism
xin jianjin zhuyi	neo-gradualism or neo-incrementalism
xing	nature
xin quanwei zhuyi	neo-authoritarianism
xin shenghuo yundong	New Life Movement
xin shiqi	new era
xintaishang de jijin zhuyi	psychological radicalism
xin wenhua yundong	New Culture Movement
xin wenxue yundong	New Literature Movement
xinxing	conformity of heaven and man in virtue
xinxing zhi xue	learning of the mind and nature
xinxue	heart-mind-centered learning
xinzheng	New Policies
xin zhengzhi baoshou zhuyi	new political conservatism
xin zhixu zhuyi	new order-*ism*
xin zhuyi	new-*isms*
xitong shuli	systematically sort out
xiuke liaofa	shock therapies
xueshu	learning; academic
xueshu guifan	academic norms
xueshushi	history of modern scholarship
xuewen	learning
xuezhe	scholar
xungen	root searching
Yan Fu *beilun*	Yan Fu paradox
yangqi	developing what is useful and discarding what is not
yihui langman zhuyi	parliamentary romanticism
yi juti de gongxiang	concrete universal
Ying Meishi jingyan zhuyi de ziyou zhuyi	Anglo-American-style empiricist liberalism
yitu lunli	intention ethics
yong	function
youdaoxing zhidu	guidance model system
youhuan yishi	crisis mentality
youhun	wandering soul
youni wuwo	where you are, I am not
yueli	experience
zenme shixian xiandaixing	how to realize modernity
zhengming	rectify names
zhengque lijie	correctly understand
zhengzhi baoshou zhuyi	political conservatism

zhengzhi langman zhuyi	political romanticism
zhidu juedinglun	system determinism
zhiqing	sent-down youths to the rural areas
zhishi fenzi	intellectual, knowledgeable element
zhixiang zhengzhi xingwei de wenhua zhuyi	culturalism directed at political action
zhizhengdang	ruling party
zhongdao lixing	middle-of-the-road rationality
Zhongguo benwei de wenhua jianshe	cultural construction on a Chinese basis
Zhongguo lichang	Chinese position
Zhongguo zhishi fenzi	Chinese intellectual
Zhonghua	Chinese
Zhonghua Kongzi Yanjiusuo	China Confucius Research Institute
Zhonghua wenhuajuan	Chinese Culture Rim
Zhonghuaxing	Chineseness
zhongji guanhuai	ultimate concerns
zhongji mudi	ultimate ends
Zhongti Xiyong	Chinese learning as the substance, Western learning as the function
Zhongxue tiyong and Xixue tiyong	Chinese learning as substance and function; Western learning as substance and function
zhuanhua	transformation
zhuliu wenhua	mainstream culture
zhutixing	subjectality
zhuti zhuyi	subjectivism
zhuyi	-*ism*
zhuyi juedinglun	-*ism* determinism
ziqiang buxi	continuous self-renewal
ziyou de yizhi he duli de jingshen	a free will and an independent spirit
zunzhong zhishi, zunzhong rencai	respect knowledge, respect talent

References

Main Journals and Periodicals

Beijing qingnianbao (Beijing Youth Daily)
Beijing zhi chun (Beijing Spring)
Dongfang (Orient)
Dushu (Reading)
Ershiyi shiji (Twenty-First Century)
Gaoxiao lilun zhanxian (Theoretical Front in Higher Education)
Guangming ribao (Enlightenment Daily)
Jindaishi yanjiu (Modern History Research)
Kaifang shidai (Open Times)
Kongzi yanjiu (Confucius Research)
Renmin ribao (People's Daily)
South China Morning Post
Tansuo yu zhengming (Exploration and Contention)
Tianya (Frontiers)
Wenxue pinglun (Literary Review)
Wenyi pinglun (Literature and Art Discussion)
Wenyi zhengming (Debates on Literature and Art)
Xueren (The Scholar)
Yuandao (True Way)
Zhanlüe yu guanli (Strategy and Management)
Zhexue yanjiu (Philosophy Research)
Zhongguo luntan (China Forum)
Zhongguo qingnianbao (China Youth Daily)
Zhongguo shibao zhoukan (China Times Weekly)
Zhongguo zhi chun (China Spring)

Interviews

Interview with Chen Lai. Beijing, August 10, 2005
Interview with Jia Xiaoye. Beijing, June 18, 2014
Interview with Jiang Yihua. Shanghai, August 8, 2006
Interviews with Ma Yong:
    (1) Beijing, August 8, 2005
    (2) Beijing, September 1, 2005
    (3) Beijing, June 6, 2006

Interview with Tao Dongfeng. Beijing, June 28, 2006
Interview with Wang Hui. Beijing, June 27, 2006
Interview with Wang Yuechuan. Beijing, June 21, 2006
Interviews with Xiao Gongqin:
  (1) Shanghai, August 4, 2006
  (2) Shanghai, June 9, 2014
Interview with Xu Jilin. Shanghai, August 6, 2006
Interview with Yue Daiyun. Beijing, July 12, 2006
Interview with Zhang Yiwu. Beijing, July 26, 2006
Interview with Zheng Min. Beijing, July 6, 2006

Books and Articles

A Cheng. "Wenhua zhiyuezhe renlei" (Culture Conditions Humanity), *Wenyibao* (Literary Gazette), July 9, 1985.
Alitto, Guy S. "The Conservative as Sage: Liang Shu-ming." Pp. 213–41 in Furth, ed., *Limits of Change*.
  ed. *Contemporary Confucianism in Thought and Action*. Berlin: Springer, 2015.
  The Last Confucian: Liang Shu-ming and the Chinese Dilemma of Modernity. Berkeley: University of California Press, 1987 [1979].
  "Postmodernism," lecture, Peking University, June 27, 2006.
[Ai Kai]. *Shijie fanwei nei de fan xiandaihua sichao: Lun wenhua shoucheng zhuyi* (Anti-modernization Thought in the Global Spectrum: On Cultural Conservatism). Guiyang: Guizhou renmin chubanshe, 1991.
Ang, Ien. "Can One Say No to Chineseness? Pushing the Limits of the Diasporic Paradigm." Pp. 281–300 in Chow, ed., *Modern Chinese Literary and Cultural Studies in the Age of Theory*.
Apter, David E. and Tony Saich. *Revolutionary Discourse in Mao's Republic*. Cambridge, MA: Harvard University Press, 1994.
Arnhart, Larry. *Darwinian Conservatism*. Exeter, UK: Imprint Academic, 2005.
Baecker, Angie. "Max Weber in Twentieth-Century China," unpublished conference paper, AAS-in-Asia, Taipei, June 23, 2015.
Baker, Keith Michael and Dan Edelstein. "Introduction." Pp. 1–24 in Baker and Edelstein, eds., *Scripting Revolution: A Historical Approach to the Comparative Study of Revolutions*. Stanford, CA: Stanford University Press, 2015.
Barmé, Geremie. "History for the Masses." Pp. 260–86 in Jonathan Unger, ed., *Using the Past to Serve the Present: Historiography and Politics in Contemporary China*. Armonk, NY: M.E. Sharpe, 1993.
  In the Red: On Contemporary Chinese Culture. New York: Columbia University Press, 1999.
  "The Revolution of Resistance." Pp. 47–70 in Elizabeth J. Perry and Mark Selden, eds., *Chinese Society: Change, Conflict and Resistance*. London: RoutledgeCurzon, 2003.
  Shades of Mao: The Posthumous Cult of the Great Leader. Armonk, NY: M.E. Sharpe, 1996.
  "To Screw Foreigners Is Patriotic: China's Avant-Garde Nationalists," *China Journal*, no. 34 (July 1995), 209–34.

"Worrying China and New Sinology," *China Heritage Quarterly* 14 (June 2008), www.chinaheritagequarterly.org/articles.php?searchterm=014_worryingChina.inc&issue=014.
Barmé, Geremie and Linda Jaivin, eds. *New Ghosts, Old Dreams: Chinese Rebel Voices*. New York: Times Books, 1992.
Barmé, Geremie and John Minford, eds. *Seeds of Fire: Chinese Voices of Conscience*. New York: Noonday Press, 1989.
Barr, Michael D. "Lee Kuan Yew and the 'Asian Values' Debate," *Asian Studies Review* 24.3 (2000), 309–34.
Baum, Richard. *Burying Mao: Chinese Politics in the Age of Deng Xiaoping*. Princeton, NJ: Princeton University Press, 1994.
"Be Firm Promoters of the Four Modernizations," *Renmin ribao* editorial, February 1, 1980. Pp. 433–38 in James T. Myers, Jürgen Domes, and Milton Yeh, eds., *Chinese Politics: Documents and Analysis, Vol. 3: The Death of Mao (1976) to the Fall of Hua Kuo-feng (1980)*. Columbia: University of South Carolina Press, 1995.
"Behind the CCP Princes Party," *Pai-hsing* (The People), no. 260 (March 16, 1992), 32–35. Translated in *Inside China Mainland* (Taipei) 14.5 (May 1992), 6–10.
Beijing daxue shehui kexuechu (Peking University Social Sciences Department), ed. *Beijing daxue jinian wusi yundong qishi zhounian lunwenji* (Collection of Articles on the Occasion of Peking University's Commemoration of the Seventieth Anniversary of the May Fourth Movement). Beijing: Beijing daxue chubanshe, 1989.
Béja, Jean-Philippe. "Introduction: 4 June 1989: A Watershed in Chinese Contemporary History." Pp. 1–12 in Béja, ed., *The Impact of China's 1989 Tiananmen Massacre*. London: Routledge, 2011.
Bell, Daniel. *China's New Confucianism: Politics and Everyday Life in a Changing Society*. Princeton, NJ: Princeton University Press, 2008.
The Cultural Contradictions of Capitalism. New York: Basic Books, 1976.
Bellah, Robert N. *Tokugawa Religion: The Values of Pre-industrial Japan*. Glencoe, IL: Free Press, 1957.
Berger, Peter L. "An East Asian Development Model?" Pp. 3–11 in Berger and Hsin-Huang Michael Hsiao, eds., *In Search of an East Asian Development Model*. New Brunswick, NJ: Transaction, 1988.
Berlin, Isaiah. "Two Concepts of Liberty." Pp. 118–72 in Berlin, *Four Essays on Liberty*. Oxford: Oxford University Press, 1969.
Bi Quanzhong. "Guoxue, zai yanyuan you qiaoran xingqi: Beijing daxue Zhongguo chuantong wenhua yanjiu sanji" (The Quiet Rise of National Studies on the Old Campus: Random Notes on Chinese Traditional Culture Research at Peking University), *Renmin ribao* (People's Daily), August 16, 1993, 3.
Billioud, Sébastien. *Thinking through Confucian Modernity: A Study of Mou Zongsan's Moral Metaphysics*. Leiden: Brill, 2012.
Billioud, Sébastien and Joël Thoraval. *The Sage and the People: The Confucian Revival in China*. Oxford: Oxford University Press, 2015.
"Bixu qizhi xianming de fandui dongluan" (We Must Take a Firm Stand and Oppose Turmoil), *Renmin ribao*, April 26, 1989, 1.
Black, George and Robin Munro. *Black Hands of Beijing: Lives of Defiance in China's Democracy Movement*. New York: John Wiley, 1993.

Bloch, Ernst. "Nonsynchronism and Dialectics," *New German Critique*, no. 11 (Spring 1977), 22–38.
Bresciani, Umberto. *Reinventing Confucianism: The New Confucian Movement*. Taipei: Ricci Institute for Chinese Studies, 2001.
Brook, Timothy. "Profit and Righteousness in Chinese Economic Culture." Pp. 27–44 in Brook and Hy V. Luong, eds., *Culture and Economy: The Shaping of Capitalism in Eastern Asia*. Ann Arbor: University of Michigan Press, 1997.
  Quelling the People: The Military Suppression of the Beijing Democracy Movement. Stanford, CA: Stanford University Press, 1998.
Brugger, Bill and David Kelly. *Chinese Marxism in the Post-Mao Era*. Stanford, CA: Stanford University Press, 1990.
Burke, Edmund. *Reflections on the Revolution in France*, ed. Frank M. Turner. New Haven, CT: Yale University Press, 2003.
Burke, Peter. *Exiles and Expatriates in the History of Knowledge, 1500–2000*. Waltham, MA: Brandeis University Press, 2017.
Cecil, Hugh. *Conservatism*. London: Williams and Norgate, 1912.
Chan, N. Serina. *The Thought of Mou Zongsan*. Leiden: Brill, 2011.
Chang, Carsun. *The Development of Neo-Confucian Thought*, 2 vols. New York: Bookman Associates, 1957–62.
Chang, Hao [Zhang Hao]. "Intellectual Change and the Reform Movement, 1890–1898." Pp. 274–338 in John King Fairbank and Kwang-ching Liu, eds., *The Cambridge History of China, Vol. 11: Late Ch'ing, 1800–1911, Part Two*. Cambridge: Cambridge University Press, 1980.
  "New Confucianism and the Intellectual Crisis of Contemporary China." Pp. 276–302 in Furth, ed., *Limits of Change*.
  "Zhongguo jin bainian lai de geming sixiang daolu" (The Revolutionary Road of China during the Past One Hundred Years). Pp. 42–56 in Li Shitao, ed., *Zhishi fenzi lichang: Jijin yu baoshou zhijian de dongdang*. Originally published in *Kaifang shidai* (Open Times), no. 1 (1999), 2, 29–47.
Chang Jiang. "Shehui zhuanxingqi de yizhong wenhua xianxiang: Ping *Gaobie geming*" (A Cultural Phenomenon in Societies at a Transitional Stage: On *Farewell to Revolution*), *Ershiyi shiji* (Twenty-First Century), no. 33 (February 1996), 68–71.
Cheek, Timothy. "Historians as Public Intellectuals in Contemporary China." Pp. 204–22 in Edward Gu and Merle Goldman, eds., *Chinese Intellectuals between State and Market*. London: RoutledgeCurzon, 2004.
  The Intellectual in Modern Chinese History. Cambridge: Cambridge University Press, 2015.
  Living with Reform: China since 1989. London: Zed Books, 2006.
  "The Worlds of China's Intellectuals." Pp. 154–72 in Timothy B. Weston and Lionel M. Jensen, eds., *China In and Beyond the Headlines*. Lanham, MD: Rowman & Littlefield, 2012.
  "Xu Jilin and the Thought Work of China's Public Intellectuals," *China Quarterly*, no. 186 (June 2006), 401–20.
Chen Baiming. "Jinnian lai guonei dui wenhua jijin zhuyi de pipan zongshu" (Summary of Mainland Criticism of Cultural Radicalism in Recent Years), *Wenyi lilun yu piping* (Literature and Art Theory and Criticism), no. 1 (April 1997), 131–41.
Chen Duxiu. "Falanxi yu jindai wenming" (The French and Modern Civilizations), *Xin qingnian (New Youth)* 1.1 (September 1915), 1–4.

"Wenxue geminglun" (On the Literary Revolution). Pp. 164–67, reprinted in Chen Duxiu, Wang Zhongjiang, and Yuan Shuya, *Xin qingnian: Minzhu yu kexue de huhuan* (New Youth: The Call for Democracy and Science). Zhengzhou: Zhongzhou guji chubanshe, 1999.

Chen, Feng. "The Dilemmas of Eudaemonic Legitimacy in Post-Mao China," *Polity* 29.3 (1997), 421–40.

"Order and Stability in Social Transition: Neoconservative Political Thought in Post-1989 China," *China Quarterly*, no. 151 (1997), 593–613.

Chen Feng and Zhi Zhong. "Kua shiji zhi jiao: Wenxue de kunhuo yu xuanze" (Stepping into a New Century: Literature's Puzzlement and Options). Pp. 219–30 in Li Shitao, ed., *Zhishi fenzi lichang: Jijin yu baoshou zhijian de dongdang*. Originally published in *Wenxue pinglun* (Literary Review), no. 6 (1994), 121–26, 34.

Chen, Fong-ching. "The Popular Cultural Movement of the 1980s." Pp. 71–86 in Davies, ed., *Voicing Concerns*.

Chen, Fong-ching and Jin Guantao. *From Youthful Manuscripts to River Elegy: The Chinese Popular Cultural Movement and Political Transformation 1979–1989*. Hong Kong: Chinese University Press, 1997.

Chen, Jianhua. "World Revolution Knocking at the Heavenly Gate: Kang Youwei and His Use of Geming in 1898," *Journal of Modern Chinese History* 5.1 (June 2011), 89–108.

Chen Kuide. "Wangchao mori de 'xinzheng'" (A Doomed Dynasty's "New Deal"), *Zhongguo zhi chun* (China Spring), no. 1 (January 1992), 24–25. Translated by David Kelly in *Chinese Law and Government* 29.1 (March–April 1996), 38–41.

Chen Lai. "Bayu: Shiji zhi jiao hua chuantong" (Afterword: On Tradition at the End of the Century). Pp. 286–89 in Chen, *Chuantong yu xiandai*.

Chuantong yu xiandai: Renwen zhuyi de shijie (Tradition and Modernity: The Scope of Humanism). Beijing: Beijing daxue chubanshe, 2006. A revised edition was published under the title *Renwen zhuyi de shijie* (The Scope of Humanism). Nanning: Guangxi jiaoyu chubanshe, 1997.

"Dui xin wenhua yundong de zai sikao: Cong 'wusi' houqi de Liang Shuming shuoqi" (Reconsidering the New Culture Movement: On Liang Shuming in the Post-"May Fourth" Era), *Nanchang daxue xuebao* (Nanchang University Journal) 31.1 (January 2000), 1–5.

"Duoyuan wenhua jiegou zhong de ruxue ji qi dingwei" (Confucianism and Its Place in Multicultural Structures), *Zhongguo luntan* (China Forum) 27.1 (1988), 21–23.

"Ershi shiji wenhua yundong zhong de jijin zhuyi" (Radicalism in Twentieth-Century Cultural Movements). Pp. 293–308 in Li Shitao, ed., *Zhishi fenzi lichang: Jijin yu baoshou zhijian de dongdang*, and pp. 68–83 in Chen, *Chuantong yu xiandai*. Translated in *Contemporary Chinese Thought* 29.4 (Summer 1998), 5–28. Originally published in *Dongfang* (Orient) 1.1 (1993), 38–44, and *Zhexue zazhi* (Philosophy Journal), no. 2 (1992).

"Ershi shiji Zhongguo wenhua zhong de ruxue kunjing" (The Predicament of Confucianism in Twentieth-Century Chinese Culture), *Zhejiang shehui kexue* (Zhejiang Social Sciences), no. 3 (May 1998), 26–32. A modified version of this text was published in Chen, *Chuantong yu xiandai*, 84–96.

"Feng Youlan wenhuaguan de jianli yu fazhan" (The Foundation and Development of Feng Youlan's Cultural Perspective). Pp. 130–62 in Chen, *Chuantong yu xiandai*. Originally published in *Xueren* (The Scholar), no. 4 (1993), 126–46, under the title "Feng Youlan wenhuaguan shulun" (Commentary on Feng Youlan's View of Culture).

"'Guoxue re' yu chuantong wenhua yanjiu de wenti" (The "National Studies Craze" and the Problem of Research on Traditional Culture), *Kongzi yanjiu* (Confucius Research), no. 2 (1995), 4–6.

"Huajie 'chuantong' yu 'xiandai' de jinzhang: 'Wusi' wenhua sichao de fansi" (Dissolving the Tensions between "Tradition" and "Modernity": Reflections on "May Fourth" Cultural Trends). Pp. 373–98 in Chen, *Chen Lai zixuanji* (Self-Selected Works of Chen Lai). Guilin: Guangxi shifan daxue chubanshe, 1997. Originally published in Lin Yü-sheng et al., *Wusi: Duoyuan de fansi*, 151–85.

"Liang Shuming zaoqi de Dong Xi wenhuaguan" (Liang Shuming's Early Views of Eastern and Western Cultures). Pp. 97–129 in Chen, *Chuantong yu xiandai*.

"Renwen zhuyi de shijie" (The Scope of Humanism), *Dongfang wenhua* (Eastern Culture) 18.1 (1997), 14–20. A modified version of this text was published in Chen, *Chuantong yu xiandai*, 1–12.

"Rujia lunli yu Zhongguo xiandaihua" (Confucian Ethics and Chinese Modernization). Pp. 188–206 in Chen, *Chuantong yu xiandai*. Originally published under the title "Shisu rujia lunli yu houfa xiandaihua" (Vulgar Confucianism and the Modernization of Late Developing Countries), *Ershiyi shiji* (Twenty-First Century), no. 22 (April 1994), 112–20.

"Rujia sixiang yu xiandai Dong Ya shijie" (Confucian Thought and the Modern East Asian World). Pp. 179–87 in Chen, *Chuantong yu xiandai*. Originally published in *Dongfang* (Orient), no. 3 (1994), 10–13.

"'Wusi' Dong Xi wenhua lunzheng de fansi" (Reflections on the May Fourth Debates on Eastern and Western Cultures). Pp. 157–74 in Beijing daxue shehui kexuechu, ed., *Beijing daxue jinian wusi yundong qishi zhounian lunwenji*. Also appearing under the title "Wusi wenhua sichao fansi" (Reflections on May Fourth Culture), *Dushu* (Reading), no. 5 (1989), 49–55.

"'Wusi' sichao yu xiandaixing" (The "May Fourth" Trend and Modernity). Pp. 60–67 in Chen, *Chuantong yu xiandai*.

"Xin lixue yu xiandaixing siwei de fansi" (New Rational Philosophy and Reflections on Modernity Thought). Pp. 163–78 in Chen, *Chuantong yu xiandai*. Originally published in *Beijing daxue xuebao* (Peking University Journal), no. 1 (1995), 57–64, 128, under the title "'Xin lixue' de xiandaihua lun yu 'xiandaixing' siwei de jiantao" (Examining the Modernization of 'New Rational Philosophy' and 'Modernity' Thought).

"Zhenxia qiyuan" (A Propitious New Start), *Ershiyi shiji* (Twenty-First Century), no. 10 (April 1992), 10–11.

"Zhongguo jindai sixiang de huigu yu qianzhan" (Retrospect and Prospects for Modern Chinese Thought). Pp. 13–30 in Chen, *Chuantong yu xiandai*. A different version was originally published in *Tianjin shehui kexue* (Tianjin Social Sciences), no. 5 (1989), 3–8.

Chen Pingyuan. "Jin bainian Zhongguo jingying wenhua de shiluo" (The Decline of High Culture in China during the Last One Hundred Years), *Ershiyi shiji* (Twenty-First Century), no. 17 (June 1993), 11–22.

Chen Pingyuan, Wang Hui, and Wang Shouchang, eds. *Xueren* (The Scholar). Jiangsu: Jiangsu wenyi chubanshe, 1991–2000.

Chen Shaoming. "Didiao yixie: Xiang wenhua baoshou zhuyi jiangyan" (Tone Down a Little: Advice to Cultural Conservatism). Pp. 507–13 in Li Shitao, ed., *Zhishi fenzi lichang: Jijin yu baoshou zhijian de dongdang*. Originally published in *Dongfang* (Orient), no. 3 (1996), 86–88.

Chen, Xiaomei. *Occidentalism: A Theory of Counter-discourse in Post-Mao China*. Oxford: Oxford University Press, 1995.

Chen Xiaoming. "Antiradicalism and the Historical Situation of Contemporary Chinese Intellectuals," *Contemporary Chinese Thought* 29.2 (Winter 1997–98), 29–44. Translation of Chen, "Fan jijin yu dangdai zhishi fenzi de lishi jingyu."

"Baoshouxing yu hefahua: Pingxi dalu zheng xingcheng yizhong wenhua lichang" (Conservative Disposition and Legitimation: Review of a Cultural Position That Is Taking Shape on the Mainland), *Zhongguo luntan* (China Forum) 16 (February 1, 1992), 93–97.

"Fan jijin yu dangdai zhishi fenzi de lishi jingyu" (Anti-radicalism and the Historical Situation of Contemporary Intellectuals). Pp. 309–20 in Li Shitao, ed., *Zhishi fenzi lichang: Jijin yu baoshou zhijian de dongdang*. Originally published in *Dongfang* (Orient), no. 2 (January 1994), 11–15.

Chen Xiaoming, Zhang Yiwu, Dai Jinhua, and Zhu Wei. "Dongfang zhuyi he houzhimin zhuyi" (Orientalism and Postcolonialism), *Zhongshan* (Purple Mountain) 88.1 (1994), 126–48.

Chen Xiaoya. "Shei yingdang dui Xinhai geming fuze" (Who Ought to be Responsible for the 1911 Revolution?). Pp. 93–102 in Li Shitao, ed., *Zhishi fenzi lichang: Jijin yu baoshou zhijian de dongdang*.

Chen Xueran. *Wusi zai Xianggang: Zhimin qingjing, minzu zhuyi ji bentu yishi* (May Fourth in Hong Kong: Colonial Context, Nationalism and Local Consciousness). Xianggang: Zhonghua shuju, 2014.

Chiu-Duke, Josephine and Michael S. Duke. "Editorial Note." Pp. xiii–xxii in Yü Ying-shih, with Josephine Chiu-Duke and Michael S. Duke, eds., *Chinese History and Culture, Volume Two, Seventeenth Century through Twentieth Century*. New York: Columbia University Press, 2016.

Chou, Grace Ai-Ling. *Confucianism, Colonialism, and the Cold War: Chinese Cultural Education at Hong Kong's New Asia College, 1949–1963*. Leiden: Brill, 2012.

Chow, Rey, ed. *Modern Chinese Literary and Cultural Studies in the Age of Theory: Reimagining a Field*. Durham, NC: Duke University Press, 2000.

Chow, Tse-tsung. *The May Fourth Movement: Intellectual Revolution in Modern China*. Cambridge, MA: Harvard University Press, 1960.

Ci, Jiwei. *Dialectic of the Chinese Revolution: From Utopianism to Hedonism*. Stanford, CA: Stanford University Press, 1994.

Cong, Xiaoping. "Road to Revival: A New Move in the Making of Legitimacy for the Ruling Party in China," *Journal of Contemporary China* 22.83 (2013), 905–22.

Cook, Alexander C. *The Cultural Revolution on Trial: Mao and the Gang of Four*. Cambridge: Cambridge University Press, 2016.

Cui Zhiyuan. "Zhidu chuangxin yu di'erci sixiang jiefang" (Institutional Innovation and a Second Liberation of Thought), *Ershiyi shiji* (Twenty-First Century), no. 24 (August 1994), 5–16.

Davies, Gloria. "Anticipating Community, Producing Dissent: The Politics of Recent Chinese Intellectual Praxis," *China Review* 2.2 (Fall 2002), 1–35.

"The Self-Made Maps of Chinese Intellectuality." Pp. 17–46 in Davies, ed., *Voicing Concerns*.

ed. *Voicing Concerns: Contemporary Chinese Critical Inquiry*. Lanham, MD: Rowman & Littlefield, 2001.

Worrying about China: The Language of Chinese Critical Inquiry. Cambridge, MA: Harvard University Press, 2007.

Davis, Edward L., ed. *Encyclopedia of Contemporary Chinese Culture*. London: Routledge, 2005.

de Bary, Wm. Theodore. "The New Confucianism in Beijing," *American Scholar* 64.2 (January 1995), 175–89.

De Jong, Alice. "The Demise of the Dragon: Backgrounds to the Chinese Film 'River Elegy,'" *China Information* 4.3 (1989), 28–43.

Deng Xiaoping. "Emancipate the Mind, Seek Truth from Facts, and Unite as One in Looking to the Future," December 13, 1978. Pp. 151–63 in *Selected Works of Deng Xiaoping (1975–1982)*. Beijing: Foreign Languages Press, 1984.

Deng Zhenglai, ed. *Zhongguo xueshu guifanhua taolun wenxuan* (Selections from the Debate on Chinese Academic Standardization). Beijing: Falü chubanshe, 2004.

Dikötter, Frank. *The Cultural Revolution: A People's History, 1962–1976*. London: Bloomsbury, 2016.

Ding Chu. "Cong 'yi' xiang 'li' de zhanlüe zhanbian" (Strategic Switch from "Principle" to "Profit"), *Zhongguo zhi chun* (China Spring), no. 1 (January 1992), 30–31. Translated by David Kelly in *Chinese Law and Government* 29.2 (March–April 1996), 55–57.

Ding, X. L. *The Decline of Communism in China: Legitimacy Crisis, 1977–1989*. Cambridge: Cambridge University Press, 1994.

Ding Xiaoqiang and Xu Zi, eds. *Wusi yu xiandai Zhongguo: Wusi xinlun* (May Fourth and Modern China: New Views on May Fourth). Taiyuan: Shanxi renmin chubanshe, 1989.

Dirlik, Arif. "Confucius in the Borderlands: Global Capitalism and the Reinvention of Confucianism," *Boundary 2* 22.3 (Fall 1995), 229–73.

Culture and History in Postrevolutionary China: The Perspective of Global Modernity. Hong Kong: Chinese University Press, 2011.

"Guest Editor's Introduction," *China Perspectives*, no. 1 (2011), 2–3.

"Mao Zedong in Contemporary Chinese Official Discourse and History," *China Perspectives*, no. 2 (2012), 17–27.

"The Past as Ideology and Critical Resource: Politics and Historical Revisionism after the Fall," unpublished conference paper, Workshop on Revisionism, Leiden, November 2005.

"Postsocialism? Reflections on 'Socialism with Chinese Characteristics.'" Pp. 362–84 in Dirlik and Maurice Meisner, eds., *Marxism and the Chinese Experience: Issues in Contemporary Chinese Socialism*. Armonk, NY: M.E. Sharpe, 1989.

"Reversals, Ironies, Hegemonies: Notes on the Contemporary Historiography of Modern China," *Modern China* 22.3 (July 1996), 243–84.

"T'ao Hsi-sheng: The Social Limits of Change." Pp. 305–31 in Furth, ed., *Limits of Change*.

"Zhongguohua: Worlding China: The Case of Sociology and Anthropology in Twentieth-Century China." Pp. 197–240 in Dirlik, *Culture and History in Postrevolutionary China*.

Dirlik, Arif and Zhang Xudong. "Introduction: Postmodernism and China." Pp. 1–17 in Dirlik and Zhang, eds., *Postmodernism and China*.

eds. *Postmodernism and China*. Durham, NC: Duke University Press, 2000.

Djilas, Milovan. *The New Class: An Analysis of the Communist System*. New York: Praeger, 1971 [1957].

Duara, Prasenjit. "De-constructing the Chinese Nation." Pp. 31–55 in Jonathan Unger, ed., *Chinese Nationalism*. Armonk, NY: M.E. Sharpe, 1996.

"Empires and Imperialism." Pp. 384–98 in Prasenjit Duara, Viren Murthy, and Andrew Sartori, eds., *A Companion to Global Historical Thought*. Hoboken, NJ: Wiley-Blackwell, 2014.

Dunlop, John B. "The August 1991 Coup and Its Impact on Soviet Politics," *Journal of Cold War Studies* 5.1 (2003), 94–127.

Eagleton, Terry. *The Illusions of Postmodernism*. Cambridge, MA: Blackwell, 1996.

Literary Theory: An Introduction, 2nd ed. Cambridge, MA: Blackwell, 1996 [1983].

Eastman, Lloyd. "The Kuomintang in the 1930s." Pp. 191–212 in Furth, ed., *Limits of Change*.

Eisenstadt, Shmuel N. "This-Worldly Transcendentalism and the Structuring of the World: Weber's 'Religion of China' and the Format of Chinese History and Civilization," *Journal of Developing Societies* 1.2 (1985), 168–86.

ed. *Multiple Modernities*. New Brunswick, NJ: Transaction, 2002.

Elman, Benjamin A. "The Failures of Contemporary Chinese Intellectual History," *Eighteenth-Century Studies* 43.3 (2010), 371–91.

Esherick, Joseph W., Paul G. Pickowicz, and Andrew G. Walder, eds. *The Chinese Cultural Revolution as History*. Stanford, CA: Stanford University Press, 2006.

Fan, Dainian. "Science, Open Society and China." Pp. 11–20 in W. H. Newton-Smith and Jiang Tianji, eds., *Popper in China*. London: Routledge, 1992.

Fan Qinlin. "Ruhe pingjia 'wusi' baihuawen yundong? Yu Zheng Min xiansheng shangque" (How to Evaluate the "May Fourth" Vernacular Language Movement? A Discussion with Zheng Min). Pp. 187–97 in Li Shitao, ed., *Zhishi fenzi lichang: Jijin yu baoshou zhijian de dongdang*. Originally published in *Wenxue pinglun* (Literary Review), no. 2 (1994), 112–17.

Fan Xing. "Fulu: Jiushi niandai de sixiang liebian" (Addendum: Thought Fission of the 1990s). Pp. 281–301 in Fan, *Shijimo wenhua sichaoshi* (History of Cultural Trends at the End of the Century). Wuhan: Hubei jiaoyu chubanshe, 1999.

Fan Yun. "Zuowei fangfa de Lusuo: Xiandai Zhongguo bainian Lusuoxue de fansi" (Rousseau as an Approach: Reflections on a Century of Rousseau Studies in Modern China), *Zhejiang daxue xuebao* (Journal of Zhejiang University) 43.1 (March 2013), 160–68.

Fang Keli. "Yao zhuyi yanjiu jiushi niandai chuxian de wenhua baoshou zhuyi sichao" (One Should Attentively Research the Cultural Conservative Trend that Appeared during the 1990s), *Wenyi lilun yu piping* (Literary Theory and Criticism), no. 3 (1996), 11–19.

Fang Wang. "Huaxia wenming chuantong yu zuguo xiandaihua de sikao: Lun He Xin de wenhuaxue yanjiu" (Reflections on Chinese Civilization and Culture and the Modernization of the Motherland: On He Xin's Research on Cultural Studies), *Zhongguo qingnianbao* (China Youth Daily), January 10, 1991, 4.

Feng Lin, ed. *Chongxin renshi bainian Zhongguo: Jindaishi redian wenti yanjiu yu zhengming* (A New Understanding of One Hundred Years of China: Research and Debates on Popular Issues in Modern Chinese History). 2 vols. Beijing: Gaige chubanshe, 1998.

Feng, Youlan. *The Hall of Three Pines: An Account of My Life*, tr. Denis C. Mair. Honolulu: University of Hawai'i Press, 2000.

Fewsmith, Joseph. *China since Tiananmen: The Politics of Transition*. Cambridge: Cambridge University Press, 2001.

"De Tocqueville in Beijing," *China Leadership Monitor*, no. 39 (Fall 2012), http://media.hoover.org/sites/default/files/documents/CLM39JF.pdf.

Elite Politics in Contemporary China. Armonk, NY: M.E. Sharpe, 2001.

"Neoconservatism and the End of the Dengist Era," *Asian Survey* 35.7 (1995), 635–51.

"Reaction, Resurgence, and Succession: Chinese Politics since Tiananmen." Pp. 468–527 in Roderick MacFarquhar, ed., *The Politics of China: Sixty Years of the People's Republic*. Cambridge: Cambridge University Press, 2011.

tr. "Wang Shaoguang Proposal (I) and (II)," *Chinese Economy* 28.3 (May–June 1995) and 28.4 (July–August 1995).

Fokkema, Douwe and Hans Bertens. *Approaching Postmodernism*. Amsterdam: J. Benjamins, 1986. Translated as *Zouxiang houxiandai zhuyi* (Postmodernism), tr. Wang Ning et al. Beijing: Beijing daxue chubanshe, 1991; Taipei: Taiwan shuxin chubanshe, 1993.

Frenkiel, Émilie. *Conditional Democracy: The Contemporary Debate on Political Reform in Chinese Universities*. Colchester: ECPR Press, 2015.

Fu Keng. "Dalu zhishi fenzi de jijin zhuyi shenhua" (The Myth of the Radicalism of Mainland Intellectuals), *Ershiyi shiji* (Twenty-First Century), no. 11 (June 1992a), 144–47.

"Langman lixiang yu shigong jingshen: Ying Fa zhishi jieceng de chayi" (Romantic Ideals and the Spirit of Cause and Contribution: Differences between English and French Intellectuals), *Dushu* (Reading), no. 1 (1992b), 30–37.

Fung, Edmund S. K. *The Intellectual Foundations of Chinese Modernity: Cultural and Political Thought in the Republican Era*. Cambridge: Cambridge University Press, 2010.

Furth, Charlotte. "Culture and Politics in Modern Chinese Conservatism." Pp. 22–53 in Furth, ed., *Limits of Change*.

"Intellectual Change: From the Reform Movement to the May Fourth Movement, 1895–1920." Pp. 322–405 in John King Fairbank, ed., *The Cambridge History of China, Vol. 12: Republican China, 1912–1949, Part 1*. Cambridge: Cambridge University Press, 1983.

ed. *The Limits of Change: Essays on Conservative Alternatives in Republican China*. Cambridge, MA: Harvard University Press, 1976.

"The Sage as Rebel: The Inner World of Chang Ping-lin." Pp. 113–50 in Furth, ed., *Limits of Change*.

Gan Yang. "A Critique of Chinese Conservatism in the 1990s," tr. Zhang Xudong, *Social Text* 16.2 (Summer 1998), 45–66.

"Debating Liberalism and Democracy in China in the 1990s." Pp. 79–101 in Zhang Xudong, ed., *Whither China: Intellectual Politics in Contemporary China*. Durham, NC: Duke University Press, 2000.

"Fan minzhu ziyou zhuyi haishi minzhu de ziyou zhuyi" (Anti-democratic Liberalism or Democratic Liberalism?), *Ershiyi shiji* (Twenty-First Century), no. 39 (February 1997), 4–17.

Tong santong (Unifying the Three Traditions). Beijing: Shenghuo, dushu, xinzhi sanlian shudian, 2007.

"Xiangtu Zhongguo chongjian yu Zhongguo wenhua qianjing" (The Future of Chinese Culture in Relation to Rural Reconstruction), *Ershiyi shiji* (Twenty-First Century), no. 16 (April 1993), 4–7.

"Yangqi 'minzhu yu kexue,' dianding 'ziyou yu zhixu'" (Discard "Democracy and Science," Establish "Liberty and Order"), *Ershiyi shiji* (Twenty-First Century), no. 3 (February 1991), 7–10.

"Zhengzhi zheren Shitelaosi: Gudian baoshou zhuyi zhengzhi zhexue de fuxing" (Political Philosopher Leo Strauss: The Revival of Classical Conservative Political Philosophy). Pp. 5–86 in *Ziran quanli yu lishi* (Natural Right and History), tr. Peng Gang. Taipei: Zuo'an wenhua, 2005. (The mainland version was published in Beijing by Sanlian chubanshe in 2003.)

"Zhongguo ziyou zuopai de youlai" (The Origins of China's Liberal Left). Pp. 110–20 in Gong Yang, ed., *Sichao: Zhongguo "xin zuopai" ji qi yingxiang* (Trend of Thought: China's "New Left" and Its Influence). Beijing: Zhongguo shehui kexue chubanshe, 2003.

"Ziyou de diren: Zhenshanmei tongyi shuo" (The Enemy of Freedom: The Unification of Truth, Goodness, and Beauty), *Dushu* (Reading), no. 6 (1989), 121–28.

"Ziyou de linian: Wusi chuantong zhi queshimian wei 'wusi' qishi zhounian er zou" (The Concept of Freedom: Loss of the May Fourth Tradition and the Making of the Seventieth Anniversary of the May Fourth Era), *Dushu* (Reading), no. 5 (1989), 11–19.

Garver, John W. "The Chinese Communist Party and the Collapse of Soviet Communism," *China Quarterly*, no. 133 (1993), 1–26.

Gasster, Michael. *Chinese Intellectuals and the Revolution of 1911: The Birth of Modern Chinese Radicalism*. Seattle: University of Washington Press, 1969.

Gay, Peter. *The Enlightenment: An Interpretation*. New York: Knopf, 1966–69.

Ge Zhaoguang. *An Intellectual History of China, Volume One*, tr. Michael S. Duke and Josephine Chiu-Duke. Leiden: Brill, 2014.

Geng Yunzhi. "Yanjiu lishi yao kao lishi shishi" (In Researching History, One Must Rely on Historical Reality). Pp. 382–84 in Sha Jiansun and Gong Shuduo, eds., *Zou shenme lu: Guanyu Zhongguo jinxiandai lishi shang de ruogan zhongda shifei wenti* (Which Way to Go? Some Major Disputes on Modern Chinese History). Ji'nan: Shandong renmin chubanshe, 1997.

Giddens, Anthony. *Beyond Left and Right: The Future of Radical Politics*. Stanford, CA: Stanford University Press, 1994.

Politics and Sociology in the Thought of Max Weber. London: Macmillan, 1972.

Goldman, Merle, ed. *Modern Chinese Literature in the May Fourth Era*. Cambridge, MA: Harvard University Press, 1977.

"Repression of China's Public Intellectuals in the Post-Mao Era," *Social Research* 76.2 (July 2009), 659–86.

Sowing the Seeds of Democracy in China: Political Reform in the Deng Xiaoping Era. Cambridge, MA: Harvard University Press, 1994.

Goldman, Merle and Timothy Cheek. "Introduction: Uncertain Change." Pp. 1–20 in Merle Goldman, Timothy Cheek, and Carol Lee Hamrin, eds., *China's Intellectuals and the State: In Search of a New Relationship*. Cambridge, MA: Council on East Asian Studies, Harvard University, 1987.

Gong Shuduo, Jin Chongji, and Song Xiaoqing. *Lishi de huida: Zhongguo jindaishi yanjiu zhong de jige yuanze lunzheng* (History's Response: Some Principal Debates in Research on Modern Chinese History). Beijing: Beijing shifan daxue chubanshe, 2001.

Gong Shuduo, Li Wenhai, Zhang Haipeng, et al. "Wusi yundong yu ershi shiji Zhongguo de daolu" (The May Fourth Movement and the Road of Twentieth-Century China), *Gaoxiao lilun zhanxian* (Theoretical Front in Higher Education), no. 6 (1996), 16–25.

Goodman, David S. G. and Gerald Segal, eds. *China in the Nineties: Crisis Management and Beyond*. Oxford: Clarendon, 1991.

Grieder, Jerome. *Hu Shih and the Chinese Renaissance: Liberalism in the Chinese Revolution, 1917–1937*. Cambridge, MA: Harvard University Press, 1970.

Gu, Edward and Merle Goldman. "Introduction: The Transformation of the Relationship between Chinese Intellectuals and the State." Pp. 1–17 in Gu and Goldman, eds., *Chinese Intellectuals between State and Market*. London: RoutledgeCurzon, 2004.

Gu Xin. "Anggelu ziyou chuantong yu Falanxi langman jingshen" (On the Anglo-Liberal Tradition and the French Romantic Spirit), *Ershiyi shiji* (Twenty-First Century), no. 6 (August 1991), 138–40.

Gu, Xin and David Kelly. "New Conservatism: Intermediate Ideology of a 'New Elite.'" Pp. 219–33 in David S. G. Goodman and Beverley Hooper, eds., *China's Quiet Revolution: New Interactions between State and Society*. New York: St. Martin's, 1994.

Gu Zhun. *Gu Zhun riji* (Gu Zhun's Diaries), ed. Chen Minzhi and Ding Dong. Beijing: Jingji ribao chubanshe, 1997.

Gu Zhun wenji (Collected Works of Gu Zhun). Guiyang: Guizhou renmin chubanshe, 1994.

Xila chengbang zhidu: Du Xilashi biji (The Greek Polis System: Notes on Reading Greek History), 2nd ed. Beijing: Zhongguo shehui kexue chubanshe, 1986.

Guo, Yingjie. *Cultural Nationalism in Contemporary China: The Search for National Identity under Reform*. London: Routledge, 2004.

"Rewriting National History: The Zeng Guofan Phenomenon." Pp. 49–71 in Guo, *Cultural Nationalism*.

Habermas, Jürgen. *The Philosophical Discourse of Modernity: Twelve Lectures*, tr. Frederick Lawrence. Cambridge, MA: MIT Press, 1987.

Hammond, Kenneth J. and Jeffrey L. Richey, eds. *The Sage Returns: Confucian Revival in Contemporary China*. Albany: State University of New York Press, 2015.

Hamrin, Carol Lee and Timothy Cheek, eds. *China's Establishment Intellectuals.* Armonk, NY: M.E. Sharpe, 1986.

Han Demin. "Chuantong wenhua de weiji yu ershi shiji fan wenhua sichao" (The Crisis of Traditional Culture and Twentieth-Century Anti-culture Trends), *Yuandao* (True Way) 1 (1994), 311–40.

Hanyu dacidian bianyuanhui (Chinese Dictionary Editorial Committee), ed. *Hanyu da cidian* (Chinese Dictionary), 13 vols. Shanghai: Hanyu dacidian chubanshe, 1995.

Hao, Zhidong. *Intellectuals at a Crossroads: The Changing Politics of China's Knowledge Workers.* Albany: State University of New York Press, 2003.

Harvey, David. *The Condition of Postmodernity: An Enquiry into the Origins of Cultural Change.* Oxford: Blackwell, 1990.

Hayek, Friedrich A. *The Collected Works of F.A. Hayek, Vol. 1: The Fatal Conceit: The Errors of Socialism,* ed. W. W. Bartley III. Chicago: University of Chicago Press, 1988.

The Constitution of Liberty. London: Routledge, 2006 [1960].

"Postscript: Why I Am Not a Conservative." Pp. 343–55 in Hayek, *Constitution of Liberty.*

"The Pretence of Knowledge." Pp. 23–34 in *New Studies in Philosophy, Politics, Economics and the History of Ideas.* London: Routledge, 1978.

[Hayeke]. *Tongxiang nuyi de daolu* (The Road to Serfdom). Beijing: Shangwu yinshuguan, 1962.

[Hayeke]. *Ziyou zhixu yuanli* (The Constitution of Liberty), tr. Deng Zhenglai. Beijing: Shenghuo, dushu, xinzhi sanlian shudian, 1997.

Hayhoe, Ruth. *China's Universities 1895–1995: A Century of Cultural Conflict.* Hong Kong: Comparative Education Research Centre, University of Hong Kong, 1999.

He, Henry Yuhuai. *Dictionary of the Political Thought of the People's Republic of China.* Armonk, NY: M.E. Sharpe, 2001.

He Pin. "'Disan zhi yan' haishi 'disan zhi shou'? Liu Huaqing nüxu Pan Yue he 'disan zhi yanjing kan Zhongguo'" (A "Third Eye" or a "Third Hand"? Liu Huaqing's Son-in-Law Pan Yue and *Looking at China through a Third Eye*), *Beijing zhi chun* (Beijing Spring), no. 17 (1994), 21–22.

He, Rowena Xiaoqing. *Tiananmen Exiles: Voices of the Struggle for Democracy in China.* New York: Palgrave Macmillan, 2014.

He Xin. *Lun zhengzhi guojia zhuyi: He Xin jinqi zhenglun* (On Political Statism: Recent Political Commentaries by He Xin). Beijing: Shishi chubanshe, 2003.

"Wode kunhuo yu youlü" (My Perplexities and Concerns), *Xuexi yuekan* (Study Monthly), no. 12 (1988), 36–37.

"A Word of Advice to the Politburo," tr. Geremie R. Barmé. *Australian Journal of Chinese Affairs,* no. 23 (January 1990), 49–76.

Higonnet, Patrice. *Sister Republics: The Origins of French and American Republicanism.* Cambridge, MA: Harvard University Press, 1988.

Hon, Tze-ki. "Global Capitalism with Chinese Characteristics: Fang Keli's New Confucian Research Project (1986–1995)." Pp. 3–18 in Tze-ki Hon and Kristin Stapleton, eds., *Confucianism for the Contemporary World: Global Order, Political Plurality, and Social Action.* Albany: State University of New York Press, 2017.

"Introduction: Confucianism for the Contemporary World." Pp. xi–xxix in Tze-ki Hon and Kristin Stapleton, eds., *Confucianism for the Contemporary World: Global Order, Political Plurality, and Social Action*. Albany: State University of New York Press, 2017.

Revolution as Restoration: Guocui Xuebao and China's Path to Modernity, 1905–1911. Leiden: Brill, 2013.

Hook, Leslie. "The Rise of China's New Left," *Far Eastern Economic Review* 170.3 (April 2007), 8–14.

Hsü, Immanuel C. Y. *China without Mao: The Search for a New Order*, 2nd ed. Oxford: Oxford University Press, 1990.

Hu Angang, Wang Shaoguang, and Kang Xiaoguang. *Zhongguo diqu chaju baogao* (A Report on China's Regional Disparities). Shenyang: Liaoning renmin chubanshe, 1995.

Hu Cheng. "Jijin zhuyi yihuo shi baoli zhuyi" (Radicalism or Ideology of Violence), *Ershiyi shiji* (Twenty-First Century), no. 13 (October 1992), 139–45.

Hu Ping. "Bitan Zhonggong jiebanren de gangling: Ruhe kandai 'Yingdui yu xuanze'" (Notes on the Program of the CCP Heirs Apparent: How to Treat "Realistic Responses"), *Zhongguo zhi chun* (China Spring), no. 1 (January 1992), 23–24. Translated by David Kelly in *Chinese Law and Government* 29.2 (March–April 1996), 38–41.

Hu Sheng. *Cong yapian zhanzheng dao wusi yundong* (From the Opium War to the May Fourth Movement), 2 vols. Beijing: Renmin chubanshe, 1981.

Hu Shi. "Duo yanjiu xie wenti, shao tan xie 'zhuyi'" (Research More Problems, Speak Fewer "-*Isms*"), *Meizhou pinglun* (Weekly Review), July 20, 1919, 1.

"Wenxue gailiang chuyi" (Some Tentative Suggestions for the Reform of Chinese Literature). Pp. 146–55 in Chen Duxiu, Wang Zhongjiang, and Yuan Shuya, *Xin qingnian: Minzhu yu kexue de huhuan* (New Youth: The Call of Democracy and Science). Zhengzhou: Zhongzhou guji chubanshe, 1999.

Hua, Shiping. *Scientism and Humanism: Two Cultures in Post-Mao China, 1978–1989*. Albany: State University of New York Press, 1995.

Huang, Guiyou. *Whitmanism, Imagism, and Modernism in China and America*. Selinsgrove, PA: Susquehanna University Press, 1997.

Huang Kewu. *Ziyou de suoyiran: Yan Fu dui Yuehan Mi'er ziyou zhuyi sixiang de renshi yu pipan* (The Raison d'Être of Freedom: Yan Fu's Understanding and Critique of John Mill's Liberalism). Taipei: Yunchen wenhua shiye gufen youxian gongsi, 1998.

Hughes, Christopher R. *Chinese Nationalism in the Global Era*. London: Routledge, 2006.

Huntington, Samuel. *Bianhe shehui zhong de zhengzhi zhixu* (Political Order in Changing Societies), ed. Li Shengping. Beijing: Huaxia chubanshe, 1988.

"The Clash of Civilizations?" *Foreign Affairs* 72.3 (Summer 1993), 22–49.

Political Order in Changing Societies. New Haven, CT: Yale University Press, 1968.

Huters, Theodore. "Appropriations: Another Look at Yan Fu and Western Ideas," *Xueren* (The Scholar), no. 9 (April 1996), 296–355.

Idema, Wilt and Lloyd Haft. *Chinese letterkunde: Een inleiding* (Chinese Literature: An Introduction). Amsterdam: Amsterdam University Press, 1996.

Ip, Hung-Yok, Tze-ki Hon, and Chiu-Chun Lee. "The Plurality of Chinese Modernity: A Review of Recent Scholarship on the May Fourth Movement," *Modern China* 29.4 (October 2003), 490–509.

Israel, Jonathan I. *Radical Enlightenment: Philosophy and the Making of Modernity, 1650–1750.* Oxford: Oxford University Press, 2001.

Jameson, Fredric [Zhan Mingxin]. *Houxiandai zhuyi yu wenhua lilun* (Postmodernism and Cultural Theory), tr. Tang Xiaobing, 3rd rev. ed. Taipei: Hezhi wenhua shiye gufen youxian gongsi, 1980.

Postmodernism; or, The Cultural Logic of Late Capitalism. Durham, NC: Duke University Press, 1991.

Jenco, Leigh. "Introduction: On the Possibility of Chinese Thought as Global Theory." Pp. 1–25 in Jenco, ed., *Chinese Thought as Global Theory: Diversifying Knowledge Production in the Social Sciences and Humanities.* Albany: State University of New York Press, 2016.

Jenks, Edward. *A History of Politics.* London: J.M. Dent, 1900.

Jenner, William J. F. "Review of *The August Sleepwalker*," *Australian Journal of Chinese Affairs*, no. 23 (January 1990), 193–95.

Ji Guangmao. "Nanyuan yu beizhe zhijian: Cong liangpian wenzhang lüekui baoshou zhuyi yu jijin zhuyi de xunxi" (In between Opposite Directions: Taking a Quick Peek at the Message of Conservatism and Radicalism from Two Texts), *Wenyi zhengming* (Debates on Literature and Art), no. 4 (1995), 12–20.

Ji, Shu-li. "The Worlds of Cultures and World 3: A Discussion of Popper's Theory of Three Worlds." Pp. 109–24 in W. H. Newton-Smith and Jiang Tianji, eds., *Popper in China.* London: Routledge, 1992.

Ji Xianlin, Liu Junning, and Pang Pu. "Zouchu chuantong yanjiu chuantong" (Out of the Traditional Research Tradition), *Renmin ribao* (People's Daily), December 6, 1994, 1.

Jiang Tao. "Wanqing zhengzhishi" (Late Qing Political History). Pp. 19–43 in Zeng Yeying, ed., *Wushi nian lai de Zhongguo jindaishi yanjiu.*

Jiang Xudong. "Lun dangdai Zhongguo wenhua baoshou zhuyi de jiazhi tezheng" (On the Value Characteristics of Contemporary Chinese Cultural Conservatism), Ph.D. diss., Zhongguo renmin daxue, 2003.

Jiang Yihua. "Ershi shiji ruxue zai Zhongguo de chonggou" (The Reconfiguration of Twentieth-Century Confucianism in China), *Ershiyi shiji* (Twenty-First Century), no. 1 (October 1990), 28–35.

"Jijin yu baoshou: Yu Yü Ying-shih xiansheng shangque" (Radicalism and Conservatism: A Discussion with Yü Ying-shih), *Ershiyi shiji* (Twenty-First Century), no. 10 (April 1992), 134–42.

"Ershi shiji Zhongguo sixiangshi shang de zhengzhi baoshou zhuyi" (Political Conservatism in Twentieth-Century Chinese Intellectual History). Pp. 57–73 in Li Shitao, ed., *Zhishi fenzi lichang: Jijin yu baoshou zhijian de dongdang.* Originally published in *Tansuo yu zhengming* (Exploration and Contention), no. 1 (1993), 30, 47–56.

Jiang Yihua and Chen Yan. "Jijin yu baoshou: Yiduan shangwei wanjie de duihua" (Conservative and Radical: An Unfinished Dialogue). Pp. 30–36 in Li Shitao, ed., *Zhishi fenzi lichang: Jijin yu baoshou zhijian de dongdang.* Originally published in *Kaifang shidai* (Open Times), no. 2 (1997), 37–41.

Jin Guantao and Liu Qingfeng. *Guannianshi yanjiu: Zhongguo xiandai zhongyao zhengzhi shuyu de xingcheng* (Studies in Conceptual History: The Formation of Key Modern Chinese Political Terms). Hong Kong: Dangdai Zhongguo wenhua yanjiu zhongxin, Chinese University Press, 2008.

Jin Yuanpu. "He yi 'baoshou zhuyi' er you 'xin'?" (Why "Conservatism" and Why "Neo"?). Pp. 385–900 in Li Shitao, ed., *Zhishi fenzi lichang: Jijin yu baoshou zhijian de dongdang*. Originally published in *Dushu* (Reading), no. 5 (1996), 84–88.

Kahn, Herman. *World Economic Development: 1979 and Beyond*. Boulder, CO: Westview, 1979.

Kang Xiaoguang. *Xin baoshou zhuyi zhenglunji* (Collected Political Essays on Neoconservatism). Beijing: n.p., 2002.

Karl, Rebecca E. *Staging the World: Chinese Nationalism at the Turn of the Twentieth Century*. Durham, NC: Duke University Press, 2002.

Kelly, David. "Chinese Marxism since Tiananmen: Between Evaporation and Dismemberment." Pp. 19–34 in Goodman and Segal, eds., *China in the Nineties*.

"The Emergence of Humanism: Wang Ruoshui and the Critique of Socialist Alienation." Pp. 159–62 in Merle Goldman, Timothy Cheek, and Carol Lee Hamrin, eds., *China's Intellectuals and the State: In Search of a New Relationship*. Cambridge, MA: Council on East Asian Studies, Harvard University, 1987.

ed. "Realistic Responses and Strategic Options: An Alternative CCP Ideology and Its Critics," *Chinese Law and Government* 29.2 (March–April 1996), 1–96.

Kenley, David L. *New Culture in a New World: The May Fourth Movement and the Chinese Diaspora in Singapore, 1919–1932*. London: Routledge, 2003.

Kluver, Alan R. *Legitimating the Chinese Economic Reforms: A Rhetoric of Myth and Orthodoxy*. Albany: State University of New York Press, 1996.

Knight, Nick. *Rethinking Mao: Explorations in Mao Zedong's Thought*. Lanham, MD: Lexington, 2007.

Kong Lingzhao. "Ba lishi de neirong huangei lishi: Ping yizhong guannianlun de wenhua shiguan" (Returning the Content of History to History: Criticizing a Conceptual Cultural View of History), *Zhexue yanjiu* (Philosophy Research), no. 4 (1995), 3–7.

Koselleck, Reinhart. *Futures Past: On the Semantics of Historical Time*, tr. Keith Tribe. New York: Colombia University Press, 2004.

"The Historical-Political Semantics of Asymmetric Counterconcepts." Pp. 155–91 in Koselleck, *Futures Past*.

Kramnick, Isaac, ed. *The Portable Edmund Burke*. London: Penguin, 1999.

Kristol, Irving. *Neoconservatism: The Autobiography of an Idea*. New York: Free Press, 1995.

Kwan, Daniel. "Stability Put Before Reform," *South China Morning Post*, May 8, 1992, 12.

Kwok, D. W. Y. *Scientism in Chinese Thought, 1900–1950*. New Haven, CT: Yale University Press, 1965.

Kwong, Luke S. W. "The Rise of the Linear Perspective on History and Time in Late Qing China c. 1860–1911," *Past and Present* 173.1 (November 2001), 157–90.

Lam, Willy Wo-Lap. "Chen's Son Bids to Expand Power Base," *South China Morning Post*, May 19, 1992, 11.

Lan Aiguo. "Shijimo wenxue: Wenhua baoshou zhuyi sichao" (End of the Century Literature: The Cultural Conservative Trend), *Wenyi zhengming* (Debates on Literature and Art), no. 6 (1994), 34–37.

Lanza, Fabio. *Behind the Gate: Inventing Students in Beijing*. New York: Columbia University Press, 2010.

Lee, Gregory B. *Troubadours, Trumpeters, Troubled Makers: Lyricism, Nationalism, and Hybridity in China and Its Others*. London: Hurst, 1996.

Lee, Leo Ou-fan. "Literary Trends: The Quest for Modernity, 1895–1927." Pp. 142–95 in Merle Goldman and Leo Ou-Fan Lee, eds., *An Intellectual History of Modern China*. Cambridge: Cambridge University Press, 2002.

Lei Yi. "Beijing yu cuowei: Ye tan Zhongguo de 'houzhimin' yu 'houxiandai'" (Background and Dislocation: Also on China's "Postcolonialism" and "Postmodernism"), *Dushu* (Reading), no. 4 (1995), 16–20.

Levenson, Joseph R. *Confucian China and Its Modern Fate: A Trilogy*. Berkeley: University of California Press, 1968.

—— "'History' and 'Value': The Tensions of Intellectual Choice in Modern China." Pp. 146–94 in Arthur F. Wright, ed., *Studies in Chinese Thought*. Chicago: University of Chicago Press, 1953.

Li Guoyan, et al., eds. *Dangdai Hanyu cidian* (A Contemporary Chinese Dictionary). Shanghai: Shanghai cishu chubanshe, 2001.

Li, He. "Debating China's Economic Reform: New Leftists vs. Liberals," *Journal of Chinese Political Science* 15.1 (2010), 1–23.

Li, Huaiyin. "From Revolution to Modernization: The Paradigmatic Transition in Chinese Historiography in the Reform Era," *History and Theory* 49.3 (2010), 336–60.

—— *Reinventing Modern China: Imagination and Authenticity in Chinese Historical Writing*. Honolulu: University of Hawai'i Press, 2013.

Li Jinquan. "Zhongguo jindaishi jige wenti pingjia de zai pingjia" (Re-evaluating the Assessments of Some Issues in Modern Chinese History). Pp. 84–92 in Li Shitao, ed., *Zhishi fenzi lichang: Jijin yu baoshou zhijian de dongdang*. Originally published in *Zhexue yanjiu* (Philosophy Research), no. 10 (1995), 3–7.

Li Liangyu. "Jijin, baoshou yu zhishi fenzi de zeren" (Radicalism, Conservatism, and the Responsibility of Intellectuals), *Ershiyi shiji* (Twenty-First Century), no. 12 (August 1992), 132–34.

Li Ping, ed. *Zhongguo xia yi bu zenyang zou: Dangdai jingying da lunzheng* (What Is the Next Step for China? The Big Debate among the Contemporary Elite). Toronto: Mingjing chubanshe, 1998.

Li Shitao, ed. *Zhishi fenzi lichang: Jijin yu baoshou zhijian de dongdang* (Intellectual Positions: The Turbulence between Radicalism and Conservatism). Changchun: Shidai wenyi chubanshe, 1999.

Li Yi. *Zhongguo Makesi zhuyi yu dangdai wenhua baoshou zhuyi sichao yanjiu* (Research on Trends in Chinese Marxism and Contemporary Cultural Conservatism). Tianjin: Tianjin shehui kexueyuan chubanshe, 1998.

Li, Youzhuo. "Will Neo-conservatism Dominate Post-Deng China?" *China Strategic Review* 2.2 (1997), 31–40.

Li Zehou. "Heping jinhua, fuxing Zhonghua: Tan 'yao gailiang bu yao geming'" (Peaceful Evolution, Reviving China: On "We Need Reform, Not Revolution"),

Zhongguo shibao zhoukan (China Times Weekly), May 3–9, 1992, 42–45 (Part 1), and May 10–16, 1992, 44–47 (Part 2).
"Li Zehou dawen" (Li Zehou Answers Questions), *Yuandao* (True Way) 1(1994), 1–3.
"Qimeng yu jiuwang de shuangchong bianzou" (The Double Variation of Enlightenment and Salvation). Pp. 7–49 in Li, *Zhongguo xiandai sixiangshi lun* (On Modern Chinese Intellectual History). Beijing: Dongfang chubanshe, 1987. Originally published in *Zouxiang weilai* (Towards the Future), no. 1 (1986), 18–38.
Zhongguo jindai sixiangshi lun (On Modern Chinese Intellectual History). Beijing: Renmin chubanshe, 1979.
Li Zehou and Lin Yü-sheng. *Wusi: Duoyuan de fansi* (May Fourth: Multiple Reflections). Taipei: Fengyun shidai chuban gongsi, 1989.
Li Zehou and Liu Zaifu. *Gaobie geming: Huiwang ershi shiji Zhongguo* (Farewell to Revolution: Looking Back at Twentieth-Century China). Hong Kong: Tiandi tushu youxian gongsi, 1995.
Li Zehou and Wang Desheng. "Guanyu wenhua xianzhuang, daode chongjian de duihua" (A Dialogue on the Cultural Status Quo and Moral Reconstruction). Pp. 74–83 in Li Shitao, ed., *Zhishi fenzi lichang: Jijin yu baoshou zhijian de dongdang*. Originally published in *Dongfang* (Orient), no. 5 (1994), 69–73 and no. 6 (1994), 85–87.
Liang Qichao. "Shige" (Explaining Revolution), December 14, 1902. Pp. 40–45, vol. 1, part 9, in *Yinbing shi heji* (Collected Works from the Ice Studio), 12 vols. Beijing: Zhonghua shuju, 1989 [reprint].
Liang Shuming. *Dong Xi wenhua ji qi zhexue* (Eastern and Western Cultures and Their Philosophies), ed. Chen Zheng and Luo Changpei. Shanghai: Shangwu yinshuguan, 1922.
Lin Gang. "Jijin zhuyi zai Zhongguo" (Radicalism in China), *Ershiyi shiji* (Twenty-First Century), no. 3 (February 1991), 17–27.
Lin, Min, with Maria Galikowski. *The Search for Modernity: Chinese Intellectuals and Cultural Discourse in the Post-Mao Era*. New York: St. Martin's, 1999.
Lin, Yü-sheng [Lin Yusheng]. *The Crisis of Chinese Consciousness: Radical Antitraditionalism in the May Fourth Era*. Madison: University of Wisconsin Press, 1979.
"Guanyu 'Zhongguo yishi de weiji': Da Sun Longji" (On "The Crisis of Chinese Consciousness": A Response to Sun Longji), *Ershiyi shiji* (Twenty-First Century), no. 3 (February 1991), 136–50.
"Radical Iconoclasm in the May Fourth Period and the Future of Chinese Liberalism." Pp. 23–58 in Benjamin Schwartz, ed., *Reflections on the May Fourth Movement: A Symposium*. Cambridge, MA: East Asian Research Center, Harvard University, 1972.
"Reflections on the 'Creative Transformation of Chinese Tradition,'" tr. Michael S. Duke and Josephine Chiu-Duke. Pp. 73–114 in Karl-Heinz Pohl, ed., *Chinese Thought in a Global Context: A Dialogue between Chinese and Western Philosophical Approaches*. Leiden: Brill, 1999.
Zhongguo chuantong de chuangzaoxing zhuanhua (The Creative Transformation of Chinese Tradition). Beijing: Shenghuo, dushu, xinzhi sanlian shudian, 1988.

Zhongguo yishi de weiji: "Wusi" shiqi jilie de fan chuantong zhuyi (The Crisis of Chinese Consciousness: Radical Anti-traditionalism in the "May Fourth" Era). Guiyang: Guizhou renmin chubanshe, 1986.
Lin Yü-sheng, et al. *Wusi: Duoyuan de fansi* (May Fourth: Multiple Reflections). Hong Kong: Sanlian shudian, 1989.
Lin Yü-sheng, Xu Jilin, and Xiao Gongqin. "'Wusi': Duoyuan de fansi: Lin Yü-sheng, Xu Jilin, Xiao Gongqin duihua lu" (Multiple Reflections on "May Fourth": Record of a Dialogue among Lin Yü-sheng, Xu Jilin, and Xiao Gongqin). Pp. 241–51 in Lin Yü-sheng et al., *Wusi: Duoyuan de fansi*.
Lipset, Seymour Martin. "Neoconservatism: Myth and Reality." Pp. 1–18 in Carl-Ludwig Holtfrerich, ed., *Ernst Fraenkel Vorträge zur amerikanischen Politik, Wirtschaft, Gesellschaft und Geschichte* (Ernst Fraenkel Lectures on American Politics, Economy, Society, and History). Berlin: John F. Kennedy-Institut für Nordamerikastudien, 1988.
Litzinger, Ralph. "Theorizing Postsocialism: Reflections on the Politics of Marginality in Contemporary China," *South Atlantic Quarterly* 101.1 (Winter 2002), 33–55.
Liu Binyan. "Ping 'Disan zhi yanjing kan Zhongguo'" (On *Looking at China through a Third Eye*), *Beijing zhi chun* (Beijing Spring), no. 17 (October 1994), 23–39.
Liu Dong. "Beida xuetong yu 'wusi' chuantong: Lishi de ling yizhong kenengxing" (The Tradition of Learning at Peking University and the "May Fourth" Tradition: Another Possibility in History). Pp. 241–51 in Li Shitao, ed., *Zhishi fenzi lichang: Jijin yu baoshou zhijian de dongdang*. Originally published in *Dongfang* (Orient), no. 4 (1994), 12–17.
"Jingti renwei de 'yangjingbing xuefeng'" (Beware of "Designer Pidgin Scholarship"), *Ershiyi shiji* (Twenty-First Century), no. 32 (December 1995), 5–13.
"Revisiting the Perils of 'Designer Pidgin Scholarship,'" tr. Gloria Davies and Li Kaiyu. Pp. 87–108 in Davies, ed., *Voicing Concerns*.
Liu Guisheng and Zhang Buzhou, eds. *Tai Gang ji haiwai wusi yanjiu lunzhu xieyao* (Selection of Essential Taiwan, Hong Kong, and Overseas Research Works on May Fourth). Beijing: Jiaoyu kexue chubanshe, 1989.
Liu Junning. "Baoshou de Baike, ziyou de Baike" (The Conservative Burke and the Liberal Burke), *Dushu* (Reading), no. 3 (1995), 77–85.
Baoshou zhuyi (Conservatism). Beijing: Zhongguo shehui kexue chubanshe, 1998.
"Dang minzhu fang'ai ziyou de shihou" (When Democracy Obstructs Freedom), *Dushu* (Reading), no. 11 (1993), 74–80.
Liu, Kang. "Is There an Alternative to (Capitalist) Globalization? The Debate about Modernity in China," *Boundary 2* 23.3 (1996), 193–218.
Liu, Lydia H. *Translingual Practice: Literature, National Culture, and Translated Modernity—China 1900–1937*. Stanford, CA: Stanford University Press, 1995.
Liu, Qingfeng. "The Topography of Intellectual Culture in 1990s Mainland China: A Survey," tr. Gloria Davies. Pp. 47–70 in Davies, ed., *Voicing Concerns*.
Liu, Xiaobo. "China's Neo-political Conservatism in the 1990s," *China Strategic Review* 1.9 (December 1996), 11–15.
Lovell, Julia. *The Politics of Cultural Capital: China's Quest for a Nobel Prize in Literature*. Honolulu: University of Hawai'i Press, 2006.
Lu Jiandong. *Chen Yinke de zuihou ershi nian* (Chen Yinke's Last Twenty Years). Beijing: Sanlian shudian, 1995.

Lu, Sheldon Hsiao-peng. "Global POSTmodernIZATION: The Intellectual, the Artist, and China's Condition." Pp. 145–74 in Dirlik and Zhang, eds., *Postmodernism and China*.
"Postmodernity, Popular Culture, and the Intellectual: A Report on Post-Tiananmen China," *Boundary 2* 23.2 (1996), 139–69.
Lu Wei. "Taizidang paozhi 'shizheng gangling' shimo" (How the Princelings Launched Their "Political Platform"), *Qianshao* (Front Line), no. 2 (February 1992), 92–93. Translated by David Kelly in *Chinese Law and Government* 29.2 (March–April 1996), 32–34.
Luo Rongqu, ed. *Cong "Xihua" dao xiandaihua: Wusi yilai youguan Zhongguo de wenhua quxiang he fazhan daolu lunzheng wenxuan* (From "Westernization" to Modernization: Selections from the Debate on China's Cultural Trends and Development since May Fourth). Beijing: Beijing daxue chubanshe, 1990.
Lynch, Catherine, Robert B. Marks, and Paul G. Pickowicz, "Introduction: Chinese Radicalism in Historical Context." Pp. 1–9 in Lynch, Marks, and Pickowicz, eds. *Radicalism, Revolution and Reform in Modern China: Essays in Honor of Maurice Meisner*. Lanham, MD: Lexington, 2011.
Lyotard, Jean-François. *The Postmodern Condition: A Report on Knowledge*, tr. Geoff Bennington. Minneapolis: University of Minnesota Press, 2010.
Ma Baozhu and Wei Zhaogai, eds., "Zhengque renshi Zhongguo jindaishi shang de geming yu gailiang" (Correctly Understanding Revolution and Reform in Modern Chinese History), *Guangming ribao* (Enlightenment Daily), March 12, 1996, 5.
Ma, Shu Yun. "The Rise and Fall of Neo-authoritarianism in China," *China Information* 5.3 (1990), 1–18.
Ma Yong. "Jindai lishi renwu yanjiu" (Research on Personages in Modern History). Pp. 659–83 in Zeng Yeying, ed., *Wushi nian lai de Zhongguo jindaishi yanjiu*.
"Yan Fu wannian sixiang yanbian zhi chonggu" (A Re-evaluation of the Intellectual Development of Yan Fu in His Later Years), *Zhexue yanjiu* (Philosophy Research), no. 4 (1992), 46–53.
1898 nian nachang weisui zhengbian (The Aborted Coup of 1898). Nanjing: Jiangsu renmin chubanshe, 2011.
MacFarquhar, Roderick. "The Post-Confucian Challenge," *Economist*, February 9, 1980, 67–72.
MacFarquhar, Roderick and Michael Schoenhals. *Mao's Last Revolution*. Cambridge, MA: Belknap, 2006.
Makeham, John. *Lost Soul: "Confucianism" in Contemporary Chinese Academic Discourse*. Cambridge, MA: Asia Center, Harvard University, 2008.
ed. *New Confucianism: A Critical Examination*. Houndmills: Palgrave Macmillan, 2003.
"The New Datong." Pp. 55–78 in Makeham, *Lost Soul*.
"The Retrospective Creation of New Confucianism." Pp. 25–53 in Makeham, ed., *New Confucianism*.
Mandelbaum, Michael. "Coup de Grace: The End of the Soviet Union," *Foreign Affairs* 71.1 (1992), 164–83.
Manela, Erez. *The Wilsonian Moment: Self-Determination and the International Origins of Anticolonial Nationalism*. Oxford: Oxford University Press, 2007.
Mannheim, Karl. "Conservative Thought." Pp. 132–222 in Mannheim, *From Karl Mannheim*, ed. Kurt H. Wolff. Oxford: Oxford University Press, 1971. Originally

published in Karl Mannheim, *Essays on Sociology and Social Psychology*, ed. Paul Kecskemeti. Oxford: Oxford University Press, 1953.
"The Problem of Generations." Pp. 276–322 in Mannheim, *Essays on the Sociology of Knowledge*, ed. Paul Kecskemeti. London: Routledge Paul, 1952 [1927–28].
Mao Zedong. "Lun renmin minzhu zhuanzheng," July 30, 1949 (On the People's Democratic Dictatorship). Pp. 4.1469–82 in *Mao Zedong xuanji* (Selected Works of Mao Zedong). Beijing: Renmin chubanshe, 1991.
"The May Fourth Movement," May 1939. Pp. 2.237–40 in *Selected Works of Mao Zedong*. Peking: Foreign Languages Press, 1965.
"Report on an Investigation of the Peasant Movement in Hunan." Pp. 1.23–58 in *Selected Works of Mao Tse-tung*. Peking: Foreign Languages Press, 1967.
Maruyama, Masao. *Nihon seiji shisōshi kenkyū* (Studies on the History of Japanese Political Thought). Tōkyō: Tōkyō Daigaku Shuppankai, 1952.
McCormick, Barrett L. and David Kelly. "The Limits of Anti-liberalism," *Journal of Asian Studies* 53.3 (August 1994), 804–31.
McGrath, Jason. *Postsocialist Modernity: Chinese Cinema, Literature, and Criticism in the Market Age*. Stanford, CA: Stanford University Press, 2008.
Meisner, Maurice. *Marxism, Maoism, and Utopianism: Eight Essays*. Madison, WI: University of Wisconsin Press, 1982.
Meissner, Werner. "New Intellectual Currents in the People's Republic of China." Pp. 3–24 in David C. B. Teather and Herbert S. Yee, eds., *China in Transition: Issues and Policies*. New York: St. Martin's, 1999.
Meng Fanhua. "Wenhua bengkui shidai de taowang yu guiyi: Jiushi niandai wenhua de xin baoshou zhuyi jingshen" (The Exile and Conversion of the Era of Cultural Collapse: The Neoconservative Spirit of the Culture of the 1990s). Pp. 287–92 in Li Shitao, ed., *Zhishi fenzi lichang: Jijin yu baoshou zhijian de dongdang*. Originally published in *Zhongguo wenhua yanjiu* (Chinese Culture Research), no. 2 (1994), 52–56, 6.
Metzger, Thomas A. *A Cloud across the Pacific: Essays on the Clash between Chinese and Western Political Theories Today*. Hong Kong: Chinese University of Hong Kong Press, 2005.
Escape from Predicament: Neo-Confucianism and China's Evolving Political Culture. New York: Columbia University Press, 1977. This book was translated as [Mo Zike], *Baituo kunjing: Xin ruxue yu Zhongguo zhengzhi wenhua de yanjin* (Escape from Predicament), tr. Yan Shi'an, Gao Hua, and Huang Donglan. Nanjing: Jiangsu renmin chubanshe, 1995.
Misra, Kalpana. "Curing the Sickness and Saving the Party: Neo-Maoism and Neo-conservatism in the 1990s." Pp. 133–60 in Shiping Hua, ed., *Chinese Political Culture 1989–2000*. Armonk, NY: M.E. Sharpe, 2001.
From Post-Maoism to Post-Marxism: The Erosion of Official Ideology in Deng's China. London: Routledge, 1998.
Mitter, Rana. *A Bitter Revolution: China's Struggle with the Modern World*. Oxford: Oxford University Press, 2004.
Moody, Peter R. *Conservative Thought in Contemporary China*. Lanham, MD: Rowman & Littlefield, 2007.
Morishima, Michio. "The Power of Confucian Capitalism," *Observer* (London), June 1978.

Muller, Jerry Z. "Introduction: What Is Conservative Social and Political Thought?" Pp. 3–31 in Muller, ed., *Conservatism: An Anthology of Social and Political Thought from David Hume to the Present*. Princeton, NJ: Princeton University Press, 1997.

Murthy, Viren. "Modernity against Modernity: Wang Hui's Critical History of Chinese Thought," *Modern Intellectual History* 3.1 (April 2006), 137–65.

The Political Philosophy of Zhang Taiyan: The Resistance of Consciousness. Leiden: Brill, 2011.

Neville, Robert Cummings. *Boston Confucianism: Portable Tradition in the Late-Modern World*. Albany: State University of New York Press, 2000.

Ng, On-cho and Q. Edward Wang. "Prologue." Pp. vii–xxiii in Ng and Wang, *Mirroring the Past: The Writing and Use of History in Imperial China*. Honolulu: University of Hawai'i Press, 2005.

Nisbet, Robert A. *Social Change and History: Aspects of the Western Theory of Development*. Oxford: Oxford University Press, 1969.

Oakeshott, Michael. *Rationalism in Politics, and Other Essays*. London: Methuen, 1962.

Olsen, Niklas. *History in the Plural: An Introduction to the Work of Reinhart Koselleck*. New York: Berghahn Books, 2012.

Owen, Stephen. "What Is World Poetry?" *New Republic* 203.21 (November 19, 1990), 28–32.

Petracca, Mark M. and Mong Xiong. "The Concept of Chinese Neo-authoritarianism: An Exploration and Democratic Critique," *Asian Survey* 30.11 (1990), 1099–1117.

Pfister, Lauren F. "A Modern Chinese Philosophy Built upon Critically Received Traditions: Feng Youlan's New Principle-Centered Learning and the Question of Its Relationship to Contemporary New Ruist ('Confucian') Philosophies," Pp. 165–84 in Makeham, ed., *New Confucianism*.

Pickowicz, Paul G. "Huang Jianxin and the Notion of Postsocialism." Pp. 57–87 in Nick Browne et al., eds., *New Chinese Cinemas: Forms, Identities, Politics*. Cambridge: Cambridge University Press, 1994.

Pilbeam, Bruce. "Conservatism and Postmodernism: Consanguineous Relations or 'Different' Voices?" *Journal of Political Ideologies* 6.1 (2001), 33–54.

Pincus, Steven C. A. *1688: The First Modern Revolution*. New Haven, CT: Yale University Press, 2011.

Popper, Karl. "Aestheticism, Perfectionism and Utopianism." Pp. 1.157–68 in K. R. Popper, *The Open Society and Its Enemies*. 2 vols., 4th rev. ed. Princeton, NJ: Princeton University Press, 1963.

[Ka'er Bopu'er]. *Caixiang yu fanbo* (Conjectures and Refutations), tr. Fu Jichong et al. Shanghai: Shanghai yiwen chubanshe, 1986.

[Ba Bo]. *Kaifang shehui ji qi diren* (The Open Society and Its Enemies), tr. Li Yingming and Zhuang Wenrui. Taipei: Guiguan tushu gongsi, 1986.

Prall, Stuart E. *The Bloodless Revolution: England, 1688*. Madison: University of Wisconsin Press, 1985.

Puett, Michael. "Classical Chinese Historical Thought." Pp. 34–46 in Prasenjit Duara, Viren Murthy, and Andrew Sartori, eds., *A Companion to Global Historical Thought*. Hoboken, NJ: Wiley-Blackwell, 2014.

Pusey, James Reeve. *China and Charles Darwin*. Cambridge, MA: Council on East Asian Studies, Harvard University, 1983.

Qi Mo, ed. *Xin quanwei zhuyi: Dui Zhongguo dalu weilai mingyun de lunzheng* (Neo-authoritarianism: Debates on the Future Fate of Mainland China). Taipei: Tangshan chubanshe, 1991.

Qian, Kun. *Imperial-Time-Order: Literature, Intellectual History, and China's Road to Empire*. Leiden: Brill, 2016.

Quirin, Michael. "Yü Yingshi, das Politische und die Politik" (Yü Yingshi, the Political, and Politics), *Minima Sinica: Zeitschrift zum Chinesischen Geist* (Minima Sinica: Journal for the Chinese Mind) 6.1 (1994), 27–69.

Rahav, Shakhar. *The Rise of Political Intellectuals in Modern China: May Fourth Societies and the Roots of Mass-Party Politics*. Oxford: Oxford University Press, 2015.

"Review Symposium: Thomas A. Metzger's Escape from Predicament." *Journal of Asian Studies* 39.2 (February 1980), 237–90.

Robertson, David. "Neo." Pp. 337–38 in Robertson, *The Routledge Dictionary of Politics*. London: Routledge, 2004.

Rosen, Stanley. "Guest Editor's Introduction," *Chinese Law and Government* 30.6 (November–December 1997), 3–7.

ed. "Nationalism and Neoconservatism in China in the 1990s," *Chinese Law and Government* 30.6 (November–December 1997), 3–100.

Rosen, Stanley and Gary Zou, eds. "The Chinese Debate on the New Authoritarianism," *Chinese Sociology and Anthropology* 23.2 (Winter 1990–91); 23.3 (Spring 1991); 23.4 (Summer 1991); and 24.1 (Fall 1991).

Rossiter, Clinton. *Conservatism in America*. Melbourne: Heinemann, 1955.

Ruan Ming. "Cong xin quanwei zhuyi dao xin baoshou zhuyi" (From New Authoritarianism to New Conservatism), *Kaifang zazhi* (Open Magazine), no. 2 (February 1992), 28–32. Translated by David Kelly in *Chinese Law and Government* 29.2 (March–April 1996), 58–70.

Said, Edward. *Orientalism*. New York: Pantheon Books, 1978.

Sakwa, Richard. *The Rise and Fall of the Soviet Union, 1917–1991*. London: Routledge, 1999.

Saussy, Haun. "Postmodernism in China: A Sketch and Some Queries." Pp. 128–58 in Yeh Wen-hsin, ed., *Cross-Cultural Readings of Chineseness: Narratives, Images, and Interpretations of the 1990s*. Berkeley: Institute of East Asian Studies, University of California, 2000.

Sautman, Barry. "Sirens of the Strongman: Neo-authoritarianism in Recent Chinese Political Theory," *China Quarterly*, no. 129 (1992), 72–102.

Schama, Simon. *Citizens: A Chronicle of the French Revolution*. New York: Knopf, 1989.

Schell, Orville and John Delury. *Wealth and Power: China's Long March to the Twenty-First Century*. London: Little, Brown, 2013.

Schneider, Axel. "Between *Dao* and History: Two Chinese Historians in Search of a Modern Identity for China," *History and Theory* 35.4 (December 1996), 54–73.

"Bridging the Gap: Attempts at Constructing a 'New' Historical-Cultural Identity in the PRC," *East Asian History*, no. 22 (December 2001), 129–44.

Schneider, Laurence A. "National Essence and the New Intelligentsia." Pp. 57–89 in Furth, ed., *Limits of Change*.

Schoenhals, Michael. *Doing Things with Words in Chinese Politics: Five Studies*. Berkeley: Center for Chinese Studies, Institute of East Asian Studies, University of California, 1992.

Schubert, Gunter. "Was Ist Neokonservativismus? Notizen zum Politischen Denken in der VR China in den 90er Jahren" (What Is Neoconservatism? Notes on Political Thought in the PRC during the 1990s), *Asien* (Asia) 65 (October 1997), 57–74.

Schumpeter, Joseph A. *Capitalism, Socialism, and Democracy*, 5th ed. London: Allen & Unwin, 1976 [1942].

Schwarcz, Vera. *The Chinese Enlightenment: Intellectuals and the Legacy of the May Fourth Movement of 1919*. Berkeley: University of California Press, 1986.

Schwartz, Benjamin I. "History in Chinese Culture: Some Comparative Reflections," *History and Theory* 35.4 (December 1996), 23–33.

In Search of Wealth and Power: Yen Fu and the West. Cambridge, MA: Belknap, 1964.

"Notes on Conservatism in General and in China in Particular." Pp. 3–21 in Furth, ed., *Limits of Change*.

"Themes in Intellectual History: May Fourth and After." Pp. 97–141 in Merle Goldman and Leo Ou-Fan Lee, eds., *An Intellectual History of Modern China*. Cambridge: Cambridge University Press, 2002.

Sha Jiansun and Gong Shuduo, eds. *Zou shenme lu: Guanyu Zhongguo jinxiandai lishi shang de ruogan zhongda shifei wenti* (Which Way to Go: Some Major Disputes on Modern Chinese History). Ji'nan: Shandong renmin chubanshe, 1997.

Shambaugh, David. *China Goes Global: The Partial Power*. Oxford: Oxford University Press, 2013.

Sheng, Anfeng. "Traveling Theory, or, Transforming Theory: Metamorphosis of Postcolonialism in China," *Neohelicon* 34.2 (2007), 115–36.

Sheng Hong. "Cong minzu zhuyi dao tianxia zhuyi" (From Nationalism to Cosmopolitanism), *Zhanlüe yu guanli* (Strategy and Management), no. 1 (1996), 14–19. Translated in *Chinese Law and Government* 30.6 (November–December 1997), 31–42.

"Shenme shi wenming" (What Is Civilization?), *Zhanlüe yu guanli* (Strategy and Management), no. 5 (1995), 88–98.

Shi Zhong. "Zhongguo de minzu zhuyi he Zhongguo de weilai" (Chinese Nationalism and the Future of China), *Mingbao yuekan* (Mingbao Monthly), no. 9 (1996). Translated in *Chinese Law and Government* 30.6 (November–December 1997), 8–27 [translated from the original, which differed from the version published in *Mingbao Yuekan*].

Shils, Edward. *Tradition*. Chicago: University of Chicago Press, 1981.

Sleeboom-Faulkner, Margaret. *The Chinese Academy of Social Sciences (CASS): Shaping the Reforms, Academia and China (1977–2003)*. Leiden: Brill, 2007.

Song Qiang, Zhang Zangzang, Qiao Bian, et al. *Zhongguo keyi shuo bu: Lengzhan hou shidai de zhengzhi yu qinggan jueze* (China Can Say No: Political and Emotional Choices in the Post–Cold War Era). Beijing: Zhonghua gongshang lianhe chubanshe, 1996.

Song, Xianlin. "Reconstructing the Confucian Ideal in 1980s China: The 'Culture Craze' and New Confucianism." Pp. 81–104 in Makeham, ed., *New Confucianism*. Special issue: "Greater China." *China Quarterly*, no. 136 (December 1993).

Spencer, Herbert. *The Principles of Sociology*, 2nd ed. London: Williams and Norgate, 1877–97.

Spira, Ivo. *A Conceptual History of Chinese -Isms: The Modernization of Ideological Discourse, 1895–1925*. Leiden: Brill, 2015.

S.R.G. "Preface to the Issue 'The Living Tree: The Changing Meaning of Being Chinese Today,'" *Daedalus* 120.2 (Spring 1991), v–viii.

Strafella, Giorgio. *Intellectual Discourse in Reform Era China: The Debate on the Spirit of the Humanities in the 1990s*. London: Routledge, 2017.

Stromberg, Roland N. *European History since 1789*, 3rd ed. Englewood Cliffs, NJ: Prentice Hall, 1981.

Su Wei. "Yifen taizidang jieban de baipishu" (A White Paper on the Princeling Faction's Succession), *Zhongguo zhi chun* (China Spring), no. 1 (January 1992), 28–29. Translated by David Kelly in *Chinese Law and Government* 29.2 (March–April 1996), 48–51.

Su, Xiaokang and Wang Luxiang. *Deathsong of the River: A Reader's Guide to the Chinese TV Series Heshang*. Ithaca, NY: East Asia Program, Cornell University, 1991.

Heshang (River Elegy). Beijing: Xiandai chubanshe, 1988.

Sullivan, Michael J. "Democracy and Developmentalism: Contending Struggles over Political Change in Dengist China, 1978–1995," Ph.D. diss., University of Wisconsin–Madison, 1995.

"The Impact of Western Political Thought in Chinese Political Discourse on Transitions from Leninism, 1986–1992," *World Affairs* 157.2 (October 1994), 79–91.

Sun Guodong. "Du Jiang Yihua 'jijin yu baoshou' shu hou" (After Reading Jiang Yihua's Writings on "Conservative and Radical"), *Ershiyi shiji* (Twenty-First Century), no. 11 (June 1992), 141–43.

Tang, Xiaobing. "The Function of New Theory: What Does It Mean to Talk about Postmodernism in China?" Pp. 278–99 in Liu Kang and Tang Xiaobing, eds., *Politics, Ideology, and Literary Discourse in Modern China: Theoretical Interventions and Cultural Critique*. Durham, NC: Duke University Press, 1993.

Tang Yijie, ed. *Lun chuantong yu fan chuantong: Wusi qishi zhounian jinian wenxuan* (On Tradition and Anti-tradition: Selected Works on the Commemoration of the Seventieth Anniversary of May Fourth). Taipei: Lianjing chuban shiye gongsi, 1989.

"Some Reflections on New Confucianism in Mainland Chinese Culture of the 1990s," tr. Gloria Davies. Pp. 123–34 in Davies, ed., *Voicing Concerns*.

Tao Dongfeng. "Baoshou ziyou zhuyi: Zhongguo wenhua jiangou de di sanzhong xuanze" (Conservative Liberalism: The Third Choice for Chinese Cultural Construction). Pp. 475–85 in Li Shitao, ed., *Zhishi fenzi lichang: Jijin yu baoshou zhijian de dongdang*. Originally published in *Kaifang shidai* (Open Times), no. 5 (1997), 32–37.

"Ershi shiji Zhongguo de baoshou zhuyi: Jianlun ziyou yu chuantong zhi guanxi" (The Conservatism of Twentieth-Century China: On the Relation between Liberty and Tradition). Pp. 217–61 in Tao Dongfeng, *Wenhua yu meixue de shiye jiaorong: Tao Dongfeng xueshu zixuanji* (The Fusion of the Horizons of Culture and Aesthetics: Self-Selections of Tao Dongfeng's Academic Works). Fuzhou: Fujian jiaoyu chubanshe, 2000.

Tao Dongfeng and Jin Yuanpu. *Chanshi Zhongguo de jiaolü: Zhuanxing shidai de wenhua jiedu* (The Anxiety of Interpreting China/Interpreting China's Anxiety: Cultural Interpretations of the Transitional Era). Beijing: Zhongguo guoji guangbo chubanshe, 1999.

Terrill, Ross. *The Life of Mao.* www.overdrive.com/search?q=E32A112B-2D31-482A-A8AA-16A00E298663.

Townsend, James. "Chinese Nationalism." Pp. 1–30 in Jonathan Unger, ed., *Chinese Nationalism.* Armonk, NY: M.E. Sharpe, 1996.

Tribe, Keith. "Introduction." Pp. vii–xx in Koselleck, *Futures Past.*

Tsai, Wen-hui. "New Authoritarianism, Neo-conservatism, and Anti–Peaceful Evolution: Mainland China's Resistance to Political Modernization," *Issues & Studies* 28.12 (1992), 1–22.

Tsu, Jing. *Failure, Nationalism, and Literature: The Making of Modern Chinese Identity, 1895–1937.* Stanford, CA: Stanford University Press, 2005.

Tu, Wei-ming [Du Weiming]. *Confucian Ethics Today: The Singapore Challenge.* Singapore: Curriculum Development Institute of Singapore, Federal Publications, 1984.

———. ed. *Confucian Traditions in East Asian Modernity: Moral Education and Economic Culture in Japan and the Four Mini-Dragons.* Cambridge, MA: Harvard University Press, 1996.

———. "'Cultural China': The Periphery as the Center," *Daedalus* 120.2 (1991), 1–32.

———. "Hsiung Shih-li's Quest for Authentic Existence." Pp. 242–75 in Furth, ed., *Limits of Change.*

———. "Huajie qimeng xintai" (Beyond the Enlightenment Mentality), *Ershiyi shiji* (Twenty-First Century), no. 2 (December 1990), 12–13.

———. "Introduction." Pp. 1–10 in Tu, ed., *Confucian Traditions in East Asian Modernity.*

———. "Introduction: Cultural Perspectives," *Daedalus* 122.2 (Spring 1993), vii–xiv.

———. *Renxing yu ziwo xiuyang* (Humanity and Self-Cultivation). Beijing: Zhongguo heping chubanshe, 1988.

———. *Ruxue disanqi fazhan de qianjing wenti: Dalu jiangxue, wennan, he taolun* (Prospective Issues in the Third Epoch of Confucianism: Mainland Lectures, Questions, and Discussions). Taipei: Lianjing chuban shiye gongsi, 1989.

———. ed. *The Triadic Chord: Confucian Ethics, Industrial East Asia, and Max Weber: Proceedings of the 1987 Singapore Conference on Confucian Ethics and the Modernisation of Industrial East Asia.* Singapore: Institute of East Asian Philosophies, 1991.

———. "'Wenhua Zhongguo' chutan" (Probing "Cultural China"), *Jiushi niandai* (The Nineties), no. 6 (June 1990), 60–61.

———. "Wenhua Zhongguo yu huayi zhishi fenzi de 'ziwo yishi'" (Cultural China and Chinese Intellectuals' "Consciousness of Self"), *Shijie ribao* (World Journal), September 22, 1991.

Tu, Wei-ming, Milan Hejtmanek, Alan Wachman, et al., eds. *The Confucian World Observed: A Contemporary Discussion of Confucian Humanism in East Asia.* Honolulu: East-West Center, University of Hawai'i, 1992.

Turner, Frank M. "Introduction: Edmund Burke: The Political Actor Thinking." Pp. xi–xliv in Edmund Burke, *Reflections on the Revolution in France*, ed. Frank M. Turner. New Haven, CT: Yale University Press, 2003.

U, Eddy. "The Making of Chinese Intellectuals: Representations and Organization in the Thought Reform Campaign," *China Quarterly*, no. 192 (2007), 971–89.

Vickers, Edward. "Museums and Nationalism in Contemporary China," *Compare* 37.3 (2007), 365–82.

Viereck, Peter. *Conservatism from John Adams to Churchill*. Princeton, NJ: Van Nostrand, 1956.

Vogel, Ezra F. *The Four Little Dragons: The Spread of Industrialization in East Asia*. Cambridge, MA: Harvard University Press, 1991.

  Japan as Number One: Lessons for America. Cambridge, MA: Harvard University Press, 1979.

von Brunner, Otto, Werner Conze, and Reinhart Koselleck, eds. *Geschichtliche Grundbegriffe: Historisches Lexikon zur politisch-sozialen Sprache in Deutschland* (Basic Historical Concepts: A Dictionary on Historical Principles of Political and Social Language in Germany). Stuttgart: Klett-Cotta, 1972–97.

Waldron, Arthur. "Warlordism versus Federalism: The Revival of a Debate?," *China Quarterly*, no. 121 (1990), 116–28.

Wang, Ban. *Illuminations from the Past: Trauma, Memory and History in Modern China*. Stanford, CA: Stanford University Press, 2004.

Wang, Chaohua. "Introduction: Minds of the Nineties." Pp. 11–45 in Chaohua Wang, ed., *One China, Many Paths*. London: Verso, 2003.

Wang, David Der-wei. "Chinese Literature from 1841 to 1937." Pp. 413–564 in Kang-I Sun Chang and Stephen Owen, eds., *The Cambridge History of Chinese Literature, Volume II: From 1375*. Cambridge: Cambridge University Press, 2010.

Wang Fansen [Wang Fan-shen]. "'Zhuyi shidai de lailin': Zhongguo jindai sixiangshi de yige guanjian fazhan" (The Advent of the "Age of *-Isms*": A Key Development in the History of Modern Chinese Thought), *Dong Ya guannianshi jikan* (Journal of the History of Ideas in East Asia), no. 4 (2013), 3–7 and 9–88.

Wang, Fanshen. "Evolving Prescriptions for Social Life in the Late Qing and Early Republic: From *Qunxue* to Society," tr. Joan Judge. *Chinese Studies in History* 29.4 (Summer 1996), 73–99.

Wang, Frédéric. "Le confucianisme et la Chine actuelle: l'héritage de Zhang Dainian (1909–2004)" (Confucianism and China Today: The Legacy of Zhang Dainian (1909–2004)), *Histoire et Missions Chrétiennes* (History and Christian Missions), no. 2 (2011), 69–87, www.cairn.info/revue-histoire-monde-et-cultures-religieuses 1-2011-2-page-69.htm.

Wang, Gungwu. *The Chinese Intellectual: Past and Present*. Singapore: Faculty of Arts and Sciences, National University of Singapore, 1983.

Wang, Hui. *China's New Order: Society, Politics, and Economy in Transition*, ed. Theodore Huters. Cambridge, MA: Harvard University Press, 2003.

  "Dangdai Zhongguo de sixiang zhuangkuang yu xiandaixing wenti," *Tianya* (Frontiers), no. 5 (1997), 133–50. Translated by Rebecca Karl under the title "Contemporary Chinese Thought and the Question of Modernity," in Wang, *China's New Order*, ed. Theodore Huters, 139–187, and in *Social Text* 16.2 (Summer 1998), 9–44.

The End of the Revolution: China and the Limits of Modernity. London: Verso, 2009.
"The New Criticism." Pp. 55–86 in Chaohua Wang, ed., *One China, Many Paths.* London: Verso, 2003.
Wang Hui and Yu Guoliang, eds. *Jiushi niandai de "houxue" lunzheng* (The Debates in the 1990s on "Post-*Isms*"). Hong Kong: Chinese University of Hong Kong Press, 1998.
Wang Hui and Zhang Tianwei. "Wenhua pipan lilun yu dangdai Zhongguo minzu zhuyi wenti" (Cultural Criticism Theory and the Issue of Contemporary Chinese Nationalism), *Zhanlüe yu guanli* (Strategy and Management), no. 4 (1994), 17–20.
Wang, Jing. "Heshang and the Paradoxes of the Chinese Enlightenment." Pp. 118–36 in Jing Wang, *High Culture Fever.*
High Culture Fever: Politics, Aesthetics, and Ideology in Deng's China. Berkeley: University of California Press, 1996.
Wang, Juntao. "Reverse Course: Political Neo-conservatism and Regime Stability in Post-Tiananmen China," Ph.D. diss., Columbia University, 2006.
Wang Meng. "Duobi chonggao" (Shunning the Sublime), *Dushu* (Reading), no. 1 (1993), 10–17.
Wang, Ning. "The Mapping of Chinese Postmodernity." Pp. 21–40 in Dirlik and Zhang, eds., *Postmodernism and China.*
Wang, Q. Edward. *Inventing China through History: The May Fourth Approach to Historiography.* Albany: State University of New York Press, 2011.
Wang Rongzu. "Jijin yu baoshou zhuiyan" (Radicalism and Conservatism: Superfluous Words), *Ershiyi shiji* (Twenty-First Century), no. 11 (June 1992), 133–36.
"Ziyou zhuyi yu Zhongguo" (Liberalism and China), *Ershiyi shiji* (Twenty-First Century), no. 2 (December 1990), 33–37.
Wang Shan. *Disan zhi yanjing kan Zhongguo* (Looking at China through a Third Eye). Taipei: Zhouzhi wenhua, 1994.
Wang Shaoguang. "'Baoshou' yu 'baoshou zhuyi'" ("Conservative" and "Conservatism"), *Ershiyi shiji* (Twenty-First Century), no. 12 (August 1992), 135–38.
"Qiubian paluan de xin baoshou sichao" (The Neoconservative Trend That Seeks Change and Fears Chaos), *Zhongguo shibao zhoukan* (China Times Weekly), March 8, 1992, 76–77.
"Zai lun Zhongguo zhengfu jiqu nengli—Jianda Yang Dali, Cui Zhiyuan, Rao Yuqing, Xiao Geng zhu xiansheng" (Further Discussion on the Extractive Capacity of the Chinese Government: Reply to Yang Dali, Cui Zhiyuan, Rao Yuqing, and Xiao Geng), *Ershiyi shiji* (Twenty-First Century), no. 22 (April 1994), 129–36.
Wang Shaoguang and Hu Angang. *Jiaqiang zhongyang zhengfu zai shichang jingji zhuanxing zhong de zhudao zuoyong: Guanyu Zhongguo guojia nengli de yanjiu baogao* (Strengthening the Guiding Role of the Central Government in the Transition to a Market Economy: A Research Report on China's State Capacity). Shenyang: Liaoning renmin chubanshe, 1993.
The Political Economy of Uneven Development: The Case of China, ed. Mark Selden. Armonk, NY: M.E. Sharpe, 1999.

"Zhongguo zhengfu jiqu nengli de xiajiang ji qi houguo" (The Decrease in the Extractive Capacity of the Chinese Government and Its Consequences), *Ershiyi shiji* (Twenty-First Century), no. 21 (February 1994), 5–14.

Wang Shi, ed. *Yan Fu ji* (Collected Works of Yan Fu), 5 vols. Beijing: Zhonghua shuju chubanshe, 1986. Originally published in Beijing by Shangwu yinshuguan chubanshe.

Wang Shuren. "Wenhua de weiji, ronghe yu chongjian" (The Crisis, Reconciliation, and Reconstruction of Culture), *Yuandao* (True Way) 1 (1994), 95–114.

Wang Sirui. "Jinri Zhongguo de xin baoshou zhuyi" (Neoconservatism in Today's China). Pp. 406–21 in Li Shitao, ed., *Zhishi fenzi lichang: Jijin yu baoshou zhijian de dongdang*. Originally published in *Beijing wenxue* (Beijing Literature), no. 3 (1999), 81–88.

Wang Xiaoming. "The Politics of Translation: Modes of Organization in the Chinese Translation Movement of the 1980s," tr. Kenneth Dean. Pp. 269–300 in Naoki Sakai and Yukiko Hanawa, eds., *Specters of the West and the Politics of Translation*. Ithaca, NY: Traces Editorial Office, Cornell University, 2001.

ed. *Renwen jingshen xunsi lu* (Collection of Reflections on the Humanist Spirit). Shanghai: Wenhui chubanshe, 1996.

Wang Yuanhua. "Guanyu jinnian de fansi dawen" (Answering Questions about Reflections in Recent Years), *Xueshu jilin* (Academic Collection), no. 3. Shanghai: Shanghai yuandong chubanshe, 1998.

"Wei 'wusi' jingshen yi bian" (In Defense of the "May Fourth" Spirit). Pp. 1–27 in Lin Yü-sheng et al., *Wusi: Duoyuan de fansi*.

Wang Yuanhua and Li Hui. "Duiyu 'wusi' de zai renshi da kewen" (Answering Questions on the Re-acknowledgment of "May Fourth"). Pp. 271–86 in Li Shitao, ed., *Zhishi fenzi lichang: Jijin yu baoshou zhijian de dongdang*. Originally published in *Wenhui dushu zhoubao* (Wenhui Reading Weekly), May 1, 1999, 8–9.

Wang Yuechuan. "Dangdai wenhua yanjiu zhong de jijin yu baoshou zhi wei" (The Link between Radicalism and Conservatism in Research on Contemporary Culture). Pp. 422–38 in Li Shitao, ed., *Zhishi fenzi lichang: Jijin yu baoshou zhijian de dongdang*.

"Xuyan" (Preface). Pp. 1–13 in *Zhongguo houxiandai huayu* (The Chinese Postmodernism Discourse). Guangzhou: Zhongshan daxue chubanshe, 2004.

Wang Zhaojun. "Xin baoshou zhuyi yu dalu zhishi fenzi" (New Conservatism and the Intellectuals in Mainland China), *Zhongguo luntan* (China Forum), July 1, 1992, 106–14. Translated by David Kelly in *Chinese Law and Government* 29.2 (March–April 1996), 83–96.

Waterman, Harold. "Which Way to Go? Four Strategies for Democratization in Chinese Intellectual Circles," *China Information* 5.1 (1990), 14–33.

Weber, Max. *Economy and Society: An Outline of Interpretive Sociology,* ed. Günther Roth and Claus Wittich. Berkeley: University of California Press, 1978.

The Protestant Ethic and the Spirit of Capitalism, tr. Talcott Parsons. New York: Scribner, 1958.

The Protestant Ethic and the Spirit of Capitalism, tr. Stephen Kalberg. New York: Columbia University Press, 2011.

The Religion of China: Confucianism and Taoism, tr. Hans Gerth. New York: Free Press, 1968.

Wende, Peter. "Radikalismus" (Radicalism). Pp. 5.113–33 in von Brunner, Conze, and Koselleck, eds., *Geschichtliche Grundbegriffe*.
Wenzhe. "Jiuyuan le, guoxue!" (National Studies, It Has Been a Long Time!), *Renmin ribao* (People's Daily), August 18, 1993, 1.
Whitehead, Alfred North. *Science and the Modern World*. Cambridge: Cambridge University Press, 1953 [1926].
Wright, Mary Clabaugh. *The Last Stand of Chinese Conservatism: The T'ung-Chih Restoration, 1862–1874*. Stanford, CA: Stanford University Press, 1957.
Wu Jiaxiang. "Xin quanwei zhuyi shuping" (Commenting on New Authoritarianism). Pp. 4–8 in Qi Mo, ed., *Xin quanwei zhuyi*.
Xiao Gongqin. *Chaoyue zuoyou jijin zhuyi: Zouchu Zhongguo zhuanxing de kunjing* (Beyond Left and Right Radicalism: Moving away from the Predicament of China's Transformation). Hangzhou: Zhejiang daxue chubanshe, 2012.
"Chuantong wenhua duoxing dui Zhongguo xiandaihua de sanzhong zuzhang" (The Three Obstacles to Chinese Modernization in the Inertia of the Traditional Culture). Pp. 338–43 in Xiao, *Xiao Gongqin ji*.
"Cong zhengzhi langman zhuyi dao zhengzhi jijin zhuyi: Dui Zhongguo zaoqi yihui minzhu sichao de lishi kaocha" (From Political Romanticism to Political Radicalism: Historical Research on the Early Parliamentary Democracy Trend). Pp. 265–80 in Xiao, *Xiao Gongqin ji*. Originally published in *Zhongguo shehui kexue jikan* (China Social Sciences Quarterly), no. 2 (1993), 82–89, under the title "Cong langman de minzu zhuyi dao zhengzhi jijin zhuyi: Dui Zhongguo zaoqi yihui minzhu sichao de lishi kaocha" (From Romantic Nationalism to Political Radicalism: Historical Research on the Early Parliamentary Democracy Trend).
"Dangdai Zhongguo xin baoshou zhuyi de sixiang yuanyuan" (The Intellectual Origins of Contemporary Chinese Neoconservatism), *Ershiyi shiji* (Twenty-First Century), no. 40 (April 1997), 126–35.
"Jindai sixiangshi shang de 'wenti yu zhuyi' zhenglun de zai sikao" (Rethinking the Debate on "Problems and *-Isms*" in Modern Intellectual History). Pp. 142–57 in Li Shitao, ed., *Zhishi fenzi lichang: Jijin yu baoshou zhijian de dongdang*.
Lishi jujue langman: Xin baoshou zhuyi yu Zhongguo xiandaihua (History Rejects Romanticism: Neoconservatism and Chinese Modernization). Taipei: Zhiliang chubanshe, 1998.
"Lishi jujue langman: Zhongguo gaige di'er sichao de jueqi" (History Rejects Romanticism: The Emergence of the Second Trend of Reform Thought in China). Pp. 109–22 in Xiao, *Xiao Gongqin ji*. Originally published in *Zhongguo xiandaihua yanjiu* (Research on Chinese Modernization), December 9, 1994. An abstract appeared in *Beijing qingnianbao* (Beijing Youth Daily), January 19, 1992, 6.
"Lishixue zai Zhongguo biange shidai de yiyi" (The Meaning of Historical Studies in the Era of Chinese Reform). Pp. 359–64 in Xiao, *Xiao Gongqin ji*. Originally published in *Shixue lilun* (History Theory), no. 4 (1988), 14–17, under the title "Rang women peiyang ziji shenshang de yonggan zhongzi: Shixue fazhan shi wo guan (Let Us Cultivate Our Own Bare Seeds of Bravery: My View of the Development of History).
"Lun dangdai Zhongguo de langman zhuyi gaigeguan: Dui 'zhidu juedinglun' de piping" (On the Romantic Reform View in Contemporary China: A Criticism of

"System Determinism"). Pp. 87–108 in Xiao, *Xiao Gongqin ji*. Originally appeared in *Zhishi fenzi* (The Intellectual), no. 1 (1989), 69–72.

"Minzu zhuyi yu Zhongguo zhuanxing shiqi de yishi xingtai" (Nationalism and Ideology during China's Transitional Era). Pp. 350–58 in Xiao, *Xiao Gongqin ji*. Originally published in *Zhanlüe yu guanli* (Strategy and Management), no. 4 (1994), 21–25.

1911 nian Zhongguo da geming (The Great Chinese Revolution of 1911). Beijing: Shehui kexue wenxian chubanshe, 2011.

"The Political Attitudes of the Various Strata in China's Society and Their Prospects for the Future," *Chinese Economy* 32.3 (1999), 56–78.

Rujia wenhua de kunjing: Jindai shidaifu yu Zhong Xi wenhua pengzhuang (The Dilemma of Confucian Culture: Modern Literati and the Collision of Chinese and Western Cultures). Guilin: Guangxi shifan daxue chubanshe, 2006.

Rujia wenhua de kunjing: Zhongguo jindai shidaifu yu Xifang tiaozhan (The Predicament of Confucian Culture: Modern Chinese Literati and the Challenge of the West). Chengdu: Sichuan renmin chubanshe, 1986.

"Ruxue de sanzhong lishi xingtai" (The Three Historical Forms of Confucianism). Pp. 315–37 in Xiao, *Xiao Gongqin ji*.

"Sixiangshi de meili" (The Charm of Intellectual History). Pp. 3–15 in Xiao, *Zhishi fenzi yu guannian ren* (Intellectuals and Men of Concepts). Tianjin: Tianjin renmin chubanshe, 2002. Also published in *Kaifang shidai* (Open Times), no. 1 (2002), 102–9.

Weiji zhong de biange: Qingmo xiandaihua jincheng zhong de jijin yu baoshou (Reform amidst Crisis: Radicalism and Conservatism in the Process of Late Qing Modernization). Shanghai: Shanghai sanlian shudian, 1999.

"Wenhua shifan yu xiandaihua de kun'e" (Cultural Anomie and the Conundrum of Modernization). Pp. 344–49 in Xiao, *Xiao Gongqin ji*.

"Wuxu bianfa de zai fanxing: Jianlun zaoqi zhengzhi jijin zhuyi de wenhua genyuan (Re-examining the Hundred Days Reform Movement: Discussing the Cultural Roots of Early Political Radicalism). Pp. 121–41 in Li Shitao, ed., *Zhishi fenzi lichang: Jijin yu baoshou zhijian de dongdang*. Originally published in *Zhanlüe yu guanli* (Strategy and Management), no. 4 (1995), 11–20.

Xiao Gongqin ji (Collected Works of Xiao Gongqin). Ha'erbin: Heilongjiang jiaoyu chubanshe, 1995.

"'Yan Fu beilun' yu jindai baoshou zhuyi biange guan" (The "Yan Fu Paradox" and the Conservative View of Change in Modern Times). Pp. 18–41 in Xiao, *Xiao Gongqin ji*. Originally published in *Zhongguo yanjiu* (China Research), no. 6 (1996).

"Yan Fu dui Zhongguo xiandaihua de sikao ji qi qishi" (Yan Fu's Reflections on China's Modernization and Its Enlightenment), *Zhongguo qingnianbao* (China Youth Daily), February 6, 1991, 3.

Yu zhengzhi langman zhuyi gaobie (Parting with Political Romanticism). Wuhan: Hubei jiaoyu chubanshe, 2001.

Zhishi fenzi yu guannian ren (Intellectuals and Men of Concepts). Tianjin: Tianjin renmin chubanshe, 2002.

"Zhongguo xin baoshou zhuyi de sixiang yuanyuan" (The Intellectual Origins of Chinese Neoconservatism). Pp. 25–40 in Xiao, *Yu zhengzhi langman zhuyi gaobie*.

"Zhongguo zaoqi xiandaihua de cuozhe ji qi lishi houguo" (The Setbacks in China's Early Modernization and the Historical Results). Pp. 199–223 in Xiao, *Xiao*

Gongqin ji. Originally published in Yang Nianqun, ed. *Jiawu bainian cha: Duoyuan shiye xia de Zhong Ri zhanzheng* (Investigating 1895 One Hundred Years Later: The Sino-Japanese War under a Pluralist Vision). Beijing: Zhishi chubanshe, 1995.

"Zhuanxingqi Zhongguo renwen zhishi fenzi de sizhong leixing" (Four Types of Intellectuals in the Humanities in Transitional China). Pp. 182–89 in Xiao, *Xiao Gongqin ji*. Originally published as "Gaige zhuanxingqi Zhongguo zhishi fenzi de leixing fenhua" (A Typological Distinction of Intellectuals in Reform Transitional China), in *Tansuo yu zhengming* (Exploration and Contention), no. 8 (1994), 3–5.

"Zixu" (Preface). Pp. 1–16 in Xiao, *Xiao Gongqin ji*.

"Zixu" (Preface). Pp. 1–13 in Xiao, *Yu zhengzhi langman zhuyi gaobie*.

"Zouxiang chengshu: Zhongguo gaige de fansi yu zhanwang" (Toward Ripening: Reflections on and Prospects for the Chinese Reforms). Pp. 123–39 in Xiao, *Xiao Gongqin ji*. An earlier version of the article appeared in *Zhongguo shibao zhoukan* (China Times Weekly), February 21, 1993, and February 28, 1993. An abstract was published in *Beijing qingnianbao* (Beijing Youth Daily), May 13, 1993.

"Zouxiang xin baoshou zhuyi" (Toward Neoconservatism), *Zhongguo shibao zhoukan* (China Times Weekly), February 21, 1993, 46–51 and February 28, 1993, 36–39.

Xiao Gongqin and Zhu Wei. "Tongku de liangnan xuanze: Guanyu 'xin quanwei zhuyi' lilun dawenlu" (A Painful Dilemma: A Record of Questions and Answers on "Neo-authoritarianism"). Pp. 13–19 in Qi Mo, ed., *Xin quanwei zhuyi*. Originally published in *Wenhui bao* (Wenhui Daily), January 17, 1989.

Xie Wujun. "Ping Zhongguo dangdai de baoshou zhuyi sichao" (Commenting on the Contemporary Chinese Conservative Trend), *Dangdai sichao* (Contemporary Trends), no. 4 (2001), 13–29.

Xu Ben. "'Di san shijie piping' zai dangjin Zhongguo de chujing" (The Predicament of "Third World Criticism" in Present-Day China), *Ershiyi shiji* (Twenty-First Century), no. 27 (February 1995), 16–27.

Disenchanted Democracy: Chinese Cultural Criticism after 1989. Ann Arbor: University of Michigan Press, 1999.

"Zai tan Zhongguo 'houxue' de zhengzhixing he lishi yishi" (Again on the Political Nature and Historical Consciousness of Chinese "Post-*Isms*"), *Ershiyi shiji* (Twenty-First Century), no. 39 (February 1997), 132–37.

Xu Jilin. "Bi piping geng zhongyao de shi lijie" (What Is More Important Than Criticizing Is Understanding), *Ershiyi shiji* (Twenty-First Century), no. 29 (June 1995), 130–36.

"Contradictions within Enlightenment Ideas," tr. Adrian Thieret. Pp. 197–234 in Cao Tianyu, Zhong Xueping, and Liao Kebin, eds., *Culture and Social Transformations in Reform Era China*. Leiden: Brill, 2010.

"The Fate of an Enlightenment: Twenty Years in the Chinese Intellectual Sphere (1978–1998)," tr. Geremie Barmé and Gloria Davies. Pp. 183–203 in Edward Gu and Merle Goldman, eds., *Chinese Intellectuals between State and Market*. London: RoutledgeCurzon, 2004.

"Jijin yu baoshou de mihuo" (The Conundrum of Radicalism and Conservatism), *Ershiyi shiji* (Twenty-First Century), no. 11 (June 1992), 137–40. Reprinted under the title "Jijin yu baoshou zhijian de dongdang" (The Struggle between Radicalism and Conservatism). Pp. 37–41 in Li Shitao, ed., *Zhishi fenzi lichang: Jijin yu baoshou zhijian de dongdang*.

Xu Jilin zixuanji (Self-Selected Works of Xu Jilin). Guilin: Guangxi shifan daxue chubanshe, 1999.

"Zhongguo zhishi fenzi de ziyou zhuyi chuantong" (The Tradition of Liberalism among Chinese Intellectuals). Pp. 98–109 in Xu, *Xu Jilin zixuanji* (Self-Selected Works of Xu Jilin). Guilin: Guangxi shifan daxue chubanshe, 1999. Originally published under the title "Xiandai Zhongguo de ziyou zhuyi chuantong" (The Tradition of Liberalism in Contemporary China), *Ershiyi shiji* (Twenty-First Century), no. 42 (August 1997), 27–35.

Xu Ming. "Wenhua jijin zhuyi de lishi weidu: Cong Zheng Min, Fan Qinlin de zhenglun shuokai qu" (The Historical Dimension of Cultural Radicalism: Explaining the Debate between Zheng Min and Fan Qinlin). Pp. 207–18 in Li Shitao, ed., *Zhishi fenzi lichang: Jijin yu baoshou zhijian de dongdang*. Originally published in *Wenxue pinglun* (Literary Review), no. 4 (1994), 114–20.

Xu Youyu. "The Debates between Liberalism and the New Left in China since the 1990s," *Contemporary Chinese Thought* 34.3 (Spring 2003), 6–17.

"Intellectual Discourses in Post-Mao China and Today," Independent Chinese PEN Center. https://protect-eu.mimecast.com/s/p2DiCJ8x8f8KL3oIzT9rK?domain=chinesepen.org.

"Shi jingjixue tiaozhan lishi, haishi luoji daiti shishi" (Is Economics Challenging History or Is Logic Replacing Empirical Facts?), *Zhanlüe yu guanli* (Strategy and Management), no. 2 (February 1996), 94–97.

Yan Jiayan. "Ping wusi, wenge yu chuantong wenhua de lunzheng" (On the Debate about May Fourth, the Cultural Revolution, and Traditional Culture), *Ershiyi shiji* (Twenty-First Century), no. 42 (August 1997), 129–36.

"Wusi, wenge, chuantong wenhua" (May Fourth, the Cultural Revolution, and Traditional Culture). Pp. 231–40 in Li Shitao, ed., *Zhishi fenzi lichang: Jijin yu baoshou zhijian de dongdang*.

Yang Chunshi. "Xin baoshou zhuyi yu xin lixing zhuyi: Jiushi niandai renwen sichao pipan" (Neoconservatism and Neorationalism: A Critique of Trends in the Humanities in the 1990s). Pp. 486–92 in Li Shitao, ed., *Zhishi fenzi lichang: Jijin yu baoshou zhijian de dongdang*. Originally published in *Hainan shifan xueyuan xuebao* (Hainan Normal College Journal), no. 2 (1996).

Yang Fan. *Gongheguo de di sandai* (The Third Generation of the Republic). Chengdu: Sichuan renmin chubanshe, 1991.

Yang, Guobin. *The Red Guard Generation and Political Activism in China*. New York: Columbia University Press, 2016.

Ye Wen. "Ying qubie zhengzhi de baoshou zhuyi he wenhua de baoshou zhuyi" (One Should Distinguish between Political Conservatism and Cultural Conservatism), *Ershiyi shiji* (Twenty-First Century), no. 40 (April 1997), 136–37.

Yeh, Michelle. "Chinese Postmodernism and the Cultural Politics of Modern Chinese Poetry." Pp. 100–27 in Wen-hsin Yeh, ed., *Cross-Cultural Readings of Chineseness: Narratives, Images, and Interpretations of the 1990s*. Berkeley: Institute of East Asian Studies, University of California, 2000.

"International Theory and the Transnational Critic: China in the Age of Multiculturalism." Pp. 251–80 in Chow, ed., *Modern Chinese Literary and Cultural Studies in the Age of Theory.*

Modern Chinese Poetry: Theory and Practice since 1917. New Haven, CT: Yale University Press, 1991.

Yeh, Wen-hsin. *Shanghai Splendor: Economic Sentiments and the Making of Modern China, 1843–1949.* Berkeley: University of California Press, 2007.

Yin Huimin. "Xin baoshou zhuyi yu Zhongguo qianjing" (New Conservatism and China's Outlook), *Jiushi niandai* (The Nineties), no. 4 (April 1993), 86–88. Translated by David Kelly in *Chinese Law and Government* 29.2 (March–April 1996), 77–81.

Yü, Ying-shih [Yu Yingshi]. "Changing Conceptions of National History in Twentieth-Century China." Pp. 155–74 in Erik Lönnroth, Karl Molin, and Ragnar Björk, eds., *Conceptions of National History: Proceedings of Nobel Symposium 78.* Berlin: Walter de Gruyter, 1994.

"'Chuangxin' yu 'baoshou'" ("Renewal" and "Preservation"). Pp. 288–95 in Yü Ying-shih, *Qian Mu yu Zhongguo wenhua.* First appeared in Yü Ying-shih, *Zhongguo wenhua yu xiandai bianqian* (Chinese Culture and Present Changes). Taipei: Sanmin shuju, 1992.

"Dai congtou, shoushi jiu shanhe" (Picking Up the Pieces for a New Start), *Ershiyi shiji* (Twenty-First Century), no. 2 (December 1990), 5–7.

"Qian Mu yu xin rujia" (Qian Mu and the New Confucians). Pp. 30–90 in Yü Ying-shih, *Qian Mu yu Zhongguo wenhua.*

Qian Mu yu Zhongguo wenhua (Qian Mu and Chinese Culture). Shanghai: Shanghai yuandong chubanshe, 1994.

"The Radicalization of China in the Twentieth Century," *Daedalus* 122.2 (Spring 1993), 125–50.

Xiandai ruxue lun (Essays on Contemporary Confucianism). Shanghai: Shanghai renmin chubanshe, 1998.

"Zai lun Zhongguo xiandai sixiang zhong de jijin yu baoshou: Da Jiang Yihua xiansheng" (Further Thoughts on Radicalism and Conservatism in Modern Chinese History: A Response to Jiang Yihua), *Ershiyi shiji* (Twenty-First Century), no. 10 (April 1992), 143–49.

"Zhongguo jindai sixiangshi shang de jijin yu baoshou: Xianggang Zhongwen daxue 25 zhounian jinian jiangzuo disi jiang" (Radicalism and Conservatism in Modern Chinese Intellectual History: Fourth Speech at the Commemoration of the 25th Anniversary of the Chinese University of Hong Kong). Pp. 1–29 in Li Shitao, ed., *Zhishi fenzi lichang: Jijin yu baoshou zhijian de dongdang.* Originally appeared on pp. 188–222 in Yü Ying-shih, *Qian Mu yu Zhongguo wenhua,* and on pp. 199–242 in Yü Ying-shih, *Youji fengchui shuishang lin: Qian Mu yu xiandai Zhongguo xueshu* (Still Remembering the Wind and the Water: Qian Mu and Modern Chinese Learning). Taipei: Sanmin shuju, 1999.

Zhongguo jinshi zongjiao lunli yu shangren jingshen (The Modern Chinese Religious Ethic and the Mercantile Spirit). Taipei: Lianjing chuban shiye gongsi, 1987.

"Zhongguo zhishi fenzi de bianyuanhua" (The Marginalization of Chinese Intellectuals), *Ershiyi shiji* (Twenty-First Century), no. 6 (August 1991), 15–25.

"Zixu" (Preface). Pp. 1–6 in *Qian Mu yu Zhongguo wenhua*.
Yü, Ying-shih, with Josephine Chiu-Duke and Michael S. Duke, eds. *Chinese History and Culture, Volume Two: Seventeenth Century through Twentieth Century*. New York: Columbia University Press, 2016.
Yuan Weishi. "Xin wenhua yundong yu 'jijin zhuyi'" (The New Culture Movement and "Radicalism"). Pp. 252–70 in Li Shitao, ed., *Zhishi fenzi lichang: Jijin yu baoshou zhijian de dongdang*.
Yue Daiyun. "Chonggu 'xueheng': Jianlun xiandai baoshou zhuyi" (Re-evaluating *Xueheng* and Concurrently Discussing Modern Conservatism). Pp. 415–28 in Tang Yijie, ed., *Lun chuantong yu fan chuantong*.
"On Western Literary Theory in China," tr. Gloria Davies. Pp. 109–22 in Davies, ed., *Voicing Concerns*.
"Shijie wenhua duihua zhong de Zhongguo xiandai baoshou zhuyi: Jianlun 'Xueheng' zazhi" (Modern Chinese Conservatism in the Global Cultural Dialogues: On the *Xueheng* Journal). Pp. 56–67 in Beijing daxue shehui kexuechu, ed., *Beijing daxue jinian wusi yundong qishi zhounian lunwenji*. The article also appeared in *Zhongguo wenhua* (Chinese Culture), no. 1 (1989), 132–36.
Yue, Daiyun and Carolyn Wakeman. *To the Storm: The Odyssey of a Revolutionary Chinese Woman*. Berkeley: University of California Press, 1987.
Zarrow, Peter. *After Empire: The Conceptual Transformation of the Chinese State, 1885–1924*. Stanford, CA: Stanford University Press, 2012.
Zeng Yeying, ed. *Wushi nian lai de Zhongguo jindaishi yanjiu* (Research on Modern Chinese History during the Past Fifty Years). Shanghai: Shanghai shudian chubanshe, 2000.
Zhang Fa, Zhang Yiwu, and Wang Yichuan. "Cong 'xiandaixing' dao 'Zhonghuaxing': Xin zhishixing de tanxun" (From "Modernity" to "Chineseness": Explorations into a New Knowledge Model), *Wenyi zhengming* (Debates on Literature and Art), no. 2 (1994), 10–20.
Zhang Guangzhao. "Wang Qishan weihe tuijian *Jiu zhidu yu da geming*?" (Why Does Wang Qishan Recommend *The Old Regime and the Revolution*?), *Renmin ribao haiwaiban* (Overseas Edition of People's Daily), January 18, 2013, 11.
Zhang Haipeng. "Jinnian lai Zhongguo jindaishi yanjiu zhong de ruogan yuanzexing lunzheng" (Several Principal Debates in Research on Modern Chinese History in Recent Years), *Makesi zhuyi yanjiu* (Research on Marxism), no. 3 (1997), 14–22.
Zhang Haipeng, et al. "Wusi yundong yu ershi shiji de daolu" (The May Fourth Movement and the Road of Twentieth-Century China), *Gaoxiao lilun zhanxian* (Theoretical Front in Higher Education), no. 6 (1996), 16–25.
Zhang, Junmai. "A Manifesto for a Re-appraisal of Sinology and Reconstruction of Chinese Culture." Pp. 2.455–83 in Carsun Chang [Zhang Junmai], *The Development of Neo-Confucian Thought*, 2 vols. New York: Bookman Associates, 1957–62.
Zhang Lin, Wang Yinhuan, Jing Jianbin, et al. "Qingnian xuesheng shiye zhong de jindai Zhongguo yilai de lishi daolu" (The Historical Road of China since Modern Times in the View of Young Students), *Gaoxiao lilun zhanxian* (Theoretical Front in Higher Education), no. 6 (1997), 31–40.
Zhang Longxi. "Duoyuan shehui zhong de wenhua piping" (Cultural Criticism in Pluralistic Societies), *Ershiyi shiji* (Twenty-First Century), no. 33 (February 1996), 18–25.

Zhang, Qiang and Robert Weatherley. "The Rise of 'Republican Fever' in the PRC and the Implications for CCP Legitimacy," *China Information* 27.3 (2013), 277–300.

Zhang Xudong. "Houxiandai zhuyi yu Zhongguo xiandaixing" (Postmodernism and Chinese Modernity), *Dushu* (Reading), no. 12 (1999), 12–20.

"Intellectual Politics in Post-Tiananmen China: An Introduction," *Social Text* 16.2 (Summer 1998), 1–8.

"The Making of the Post-Tiananmen Intellectual Field: A Critical Overview." Pp. 1–75 in Zhang, ed., *Whither China? Intellectual Politics in Contemporary China*. Durham, NC: Duke University Press, 2001.

Zhang Yiwu. "Chanshi 'Zhongguo' de jiaolü" (The Anxiety of Interpreting "China"), *Ershiyi shiji* (Twenty-First Century), no. 28 (April 1995), 128–35.

"Chonggu 'xiandaixing' yu Hanyu shumianyu lunzheng" (A Re-evaluation of "Modernity" and the Debate on Written Chinese), *Wenxue pinglun* (Literary Review), no. 4 (1994), 107–13, 120.

Zhao, Suisheng. "Chinese Intellectuals' Quest for National Greatness and Nationalistic Writing in the 1990s," *China Quarterly*, no. 152 (December 1997), 725–45.

"The Ideological Campaign in Xi's China: Rebuilding Regime Legitimacy," *Asian Survey* 56.6 (2016), 1168–93.

A Nation-State by Construction: Dynamics of Modern Chinese Nationalism. Stanford, CA: Stanford University Press, 2004.

"A State-Led Nationalism: The Patriotic Education Campaign in Post-Tiananmen China," *Communist and Post-communist Studies* 31.3 (1998), 287–302.

Zhao Yiheng [Henry Y. H. Zhao]. "'Houxue,' xin baoshou zhuyi yu wenhua pipan" ("Post-*Isms*," Neoconservatism, and Cultural Criticism). Pp. 343–56 in Li Shitao, ed., *Zhishi fenzi lichang: Jijin yu baoshou zhijian de dongdang*. Originally published in *Huacheng* (Flower City), no. 5 (1995), 201–81.

"'Houxue' yu Zhongguo xin baoshou zhuyi" ("Post-*Isms*" and Chinese Neoconservatism), *Ershiyi shiji* (Twenty-First Century), no. 27 (February 1995), 4–15.

"Post-*Ism* and Chinese New Conservatism," *New Literary History* 28.1 (1997), 31–44.

"Ruhe miandui dangjin Zhongguo wenhua xianzhuang: Haineiwai dalu xuezhe de yichang bianlun" (How to Confront the Status Quo in the Present Chinese Culture: A Debate among Mainland and Overseas Scholars). Pp. 357–67 in Li Shitao, ed., *Zhishi fenzi lichang: Jijin yu baoshou zhijian de dongdang*. Originally published in *Wenyi zhengming* (Debates on Literature and Art), no. 5 (1996), 55–60.

"Wenhua pipan yu houxiandai zhuyi lilun" (Cultural Criticism and Postmodernism Theory), *Ershiyi shiji* (Twenty-First Century), no. 31 (October 1995), 147–51.

Zhao Yuesheng. "Xin faxisi zhuyi de xuanyan" (A Manifesto of Neofascism), *Zhongguo zhi chun* (China Spring), no. 1 (January 1992), 29–30. Translated by David Kelly in *Chinese Law and Government* 29.2 (March–April 1996), 52–54.

Zheng Dahua. "Xiandai Zhongguo wenhua baoshou zhuyi sichao de lishi kaocha" (A Historical Investigation into Trends in Modern Chinese Cultural Conservatism). Pp. 2.439–50 in Feng Lin, ed., *Chongxin renshi bainian Zhongguo*.

Zheng Dahua, He Xiaoming, and Yu Zuhua. "Guanyu 'Zhongguo jindaishi shang de jijin yu baoshou' de duihua" (Dialogue on "Radicalism and Conservatism in Modern Chinese History"). Pp. 1–11 in Zheng Dahua and Zou Xiaozhan, eds., *Zhongguo jindaishi shang de jijin yu baoshou* (Radicalism and Conservatism in Modern Chinese History). Beijing: Shehui kexue wenxian chubanshe, 2011.

Zheng Dahua and Jia Xiaoye. "Ershi shiji jiushi niandai yilai Zhongguo jindaishi shang de jijin yu baoshou yanjiu shuping" (Commentary on Research on Radicalism and Conservatism in Modern Chinese History since the 1990s), *Jindaishi yanjiu* (Modern Chinese History Research), no. 4 (2005), 289–314.

"Jiushi niandai yilai Zhongguo jindai sixiangshi yanjiu zhong de zhongda wenti zhenglun" (Discussions on Major Issues in Research on Modern Chinese Intellectual History since the 1990s), *Huaihua xueyuan xuebao* (Journal of Huaihua University) 24.3 (June 2005), 51–57.

"'Zhongguo jindai sixiangshi shang de baoshou yu jijin' xueshu taolun hui zongshu" (Summary of the Academic Symposium on "Conservatism and Radicalism in Modern Chinese Intellectual History"), *Jindaishi yanjiu* (Modern History Research), no. 2 (February 2004), 291–301.

Zheng Dahua and Zou Xiaozhan, eds. *Zhongguo jindaishi shang de jijin yu baoshou* (Radicalism and Conservatism in Modern Chinese History). Beijing: Shehui kexue wenxian chubanshe, 2011.

Zheng Min. "Guanyu 'Ruhe pingjia "wusi" baihuawen yundong?' Shangque zhi shangque" (A Rejoinder to the Rejoinder: "How to Evaluate the 'May Fourth' Vernacular Language Movement?"). Pp. 198–206 in Li Shitao, ed., *Zhishi fenzi lichang: Jijin yu baoshou zhijian de dongdang*. Originally published in *Wenxue pinglun* (Literary Review), no. 2 (1994), 118–22.

"Hewei 'dalu xin baoshou zhuyi'?" (What Is "Mainland Neoconservatism"?), *Wenyi zhengming* (Debates on Literature and Art), no. 5 (1995), 40–48.

"Shijimo de huigu: Hanyu yuyan biange yu xinshi chuangzao" (Retrospect at the End of the Century: The Chinese Language Reform and the Creation of New Chinese Poetry). Pp. 158–86 in Li Shitao, ed., *Zhishi fenzi lichang: Jijin yu baoshou zhijian de dongdang*. Originally published in *Wenxue pinglun* (Literary Review), no. 3 (1993), 5–20.

"Wenhua, zhengzhi, yuyan sanzhe guanxi zhi wo jian" (My Views on the Relationship among Culture, Politics, and Language), *Ershiyi shiji* (Twenty-First Century), no. 29 (June 1995), 120–24.

Zhongguo qingnianbao sixiang lilunbu (*China Youth Daily* Ideology and Theory Department). "Sulian zhengbian hou Zhongguo de xianshi yingdui yu zhanlüe xuanze" (Realistic Responses and Strategic Options for China after the Soviet Upheaval), *Zhongguo zhi chun* (China Spring), no. 1 (January 1992), 35–39. Translated by David Kelly in *Chinese Law and Government* 29.2 (March–April 1996), 13–31.

Zhongguo shibao zhoukan bianji (Editors of *China Times Weekly*). "Dalu xin baoshou zhuyi de jueqi: Fangwen dalu 'di'er sichao' lilunjia Xiao Gongqin" (The Rise of Mainland Neoconservatism: An Interview with Mainland "Second Trend" Theorist Xiao Gongqin), *Zhongguo shibao zhoukan* (China Times Weekly), January 26, 1992, 66–69 and February 2, 1992, 98–100.

Zhongwai mingren yanjiu zhongxin (Research Center on Chinese and Foreign Eminent Persons), ed. *Zhongguo dangdai mingrenlu* (Record of Contemporary Chinese Eminent Persons). Shanghai: Shanghai renmin chubanshe, 1991.

Zhou, Lian. "The Debates in Contemporary Chinese Political Thought." Pp. 26–45 in Fred Dallmayr and Zhao Tingyang, eds., *Contemporary Chinese Political Thought: Debates and Perspectives*. Lexington: University of Kentucky Press, 2012.

Zhou Yangshan, ed. *Cong wusi dao xin wusi* (From May Fourth to the New May Fourth). Taipei: Shibao wenhua chuban qiye youxian gongsi, 1989.

Zhou Yangshan and Yang Suxian, eds. *Jindai Zhongguo sixiang renwu lun: Baoshou zhuyi* (Modern Chinese Thought and People: Conservatism). Taipei: Shibao wenhua chuban shiye youxian gongsi, 1980.

Zhu Xueqin. "For a Chinese Liberalism," tr. Wu Shengqing. Pp. 87–107 in Chaohua Wang, ed., *One Road, Many Paths*. London: Verso, 2003.

"Wusi sichao yu bashi niandai, jiushi niandai" (May Fourth Trends and the 1980s and 1990s), *Xiandai yu chuantong* (Modernity and Tradition), no. 1 (1995), 29–37.

Zou Dang [Tsou Tang]. "Du 'Gaobie geming': Zhi Li Zehou, Liu Zaifu" (Reading *Farewell to Revolution*: To Li Zehou and Liu Zaifu), *Ershiyi shiji* (Twenty-First Century), no. 33 (February 1996), 62–67.

Zurndorfer, Harriet T. "Confusing Confucianism with Capitalism: Culture as Impediment and/or Stimulus to Chinese Economic Development," paper presented at the Third Global Economic History Network Meeting, Konstanz, Germany, June 3–5, 2004, www.researchgate.net/publication/237385777_Confusing_ Confucianism_With_Capitalism_Culture_As_Impediment_AndOr_Stimulus_To_ Chinese_Economic_Development.

Index

academic norms, 26, 129–30, 198
Academy of Chinese Culture, 96, 99, 131, 144, 221
anti-radicalism, 183, 195, 204
   and official ideology, 117
   criticisms, 116–20
anti-traditionalism, 91, 102, 142, 146, 158
   radicalism, 122
anti-Westernism, 181
Asian values, 157

baihua, 169, 171
Bao Zunxin, 96
Bell, Daniel, 133, 150, 158, 167, 201
Berlin, Isaiah, 105–6, 116, 123, 208
Bo Yibo, 38
Boston Confucianism, 137
British conservatism
   and preserving the status quo, 107
Burke, Edmund
   influence on Chinese intellectual debates, 107–9
Burkean conservatism, 17, 73, 87–88, 90, 121, 150
   Xiao Gongqin's observations on, 73

Campaign Against Spiritual Pollution, 5
capitalism, 167
   and Confucianism, 153–58
   Confucian views on, 160
   Confucianism as antidote and facilitator of, 158–61
Cecil, Hugh, 107, 110
Chang Hao [Zhang Hao], 137
Chen Duxiu, 26, 103, 149, 169, 171
Chen Feng
   criticism of Zheng Min, 177
Chen Lai, 132–33, 137, 140, 145–48, 158, 206, 218
Chen Lai
   Confucianism, 140–44
   cultural conservatism, 149–51

cultural inheritance, 159
   dialectical denial, 159
   on Confucianism and capitalism, 156–57
   on Weber, 156–57
   use of Max Weber, 141–49
Chen Tianhua, 79
Chen Xiaoming, 48
Chen Yinke, 26, 128
Chen Yinke de zuihou ershi nian (Chen Yinke's Last Twenty Years), 128
Chen Yizi, 52
Chen Yuan, 58
Chen Yun, 38, 58, 61
Chen Ziming, 97
China Can Say No, 45
Chinese and Western cultures
   debate over, 20
Chinese Culture Rim, 179–80
Chinese Revolution
   Glorious Revolution as counter model, 12
Chinese University of Hong Kong, 3, 95, 100–1, 110, 218–21, 223
Chineseness, 27, 103, 165, 168, 171, 173, 175–76, 179–80, 187, 193, 195, 198, 200
Clash of Civilizations, The, 176
Cold War, end of, 2
commercialization, 8, 25, 32, 95, 150, 164–65, 167, 182, 185, 187–88, 192–93, 195–96, 210
   of Confucianism, 133
concepts of movement, 15, 69, 95, 130, 164, 202
conceptual history, 13, 15, 28–29, 47, 49–50, 69, 88, 126, 202, 214
Confucianism, 92–93, 103, 127, 131–32, 136–40, 155–56, 211
   after 1949, 147
   as antidote and facilitator of capitalism, 158–61
   as moral cure, 152
   Boston, 137

Index

Chen Lai, 140–44, 146–47, 163
Chen Sihe, 185
  Neo, Cheng-Zhu school, 137
  Neo, Lu-Wang school, 137
  relationship to capitalism, 153–58
  revival of, 133–34
  role of ethics vs imperial ideology, 157
  Tu Wei-ming, 140, 152
conservatism, 16, 28, 121, 184, 192, 199, 215, *See also* cultural conservatism *and* political conservatism
  and balancing with radicalism, 109
  and modernization, 101
  and radicalism, 15
  as adherence to familiar things, 107
  change in meaning of, 114–15
  critique of modernity, 194
  history as object of discussion, 215
  modernization, 197–201
  positive re-evaluation, 130
  postmodernism, 128, 177, 180–84
  ruxue-centered cultural nationalism, 122
  turn towards, 9
  variated uses, 216
  vs gradual reform, 113
  vs radicalism, 106–9
  Xueheng zazhi (Critical Review), 20
  Yü Ying-shih on, 101
conservative liberalism, 31, 95, 111, 114, 120–23, 209
conservatives, 214
constructivist rationalist liberalism, 121
counter-concepts, 27, 29
Crisis of Chinese Consciousness, The, 128
crossing the river by feeling for the stones, 7, 115, 122
Cui Zhiyuan, 185
Cultural China, 138, 200
cultural conservatism, 9, 17, 69, 191, 201
  Chen Lai, 149–51
  intellectual diversity, 150
cultural conservatives, 107, 148–50
  Chen Lai, 150
  influences on, 149
  modernization, 150
cultural nationalism, 200
cultural radicalism, 143, 145, 158, 194
  Chen Lai, 141, 161
  Zheng Min and Fan Qinlin, 177
Cultural Revolution, 106–7, 145
  as part of Chinese tradition, 108
  debates on reasons for disaster, 146
  radical characterization, 107
  Tiananmen generation, 24

culture fever (*wenhua re*), 6, 97, 131, 166, 219
  Academy of Chinese Culture, 97

de Tocqueville, Alexis, 105–6, 211
Debate on 'Problems and *-Isms*', 82
Debate on science and metaphysics (*renshengguan*) or *Weltanschauung*, 19
de Maistre, Joseph, 73
Deng Liqun, 28, 38, 41
Deng Shi, 19
Deng Xiaoping, 60–61, 64, 118
  Southern Tour, 2, 7
Dongfang (Orient), 8, 11, 19, 30, 106, 122, 143–45, 148–50, 185, 188
Durkheim, Émile, 70
Dushu (Reading), 11, 29–30, 96, 100, 105–6, 113, 121, 123, 129, 148, 166, 176, 185–86, 190, 208
Du Yaquan, 19

Eisenstadt, 78, 102, 154, 216
Eleventh Party Congress, Third Plenary Session, 5
empiricism, 26, 63, 78, 83, 89–91, 105, 198, 204
English vs. French models, 106
Enlightenment mentality, 104
Ershiyi shiji (Twenty-First Century), 3
evolution, theory of, 86

Fan Qinlin, 173, 177
Fang Keli, 159
Farewell to Revolution, 118
Feng Youlan, 159–60
Four Basic Principles, 34
Four Mini Dragons of East Asia, 38, 131
Four Modernizations, 34
Fourteenth Party Congress, 2, 7, 65
Frankfurt School, 161
French Enlightenment, 141
French Revolution, 12
  ideal types, 197
Fu Keng, 112–13
Furth, Charlotte, 16–17, 86, 201
Fuxing zhi lu (Road to Revival), 212

Gan Yang, 104–6, 116, 122, 160, 185, 207, 209, 218
Gaobie geming (Farewell to Revolution), 11
Ge Zhaoguang, 205
geming, 13, 125
Geng Yunzhi, 120
Global Modernity, 10, 14
globalization, 13, 32, 163–81, 184, 195–96, 201, 208

Glorious Revolution (1688–89), 12, 105
  ideal types, 197
Gorbachev, Mikhail S., 36, 38
gradualism (*wenjin zhuyi*), 54, 57, 74, 112
gradualist liberalism, 122
Greater China, 193, 214
Gu Zhun, 123
Guo Yingjie, 162, 174, 180, 193
guocui (national essence), 18, 21
Guocui xuebao (Journal of National Essence), 21, 103, 107

Hayek, Friedrich, 78, 89, 105, 197
He Xin, 45–46, 51, 218
Henry Y.H. Zhao. *See* Zhao Yiheng
Heshang (River Elegy), 6, 97, 215
historiography, 215
history
  as cyclical, 127
  as moral example, 126
  role of, 203–4
  use of, 213
Hong Kong, 27
horizons of expectations, 14, 198
Hu Angang, 41–42, 218
Hu Cheng, 113
Hu Jintao, 211
Hu Ping, 58
Hu Qiaomu, 28, 38
Hu Sheng, 136
Hu Shi, 26, 81–82, 103, 123, 141, 164, 169, 171
Hu Yaobang, 8, 46
Huang Jie, 19
humanist spirit, 186
Hundred Days Reform (1898), 73–74
  Xiao Gongqin, 75–78
Huntington, Samuel, 59, 75–76, 78, 106–7, 176

instrumental rationality (*gongju lixing*), 60, 148, 160
intellectuals, 1–3, 187, 199
  changing role of, 193–95, 200–1
  crisis of, 22–27
  debates on role in society, 126
  definition, 22, 26
  during May Fourth period, 23
  establishment intellectuals, 23–24, 29, 195
  generations, 2, 6, 15, 24, 100, 102, 112, 126, 138
  humanistic and technocratic, 25, 29, 204
  in United States, 4
  self-identification as scholars (*xuezhe*), 128
  under Mao, 23
  zhishi fenzi, 3, 22–23, 25, 62, 70, 72, 74, 98, 102, 104, 108, 111, 112, 155, 186
intellectuals, public, 206

intelligentsia. *See* intellectuals
irrationalism, 59–60, 63
-*isms*, 15, 28, 34–65, 69, 82, 88, 94, 95, 113, 116, 125, 126, 130, 164–89, 202, 203

Ji Guangmao, 126
Jia Xiaoye, 199, 204, 219
Jiang Yihua, 3, 219
  debate on Yü Ying-shih's thesis, 107–9
Jiang Zemin, 53, 65, 212
Jin Guantao, 94, 219
Jin Yuanpu, 47
June Fourth, 5, 10, 35, 47, 57, 196

Kang Xiaoguang, 42
Kang Youwei, 73, 75–76, 79, 84, 103, 107, 118
Koselleck, Reinhart, 28–29, 49
Kristol, Irving, 47
Kuomintang, 18

language, 178, 180
  debate over Chinese vernacular, 171–74
Last Confucian, The, 18, 151
learning (*xueshu*), 95
Lei Yi, 189–90
Levenson, Joseph, 16
Li Dazhao, 49, 115
Li Liangyu, 111
Li Zehou, 8, 11, 25, 118, 120, 122, 141, 150, 219
Liang Qichao, 19, 73, 118, 124, 132, 135, 149, 186
Liang Shuming, 18–20, 138, 151, 159, 184, 213–14, 223
liberalism, 115, 199
  and gradualism, 111
  Gan Yang on, 122
Limits of Change, The, 16, 21–22
Lin Gang, 106
Lin Yü-sheng [Lin Yusheng], 24, 70, 76, 81–82, 92, 99–100, 103, 113, 127–28, 201, 219
Literary Revolution, 25, 32, 143, 165, 168–72, 174–75, 186, 204, 208, 224
Liu Dong, 143, 165, 190, 210, 220
Liu Junning, 114, 121, 207, 220
Liu Qingfeng, 94, 219–20
Liu Shipei, 18–19
Liu Xiaobo, 45
Liu Zaifu, 11, 97, 118, 208, 220
lixue, 92, 137, 148, 159–60
Looking at China Through a Third Eye, 40–41
Luo Rongqu, 78
Lu Xun, 26, 50

Index

Ma Yong, 72, 202, 220
Mandate of Heaven (*tianming*), 127
Mannheim, Karl, 17, 24
Mao Zedong, 1, 50, 61, 83, 103, 118
   commercialization of legacy, 8
   Thought, 34, 64, 210
Marx, Karl, 12
Marxism, 212
   argument for, 45
Marxism-Leninism and Mao Zedong Thought, 34
Max Weber dilemma, 131–33
May Fourth Movement (1917–21), 1, 6, 10, 70, 74, 96–98, 108, 141–42, 145–46, 153, 170, 177, 181, 194, 198
   anti-traditionalism, 142, 146
   cultural nihilism, 143
   debates on, 95, 98
   intellectuals, 100, 172, 178, 214
   modernization, 144–47
   radicalism, 117
Meiji Restoration, 118
Metzger, Thomas A., 199
modernity, 14, 175, 179, 183, 190, 194, 199
   language, 178
modernization, 69, 83–90, 93, 98, 124, 132, 144–47, 157–58, 161, 167, 184, 196, 199, 202
   Chen's views on Confucianism and, 146–47
   conservatism, 101, 197–201
Mou Zongsan, 137, 139

national conditions (*guoqing*), 60
national studies (*guoxue*), 10, 19, 107, 134–36
nationalism, 41, 64, 190
   and neoconservatism, 43–47
neo-authoritarianism, 38–39, 51–53
   Northern and Southern schools, 52–53
neoconservatism, 40, 114, 186, 199, 210
   American context, 47
   and nationalism, 43–47
   as criticism of radicalism, 93
   as middle path, 37–43
   as political label, 191
   definition, 48
   Marxist perspective on, 65
   of Xiao Gongqin, 70
   radicalism, 60
   rejection of label, 190
   rise of, 36
   turn to non-Marxist thinkers, 65
   Zhao Yiheng, 188
neologisms, 28, 85, 95, 125
New Asia College, 99, 101, 110, 139, 222
New Confucianism, 158, 162–63
   capitalism, 160
   'manifesto', 139
New Enlightenment Movement, 4–6, 198, 207
   repression of, 23
new *guoxue*, 20
New Left, 4, 6, 29, 123n.35, 185, 207–10
New Literature Movement, 170
New Policies, 77, 113
nihilism, 177

Old Regime and the Revolution, The, 211
Orientalism, 176
Otherization, 178–79

Patriotic Education Campaign 1991, 46
peaceful evolution, 45, 47, 60, 193
Peng Zhen, 38
piecemeal engineering, 115–16, 122
political conservatism, 67, 108, 112, 116, 201
Political Order in Changing Societies, 59, 75, 106
Popper, Karl, 197
   piecemeal social engineering, 78, 89–90, 110–12, 114–16, 122
   utopian social engineering, 112, 115
postcolonialism, 176, 178, 189–90, 193
post-*isms*
   criticism of, 187–89
   Xu Ben criticism, 188–89
postmodernism, 166–68, 178, 186, 190, 193
   and neoconservatism, 180, 186–89
   critique of modernity, 194
   de-revolution, 182
   Marxist perspective on, 183
   radicalism, 180–84
postsocialism, 182
poststructuralism, 166, 172, 174, 186–88, 191
practice as the sole criterion of truth, 64
primary stage of socialism, 8, 65, 183
princelings (*taizidang*), 30, 40, 63–64
Protestant Ethic and the Spirit of Capitalism, The, 153, 156
public intellectuals, 206

Qian Mu, 97, 101, 110, 138–39
Qin Hui, 207

radicalism, 1, 9, 11, 14–15, 17, 22, 24, 26–27, 30–32, 36–37, 45, 47, 49, 54–56, 59, 62, 65, 67–68, 71–72, 76, 78, 80–81, 115, 117, 120, 125, 132, 142, 145, 149, 165, 170, 196, 202, 210, 214, 219, 225–27, 229–30
   and debate on conservatism in modern Chinese history, 181

radicalism (cont.)
  and Leninist organization in China, 126
  and liberalism, 111
  and self-censorship, 10
  and the CCP, 109
  anti-traditionalism, 91
  as counter-concept, 29
  Chen Lai's critique, 146
  criticism of debate about, 124
  cultural vs. political, 112
  debates on, 25, 100, 124, 161, 168, 187, 205, 213
  discussion on May Fourth, 20
  First Opium War, 2
  French Revolution, 113
  Hundred Days Reform Movement 1898, 75–78
  in *Realistic Responses*, 60
  in Xiao Gongqin, 103
  liberalism, 122
  Lin Yü-sheng's criticism of, 127
  May Fourth Movement, 99, 117, 144–47
    rejection of, 131
  narrative, 125
  natural law, 83
  negative connotation, 114
  neoconservatism, 60
  origin of, 67, 118
  postmodernism, 180–84
  princelings' view of, 63
  rejection of, 128
  roots of, 201
  shift in meaning, 114
  Soviet crisis, 4
  types of, 74, 80
  views of Chinese intellectuals on, 111
  Westernization, 79
  Xiao Gongqin's three kinds of, 73–75
  Yü's stages of, 102–3, 125
radicalization thesis, 108, 113
rationalism, 55–56, 63, 78, 89, 105, 114, 141, 184, 204
  critique of, 198
  French Revolution, 81
  radicalism, 26
  Yan Fu, 83
realism, 60, 95, 115, 194, 196
Realistic Responses and Strategic Options for China after the Soviet Upheaval, 30, 57–62, 64, 196
  romantic reform view, 61
realistic revolution, 196–97
Reflections on the Revolution in France, 16, 108
Religion of China, The, 157

ren (benevolence), 92, 137, 163
Republic (1912), parliamentary democracy of, 74
Resolution 1981, 65
Revolution (1911), 118, 120
revolutions
  definition, 125
  English vs. French models, 80, 124, 204
Road to Serfdom and *Constitution of Liberty, The*, 123
romanticism, 81–83
Rousseau, Jean-Jacques, 89
ru/rujia, 140, 147, 162
Russian Revolution, 124

scholarship
  debates over meaning, 130
Schwartz, Benjamin, 17, 84, 99, 126, 127
Sheng Hong, 44, 220
shock therapies, 59
Social Darwinism, 86, 88
social evolutionism, 88
socialism with Chinese characteristics, 60
socialist humanism, 143
socialist market economy, 65
Southern Tour, 2, 7, 30, 35, 93, 95, 106, 167, 185
Soviet coup
  Realistic Responses and Strategic Options for China after the Soviet Upheaval, 57–62
Soviet Union, 35–36
special economic zones (SEZs), 80
Spencer, Herbert, 85
Strauss, Leo, 209
statism (*guojia zhuyi*), 35, 38, 45, 48, 198
Sun Guodong, 110
Sun Yat-sen, 79

Taiping rebellion, 99
Taiwan, 3, 27
Tan Sitong, 73
Tang Junyi, 81, 136, 139
Tang Yijie, 96, 221
Tao Dongfeng, 122, 190, 221
Tao Xisheng, 18
Third Wave, The
  Chinese translation of, 4
Third Way, 61
thought (*sixiang*), 94
Tiananmen, 5, 52, 74, 80, 125
  debate around, 124

Index

demonstrations, 62
massacre. *See* June Fourth
tiyong, 14, 86–87
totalistic iconoclasm, 29, 100, 170, 177
Tianya (Frontiers), 11
tradition, 2, 16, 53–54, 65, 76, 90–93, 95, 101, 107, 127, 146, 158, 174
Tu Wei-ming [Du Weiming], 24, 100, 103–4, 137–38, 140, 152–53, 157, 160, 211, 216, 221

unhistorical history, 126
utopian capitalism, 59
utopian socialism, 59, 115–16, 116, 196, 217

value rationality (*jiazhi lixing*), 92, 147–49, 151, 152, 157, 160–63

Wang Fansen [Wang Fan-shen], 49
Wang Guowei, 20, 26, 128
Wang Hui, 6, 28, 39, 114, 116, 121, 124, 199, 207–8, 215, 221
Wang Huning, 52
Wang Juntao, 37, 48
Wang Ning, 166
Wang Rongzu, 109
Wang Shan, 40–41
Wang Shaoguang, 41–42, 110–11, 221
Wang Shuo, 186
Wang Xiaodong (pseudonym Shi Zhong), 43–44, 58, 222
Wang Xiaoming, 185
Wang Yuanhua, 129, 143–44, 222
Wang Yuechuan, 48, 168, 190, 222
Weber, Max. *See* Max Weber dilemma
  introduction into the Chinese debate, 161
  Max Weber dilemma, 158–61
  on Confucianism and capitalism, 153–58
  sociology at Chinese universities, 147–48
  tension between value and instrumental rationality, 160
Wenhua: Zhongguo yu shijie (Culture: China and the World), 96
Wenxue pinglun, 130, 143, 166, 170, 173, 175–78
Westernization, 79, 143, 160, 179, 217
Wu Jiaxiang, 52

Xi Jinping, 212
Xiao Gongqin, 50–57, 62–63, 66, 210, 222
  and Burke, 89, 93
  Hayek, 89
  Hundred Days Reform Movement 1898, 75–78
  political romanticism, 81–83
  psychological radicalism, 54–55, 174–76, 80

on radicalism, 63
on Yan Fu, 84
role in intellectual debates, 69–72
social evolutionism, 89
system determinism, 78–80
tradition, 90–93
theory of the social organism, 85–86
Yan Fu and Burke, 85
Xie Wujun, 120
Xu Ben, 117, 188–89
Xu Fuguan, 136, 139
Xu Jilin, 6, 24, 94, 111, 115–16, 122, 131, 181, 191, 201–2, 207, 209, 222
Xu Ming, 177
Xu Youyu, 123
Xueheng zazhi (Critical Review), 20, 22, 128, 143
Xueren (The Scholar), 26, 129

Yan Fu, 53, 56–57, 68, 70, 103
  and Burke, 87, 89
  break in thought of, 84
  criticism of natural law, 83
  neoconservatism, 85
  paradox, 83–90
  theory of the social organism, 85–86
  Western liberalism, 85
  Xiao Gongqin on, 67
Yan Jiayan, 19
Yang Baikui, 52
Yang Ping, 58
Yin Haiguang, 123
Yinhe cargo ship incident, 44
Yuandao (True Way), 266, 106, 129, 135, 143
Yü Ying-shih [Yu Yingshi], 3, 21, 24, 99, 107, 113, 125, 128, 138–39, 184, 206, 214, 222
  Jiang Yihua and debate on the Cultural Revolution, 107–9
Yü Ying-shih
  political stand, 127
Yuan Shikai, 18
Yue Daiyun, 144–45, 176, 221, 223

Zeng Guofan, 99
Zhang Bingjiu, 52
Zhang Chengzhi, 185
Zhang Dainian, 132
Zhang Junmai [Carsun Chang], 19, 139
Zhang Longxi, 189
Zhang Shizhao, 19, 149
Zhang Taiyan, 19
Zhang Wei, 185
Zhang Xudong, 117, 223
Zhang Yiwu, 166, 168, 178–82, 189–90, 192–93, 223

Zhanlüe yu guanli (Strategy and Management), 30, 42–44, 70, 176, 190
Zhao Yiheng [Henry Y.H. Zhao], 187–88, 191, 223
    criticism of, 191
Zhao Ziyang, 8, 38, 46, 53, 65, 114
Zheng Dahua, 71, 84, 120, 205, 223
Zheng Min, 170–75, 188, 191–92, 223
    postmodernist critique of, 178

Zhexue yanjiu (Philosophy Research), 30, 84, 106, 119, 136
Zhishi fenzi lichang, 29–30, 48, 71, 101, 120, 122, 170, 175, 187, 204, 206
Zhou Yang, 5
Zhou Zuoren, 18
Zhu Xueqin, 6, 116, 124–25, 205, 207, 216, 224
Zouxiang weilai (Towards the Future), 96

Printed in the United States
By Bookmasters